Simon Callow

Simon Callow is an actor, director and writer. He has appeared on the stage and in many films, including the hugely popular *Four Weddings and a Funeral*. Callow's books include *Being an Actor*, *Shooting the Actor*, a highly acclaimed biography of Charles Laughton, a biographical trilogy on Orson Welles (of which the first two parts have now been published), and *Love is Where it Falls*, an account of his friendship with the great play agent, Peggy Ramsay.

Simon Callow

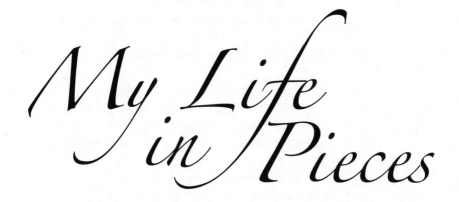

My Life in Pieces

An Alternative Autobiography

NICK HERN BOOKS

London

www.nickhernbooks.co.uk

A Nick Hern Book

MY LIFE IN PIECES

First published in Great Britain in 2010
by Nick Hern Books Limited,
14 Larden Road, London W3 7ST

Copyright © 2010 Simon Callow

Sources of material previously published elsewhere
are given in the list of Acknowledgements on p. 419
Extract on p. 411 from *Four Quartets* by T.S. Eliot
reproduced with permission of Faber and Faber Ltd.

Simon Callow has asserted his right
to be identified as the author of this work

Cover design by Ned Hoste, 2H
Front cover photograph by Kevin Davis, imagecounterpoint.com
Back cover photograph by Camilla Jessel Panufnik

Typeset by Nick Hern Books, London
Printed and bound in Great Britain by
Cromwell Press Group, Trowbridge, Wiltshire

A CIP catalogue record for this book
is available from the British Library

ISBN 978 1 84842 054 0

Mixed Sources
Product group from well-managed
forests and other controlled sources
www.fsc.org Cert no. TT-COC-2082
© 1996 Forest Stewardship Council
FSC

This book is dedicated to my very dear friend, Vernon Dobtcheff, who, it can safely be said, has – across many decades and several continents – seen, relished and remembered, in dazzling detail, more actors and acting than anyone on the planet.

Contents

Foreword

A word about the title. It may seem to suggest a certain degree of disintegration. The opposite is intended, though the possibility, of course, is always there.

I've been writing for newspapers pretty well continuously for thirty years (unless you count – which I don't think you should – a piece knocked off forty years ago for the student newspaper of my university). I have written features, weekly columns (for the *Independent*, for the *Sunday Express* and, under the nom de plume Autolycus, for *Country Life*), a monthly column for *Gramophone* magazine, travel pieces, book reviews, restaurant reviews. As well as newspapers, national and local, I've written features for magazines, theatre programmes, in-house journals; and I have written introductions and forewords and articles for books. I have written about many, many things, but most of my writing by far has been about acting and the theatre. Looking at them again, these literally hundreds of thousands of words, I seem to have been in the grip of a virulent form of logorrhœa. The fact is, my overriding ambition, through all the years of my childhood, and long before I had any notion of being an actor, was to be a writer. I have always had a compulsion (noted on many school reports) to communicate in words – audibly, normally, and in class, to the intense irritation of my teachers. But even then, in those garrulous days of childhood, I was writing: mostly what in America is called journaling, which even I could see was a hiding to nowhere. I had no subject other than myself. So at a certain point, bored and disgusted with that self, I put my writing on hold.

When I found the theatre, I knew I had my subject, and I started writing again. I felt like an anthropologist who has had the good fortune to discover a lost tribe. *Being an Actor,* my first book, published in 1984, was the culmination of nearly fifteen years of writing about this new world I had discovered and which had proved so hospitable to me. No one, of course, had read what I wrote, though occasionally it would spill over into letters. Then, in 1981, the *London Evening Standard* asked me – to be precise was cajoled by desperate publicists into asking me – to write about the play I was in, and from then on I have been asked on a pretty regular basis to commit my deathless thoughts on the subject to print. I've been at my happiest celebrating actors and acting, directors and writers. Sometimes this has taken the form of interviews, sometimes profiles, increasingly often obituaries.

It will be evident to anyone who so much as dips into the book that, like my hero, Kenneth Tynan, I am a bit of a hero-worshipper. My luck is that I have encountered so many people whom I could admire. Taken together, the celebration of performers, directors and writers amounts to a view of acting and the theatre; in some pieces, I have spelled this view out. I have sought to fascinate the reader with those aspects of the life of the theatre (and of film) that have fascinated me. Like another hero of mine, Laurence Olivier, who said he wanted to interest the public in the art of acting, I have tried to spark a debate about it, to alert people to the fact that there is no single truth in this art, and to the possibility of gloriously different modes of expression within it. I am also writing for those who, like my fifteen-year-old self, are doing their theatre-going in their rooms at home. I am aware that to a large extent, I am writing about a theatre which no longer exists or will soon cease to. The theatre constantly remakes itself. Perhaps this book might sow a seed, encourage a few people, not to turn the clock back, but to take note of what heights the theatre and acting has from time to time attained, and strive to match it.

Put together, the pieces form an account of my relationship, over more than fifty years, to the theatre and, to a somewhat lesser degree, because I have been rather less involved in it (and over a much shorter period), to film. I've arranged them, not in chronological order of composition, but as their subjects came up in my life, so I suppose they amount to a sort of alternative autobiography, or at the very least, a growing narrative of my theatrical preoccupations. I have written about my career as such in *Being an Actor* and *Shooting the Actor.* Here I write about my passions, my concerns and my dreams. Theatre has been at the centre of my life for four decades, so to that extent, this book is the story of my life.

Learning

My background was, I suppose, theatrical, but in the unimaginable past and swathed in myth: my Danish great-grandfather Jules Guise had been first a clown, then a ringmaster, then a theatrical agent: his star clients were a fourteen-strong troupe of midgets called Dr Zeynard's Lilliputians. His French wife Thérèse, whom he met when she was riding bareback in the circus of which he was ringmaster, came from a long and distinguished line of circus equestrians; her grandfather had opened a hippodrome in St Petersburg, and when he left, the Tsar, who had grown fond of him, gave him, as a farewell present, Napoleon's horse, Splendid, which he then showed off in the capital cities of Europe for the rest of his life. Jules and Thérèse had a son, also Jules, whose wife, my maternal grandmother, was a gifted singer, and had briefly been a chorus girl on tour, until she ran away, she told me with characteristic candour, after an unwelcome advance of an amorous nature from one of the other girls. I was seven years old when I received this baffling piece of information. My father's mother, who was French, had memories of the divine Sarah Bernhardt coming to their house in Lyon for tea; her father was teaching Bernhardt the role of Hamlet. Less sensationally, she had been best friends with Lilian Baylis's Box Office Manager at the Old Vic, Miss Clarke.

This ancient history was of purely romantic interest to me. We did just about as much theatre-going as any normal middle-class family, no more, no less: in other words, we were not really theatregoers at all. The annual season of Peter Pan *at the now long-demolished Scala Theatre was more or less de rigueur, however. I wrote this piece about my visit to it for Snowdon's Christmas edition of* Country Life *in 1997.*

1

I am standing in a queue in a London street on a cold dark November night in 1953 with my Uncle Maurice and my grandmother. I am four years old and howling with all the considerable power of my infant lungs. My fingers and toes are frozen and I don't know why we're here, lined up with all these other people. The bright lights on the front of the building are getting closer as the queue shuffles forward. I howl louder and louder, not in the least mollified by assurances that I'll love it when we get inside. We pass through the front doors and into a sort of hallway and then on into a vast room with rows and rows of seats covered in red velvet. At the end of the room is a huge curtain, with gold tassels and braid in figures of eight down the sides. I am more upset than ever, only wanting to be back home in familiar suburban Streatham. Then music starts, and the lights go out. Terror. The great curtain goes up, and there before me is the inside of a big house filled with beds and children and their nanny, who happens to be a dog. And my jaw drops and I immediately stop howling. And then a boy in a green costume flies in at the window, looking for his shadow, which turns out to be in a drawer, and a fairy flickers around the stage, and soon all the children fly out of the window as the music surges up. And my eyes open so wide it hurts, and I don't want to go back to Streatham; in fact, I never want to go back to Streatham again. I want to fly out of the window, I want to fight pirates and rescue Indian maidens, I want to clash swords with Captain Hook, I want a twinkling fairy of my own. And I want to do it to the roars of approval and disapproval that well up from the hundreds of children in the theatre that evening.

In short, my destiny has been fixed. And throughout my childhood, I am haunted by Peter Pan, moved by him in ways I don't understand, and captivated by Wendy, and Nana the dog, Tiger Lily, Smee, and Noodler, colouring them in in my copy of *Peter Pan in Kensington Gardens*; above all, I am haunted by the ringleted, saturnine ex-Etonian Captain Jas. Hook, sardonic, dashing, and bad to the core. I too might have cried out with the little girl who, on the very first night of the play, in November of 1908, shouted during the terrible scene in which Hook poisons Peter, 'I love that man!' But as time passes, I forget *Peter Pan*; Shakespeare replaces Barrie, and I have left the Mermaids' Lagoon and the Wendy House far behind.

Until 1982, that is, when, purely out of curiosity, I go the Barbican Theatre to see the Royal Shakespeare Company's production of this funny old play, this dim memory of my childhood, and sitting there sceptically in that unlovely auditorium, the moment the chrome drawbridge that replaces the curtain is raised, and the Darlings' nursery is revealed, my heart is in my mouth, and when Nana the dog appears, I feel my eyes opening wide. The whole first scene passes in a sort of blur of emotion for me until, to Stephen Oliver's glorious ascending theme, Peter and the Darling children fly out of the window, and I find myself sobbing. I squint sideways to see if anyone else has been similarly afflicted, and sure enough, down the cheeks of my fifty-something neighbour, large tears are trickling as he tries to assert control over his twitching facial muscles. The children in the audience, meanwhile, are craning their necks, staring up, their jaws locked open as Peter and Wendy and John and Michael ('I flewed!') soar above their heads on the way to Never Land, and now the babble of childish voices from the auditorium threatens to drown the music. And all the other locations, and the other characters, produce this same dual effect, stirring the children to wonder and the adults to intense and ineffable emotion, painful and tender, and so it has always been, from the very first performance. Barrie produced, out of his own longings and disappointments, a story which is both a stupendous *divertissement* and a potent myth, which, at least for Anglo-Saxons, seems to speak to some very deep places of the human heart, more so even than its close relation *Alice in Wonderland* – also the product of a man who became obsessed by the offspring of others and strove to glorify and immortalise their childhoods.

My parents had broken up when I was eighteen months old; my father lived in Africa. I began to form romantic and complex ideas about his life there. No doubt the transformation of Mr Darling (the sort of father I would very much like to have had) into Captain Hook, who hated children and wanted them dead, had deep resonances for me; certainly the father who was so unimaginably far away figured in my imagination as both frightening and hugely exotic. The photographs I had of him showed a piratical figure, bearded, with a fierce brow. He had, I had been told, a metal kneecap, and in my favourite photograph of him, which showed him on the bonnet of the racing car he drove as an amateur, surrounded by trophies he'd won, his leg was indeed stretched out rigidly ahead of him. He has a devil-may-care look in his eye. I took great pleasure in colouring in with my crayon Hook's black locks in my picture book of

Peter Pan, going over and over them till they were three-dimensional; to fill in his cruel, leering mouth I used my mother's lipstick. The vividness of my feelings about Captain Hook must owe a great deal to the fact that in the production I saw, the part was played by the late Sir Donald Wolfit; no doubt my entire subsequent development as an actor owes a great deal to that formative exposure.

When I was five, my mother uprooted us to the country, taking a job as school secretary at an unusual establishment called Elmcroft School in the village of Goring-on-Thames, run by a schoolmaster with the highly satisfactory name of Birch. Run as a normal prep school in term time, during the vacation it became a crammer for Spanish students going to Oxford or Cambridge. My education was thrown in as part of my mother's salary; the teachers were horribly overstretched, so the task fell to the headmaster's mother. This turned out to be one of the best strokes of luck of my childhood, perhaps of my life. This wonderful woman it was who taught me to read. When I ran to find my mother to inform her of this (rather late) development, she said, with impressive gravity, 'Now you have a key with which to unlock the riches of the world.' I wrote this piece for the programme of a show I did in Stratford, Ontario, in 2008.

I'm six. My mother is the secretary of a school deep in the Berkshire countryside. The headmaster's mother, Mrs Birch, a hirsute, full-breasted old Cockney whom I adore, and on whose breath there is always the sickly sweet scent of Madeira, gathers me up onto her hospitable lap one afternoon and switches on the radio. Eerie music. The announcer says, in his crisp cut-glass accent, '*Macbeth, A Play by William Shakespeare.*' It was scary and very strange, this *Macbeth*, and thank God for Mrs Birch's ample bosom into which I could sink for comfort. I realise now that this was the first play I ever saw. I use the word 'saw' advisedly. The images conjured up, of battlements and blasted heaths, of witches and kings, of children murdered and dead men walking, augmented by the sound of wind and rain and marching feet and haunted by the music of the words, most of which I could barely understand, imprinted themselves on my brain and have never faded from it. A certain landscape, Shakespeare's landscape, entered my consciousness, like a dream that is more vivid than experience itself. Scholars talk of the Shakespeare Moment, meaning the moment in time, the crossroads – historical, linguistic, theatrical – at which Shakespeare stood; but my personal Shakespeare Moment was then, in that cosy room in Goring-on-Thames, on that familiar lap, enveloped by the scent of that sweet warm breath. Ever after, I craved the poetry, the power, the sense of history, of great conflicts, and of the other world – the overwhelming atmosphere, in a word – that this astonishing writer purveyed.

What my mother had said was true. Learning to read seemed to unleash in me a passion for language which became insatiable. Above all, I loved to read out loud, a compulsion more or less indulged by my family. It was the sound of the words rather than their sense which captivated me: they had a magical, incantatory quality which intoxicated me, put me under a spell. And in my family, beauty of speech was highly prized. My grandmother, who was a fine singer, had an infinitely melodious speaking voice, caressing and beguiling. Her daughters had not inherited that, any more than they had, to her chagrin, inherited her perfect pitch, but they had vivid, crisp, eminently audible voices. I was told from the earliest age that speaking well – correctly, audibly, articulately – would open all doors. It was a Shavian proposition, one I accepted wholeheartedly. My grandmother had a further mystical belief in the power of personality. Being herself endowed with vast quantities of this precious commodity, and very little else, she naturally placed a high premium on it, one I found I rather agreed with. Sometimes perfectly pleasant people would visit the house, and when they left my grandmother would deliver the damning verdict: 'Nice, but NO PERSONALITY.' It was if they lacked a limb or an organ, and in a way, I suppose they did.

Theatre still barely featured in my life. My mother and I returned to London when I was seven. I remember A Christmas Carol *in-the-round at Croydon; and panto at Streatham Hill Theatre. Beyond that, nothing that I can recall.*

I was nine when, quite out of the blue, my parents attempted a reunion, and my mother and I found ourselves in September 1958 taking a huge aeroplane to Africa, three long days in unpressurised cabins, landing every twenty-four hours to refuel in, first, Rome, then Wadi Halfa. It was an epic adventure; tossed about in the air, sucking fiercely on our anti-emetic boiled sweets, we felt as though we were intrepid pioneers. Waiting to meet us in Kenya was Captain Hook in person, my father, who, with his heavy limp and his fiercely staring eyes, scared me rigid, though his words were kind and his body warm. We drove all the way from Nairobi Airport through Tanganyika (a country seven times the size of Britain) to the tiny township of Fort Jameson in what was then Northern Rhodesia, stopping overnight at various watering holes, awakening every morning to the roaring dawn chorus of crickets chirping. When we arrived in Fort Jimmy, as it was known, we were introduced to the sharply appraising colonial community. To my huge relief, and as if to prove my family's convictions, I immediately scored a big hit because of my accent, which reminded everyone of 'back 'ome', as they pronounced it in their almost impenetrably thick Rhodesian brogue. I was made to stand on the table and say things. Anything, really, would have done, but the words of the National Anthem proved a particular success. There were approximately two hundred white people in this village in the middle of Central Africa, so one might have thought that any hope of seeing theatre was absurd – except that, as if in token of the unstoppability of the theatrical impulse, I have a vivid recollection of an amateur production at the Victoria Memorial Institute of a Whitehall farce called Simple Spymen, *which knocked me dead with its wit and brilliance. One of the characters was called Forster-Stand. Whenever anyone new came on stage, he would introduce himself. 'I'm Forster-Stand,' he would say, to which the newcomer would invariably reply, 'Oh, I am sorry.' I think this deathless exchange got me through three largely miserable years in Africa, as my parents' reunion foundered, and my mother and I found ourselves alone and adrift in the vast alien continent, scheming how to get home; by night I dreamed of Streatham High Street.*

Then things started to look up. I explained why in a Zambian expatriates' magazine in 1998; the journal is called, oddly enough, Spotlight.

After my parents failed to reignite their marriage, my mother decided to move from Fort Jimmy to the capital. Everyone said the same thing: jobs were more plentiful there, there were better educational opportunities, it was safer for a woman and child in the big city than alone in the middle of nowhere. She secured a rather grand government job as Secretary to the Tender Board, and I was enrolled in the Lusaka Boys' School. Here something marvellous happened to me for the first time: acting. The lovely Miss Isabelle, a classic 1950's beauty, with shiny bouffant hair, luscious glossy lips, fine rounded figure and a bee's waist, was in charge of theatrical performances. Despite my lack of experience I was cast in the lead in the big show. I was wearing a very swish purple robe with gold frogging run up for me by my mother. At this age, and for some years to come, all I ever wanted for Christmas was fancy dress; this costume was an early Christmas present. I was playing a king who suffered from seeing spots before his eyes. The kingdom was scoured for someone – anyone – who could cure me; those who failed were arrested or executed. At the end of the play, when every option seemed to have been exhausted, my tailor arrived, insisting on seeing me. Finally granted an audience, he said that he was worried because he'd made my collar too small. 'What effect would that have?' I enquired haughtily. 'Well,' he said, 'you could, for example, find yourself seeing spots before your eyes.' Curtain. End of play.

During rehearsals, I suggested to the lovely Miss Isabelle that I could at this point faint. I demonstrated, keeling right over backwards. No, said Miss Isabelle briskly, with that lovely, firm smile of hers, she didn't think it was a good idea. I saw that opposition was fruitless, and gracefully deferred to her superior wisdom. At the performance, needless to say, having practised my fall for hours in our little bungalow in the Lusaka suburbs, I keeled right over backwards, and brought the house down. Things were never the same between Miss Isabelle and me after that.

Not much later, there was a positive development (never fully explained to me) in the family fortunes, and I was despatched to a very grand school in South Africa, St Aidan's Jesuit College in Grahamstown. Education suddenly became a much more intense affair. It was all Latin and serious praying and corporal punishment, and definitely no keeling over backwards. I felt intense nostalgia for Northern Rhodesia, not least for Miss Isabelle. I was sure we could have resolved our artistic differences. But alas it was never to be.

The train ride to school was via the Victoria Falls, the Kalahari Desert, the Boer War towns of Mafeking and Ladysmith, down the Cape coast, past Table Mountain and on into the very English cathedral town of Grahamstown. St Aidan's was a school of some rigour, and I was only there for nine months, because yet again my father's maintenance payments had stalled. Before I left, though, I appeared for the first time on a proper stage. Of the play I remember nothing, but I have a Proustian memory of the smell of the size used to stick the set together and the canvas out of which it was constructed and the extraordinary sense of warmth and light as I walked on stage. This was purely the effect of the lights, of course, but it immediately struck me as a beatific state. There survives a photograph of me in the play. I'm impersonating a middle-aged gentleman, perhaps of the military persuasion; the word 'Colonel' comes unbidden to mind. In this scene I'm in pyjamas, a dressing gown, and a raincoat, raising my fist against a hapless boy, taller than me, who is in his street clothes. He carries a lamp; I am very, very angry. The photo is in black and white, but you can see I'm red in the face, my fist genuinely threatening, my false moustache on the point of falling off under the pressure of so much anger. My fellow player looks at me nervously, as if he were unsure whether the anger was the character's or the actor's.

There is another memory: a Christmas concert in the school hall in Lusaka. I have been designated to read the Nativity story from the Gospel according to St Matthew. My fellow pupils have to sing songs and read poems. I – due to the nature of my text – am top of the bill. We sit in a row at the front of the stage. I am restless, bored, squirming on my seat, occasionally giggling inappropriately, looking out into the audience, unimpressed by my colleagues, aching to make my contribution. The other readers and singers must loathe me; parents in the body of the hall are looking daggers at me. Finally it's my turn. I stand up and I read, and something happens – something in the hall, but also something in me. The story comes to life; I have a sensation of enormous power and profound poetry; the words seem to hang in the air; it's as if these hoary old words were being spoken for the first time. I come to the end of the passage, but the spell lasts for a few seconds afterwards. Somebody makes announcements, and expresses thanks, and I am again a squirming, restless child on a stool. Afterwards, my mother, severely berating me for my selfishness and my lack of discipline (a quality by which she set great store), ends by saying, 'But you read marvellously. It was thrilling. Everybody was spellbound.'

Africa saw the height of my religious, or rather my ecclesiastical, aspirations. I was an altar server, and rose quite high in the ranks, to the extent that I participated prominently in the ordination of a bishop in Lusaka. In Grahamstown, I had gone so far as to found my own sodality, and even held services, spontaneously improvising prayers. The rubric of the Catholic Church, before the second Vatican Council, was theatrically uninhibited: Latin, incense, processions, prostrations. We wore very colourful vestments, there was a backstage and an onstage, and I yearned to be a priest, leading the congregation in obscure prayers in a dead language, moving them to tears in my sermon, distributing Christ's body and blood from golden chalices, communing privately in a whisper with my God. I might have become a priest, too, until Latin was abolished overnight and the Vulgate suddenly revealed the tawdriness of the whole thing.

We finally returned to England, my mother and I, when I was nearly twelve. On the boat coming across, I entered a fancy dress competition as a cancan girl; I won first prize. The best thing was being wolf-whistled as I went up to collect it. I came back to England at the wrong time of the academic year, and missed the 11-Plus, but by sheer persistence my mother managed to get me into a Catholic grammar school, the London Oratory, which – though it was in smartest Sixties Chelsea, with the ultra-modish pop singer Georgie Fame living literally on our doorstep in Stewart's Grove – was a rather thuggish place. It had once been very good and is now very good again, but then, under a repressive and unimaginative headmaster, it was deep in the doldrums. It had been used as a detention camp during the war, and the bars were still up at the windows. This seemed to us to say it all.

One of the school's many deficiencies was an absence of drama. Instead, we had Elocution. This poisoned chalice had been handed to an elegant middle-aged woman by the name of Mrs Williams. In my mind's eye, she was always dressed in a black cocktail gown flecked with silver and blue scintillants, her lovely grey hair gaily coiffed and full of bounce, her spectacles, à la mode, curving upwards, pink, with shiny speckles. I realise now that this cannot have been so, but it conveys the degree to which she seemed out of place in the rough environs of the London Oratory School. She struggled to command attention. Challenged almost beyond endurance by the task of trying to inculcate the virtues of open vowels and precise plosives into her Sarf London pupils, she had a slightly deranged quality. 'Ray of the Rainbows,' she would chant ecstatically at us, caressing and shaping the air with her hands and arms, as if conducting an invisible Aeolian orchestra, extending every vowel to breaking point, seductively rolling her r's like a tiger purring: 'Raaaaaaay of the Rrrrrrrraaaaaain-boooowsss.' Meanwhile, her charges went serenely about their usual daily lives, stabbing each other, carving lewd messages into their desktops or closely inspecting the contents of their nostrils. Because my vowels and plosives were, in their native state, pretty much what she thought vowels and plosives should be, I was smiled on by Mrs Williams. One term, with a misplaced enthusiasm that bordered on the delusional, she attempted to stage some scenes from A Midsummer Night's Dream. She gave me the part of Bottom, so – although I had no inkling of it myself – she must have glimpsed the latent thespian in me. Or perhaps it was just the plo-sives and vowels.

> And Phoebus' car
> Shall shine from far
> And make and mar
> The foolish fates –

I declaimed, as I strode up and down Room 3. Like Bottom himself, I longed to play all the parts, and I frequently did, because people would find any excuse not to show up for the class. I'd leap in to fill the breach, often happily playing scenes with myself. But Mrs Williams's purpose was not to produce a one-man show, and in the end, she threw the towel in, a beaten woman, and we went back to 'Raaaaay of the Rrrrrainbooowssss.' But it was never the same after that, and she went through the motions increasingly mechanically, the Aeolian orchestra sadly muted.

My Shakespearean explorations were not confined to school. My family were not great readers, but like most British people of the time, they had a Complete Works of Shakespeare on the bookshelf. This particular one belonged to my maternal grandmother, another ample-bosomed, sweet-breathed, spirited old personage like Mrs Birch, and it was a rather splendid affair, in three volumes – Comedies, Tragedies and Histories – edited by Dr Otto Dibelius of Berlin, and illustrated with Victorian black-and-white engravings which suggested some of what I had imagined on the radio on Mrs Birch's knee (though as it happens the illustrations for Macbeth itself disappointed me by comparison with what had filled my listening imagination, as has every production I've attended ever since).

As a no doubt somewhat overwrought twelve-year-old I would stretch out with the precious volumes on the tiger-skin rug in my grandmother's front room, reading aloud from them, weeping passionately at the beauty and the majesty of it all, though I had only the vaguest idea what it was that I was saying. Big emotions, big beautiful phrases, big expansive characters

– it was a better world than any my daily life afforded me, that was for sure.

School did its best to destroy my love of Shakespeare by reducing him to a Set Subject, whose works had to be broken down into formulas which would lead to exam success. Whenever I could swing it, I took the leading parts in the ghastly droned, fluffed, misinflected classroom readings of the plays during English classes. Armed with footnotes and glossaries and starting to become acquainted with the critical literature, I was now, finally, making sense of what I was saying.

This is the second part of Shakespeare and Me, *written for the booklet for my sonnet programme at Stratford, Ontario.*

I had at last seen some of the plays. My paternal grandmother had some personal connection with the Box Office Manager of the Old Vic in its dying days, in the early 1960s, before Olivier and his glamorous cohorts stormed its bastions and installed the refulgent new National Theatre Company there. Grandma dutifully took me down the Waterloo Road, and there I began to realise something of the diversity of this author, the different worlds – so very different from that of *Macbeth* – that he had brought to life. And I began to hear the language more and more precisely, not as undifferentiated music but as a succession of images and metaphors with a life of their own.

It always seemed to be somehow part of my life, and my family history – somewhat spuriously, as it now seems to me. In a typically Edwardian association, my maternal grandmother claimed a connection because she and her family had worshipped in St Agnes' Church in Kennington, at the next pew but one down from Emma Cons and her niece Lilian Baylis, successive directors of the theatre; after the service my grandmother's family would exchange nods and greetings with the Misses Cons and Baylis. That was the entire extent of the familiarity, but for an Edwardian it was significant, and placed us, in my grandmother's eyes at any rate, rather closer to the Vic (as she always called it) than ordinary theatregoers. My mother and her brother and sister duly attended plays there, feeling rather special (though they were more often to be found at ballet or opera performances at Sadler's Wells, that new theatre with an old name which was a late outcrop of Miss Baylis's missionary passion to spread improving culture to the people). The contact with the Old Vic claimed by Grandma Toto was more personal, less spiritual: she played bridge with Annette Clarke, Lilian Baylis's loyal Box Office Manager and later assistant, and this pastime resulted in my father and his brothers receiving free tickets for everything at the Vic.

Clarkie was long dead by the time Toto started taking me there, in the early 1960s, when the theatre was under the direction of Michael Elliott, later creator of the Royal Exchange Theatre in Manchester. She and I had occasionally been to plays in the West End, but this was a very different experience. For a start, Waterloo was, in those days, a far from salubrious quarter, just as it had been in the 1880s when Emma Cons had transformed the disreputable Old Vic (as the Royal Victoria Theatre was quickly dubbed) into the Royal Victoria Hall and Coffee Tavern. Her plan was to lure the locals out of the pubs and gin palaces and into the warm, clean and alcohol-free auditorium, where they would be diverted and improved by classical concerts and the occasional scene from Shakespeare; little by little, under Lilian Baylis's direction, this evolved into performances of operas and the first full cycle of Shakespeare's plays, and in the 1920s and '30s, still underpinned by evangelical inspiration and desperately underfunded, it had become the great breeding ground of English classical actors. By 1962, when I started going there, it was as chronically short of money as ever, and the evangelical fervour was flagging. Waterloo itself was of course dominated by the station, at the back end of which the theatre was to be found, a far cry from the ultra-modern glamour of the Royal Festival Hall on the South Bank, with its fine position on the river and its commanding view of the West End.

The Vic itself was a somewhat unprepossessing four-square building, part of a block which included a large branch of the grocer David Greig. The effects of bombing were still apparent and the impression was functional rather than glamorous. The Lower Marsh, just behind the station, was a busy market, selling clothes and household goods rather than food; to the left of the theatre as you entered was The Cut, a run-down suburban street of butchers, greengrocers, pubs and caffs. Directly opposite the theatre was a little green on which were to be found the successors of Miss Cons's original target audience, the so-called winos, though methylated spirits was their more likely tipple, with an occasional Brasso chaser.

One was nipped pretty smartly past these ladies and gents and into the foyer. This was no vision of loveliness, no prelude to romance: plain, practical, unembellished, it was simply the doorway to the auditorium, the general impression of which was dim, the burgundy seats further darkened by the sweat of thousands of backs and buttocks, the gold paint on the balconies and boxes dulled and peeling, the curtain moth-eaten and sagging. Inexplicably, this tattered and tired interior had a thrilling effect: redolent of past excitements, archaic and mysterious, full of shadows and stray shafts of golden light, it was utterly unlike the outside world. To enter it was to be inducted into a space which was halfway between waking and dreaming, one in which something momentous seemed about to happen. Sometimes, bravely, I took myself to see plays there alone, which meant going to the gallery, to the *gods*, as I quickly learned to call them. One entered by a side entrance, struggled up what seemed like hundreds of stairs and found oneself sitting on wooden benches, clinging vertiginously onto the metal railings. From this position the auditorium seemed even more dramatic, incorporating as it did a view of the rest of the audience, on whom one looked down, in rather, well, godlike-fashion. Emanating from the Gallery Bar, an aroma of coffee (a direct legacy of Miss Cons, perhaps) permanently hung in the air. And then suddenly the fanfares would sound – it was generally Shakespeare – and one was immediately in the midst of dynastic struggles, or fearing for star-cross'd lovers or chilled by the dank mists enshrouding some Scottish castle.

These productions which so enthralled me were, I realise in retrospect, for the most part serviceable rather than inspired. The days of the Old Vic Company under Elliott were numbered: it had already been announced that the newly created National Theatre under the direction of Laurence Olivier would be taking up residence in the building. And when, in short order, they did, they brought with them – to say nothing of the greatest actor in the world, a superb ensemble and a clutch of challenging directors – a team of brilliant theatre managers, architects and press officers (many from Sadler's Wells) who radically altered the experience of seeing a play at the Old Vic.

As it happens, in those radiantly enlightened days of the now defunct Inner London Education Authority, we started going in school parties to matinees at the new National Theatre, an electrifying, and, for this particular schoolboy, life-changing experience. Week after week, we were astounded by, say, Colin Blakely and Joyce Redman in Juno and the Paycock, *or Olivier's heartbreaking production of* The Three Sisters, *or maybe*

13

the asphyxiatingly hilarious Feydeau farce A Flea in Her Ear. *Almost beyond belief for sheer delight was* Much Ado About Nothing, *with Maggie Smith and Robert Stephens at their outrageous brilliant best in Zeffirelli's stupendously Sicilian production, utterly incorrect, in a rewritten text, as our teachers carefully explained to us, replete with anachronisms and cod Italian accents, but releasing more of the pain, the wit and the tenderness of that play than any production I have ever seen. This was an Old Vic transformed.*

The exterior of the theatre hardly changed, though the stage door was switched from the left of the theatre to the right, but internally everything was different, from the arrangement of the foyer, which now contained a bookstall and a wide-open box office which radically broke from the tradition of the enclosed, latticed lair of the typical West End theatre, to the graphics announcing the exits and the whereabouts of the bars (very modern), to the colour of the seats (blue) and their arrangement – there was now a gap at row O – and then, most significantly, to the proscenium, which Sean Kenny, Olivier's first designer, reshaped, thrusting the stage forward and eliminating the stage boxes, which were faced with grey boards. The splendour of the old proscenium arch (however dimmed with age) was now replaced with something functional, even ugly, and the auditorium accordingly lost some of its mystery and charm. The gain was obvious, however, the moment the curtain went up. After the solid and sensible productions of the last days of the Old Vic Company, Olivier and his cohorts offered a riot of colour, in costume, set and performances: sensuality and glamour had returned to the theatre, made all the more dazzling because of the new austerity of the auditorium.

The old place was transformed, and my first visits there, with my school on a typical ILEA matinee outing, instantly revised my understanding of what was possible in the theatre. The acting company was a crack unit, strong at every level, with the old warrior, Olivier, leading from the front; but everybody there – ushers, bookstall staff, coffee vendors, all in their smartly functional uniforms – seemed part of the enterprise, which had a swaggering sense of itself that stemmed directly from the boss. Some fairly brutal alterations had been made to the original scheme of the foyers, the walls covered with brown hessian which could be covering hardboard as likely as bricks. Olivier, he claimed, had never liked the Old Vic, where he had his first classical triumphs, and he certainly remade the old place. But it remained recognisably Lilian Baylis's theatre. When, later, I became an usher, I discovered that the password in case of fire was 'Miss Baylis is in the house', which struck me as rather risky, since many of her original customers, now elderly, were regular visitors to the National: the thought of her suddenly wheeling lopsidedly round the corner, frying pan in hand, to take up her usual position in the stage box, there to cook her supper, as was her nightly wont, could easily have given them a heart attack.

As a supplement to theatre-going, I was reading insatiably. I found plays wonderfully easy to read: I seemed to see them in my mind's eye as I turned the pages, and raced my way through all of Congreve, Racine, Molière, Goethe, Wilde, Ibsen, Chekhov, Shaw, Maugham, Wesker, Osborne, Jarry, in a state of high excitement, further fanned by Shaw's theatre reviews, the manifestos of Artaud and Edward Gordon Craig, and Eric Bentley's brilliantly lucid theoretical writings. But best of all was Kenneth Tynan, whose reviews were still coming hot off the press every week in the Observer. *I had read him from the early Sixties and began to find his collections in second-hand bookshops. His sense of occasion, his power of sensuous evocation, his youthful audacity, his political provocativeness, his visceral response to great acting – all these spoke of the theatre as both wildly exciting and very important. The following is a review of Dominic Shellard's biography.*

Tynan's career as a critic was brief out of all proportion to his subsequent *réclame*. First at the *Evening Standard*, and then, triumphantly, at the *Observer*, his survey of the British theatre lasted just over ten years, after which the poacher turned gamekeeper, and he took up his post at the Old Vic, where he attempted to put into effect the vision he had so vividly articulated in print. With the publication of the remarkably frank and searching *Life* by his widow, Kathleen, and the subsequent appearance of his *Letters* and *Diaries*, and a memoir by his first wife, Elaine Dundy, he has become the best known theatre critic who ever wrote. Even James Agate, the legendary critic of the *Sunday Times*, the many volumes of whose ongoing Diary, *Ego*, fill most of a bookshelf, is obscure by comparison. All this is just as Tynan would have wished. What would surely have surprised him is that, despite the availability in print of his dazzling collection of *Profiles*, none of his critical work – published during his lifetime in various manifestations as *Curtains, Tynan on Theatre, Tynan Right and Left* – can currently be bought; not even the most brilliant of them all, his precocious first volume *He That Plays the King*, a Cyril Connollyesque study of theatre with the critic as hero at its centre. Tynan himself has eclipsed his work. This is a grievous loss for anyone remotely interested in theatre in the twentieth century, or indeed in theatre *tout court*. It is the purpose of Dominic Shellard's scholarly and rather sober book to focus attention again on what he feels is Tynan's real achievement.

He is quite right to do so. Tynan's account of the dramatic life of his times is not only irresistibly entertaining, but also gives a vivid if unashamedly prejudiced picture of one of the great turning points in the history of the British theatre; perhaps of equal importance, it is as good an advertise-ment for the delights of theatre-going as has ever been written. Anyone reading those reviews would be irresistibly impelled – as I, a portly sub-urban child in the mid-Sixties, most certainly was – to go and see a play. Any play, really: Tynan had the uncommon gift of making flops sound as intriguing as hits. For him, theatre was an arena, a corrida: glory to the victor, but glory to the loser for having fought. He started writing reviews in the early 1950s when the theatre was at its most becalmed, and his attempts to stir it up were instrumental in creating the climate in which a new sort of theatre, represented by the Royal Court, by Peter Hall's Arts Theatre and by Joan Littlewood at the Theatre Workshop, arose. He was for a while this new theatre's prophet, its chronicler and its conscience, but then he felt the need to be involved in creating theatre rather than observing it.

This tension between participating and observing is central to his life; the central problem of his life, one might say. To him criticism was a con-scious act of performance, and the persona he adopted was securely in place by the time he arrived at Oxford, like Oscar Wilde, in fancy dress, dispensing brilliant judgements and outrageous provocations to his astounded contemporaries. The theatre was his chosen arena, and he set about directing with some energy. His quest to be associated with celebrity was already well-established; Donald Wolfit, Paul Scofield and

Robert Helpmann all attended the first night of his production of the First Quarto of *Hamlet* (he had previously directed it at school). From Oxford he went to Lichfield Rep, where he staged twenty-four plays in as many weeks; subsequently he directed for Binkie Beaumont at the Lyric Hammersmith and leased the Bedford, Camden for a somewhat unsuccessful season. But he was already writing, and it was that, rather than his solid work in rep, from which he accrued the attention and excitement that he craved. His career as a director came to an end when he was ignominiously removed from a production of *Les Parents Terribles*; and Alec Guinness's eccentric casting of him as the Player King in his own ill-fated production of *Hamlet* led to universal derision. But the inside knowledge of the processes of theatre thus gained, allied to his cocky, bobby-dazzling style, gave a unique vividness to his reviews. He was, as a bonus, one of the funniest writers of his time; his best jokes still make one laugh out loud. 'Theatre cramps him,' he wrote of the barnstorming Donald Wolfit. 'He would be happiest, I feel, in a large field.' John Gielgud's mellifluous production of *Richard II*, with Paul Scofield in the title role, was 'an essay, on Mr Gielgud's part, of mass ventriloquism'; he remarks on Vivien Leigh's 'dazzling vocal monotony'. His comment on Edwige Feuillière's acclaimed Phèdre is funny, too, but an utterly brilliant vivisection of a performance which perfectly describes something with which we are all familiar: 'Her performance is an immensely graceful apology for Phèdre, a sort of obituary notice composed by a well-wishing friend: but it is never a life, nakedly lived.'

The final phrase of this sentence, if it does not summarise the whole of Tynan's aspiration for the theatre, is certainly a vivid indication of what he expected out of it. His appetite for the stimulation that he felt the theatre could uniquely offer was immense, and informs all his criticism. He *needed* good theatre, as an addict craves his drug, as a starving man craves nourishment. This is what makes his reviews so urgent and so personal and quite unlike those of any other critic who has ever written. He announced his credo with absolute clarity: 'The critic [has done his job] if he evokes, precisely and with all his prejudices clearly charted, the state of his mind after the performance has impinged upon it... he will find readers only if he writes clearly and gaily and truly; if he regards himself as a specially treated mirror recording a unique and unrepeatable event.' Somewhat disingenuously, he claims that 'the true critic cares little for the here and now... his real rendezvous is with posterity. His review is better addressed to the future; to people thirty years hence who may wonder exactly what it felt like to be in a certain playhouse on a certain distant night.' In reality, of course, his review can only tell us what it felt like to be Ken Tynan in a certain playhouse on a certain distant night; but that is more than enough when Ken Tynan is as interesting and perpetually interested as he was. It is equally disingenuous to pretend that he had no desire to influence his own times. On the contrary, his agenda in that regard was quite naked. He savagely attacked the institution of censorship in the form of the Lord Chamberlain ('the ex-Governor of Bombay', as he relentlessly calls him), the moribund West End, the perceived inadequacies of certain actors, the life-denying philosophy, as he saw it, behind the Theatre of the Absurd. He provoked mercilessly, and without regard to friendship. He caused much pain. The actor and director Sam Wanamaker was driven to great epistolary lengths to rebut Tynan's wickedly negative account of one of his performances: 'I will not accept and will fight against your almost psychopathic desire to denigrate me and my work,' raged Wanamaker. 'You have no real convictions except those of an avant-garde opportunist… you are a fraud as a critic and will never grow into a great one (which potential you have) until you develop humility and respect for honest work, integrity and sincerity… the most vitriolic piece of critical groin-kicking I have ever come across.' Tynan was bewildered by this response, just as he failed to understand why Orson Welles didn't welcome him backstage after he had reviewed Welles's performance of Othello as 'Citizen Coon'. He wanted to be a licensed jester in the Shakespeare manner, allowed to say the unsayable, to make the forbidden joke. He loved, he said, *testing* people; Dundy, in a marvellous phrase, alludes to his primary tactic: to 'pour oil on troubled waters and then light it.'

To him it was all a game, a serious game, but a game nonetheless. There is an obvious analogy here with the aspect of his life that has now become notorious, his addiction to sadomasochistic sex. The pain is not the point, Tynan argues, and anyway, it doesn't *really* hurt. Oh yes it did, says Elaine Dundy, whom he liked to cane, and oh yes it did, cry the many victims of his lashing prose. What is startlingly clear from Shellard's book is that the rift between Tynan's persona and his private longings rapidly grew to the point that it was increasingly difficult for him to sustain. He needed to out himself in order to get a sense of his own reality, always an elusive matter with him. 'You are the only proof that I exist,' he told Dundy during one of their many separations; in his diary he notes 'My persona and myself have never properly matched.' After leaving the National he persistently tried to produce a film about his erotic tastes; in his erotic revues, *Oh! Calcutta!* and *Carte Blanche*, he attempted to persuade his collaborators to include sketches celebrating them. Rather riskily, he even makes an allusion in a jolly letter to Laurence Oliver thanking him for securing his severance pay for him, among the beneficiaries of which will be 'Miss Floggy's finishing school in Maida Vale'. Shellard does not seek to psychoanalyse Tynan, but this is all pretty standard textbook stuff: he grew up not knowing that he was the illegitimate son of a father who had an entirely separate family elsewhere, and that his very existence was a secret. He felt all his life the compulsion to share the secret, and to announce and re-announce his existence to the world at large, obsessed with greatness ('that inner uproar') in others.

Apart from theatre, music was the great passion of my life, although I was quite slow in discovering music theatre. Everything in my grandmother's house revolved around music; there was music to get up to, music to eat to, above all music to drink to, mostly provided by the radio, but for special occasions there was the collection of a hundred or so shellac records, scratched, cracked, bitten into. On what must in that early stereophonic era have been one of the last fully functioning 78 rpm radiograms, we untiringly listened to them. Most of them were of operatic arias, almost without exception from the Italian verismo repertory, and of these, more than ninety per cent were from operas by Puccini. A remarkably large number of them were tenor arias; Gigli – seen in the substantial flesh from the gods at Covent Garden by my mother and aunt in the late Thirties – was the presiding genius, his caressing liquidness swooned over, his sobs sobbed along with. Di Stefano and the briefly famous Luigi Alva were similarly lauded for their sweetness, while for heft, Björling was the man, 'Nessun Dorma' and 'Ch'ella Mi Creda Libero' thrilled to over and over. My aunt was quite frank about the sexually stirring effect of those Nordic high Cs flung out like javelins. 'Oomph! Gorgeous. Let's hear it again!' Sopranos were less loved; the house diva was plump-toned Joan Hammond – 'Ah, love me a li-toll' – while Callas – briefly heard on the radio – was despised. *'Ugly, ugly, ugly.' Baritones were rare: I can recall only Tito Gobbi; non-operatic Gobbi, actually:* The Legend of the Glass Mountain.

But it was Gobbi, as it turned out, who fixed for ever in my mind the ideal of what opera might be. In Opera and Me, *written for the* Independent *in 1995, to coincide with my production of* Il Trittico *at Broomhill, I explain how.*

It must have been 1965. A Friday night. Two school chums and I were wandering about the centre of town as we usually did at the end of the school week, on a sort of tea-crawl from one Joe Lyons to another, gossiping, dreaming, showing off, smoking furiously, when we happened to drift into Floral Street, down by the Royal Opera House, past the entrance to the gallery. People were filing in; idly I glanced at the poster and saw that they were doing something called *Il Trittico*. Never heard of it. 'It's by Puccini,' I suddenly noticed. 'Never heard of him,' my chums said. I scorned their ignorance. Then I saw that Tito Gobbi was singing in it; had indeed directed it, whatever it was. That settled it. 'We have to see this,' I said. They were aghast. We were not what you might call theatregoers at the best of times: and were we now going to submit to an evening of foreign yowling written by one unknown wop, starring another? Somehow I swung it, we paid our three shillings and we found ourselves in the slips, hanging suicidally through the bars at right angles to the stage like three culture-loving gargoyles.

The first shock was the sound. I'd never been to a concert, never (apart from my grandmother) heard a live singing voice, and by that marvellously democratic trick of the architects of the Opera House, here, clinging to the rafters, we were exposed far more vividly to the full glory of that swelling, complex orchestra bringing Paris to life than were the toffs sitting a hundred miles below. The voices seemed only a yard away. The physical impact of Gobbi's voice was sensational, his unmistakable tone, here, in the first of the three operas, *Il Tabarro*, hardened to reveal the bargee's bitterness, frustration and despair. It was completely direct: like someone talking to you, someone you knew inside out. I had not heard this before: Björling was always Björling, Gigli always Gigli. They were the noise they made. This was different: a character, a human being. I risked decapitation or at the very least traction as I strained for a glimpse of the physical embodiment of this person so far only heard, not seen. There, finally, at the centre of the grim stage picture, was a man wearing a polo-neck jumper, rough trousers and jacket and some kind of a cap, a man who might have just come off the street. But one was riveted by this ordinary man; the impacted force of his pain sucked you into him. Suddenly, shockingly, by some turn of the head which seemed wholly natural, his eyes would rake the auditorium and you saw the anguish through them as clearly as if you had X-rayed his heart. Puccini's unforgiving, unrelenting river welled up and up and with it my tears.

The interval was a little embarrassing, me snuffling, them bored. The chums had not been having the best time; we went off and smoked passionately then returned for more, they somewhat as if they were about to settle in for double maths. There's no point now in my pretending that I enjoyed *Sister Angelica* any more than they did though at the time I worked myself up into some sort of synthetic ecstasy. For Catholic schoolboys to spend an unrelieved fifty-three minutes with twenty nuns *after* school stretched aesthetic aspiration to breaking point, and anyway, where were the tunes? After the next interval and five more cigarettes each, they decided that it could only get worse and jacked it in. I stubbornly stayed, and so set my life on its future course.

I had been totally unprepared for Gobbi's comic genius. That the granite figure of *Il Tabarro* should within an hour or so be replaced by this gargoyle, tip-nosed, rubber-mouthed, agile as a monkey, was, and is, uncanny. What was going on around him on stage and in the pit was pretty lively too, but he positively became the music, mercurially transforming himself from bar to bar. He seemed constantly to take – and I do not doubt did take – his fellow singers by surprise, an anarch at the centre of things, pure energy, only finally coming to seem benevolent in time for Schicchi's final address to the audience, and then only temporarily. Simply the thing he was, made him live.

Well, this was IT. I rushed home to proclaim the new gospel. Björling and Gigli, brassy top Cs and creamy cavatinas OUT; character in music and music in action IN. With cruel indifference to the feelings of those with whom I had but days before sobbed and cooed over the old discs, I found a new mentor. I disappeared for long periods to my best friend Billy Brown's next door. His father Andrew was my guru. He seemed to have stepped out of a Grimm Brothers fairy tale: nearly seventy then, a violinist with the Royal Philharmonic Orchestra, but also a student of the Koran, a practitioner of yoga, a brewer of mead, a painter, a clockmaker and a reconstructor of ancient instruments. And all this in Streatham. At my urgent demand he regaled us, Billy and me, from his vast experience of playing in orchestra pits since the early Twenties, with the stories of the operas. Not perfunctorily: he described the characters, explained their predicaments. Nobody could have done it more vividly. No opera producer could have conveyed the story as simply, as powerfully. Operas, he made clear, were simply plays told in music. I understood.

Shellac was out, now. I put together a gramophone from various spare pieces; then began my love affair with vinyl as I discovered not golden gobbets but whole operas. The sequence, I found, was everything. When I first heard the chain of two arias and a duet at the end of the first act of *La Bohème* together instead of separately, I thought I'd explode (as I must say I have thought I'd explode on every subsequent hearing). There was no end it seemed to the territories in this new universe. With Stephen Williams's masterful *Come to the Opera* as my vade mecum, I more or less moved in to Sadler's Wells, where the entire repertory crammed itself onto that unaccommodating stage: operettas, early Verdi, Britten, Kurt Weill, Janáček, Thea Musgrave. I could see that the productions were somewhat hastily put together, that the chorus were barely numerous enough to do what was called of them – in *The Flying Dutchman* the sailors were unmistakably running round the back of the stage to take their place at the end of the rope again. But what the hell. Norman Bailey was singing Daland, for goodness' sake, Rita Hunter was Senta. Then after some years came the staggering culmination of everything everyone – Lilian Baylis, Tyrone Guthrie, Constant Lambert, Colin Davis and indeed the audience, because we felt ourselves part of the Wells – had worked for, the monumental evening when the Sadler's Company and the Wells Company joined forces to mount *The Mastersingers of Nuremberg* on that impossibly tiny stage, Reginald Goodall weaving his immense gold-threaded tapestry in the pit, every strand clear, the whole picture radiant, while all those singers whom we had watched and relished, who had grown in artistic stature from performance to performance as we watched them, were now constituted into the noblest thing the theatre has to offer: a great ensemble, integrated yet individuated, a living organism, a huge celebration of human life.

In fact, opera was rather closer to home than theatre. This is the first part of Opera and Me.

Opera was in the air from the very beginning. My grandmother had been a singer. Never fully professional, she was a member of that substantial army of part-timers who, before and after the First World War, sang for private gatherings, above all for those mysterious events, *Masonics*. The zenith of her career had been public, however: at the great Peace Concert at the Albert Hall in 1919, she had sung 'Land of Hope and Glory', under the shamelessly allusive name of Vera Melbourne, with such unbridled fervour that the acoustical apparatuses had shattered. Even in her sixties when I first knew her, the voice was huge and rich, almost uncomfortably so at close quarters, as she crooned for my personal pleasure those Masonic favourites 'Down in the Forest' by Sir Landon Ronald, or Teresa del Riego's 'Homecoming'. Droopy pieces, they seemed to me; better by far was her *pièce de résistance*, 'Softly Awakes My Heart' from *Samson et Dalila*, produced at the climax of the Friday evenings at my grandmother's house which, awash with booze and racy talk, were such a feature of my childhood. Slowly (good living and phlebitis having taken their toll over the years) she would make her way around the room, inhabiting the sinuous curve of the melody, pausing to address each male in her path, boldly locking her eyes with his. She sang it quite wonderfully, sexily, dangerously. All her bulk and all her years disappeared and we all of us, her silent partners, felt a little hotter under our collars as she sang to us, us alone, excluding all the others.

This, I suppose, was my first experience of opera, of the medium where, pre-eminently, physical circumstances are triumphantly transcended to reach a different kind of truth.

By now – 1966, when I was seventeen or so – I had seen a good deal of theatre, both lyric and dramatic. Unlike almost all my contemporaries, I was largely ignorant of films: it was not a family pastime. Grandma Toto, whose christened name, incidentally, was Marie Élisabeth Eugénie Lénore, had introduced me to Chaplin on faintly illicit visits to the Movietone Theatre in Waterloo Station after seeing Julius Caesar *or* The Merchant of Venice *at the Vic. We'd watch the whole programme, and sometimes stay and watch it all over again. I wrote this piece for the booklet of a London Philharmonic Orchestra concert in which Carl Davis conducted his own newly composed score for* The Circus.

SIMON CALLOW

During my lifetime, Charlie Chaplin, that multifaceted genius, more famous in his day than Jesus or the Buddha, has been consistently under-rated, not least by actors, who for the most part profess themselves scornful of the ostentatiousness of his technical skills, nauseated by his sentimentality, and unamused by his comedy. I have always been bewildered by this view. I was introduced to his work by a grandmother who was addicted to it. In those pre-NFT, pre-video, prehistoric days, we would go all over London to catch them. Sometimes the tiny Clifton cinema on Brixton Hill would be showing a three-reeler alongside a Tarzan movie, and the cinema in Waterloo Station was a pretty good bet, too, though you never knew what you might get. Of the feature films, especially the ones in sound, there was very little sight. My dear old grandma, a woman who otherwise betrayed very little sense of humour, would shake with laughter, tears rolling down her cheeks, as she re-enacted the scene in *The Gold Rush* where Chaplin eats his boot. She had no particular mimetic gifts, but somehow she managed to suggest the incongruous delicacy with which the little tramp addresses his task. When I finally saw the film, it was remarkable how much of it she had been able to convey, which I take to be a great tribute to him: it had made such an extraordinary impact on her. His absolute mastery of his own physical instrument is phenomenal, his expressiveness unparalleled. When, as a very young man, he was appearing with Fred Karno in a theatre in Paris, playing the drunken toff which was his most famous role before he created The Tramp, he was summoned at the interval to a box where he was gravely informed by a stocky bearded man with peculiarly penetrating eyes, '*Monsieur Chaplin, vous êtes un artiste.*' It was Debussy.

Both in conception and execution, Chaplin was in a league of his own. The character of The Tramp is a creation of the highest brilliance. In his great book *Chaplin: Last of the Clowns*, the American critic Parker Tyler identifies the elements – the hat, the walk, the moustache – showing where they came from and how Chaplin assembled them; what is harder to explain is why the strange child–man with his tottering, oscillating walk, his bowler hat and his bendy cane is at the same time so funny and so affecting, or how Chaplin makes of him a universal image of humankind, indestructibly optimistic regardless of the setbacks inflicted on him by a capricious destiny. Where is he from, who is he? He has no name, being known only as The Tramp, though he is scarcely what we think of today as a street person. He has distinct sartorial and social aspirations; he is gallant and fastidious, and is a defenceless victim of Cupid's dart, endlessly falling unsuitably in love at first sight. But he comprehends nothing of the world. He fails to understand that his adorable *moues* and dazzling smiles hold no sway against the musclemen and plutocrats to whom the women for whom he falls are attached, nor has he the confidence to assert himself against bullies and figures of authority, or the skills to hold down a job. In love and in work, he is unceremoniously shown the door, ending up over and over again in the gutter. But he always picks himself up, brushing himself down with some elegance, as if he were his own valet, proceeding, generally in the company of someone equally ill-favoured, to the next rejection, the next infatuation, the next dashed dream. Hope springs eternal. It is the inevitable repetition of failure, and the constant witty assertion of dignity, that speaks so deeply to us.

From the beginning, even before the arrival of The Tramp, Chaplin the writer and director was ceaselessly inventive, and his increasingly ambitious structures take the modern world on board with growing complexity. In *City Lights*, The Tramp is nearly overwhelmed by the sprawling vastness of the metropolis; in *Modern Times*, he is literally chewed up and spat out by the great heartless machines he is called on to operate. He scarcely belongs to the world in which he finds himself, but, like a cat or a drunk, he negotiates it with crazy grace, dancing away from danger as the structure disintegrates around him. Politically speaking, Chaplin was a radical populist in the mould of Dickens: instinctively identifying with the disadvantaged, naturally suspicious of the establishment, acutely conscious of the dehumanising effect of organised capital. In the America of the Fifties, this meant that he was a *de facto* Communist, though he was no such thing.

It was inevitably difficult for Chaplin to maintain the reckless improvisatory brilliance of his early movies. His projects took longer and longer to gestate and indeed to shoot, with a resultant loss of brio; his reluctant embrace of sound robbed them of some of their expressiveness, and led to his adoption of somewhat ponderous narrative procedures. There is scarcely a moment of his own performances within them, however, that is without some touch of genius: in *The Great Dictator*, Hynkel's dance with the globe and the barber shaving a customer to Brahms' Fifth Hungarian Dance, the murderous bigamist's dazzling prestidigitation as he counts up his ill-gotten gains in *Monsieur Verdoux*. It is in such moments that the golden legacy of Chaplin's Music Hall background is at its most evident. Elsewhere characterisation and even *mise-en-scène* tend to creak; the liberal humanitarian message of the films is spelt out rather too clearly, no doubt. The truth is that Chaplin's art was perfectly suited to the early cinema, and he exploited it more brilliantly than anyone else had done: the medium and the man were made for each other. Then the medium changed, and nothing that he was able to do, despite all his wealth and power, could stop it in its evolution. The Music Hall, too, had died, leaving him stranded in a different world of expression, a point movingly made in *Limelight*, which should, by rights, have been his last film.

No actor and no film-maker can fail to learn from the early, pre-sound films, which, especially when shown with live accompaniment as intended, achieve a kind of perfection and create a kind of exhilaration which later cinema has found hard to match.

Toto's other favourite was Danny Kaye, and we saw that master's The Court Jester *twice. I was rather keener on* Tarzan, *for reasons that I dimly began to understand: how bored she must have been by the acres of Gordon Scott's scantily clad flesh of which I could never have enough, sitting in the dark, silently willing that loincloth to slip. When I came back from Africa, television – the early days of which I had completely missed – became something of an obsession. Grandma Toto never had a television, all the days of her life, but Grandma Vera did, and I immediately became an addict. To begin with it was* Coronation Street *I loved (my impersonations of Ena Sharples and Minnie Caldwell and Leonard Swindley were much sought after), but when my mother finally succumbed and got a set, around the time that BBC2 started, I saw the classic films they so regularly broadcast, and fell in love with the work above all of Jean Renoir and Ingmar Bergman. Film had its classics, I discovered, just as much as theatre. When I was seventeen, I abruptly stopped watching television – my mother had now become the addict – and I continued my celluloid education in the art-house cinemas scattered around London and at the National Film Theatre under Waterloo Bridge. But though I had begun to grasp the role of the director, and in time was to be able to tell the work of one from another, it was always the actors that made my pulse beat faster. Peter Ustinov was, I knew, a distinguished actor–writer–director, but his fascination to me was as a personality. Indeed, for quite a time when people asked me what I wanted to be, I would answer, 'A Personality,' and it was always Peter Ustinov I had in mind. I got to know him a little, eventually: I wrote this review of John Miller's biography of him in September 2002.*

Last year Peter Ustinov, that Puckish polyglot twinkler, that elegant cosmopolitan anarch, turned, improbably, eighty, and much credit he received in the land of his birth. The Germans went crazy; the French offered various *hommages*; the Italians were effusive; but the British could scarcely manage a newspaper interview. The present volume is celebratory in intent, but the great man deserves something more illuminating, and so do we. Mr Miller is a sympathetic and intelligent chronicler of thespian extravagance, having previously done solid service in the matter of Sir John Gielgud and Sir Ralph Richardson: but though his appreciation of Ustinov and his delight in him are not in doubt, he is unable to draw our attention to quite how astonishing a phenomenon he is.

He has written, in fact, a very nice book about a jolly talented chap, a bit of a genius, perhaps, but frightfully nice with it. The books, the plays, the films, the documentaries, the stories, the epigrams, the languages simply roll out one after another as if it were the most normal thing in the world.

But hold on just a second. This is a man who was an instant star in revue at the age of eighteen, appearing with serene confidence alongside such sainted gargoyles as Robert Helpmann and Edith Evans, and garnering rather better notices; whose first West End play was written when he was nineteen and performed two years later while he was still in the army, to be acclaimed as the Best Play of the War; whose first feature film, in which he also starred, was made when he was twenty-five; who thereafter produced play after play (twenty-one of them eventually), some of which he also directed, and in many of which he starred, not merely in the West End and on Broadway but also in Paris, in Berlin and in Rome, in the languages of their respective countries; who has in addition written admirable novels (one of them something of a masterpiece), short stories, history, political commentary; who created the trailblazing radio programme *In All Directions*, without which The Goons would scarcely have been possible; who has been a roving and highly effective ambassador for international organisations and a fiercely proactive rector of both Dundee and Durham Universities; who has toured the world making hard-hitting documentaries which often involved him in challenging interviews with the great statesmen and women of the day; and who has done all of this on a bubble of irrepressible and epidemically contagious mirth. He is utterly, magnificently unique, and Mr Miller is unable to convey this, nor to wonder how it came about.

Part of the problem stems from his subject. For one thing, Ustinov has, in *Dear Me*, written one of the most deliriously funny and provocative theatrical autobiographies in the canon, original in form and beguiling in expression, and Miller is sadly doomed to retelling many of its best stories in leaden paraphrase; for another, his constant activity, both professionally and in the charitable and educational spheres, serves to obscure the man. There seem no moments of repose, of reflection, of doubt. *Dear Me* was more revealing in these areas, often, admittedly, in the things it refused to address and in the way they were deflected. There is a brief meditation in *The Gift of Laughter* on the probable melancholy at the heart of his preponderantly Slavic soul, but like so much else in the book, it turns out to be just one of those things – now and then a chap gets a bit blue, but he always rises above it.

In Miller's account, personal matters – parents, wives, children, all of whom, it would appear, have been not unproblematic – are discreetly touched on then swiftly passed by. An arresting fact occasionally appears but is allowed to scurry on, unexamined: his father's flirtatiousness turned him as a youth, Ustinov says, into a puritan; he discovered 'a lot of things' too late; when you play King Lear 'you're going out to sea in a boat alone with Shakespeare'. These are tiny cracks in the otherwise unendingly polished and accomplished façade, but Mr M is too polite to let us see what might lie behind them. *Billy Budd*, he quite rightly asserts, is a fine film, but he does not enquire what it was that drew Ustinov to that disturbing story, nor why it should be so much the best of his films as a director. He never speculates on how Ustinov's many skills were acquired. Make a film? Easy. Hold a thousand people rapt for two hours on your own? A doddle. The subject and the author are equally incurious about what it is actually like to be Peter Ustinov. Perhaps he would prefer not to go into awkward and possibly painful places, but if he is to be part of the human race we, the readers, need to.

What Miller gets absolutely right, in his title and in his text, is the supremacy of humour in Ustinov's life and work. His talent is indeed prodigious and prodigal, exploratory and innovative (his 1960 play *Photo Finish*, for example, anticipates and eclipses the formal conceit of Edward Albee's wildly over-praised *Three Tall Women* of thirty-five years later). But his genius, and that is what it is, is unquestionably for comedy. His recorded turns – the *Mock Mozart* opera, the *Phoney Folk Songs* (Russian: 'the song of a peasant whose tractor has betrayed him'; Norwegian: 'the lament of a young woman rejected by a dilatory troll'), his impersonation of the entire Gibraltar Grand Prix – are perfect works of art, and their present unavailability is a crime and a disgrace.

He is funny enough on the page, on the air and on screen, but in the flesh he is discombobulatingly funny, as only the greatest comedians are: he engenders an air of surreal fantasy which turns the world into a madhouse peopled by meticulously observed loons, megalomaniacs and doubters. His incomparably brilliant ear, both for accent and for phrase, his facial and physical versatility, his emotional flexibility produce transformations so instant and so complete that he seems to be possessed, like a sort of droll shaman. This atmosphere of hilarity he commands is as potent as a powerful sexual attraction, and as hard to control.

I once had occasion to interview him on television on the subject of Charles Laughton. Before the cameras had started to roll, only minutes after meeting the man, I was already, after a few preliminary pleasantries, in serious trouble. He told his Lew Grade story: about how Grade had received a telegram from a rabbi saying that if only *Jesus of Nazareth* had been made at the time, the crucifixion need never have happened. Whimpering, gurgling noises started to emerge from my mouth as he proceeded. I was delirious, out of control. The cameras rolled. It was a struggle to ask my simple questions. He continued, unforgiving, describing the visit of his son Igor to the set of *Spartacus* during the filming of the bathhouse scene. Igor pointed at Laughton, asking, 'Who is that lady?' 'That is not a lady,' Ustinov gently pointed out, 'it is Mr Laughton, a very famous actor.' 'Well,' said the boy, not unreasonably, 'if he's not a lady, why has he got breasts?'

His evocation of Laughton gathering up the skirts of his toga and withdrawing to consider the scale of the insult he had just received destroyed us all – the cameramen, the director, the continuity girl. I've never experienced anything quite like it – mass hysteria on the part of six people trained to maintain absolute silence. Now *that's* genius. 'I was irrevocably betrothed to laughter,' he tells Miller, 'the sound of which has always seemed to me the most civilised music in the universe.' He has spoken his own perfect epitaph.

Although I rejoiced in Ustinov's comic performances, I was aware that there were greater heights to which actors could aspire. Two performances in particular had scorched themselves on my imagination, Laurence Olivier's as Richard III, and Charles Laughton's in The Hunchback of Notre Dame, *two men with mangled bodies, one revenging himself on the world for it, the other impossibly looking for love despite it. Laughton's was the one I identified with; it moved me in ways I simply didn't understand. Olivier's film was much more straightforward, pure Grand Guignol, in lurid Technicolor as against Laughton's muted black and white. I had first seen it as a six-year-old, and it had given me screaming-out-loud nightmares, especially the terrifying scene with the young princes. This was a Captain Hook who could really kill you. I caught up with the film again when I was thirteen or fourteen, consumed with adolescent self-disgust, feeling myself to be deformed in some way. This time, identifying with Richard, I was excited by his superbly expressed contempt for the beautiful and the shapely. I was also by now aware that there was such a thing as acting. Having seen other examples of Olivier's film performances –* Hamlet, Henry V, Khartoum, Spartacus – *I could see and hear how he was using himself physically and vocally, the way in which he was able to command his voice and body to do his will. This I found exhilarating and inspiring, and lodged in my brain the liberating possibility of transformation. One did not have to be stuck, it appeared, with the face and the form that nature had given one. Olivier's voice, in particular, astounded me. I spent my days – far away from anyone who might hear me – shrieking out phrases like 'Cry God for Harry, England and St George!' and 'A horse! A horse! My kingdom for a horse!' It's a wonder I didn't give myself nodules. Both his Richard and Laughton's Quasimodo stuck in my mind, became part of my mental landscape, in a way which I began to understand was the defining characteristic of great performances: they wouldn't let go of you.*

I began to learn something about the history of the stage, to read about actors past. Garrick is the first actor about whom we know a great deal. I reviewed Ian McIntyre's biography in the Sunday Times *in 1999.*

Every age redefines acting, almost without exception in terms of greater realism. The New Actor, fresh on the scene, startles by his immediacy and truthfulness, making other actors seem stagey, hammy, corny. In time, the new truthfulness becomes widely current, and is in turn revealed as stagey, hammy, corny, to be replaced by the new New Actor; a familiar process across the whole range of human activity.

It occurred with particular abruptness in the case of David Garrick. His sudden eruption into London's theatrical life in 1742 with his sensational portrayal of Richard III shocked the city and the profession.

The almost unknown twenty-five-year-old wine merchant from Lichfield gave an account of the role of such vividness and confidence that older actors of the day were immediately thrown onto the defensive. 'If this young fellow is right,' said James Quin, one of the reigning stars of the time, 'then we have all been wrong.'

What was it that so electrified Garrick's contemporaries? In a word, actuality. The actors of the mid-eighteenth century were still recycling the rhetorical French style which they had adopted with the reopening of the theatres at the Restoration: the manner was declamatory, impressive, ponderous; Quin himself – the mighty Quin, a great barrel of a man with a deeply sonorous voice and the swaying motion of an ocean-going vessel – was the supreme exemplar of this style. The impact of Garrick, slight (only 5'3"), nimble, swift in thought and flexible in utterance, responsive to every impulse in the language, each development in the character, was clearly breathtaking.

Audiences felt that they were for the first time in the presence of the character, rather than a stylised representation of him, because they were able to see his thinking, minute by minute; moreover, the quite exceptional expressiveness of Garrick's somewhat bland features, which seemed to be inhabited by the whole gamut of human emotions in rapid succession, was a marvel in itself, a sort of conjuring trick that defied disbelief. His senior contemporaries preferred on the whole to demonstrate the conventionalised lineaments of a role; they were reproducing the past. Garrick was thrillingly, hair-raisingly present.

His career took off instantly and with bewildering variety; his range encompassed high comedy, farce and tragedy – often on the same evening. When he played King Lear for the first time (at the ripe age of twenty-six) he followed it on the same bill with Cibber's after-piece *The*

31

Schoolboy, in which he played the fifteen-year-old Master Johnny. Needless to say, his fellow players did not take his sudden ascendancy lying down. 'This might be a proper representation of a mad tailor,' sniffed the comedian Samuel Foote, 'but by no means corresponds with my idea of King Lear.'

The criticisms of his contemporaries bear a striking similarity to those offered to one of this century's thespian mould-breakers, Laurence Olivier, whose early performances in Shakespeare were held to be a smack in the face for the values of nobility, lyricism, elevated tone and resonance. In fact, Olivier and Garrick have a number of things in common; how Garrick would have enjoyed Olivier's famous doubles of Oedipus and Mr Puff, Hotspur and Justice Shallow. Like Olivier, Garrick was criticised for his naturalistic phrasing; his pauses were analysed in minute detail.

It was an age when theatre was the great metropolitan sport: the rival companies at Covent Garden and Drury Lane had their supporters and their detractors, whose conduct makes the most extreme football hooligans seem like pussycats. The best job to have in London c.1750 was a theatre repairer: at the slightest provocation the denizens of the pit would smash the benches, tear down the lighting sconces, and set fire to the curtains. The workmen would move in, swiftly reconstruct the auditorium, and the next day or the day after it would be business as usual, until the next offence from the stage, which could be almost anything: inaudibility, price increases, political incorrectness (betraying Francophilia, for example). Even Garrick, on whom the audience bestowed almost continuous favour, was hauled over the coals in this manner from time to time, though there is no record of him being made to kneel to the audience in contrition, the fate of many of his fellow players.

By 1747, a mere five years after his debut, Garrick was co-manager of Drury Lane, his reign inaugurated with a prologue written by his former schoolmaster and fellow Lichfielder, Samuel Johnson, with whom he had a somewhat uncomfortable lifelong friendship. ''Tis yours this night to bid the reign commence,' the prologue proclaimed, 'Of rescued nature and reviving sense.' And he was true to his word. Over the next twenty years of his tenure, he raised standards, of acting, lighting, scenic design and of the general conditions of theatre-going. The eighteenth-century playhouse was not the cesspit of the Restoration, but it was very noisy and the division between backstage and front of house not always clear.

Garrick helped reform all this. As far as his encouragement of new writing is concerned, his record is mixed, but it is greatly to his credit that he brought back into circulation a number of Shakespeare's plays, in more or less mutilated versions, but nonetheless always done with great vivacity and imagination.

It was inevitable that he should have been the frontman for the Shakespeare Jubilee of 1769; the beginnings of the Shakespeare industry can readily be discerned in this event, which passed uncomfortably from pageant to pomposity until it was rained off. It confirmed Garrick's position not only at the head of his profession but as a distinguished member of society long before Henry Irving's symbolic knighthood supposedly made acting respectable; his acquaintance included dukes and marquesses, and indeed the intelligentsia of Britain and Europe.

His acting was immensely influential on both sides of the Channel, not simply in theatrical terms, but philosophically. As part of the great rationalist inquiry into the human condition, the Enyclopédistes, and particularly Diderot, were fascinated by his ability apparently to create emotions at will: what did this tell us about the human brain? *The Paradox of Acting*, Diderot's famous dialogue, identifies what has become the central issue of acting: to feel or not to feel? 'Garrick will put his head between two folding doors and in the course of five or six seconds his expression will change successively from wild delight to temperate pleasure, from this to tranquillity, from tranquillity to surprise, from surprise to blank astonishment, from that to sorrow, from sorrow to the air of one overwhelmed, from that to fright, from fright to horror, from horror to despair, and thence he will go up again to the point from which he started. Can his soul have experienced all these feelings, and played this kind of scale in concert with his face? I don't believe it; nor do you.' If this was face-pulling, it is on a titanic scale. Johnson crushingly observed: 'David looks much older than he is... such an eternal restless fatiguing play of the muscles must certainly wear out a man's face before its real time.'

To the day of his retirement, audiences were astonished by his performances. He had few failures – Othello, Romeo, Hotspur – and seemed to understand his own range. He had a repertory of more than ninety roles; small wonder that, exhausted by management, acting, directing and writing – innumerable prologues and after-pieces and a number of very enjoyable full-length plays – he took a long sabbatical; he was forty-six, had acted for twenty-one years, and seriously wondered whether he hadn't lost the taste for it. After eighteen months, he returned, renewed, and finally retired at the early age of sixty. His health was by now poor, and death – from the same savage kidney condition which claimed Mozart (uraemia: 'the stone') – came quite soon after. His obsequies were of the most splendid; the nation mourned.

Hesketh Pearson's wonderful book about Beerbohm Tree, for whom he had worked, superbly evoked the late Victorian theatre; while Edward Gordon Craig's book about Henry Irving was a kind of Blakeian vision of acting. Next to that, I read Shaw's sceptical journalistic account of Irving, and Laurence Irving's magisterial three-volume Life. *Such conflicting opinions seemed to surround any great actor; there was no consensus. In 2005, I reviewed a recent and brilliantly perceptive book about the great actor which shows him as one of the key figures of his age.*

When the actor-manager Henry Irving appeared for his curtain call in Swansea on his farewell tour in 1905, someone started softly singing 'Lead Kindly Light'; soon the whole audience joined in. Not long afterwards on the same tour, after playing the title role in *Becket* in Bradford, he died. The last lines he uttered on stage were 'Into thy hands, O Lord, into thy hands.' When his lifeless body was borne through the streets at the beginning of his final journey back to London, thousands of people assembled along the way in perfect silence, a response repeated tenfold in London when he was interred amidst high pomp in Westminster Abbey; the cabmen going about their work that day wore black bows on their whips. All this for an actor? A mere actor? As it happens, the intense national mourning for Irving was the culmination of everything he had striven for in his life: the elevation of the status both of the actor and the theatre itself from bawdy disrepute and intellectual dismissal to a central place in the national landscape. His knighthood, bestowed in 1895, the first awarded to an actor, was powerfully symbolic of the respectability the theatre had acquired in the forty years since he had been acting professionally. That he was personally responsible for this transformation was in no doubt. 'The actor's world he lifted up,' said one of the many poems inspired by his demise, 'From base report and evil sway / Into the purer light of day / Where art and beauty rule the play.'

34

A crucial figure in the development of the theatre, Irving is equally significant as a man of his times, a phenomenon of the Victorian age, and it
is as such that Jeffrey Richards considers him in a book which, though
academic in design, is commendably clear in expression (when the non-
word 'performativity' crops up in his otherwise jargon-free text, it is a
bit of a shock). The details of Irving's extraordinary life are briskly
despatched in an opening paragraph, and then reappear in different con-
texts in Richards's thematically headed chapters, in each of which a key
concept of the Victorian world is explored. The thematic approach yields
remarkable and unexpected glimpses of him. Focusing on Irving's evangelical convictions, his Christian socialism, for example, reveals the
central position in his world view of the ideal of gentlemanliness, of
chivalry; this sense of the ennobling power of gentle strength was
brought to its apotheosis in his production of *King Arthur*. Similarly his
commitment to the educative potential of the theatre has its roots in the
same philosophy, and resulted in the commission of a large number of
historical dramas (*Charles I, Becket, Robespierre, Dante*), all scrupulously
researched historically and archaeologically, none undertaken without
extensive consultations with the British Museum.

The designs of his shows – entrusted to the leading painters of the day –
were universally acknowledged to be miracles both of stagecraft and
aesthetic accomplishment; when the curtain went up on the first scene
of *Charles I,* the set painter had to be given a round of applause before the
play could continue. Irving's exploration of the possibilities of light
(always evocative gas or limelight, never harsh and unpoetic electricity)
was exhaustive and innovative, constantly aspiring to ever greater
patination of texture. Richards's book is especially thought-provoking in
its account of Irving's achievements as a director. He endlessly strove for
a Wagnerian *Gesamtkunstwerk,* the integration of all the elements –
scenic, musical, thespian – into one artistically overwhelming gesture,
hypnotising his audiences with a succession of sustained and deeply
harmonised visions. The intention was spiritual as much as theatrical: by
sheer force of will and intensity of belief, he turned Tennyson's indifferent
verse drama *Becket* into an act of worship. Even his (many) detractors
admired the physical productions at the Lyceum Theatre, achieved with
the aid of veritable armies of collaborators, on stage and off: in one of his
shows, *Robespierre,* the company of sixty-nine actors was supported by
three hundred and fifty staff backstage; the regular standing orchestra
consisted of thirty-five players. In one sense, his work was old-fashioned,

the culmination of the nineteenth-century stagecraft of illusion, but in another he looked forward to the cinema: had he lived only thirty years later, that is surely where his great talents would have found their proper place. The most remarked-on scene in his production of *The Merchant of Venice*, for example, was one not envisaged by Shakespeare at all, in which Shylock returned to his empty house, knocked at the door and was greeted by silence. The curtain fell as he turned his grief-stricken face to the audience. In the parlance of Hollywood, Irving was 'opening the play out'.

Richards fascinatingly proposes that Irving's passion to create theatrical harmony was fuelled by his sharp awareness of one of the central Victorian experiences: doubleness, the schism in the soul, the lie in the heart. Many of the age's most famous citizens led double lives: Charles Dickens, Wilkie Collins, Oscar Wilde. Wilde and Robert Louis Stevenson provided the great fictional exemplars of this doubleness, and Irving's repertoire encompassed many plays in which he played twins, one brother noble, the other dastardly. Most famously he brought to the stage the portrayal of stricken conscience: Eugene Aram, Faust, Vanderdecken in *The Flying Dutchman*. Supreme among these guilt-racked figures was Matthias in *The Bells*, his first and perhaps greatest success: 'The feverish alertness engendered by the strife of a strong will against a sickening apprehension,' as a contemporary wrote, 'the desperate sense, now defiant and now abject, of impending doom, the slow analysis of the feelings, under the action of remorse – these indeed were given with appalling truth.'

Few disputed Irving's greatness as Matthias, but despite his pre-eminence as a manager, his gifts as an actor were by no means universally acknowledged. 'Nature has done very little to make an actor of him,' wrote Henry James. 'His face is not dramatic, it is the face of… anything other than a possible Hamlet or Othello. His figure is of the same cast, and his voice… is apparently wholly unavailable for the purposes of declamation.' The playwright Henry Arthur Jones identified the doubleness at the heart of his art, writing of him that 'he was supremely great in what was grim, raffish, ironic, crafty, senile, sardonic, devilish; he was equally great in what was dignified, noble, simple, courtly, removed, unearthly, saintly and spiritual. The core of them was in himself. The sly impishness, the laconic mockery and grim *diablerie* that were the underwoof of his character were the strange, harmonious complements of his hauteur, asceticism and spirituality.' It is a paradox that such an exotic and complex actor, with no access to straightforwardly heroic or romantic characters, should have become the outstanding actor of the day. He achieved his pre-eminence by will-power, by unremitting hard work and by shrewd manipulation. He imposed himself on the British theatre, and the British theatre on the nation.

Richards's book is wonderfully informative about the Victorian cult of celebrity (a word which, surprisingly, was current in more or less its present meaning from the 1850s) and Irving knew exactly how to turn it to his advantage. The first London manager for whom he worked – 'Colonel' Hezekiah Linthicum Bateman, who occupied roughly the same position in his life that 'Colonel' Parker did in Elvis Presley's – taught him the black arts of promotion. Irving and his general manager, Bram Stoker (author of *Dracula*), engineered sensational atmospheres at first nights, and cleverly paid court to friendly critics; Irving's intimate dinner parties backstage for the greatest celebrities of the day – Liszt, Gladstone, Buffalo Bill, Whistler – make him the Elton John of his days. His cultivation of royalty knew no limits: he personally paid for the Command Performances he gave at Windsor. He became something of a cult himself, his idiosyncratic appearance – long hair, pince-nez, tall broad-rimmed hat, low collar, and flowing-collared coat – widely imitated.

Alongside all this commercial calculation was his mission to transform public attitudes to the theatre. His strictly Nonconformist mother had cut him off the moment he decided to make the stage his profession, and after the first night of *The Bells* his upper-crust wife Florence asked him: 'Are you going to go on making a fool of yourself like this all your life?' As soon as she said the words, he stopped the carriage, got out, and never spoke to her again; nor was he ever reconciled to his mother. But he determined to prove them wrong: that the stage was both moral and serious. Tirelessly making speeches, cultivating academic, journalistic, ecclesiastical and aristocratic patronage, he succeeded triumphantly. 'I know of nothing in the history of modern civilisation,' wrote a contemporary, 'that can compare with the revolution in thought and idea caused by Irving's work in connection with the theatre as a national institution.' For the Coronation of his patron and supporter Edward VII, he threw – at his own expense – a banquet on the stage of the Lyceum for all the colonial premiers, princes and their retinues. His knighthood (announced the day that Oscar Wilde was convicted of gross indecency) seemed to confirm that the theatre was now part of the establishment. This did not mean that it was reactionary: Irving himself was socially and intellectually progressive; his Shylock was a radical reassessment of the character from a characteristically liberal perspective. But it meant that the theatre now operated from within society rather than from its traditional position, at its barely respectable fringes.

Towards the end of his life, Irving unveiled a plaque to one of his great predecessors, James Quin. The stage journal *The Era* commented: 'The present generation, with its keen sensitiveness, its intellectual activity, its moderation, its humanity, and its self-control, paid honour on Friday to the eighteenth-century ideal of an actor: the three-bottle or six-bottle man, the rake, the duellist and the beau. How much humanity has advanced since those days of limited ablution and unlimited paint, powder and perfume; of foolish fighting and intemperate indulgence; or heartless repartee and scandalous epigram, it is hardly necessary to note.' From this distance, it is hard not to lament what has been lost: the great alternative carnival tradition, embracing the antipodes so alarming to the Victorians, celebrating the continuum of existence, exalting the communal body. Thanks to Irving, the theatre ceased to be part of *us* and became part of *them*. It has yet to be fully reclaimed.

My knowledge of the theatre, past and present, was becoming encyclopedic. Immersing myself in it in almost scholarly fashion, I was at a loss to know what to do with these insights, these overwhelming emotions. I had a small – a tiny – outlet in the Sixth Form Literary and Debating Society, which I had founded with the sole purpose of giving myself the opportunity of reading great roles in dramatic masterpieces, which I accordingly did. As the price of that indulgence, I reluctantly submitted to the tedious horrors of the weekly debate. I was also involved in another form of play-acting, in that I had been appointed Head Boy of the school. It was a part I took to enthusiastically, seeing myself as a Reform candidate, which I suppose I must have been. I was a dunce at sport, success in which area had hitherto been the sole criterion for Head Boyship; they must, I reasoned, have wanted something different. So I gave it to them. I vigorously set about transforming the prefectorial system, attempting to increase the prefects' power and responsibilities and diminish those of the teachers. The headmaster, like many another absolute ruler who has wanted to make a gesture in the direction of change, found that he didn't in fact want to change anything, and blocked my reforms. I handed in my notice. Like Lady Bracknell, he told me that if I should cease to be Head Boy, he would inform me of the fact; until then I was to go back to doing what every other Head Boy had done. As this amounted to being tall and handsome and doing dashing things with balls, I was unable to oblige, and sulked my way through my year of tenure, in office but not in power.

I left school in a state of high disgust, reviling the academic life in any form, determined above all not to go to university. Instead, I went to work in Oppenheim's Library Wholesalers in South Kensington, which was a mistake for someone who loved books, as it involved carrying large piles of Mills and Boon romantic novels from one shelf to another. My visits to the National at the Old Vic became compulsive. As I have recorded elsewhere, my passion for it, and especially for what I perceived to be the company spirit that seemed to touch every part of that organisation – ushers, book- stall, ice-cream sellers – led me to write a three-foolscap-page letter to Olivier himself. I stood by the letter box trembling before I finally bit the bullet and shoved the letter in. Astoundingly, he wrote back by return of post, inviting me to come and work at the Old Vic, in the box office. This was my first professional connection with the theatre. I could scarcely have hoped for a more exhilarating one. The National, though it was going through a slightly sticky patch, was still close to its golden zenith. When I went to work there in 1967, it was only five years after it had opened, and I sold tickets for some of the productions which had made it world famous, bringing a level of glamour to the classical theatre that it had scarcely known since the days of Irving and Tree. Olivier's combination of absolute mastery of the physical aspects of acting with a determination to make his work speak directly to the audience about their own lives per- meated the organisation he had created, which felt dedicated in every fibre of its being to creating the nightly miracles on stage that I was now able to see as often as I liked.

Ken Tynan's influence was everywhere too. He would appear in a foyer or down a corridor, a haunted, brooding presence, immensely tall, his legs stick-thin, the skin pulled tight over his skull, eyes bulging with intelli- gence, a lit cigarette always delicately held between second and third fingers. At the age of forty-two he was already the figure he later described himself as being, Tynanosaurus Rex, his best work behind him. To me he seemed mythic, more so, curiously, than Olivier himself, whose offstage persona of absent-minded senior clerk of a city company was unimpressive, if endearing. At the time, Tynan was notorious: he had just

39

said 'fuck' on television, he was talking about producing an erotic revue, and he was publicly at war with the Board of the National. I of course knew nothing about the dramas that were at the time engulfing the organisation; I simply knew that if the National were anything like the sort of theatre Tynan lauded in his reviews – glamorous, cosmopolitan, provocative – then I wanted to be part of it. On the whole, it was, and that it was, was in no small measure thanks to him; but it was a brief golden age, and it ended badly for both Olivier and Tynan. When he left the National, Tynan lost an empire, and never thereafter found a role. Even I was vaguely aware that there was dissent in the ranks, that my hero was on the way out as a result of titanic boardroom struggles, that Sir Laurence was not as well as he might be. All this gossip was thrilling: the National was always in the newspapers, the world and his wife wanted tickets, there was a constant sense of its place at the centre of cultural life. For me this was exactly what I had dreamed of. However menial my position might be (and it was), Life seemed suddenly to matter; I seemed to have escaped the rut of the ordinary, to be condemned to which was the thing I dreaded more than anything in life.

But more than that, I was able, eventually, to observe the life of the theatre. It was a real company, over a hundred people uncomfortably squeezed together in that cramped and antiquated building. Olivier had with brilliant cunning insisted on a cheap but excellent canteen in the Old Vic, so that everyone would eat there. There I met people central to the running of the theatre but of whose existence I had hitherto scarcely been aware: electricians, stage carpenters, wardrobe mistresses, wig masters, stage managers, all evidently feeling themselves part of some mad dysfunctional family, rubbing up against each other with a boisterous and occasionally venomous esprit de corps. The Stage Manager Diana Boddington was one of the first of the technical staff I got to know. Nearly forty years after I met her, I wrote her entry in the Dictionary of National Biography.

Diana Boddington was born in Blackpool on July 30th, 1921; she died in London on January 17th, 2002. She had retired from the National Theatre, where she had been the senior stage manager, in 1987, after a career in that profession which had lasted over forty-five years. She started out as an assistant electrician at the Old Vic – the de facto National Theatre – in 1941 during the Second World War; after the Vic was bombed, she stayed with the company when it transferred its operation to the New Theatre under the aegis of John Burrell, Ralph Richardson and Laurence Olivier. She and Olivier formed a strong working relationship on, among other productions in that legendary season, *Richard III, Henry IV Parts One* and *Two* and the famous double bill of *Oedipus* and *The Critic*, and she continued to work for him when in the late 1940s he became, under the banner of Laurence Olivier Productions, a commercial manager; she was stage manager on the LOP presentation of Orson Welles's *Othello* in 1951, and proved more than a match for that legendary temperament. Her lifelong bond with Olivier was essentially one of camaraderie; they had once taken refuge together under a table at the National Portrait Gallery when surprised by an air raid, and something of the spirit of those days continued to characterise their relationship. When, in 1962, Olivier was appointed to the Chichester Festival Theatre as its first direc-tor, Boddington went with him, and then accompanied him to the National Theatre at the Old Vic in the following year.

Her working partnership with Olivier was explosive, her occasionally excessive candour resulting in fierce arguments which frequently ended with him angrily dismissing her; she would be reinstated the following day amid emotional apologies and reconciliations. She remained at the National Theatre for some thirteen years after Olivier's departure from the company and its transfer to the South Bank, providing a vital living continuity between Olivier's regime and that of his successor Peter Hall. In truth, she was always something of an anomaly in Denys Lasdun's great concrete emporium, with her flat sandals, her check dresses, her round spectacles and her straight up-and-down haircut, making her look for all the world like someone in charge of the tombola at a parish fête, though her vigorous use of four-letter words might have curled the vicar's hair. (In fact, she was an ardent Roman Catholic and cycled to work every morning after having attended six o'clock mass.) She never entirely mastered the new stage technology which developed so rapidly in the 1970s: the Tannoy system was a particular pitfall for her. Giving the actors their calls, she would often forget to remove her finger from the button, thus continuing to broadcast her private thoughts to the entire theatre: 'Ladies and gentlemen of the *Henry VIII* company, at this after-noon's performance the part of Cardinal Wolsey will be taken by Mr Henry Jones... I can't think why, I worked with him twenty years ago and he was useless then.'

It was not for her technical skills that she was cherished. It was for her sense of what the human beings involved in the process required in order to do their best work: directors, wardrobe department, make-up, stage-management team, above all, actors, of whom she was especially fond, in her no-nonsense way. 'Marshal Boddington' she was dubbed by the intake of '64 (which included Michael Gambon and Derek Jacobi), bluffly organising and rallying her troops. She was not a democrat, was, indeed, a famously devoted monarchist, and insisted on proper titles and a sense of the natural hierarchy within the company. Whatever she called Olivier to his face, behind his back she defended him like a tiger. Even on the impersonal South Bank, she managed to maintain a quality which is seriously imperilled in the vast theatrical organisations of today: theatre as family. Her sense of *esprit de corps* was profound; somewhere inside her lived the spirit of the wartime Old Vic, speaking for England – the theatre as a gallant enterprise made up of individual human beings, a human pyramid of which every member was made to feel his or her vital importance. It was an inestimable boon for actors and directors, and an inspiring example for generations of stage managers who worked with her or were trained by her, an example on which the future of the theatre as a human enterprise greatly depends. Very properly, in view both of her services to the stage and her devotion to the Royal Family, she was the first (and so far the only) stage manager to be appointed MBE.

The theatre was her life, so it is remarkable that she led such a cheerfully happy domestic existence with her husband, the actor Aubrey Richards, who predeceased her by some two years. Boddington is survived by her two children, Claudia and David, whose upbringing and indeed whose very existence, given the extraordinary length of their mother's working day, were, in the words of a witty colleague, something of a mystery.

This sense that the theatre could become one's life was intoxicating to me. I felt something that those who have undergone religious conversions feel: a huge, a relieving, a joyful sense of the rightness of things, of belonging, of having a purpose. I scarcely knew what my contribution could be, and for the time being simply gloried in being part of it. To my surprise, it was perfectly possible and indeed easy to talk to the actors – especially the young ones, like Mike Gambon or Jane Lapotaire or Derek Jacobi. Far from being members of some rarefied caste, they were eminently human – almost too human: noisy, expansive, tactile, emotional, hilarious. Of course, I didn't know who they were: they were just the young bloods of the company. What was more remarkable was that the famous ones – Maggie Smith, Bill Fraser, Jeremy Brett – were just the same, and though they perhaps appeared more preoccupied than the others (because, I assumed, they were playing leading parts), they were just as much part of the family, and just as prone to shriek or roar or burst into tears. Astonishingly, Laurence Olivier was quite likely to be found at one's table in the canteen. The anxious thought that one was eating one's scampi and chips with Richard III was dispelled by the amiable, slightly distracted manner of the man himself. When I finally saw him on stage, at the Vic, in The Dance of Death, it was almost impossible to connect him with the man I had eaten with in the canteen, who would occasionally drop in to the box office for a cheery chat, but his slightly dotty affability, his wonderment at the fact that money was changing hands, that tickets were being sold, that we had cash tills and calculators, booking plans and specially printed stationery, seemed to have nothing whatever to do with the animal that prowled the stage night after night.

It is pretty well impossible to convey in words the physical impact of Olivier's presence in the flesh as an actor; I have spent many years on and off trying to do so with only middling success. It seemed to me important to make the effort, since his film work, even the magisterial performances in his Shakespeare trilogy and The Entertainer, for example, gives little hint of what it was like to see him on stage – of the sheer sexual energy he unleashed into the auditorium. Only rock stars or great singers and dancers can compare, but he had no microphone to amplify his voice, nor any orchestra to support him except the music of speech – no choreography but his own instinctual expressivity. He bent every muscle in his body, every note in his voice, to ravish the audience, to take us – by force, if necessary. It was a seduction on the grandest and most extravagant scale, perilously close to rape; above all, it was dangerous. By now, I had seen Gielgud, Guinness, Richardson, Redgrave and Ashcroft on stage, all superb actors, who had the gift of drawing you nearer to them. But this was something else. It was domination. It was a head-on assault. It was total war.

I still have difficulty in putting together the man from the canteen and the man on stage. Whatever the alchemy that transformed the one into the other was, I began to grasp, another essence of acting. I tried to sum him up for an entry in Cassell's Encyclopaedia of Theatre in the Twentieth Century.

The son of an Anglo-Catholic priest, Laurence Olivier (b. 1907), demonstrated few gifts as a child for anything other than acting, but at this he was from the earliest age exceptional. As a ten-year-old, he was spotted as Kate in *The Taming of the Shrew* by Ellen Terry, who said, 'This child is already a great actor.' His early career was however far from meteoric. Slight of build, gap-toothed, his face burdened with continuous eyebrows and a very low forehead, he presented a somewhat wild appearance. In conjunction with his enormous high spirits and propensity for uncontrollable giggling on stage, he needed taming. This was provided first of all by the Central School, then run by its founder Elsie Fogerty, by a season or two at the Birmingham Rep, and finally by a longish stint in the unrewarding role of Victor Prynne in the London and New York runs of Coward's *Private Lives*, with the author in the cast to keep a sharp eye on him. At this stage, Olivier's ambitions were entirely directed towards achieving the status of romantic leading man. He made a number of miscalculations however: instead of continuing with the role of Stanhope in *Journey's End*, which he had created, he chose to star in *Beau Geste*, a conspicuous catastrophe: and a brief visit to Hollywood had left him disenchanted with film. The turning point in his career came when, in 1935, John Gielgud, who had previously directed him in *Queen of Scots*, invited him to alternate the roles of Romeo and Mercutio with him at the New Theatre. Olivier, having by now had his teeth and his hairline adjusted, and acquired a degree of professional discipline, came to Shakespeare with a passionate conviction that the plays were essentially realistic. His performances, as a highly sexed Mediterranean Romeo and a dangerous, wild Mercutio, created a sensation, most particularly by contrast with the lyrical and aesthetically modulated performances of Gielgud. His verse-speaking was disparaged ('Mr Oliver does not speak verse badly; he does not speak it at all'), but it was clear that an actor capable of reinventing the tradition of classical acting had arrived. This was confirmed when in 1937 he joined the Old Vic company under the direction of Tyrone Guthrie, playing in quick succession Hamlet, Henry V, Macbeth, Coriolanus and Iago. Thus established as a leading classical actor, he returned to Hollywood for *Wuthering Heights*. His Heathcliff gave him international stardom, but with England at war, he returned home as quickly as possible (against the advice of the British Embassy), first of all to join the Fleet Air Arm, then to direct a film of *Henry V*, as part of the war effort. This triumphant realisation was followed in 1944 by the assumption of the co-directorship with Ralph Richardson and

Michael Benthall of the Old Vic Company. The productions of *Peer Gynt*, *Henry IV*, *Arms and the Man* and *King Lear* became a focus of national pride to such an extent that the productions and his own performances, above all as Richard III and in the audacious double bill of *Oedipus Rex* and *The Critic*, represent high watermarks in the history of the British theatre. It is all the more astonishing that when plans were laid to establish the National Theatre at the Old Vic in 1946, in one of the most disgraceful episodes of modern theatre, it was decided that Olivier and Richardson would not head it; actors, it was felt, were unsuitable for the task of running so important and complex an organisation. The National Theatre took another twenty years to come into existence; Olivier went into theatre management on his own, and for some four years was more involved in directing or presenting than acting. He re-entered the lists as a tragic Shakespearean actor with *Macbeth* and *Titus Andronicus*, both at Stratford, the latter directed by Peter Brook. Both performances were acclaimed; the Titus particularly as a radical interpretation in a startling production.

It seemed to prepare him for the great leap which he took two years later, when he appeared at the Royal Court Theatre as Archie Rice in John Osborne's *The Entertainer*. The first actor of his generation or stature to associate himself with the new wave of playwrights, he scored an enormous personal success and boosted the new movement. His straddling of the old and the new, added to his managerial experience and personal authority, made him the inevitable and only choice for the directorship of the National Theatre when in 1962 it was finally voted by Parliament. Drawing together the best talents from the various theatrical worlds he had inhabited – the Royal Court, the West End and the Classical theatre – he created an organisation which for some years set new standards of excellence. Directing, acting (his Othello, Shylock, Edgar in *Dance of Death*, James Tyrone in *Long Day's Journey Into Night* and Tagg in *The Party* were among the outstanding creations of those years) and leading very much from the front, he brought the century-old dream of a National Theatre to life in a way that no one else could have done. Towards the end of his tenure, tiredness and ill-health led to a slight decline in the vigour of the work, but he laid the foundations for a flourishing organisation. After retiring from the National Theatre in 1973 he never appeared on stage again, though he continued and continues to make film appearances. Since the war, in fact, he has acted in over twenty films, often with great distinction, but without ever quite seeming to belong in the medium. It is his work on the stage that has brought him the immortality he so fervently sought, and from the early Fifties it has been a commonplace for English-speaking actors (Americans as well as British) to refer to him as the greatest living actor. Certainly no one in our century has challenged himself more. Transforming himself vocally and physically for every part, he has left an indelible stamp on a number of the greatest roles in the repertory. He always sought a realistic core to his characterisations which sometimes robbed them of their poetry or their grandeur; but in compensation he brought comedy verging on the vulgar, physical audacity bordering on the reckless and an emotional intensity that could be terrifying. Olivier never concealed his virtuosity: he wanted his audiences to be as interested in the mechanics of acting as he was. His ambition was so huge, his achievement so great, that his disappearance from the stage has left something of a vacuum. This was to some extent deliberate. Asked who would inherit Kean's sword (given to Olivier by John Gielgud after a performance of *Richard III*) he replied: 'No one: it's mine.' A question mark thus hangs over the very idea of great acting in our age.

It was often said of him that Olivier ruthlessly eliminated the competition, and this was no doubt true of his peers in his own generation, with whom he rarely appeared on stage after his wartime seasons at the Old Vic. But at the National Theatre, his ideal, like that of Peter Hall at the Royal Shakespeare Company, was an ensemble, a group of people who stay together, committed to each other and to an idea. Olivier surrounded himself with the very best of the younger generation; he carefully modelled their careers, noting what challenges would most benefit them, giving advice and encouragement, teaching by example, leading from the front. They adored him, these young actors. 'Captain, my Captain,' they might have cried, and they would have followed him, at the beginning at least, to the ends of the earth. I wrote this piece about companies for The Times *in the late 1980s at a time when arts organisations were severely threatened by cutbacks – a cyclical phenomenon of which we can no doubt expect a great deal more in the near future.*

The creation of any artistic company or organisation – an orchestra or a theatre group, an art gallery or a drama school – is a slow and arduous business, dependent on vision, determination, cunning and skill. It generally starts small and poverty-stricken, its beginnings modest and uncertain; then, thanks to blind faith, hard work and an unwavering commitment to standards, the growing organism begins to get stronger, to expand, to flourish. At this point the judicious application of extra funds can have a transformative effect; the solid struggling work of the earliest days begins to pay off in gorgeous blooms. From the beginning, too, the company will have been cultivating its audience, exciting and involving them with the nature of the work, charming and challenging them, giving them something of what they know they like along with some of what they're not really sure about. Carefully but purposefully, the company creates a loyalty and a trust in its audience; they adventure into the unknown together.

Somewhere about this point, the critics discover it, and heap trowels of praise on the work in rather indiscriminate manner, till suddenly the company is fashionable, and the world rushes to see it. The company grows still more; it becomes an institution; the board is stuffed with the great and the good; costs spiral. Then the critics reach for their shovels again and start to heap the opposite of praise on it. Then questions are asked in Parliament, and people get weary of the whole thing and the bully-boy phrases 'pulling the plug' and 'starting from scratch' are bandied about. And sometimes, after an episode of mismanagement or scandal, the company/school/museum is shut down. And then it's gone, gone for ever.

Because make no mistake, the tree thus felled will not grow again overnight. The process has to start all over again, but the skills and the confidence and the trust and the continuity have been destroyed for good and all. An arts organisation is not a Millennium Dome, some gaudy palace thrown up ostentatiously to celebrate the awful emptiness of the age; it is a growing, living thing, which exists to enrich and sustain the whole of society. This is not brainwashing, nor is it an imposed discipline: it's about building some sort of inner resource within individuals so they don't have to keep looking to superficial stimulation to feel alive, but are able to build their understanding and experience, to develop what's naturally within them.

*Around the late 1960s, Olivier became ill, there was dissension among the National Theatre Associates, and things began to fall apart. At exactly the point I arrived, there was a rather bad wobble – two ill-fated productions by an ailing Tyrone Guthrie (*Volpone *and* Tartuffe*), then an experimental* Triple Bill *which included an adaptation of John Lennon's* In His Own Write *and which pleased no one, and finally a deeply shocking production of Seneca's savage* Oedipus *by Peter Brook which turned the place upside down and culminated in a fierce row between Brook and Olivier (about whether 'God save the Queen' should be played at the end of the evening, of all absurd things), a row which Olivier bruisingly lost. A notice went up at the Stage Door officially abandoning the practice of playing the National Anthem. The old lion had been bested by a whelp. From my vantage point in the box office, I was privy to all this. News of each and every development swept through the building, even as it was happening – sometimes before it happened; there was a lot of tutting and long faces and sage head-wagging, as in any organisation. At the National, things were never quite the same again, people said, after Sir Laurence lost his battle with Peter Brook.*

Oedipus was nothing but trouble. It was the occasion of another, very public, battle, but of an entirely different kind: the unequal struggle of an actor with his role, or perhaps, more accurately, with his role in the production. Sir John Gielgud was palpably uncomfortable playing Seneca's Oedipus in a brown polo-necked jumper, surrounded by sobbing, moaning, panting actors similarly attired, strapped to pillars, on a golden set dominated by a huge spike on which Irene Worth finally impaled her vagina. Rumours from the rehearsal room had suggested imminent catastrophe, and certainly the dress rehearsal (which, like all members of the company, I attended) was an unhappy affair, with Sir John wandering aimlessly about, his face contorted in a pained expression which seemed to have nothing to do with Oedipus's dilemma and everything to do with his own. I made a point of watching all the previews and saw the production gain power, releasing the horror in a way that no conventional production could have done, while Gielgud, too, little by little, seemed to find his bearings, though not quite by the first night, when he still had the demeanour of a deer caught in headlights. I kept going back, though, and was amazed and eventually deeply moved to see the actor start to become part of the production, then to lead it, and finally to create a performance of such economical anguish that it was almost unbearable to watch, in its disci-

plined pathos. I had to revise my opinion of Gielgud, whom I had just seen foundering as an absurdly miscast Orgon in Tartuffe *and had dismissed, bewildered that he was considered, by shrewd judges, to be Olivier's equal, if not, murmured some, his superior. Now I saw the point, and never missed any performance he gave thereafter. Later, I came to know him personally a bit, and understood something of the depth and brilliance of his talent. This is a review of Sheridan Morley's 2001 authorised biography.*

It really did seem as if Gielgud would be with us for ever, the living embodiment of another time, another world. There was nothing old-fashioned or *derrière-garde* about him though: he seemed younger and more modern with every passing year, an elderly newborn baby, brimming over with curiosity and mischief, spontaneous and affirmative. Often he appeared in preposterous pieces of work, but however absurd or feeble the piece, it was always good to see him; sometimes, for a gala or a memorial, he would speak some verse, and then time would stand still, and one knew that he was not just charming and gracious and stylish and funny, but that he was one of the Immortals.

He made the surprising provision in his will that there must be no memorial of any sort after his death – surprising, because he of all people must have known that no matter what the actor feels, the audience needs to applaud at the end of the show. In his case, the need was even more compelling than usual, since he commanded a unique degree of affection and admiration from both profession and public, quite different in kind from the feelings inspired by his great contemporaries Richardson and Olivier, both of whom predeceased him. Certainly, the pomp and more than slightly gaudy spectacle of Olivier's state funeral at Westminster Abbey – all fanfares and fulsome farewells, the theatre on its knees, Joe Allen at prayer – would have been quite inappropriate for a man who throughout his long life had stood for a certain fastidiousness, an impeccability of taste and a precision of communication quite inimical to the grander gestures so easily commanded by the man who over the course of both their nearly overlapping careers had waged a unilateral war of rivalry against him. Gielgud in later years had even been reluctant to celebrate his important birthdays, not wishing to advertise his great antiquity. Nonetheless, from very near the start of his career, he had been celebrated, willy-nilly, in interviews, in articles and in books: in 1937, when he was thirty-four, the most brilliant of American theatre writers, Rosamond Gilder, had devoted an entire long and well-illustrated volume to his Broadway *Hamlet*. During the remaining sixty years of his life, many other books were devoted to his art; and he himself maintained a steady flow of vividly written reminiscences, mostly, and typically, centred on the extraordinary people he had worked with or simply admired. Inevitably, when he died, a couple of books immediately appeared, one, engagingly chatty, by Gyles Brandreth, the other scholarly and monumental, by Jonathan Croall. But the book that was most eagerly awaited was the one that Gielgud himself had commissioned, the authorised biography by Sheridan Morley. Perhaps this would be the memorial, the monument his will proscribed?

Gielgud himself was hilariously ambivalent about the book, which he invariably referred to as The Book. Whenever one met him over the last ten years of his life, the conversation would quickly advert to it. 'Sheridan's been writing The Book for ever. I wish he'd hurry up. I think he's waiting for me to die. Perhaps it would be better if I did. I rather dread him writing about all the queer stuff. I suppose it has to be done, but I don't want to be here to read the reviews. Perhaps I should stop him. Oh dear, I wish he'd get on with it.' It was, of course, the queer stuff that he had had in mind when he had proposed the book to Morley, specifically his arrest in 1953 for soliciting in a public lavatory, which, after a brief furore in the press at the time, and despite its being fairly common knowledge thereafter, had scarcely been alluded to in public since. It is indeed good to have the story told in precise detail, not least from a sociological point of view. Morley carefully creates the background of repression and hysteria against which the incident took place, relating the details which though nightmarish at the time now have an *Alice in Wonderland* quality to them – Gielgud, giving his name as Arthur, told the police in that inimitable voice that he was a clerk earning £1,000 a year, living in Cowley Street (then as now one of the most expensive parts of town) – and recording the panic and anger of other homosexuals, like Noël Coward and Frederick Ashton and the all-powerful West End producer Binkie Beaumont, his principal employer, who felt that Gielgud had acted selfishly and thoughtlessly. Morley quotes the interview Gielgud gave him (the only time he ever spoke about the incident on the record) to moving effect: 'Why didn't I call on Binkie's help…? I was thoroughly ashamed, not of what I had done but of being caught, and I couldn't bear to hear the anger and disappointment in Binkie's voice. Then again, I had some vague Westminster-schoolboy idea that when you were in trouble you had to stand on your own two feet, and "take it like a man".' Morley gives us the astonishing scene of the council of war summoned by Binkie to determine how to handle the crisis. For sheer horror, the arrest and subsequent fine pale by comparison with the prospect of being advised in such a delicate matter by a committee consisting of Laurence Olivier, Vivien Leigh, the extremely homophobic Ralph Richardson and his wife, Glen Byam Shaw (then running Stratford) and his wife. All of them, except for – perhaps predictably – Olivier, urged him to carry on regardless with the production of *A Day by the Sea* in which he was about to open as star and director. Most touchingly of all, Morley describes in loving detail, the courage and heroic professionalism this course of action called for, and the wonderful generosity of fellow actors (above all, the doyenne of them all, Sybil Thorndike, who greeted him when he returned to rehearsals with the incomparable remark, 'Well, John, what a very silly bugger you have been,' and then gently and lovingly steered him through the subsequent storm). He was nobly supported by the public, too, who gave him a huge ovation on his first appearance in the play, capped by an even greater one when he uttered his first line: 'Oh dear, I'd forgotten we had all those azaleas' – a response which suggests what, contrary to received opinion, some of us have believed for a long time: that Britain is rather fond of its homosexuals.

This chapter of the book is very fine, and almost self-contained, as was the episode itself in Gielgud's life, despite the lifelong reluctance it inspired in him ever to raise the matter in public. Throughout the book, Morley heroically strives to give due weight to his subject's sex life, but it is something of a losing battle, because sex – though pleasurable – genuinely seems to have been of peripheral importance for him; certainly here you will find none of the 'filthy details' that Gielgud confessed to so relishing in the novels of Harold Robbins and Jacqueline Susann. It is hard to deduce from Morley's pages what Gielgud's feelings were for his two longest-serving partners, the glamorous, hedonistic John Perry, who left him for Binkie, and the acidulous Hungarian, Martin Hensler, with whom for the last forty years of his life he was locked in a relationship that seemed hellish to most outsiders but was clearly sustaining and profound for him. The absence of photographs of either doesn't help. When Hensler (twenty years younger) died, Gielgud, like any spouse bereft of the central feature of his domestic landscape, was bewildered and soon started to allow himself to slip away – in harness, as he would have wished, on his ninety-sixth birthday filming a Samuel Beckett script, which, to his chagrin, was wordless: a poignant prediction of the imminent silencing of the most beautiful speaking voice of the twentieth century, which finally occurred a few weeks later.

The great bulk of *John Gielgud* is devoted to recording the career of that voice's owner, and it does so thoroughly and engagingly. Morley is of the chronicle school of biographers, eschewing dry analysis in favour of an enthusiastic evocation of the ambience and aura of his subject. He is the John Aubrey of biographers, irresistibly drawn to gossip, believing – rightly – that an anecdote is often more revealing than an autopsy. His affection for Gielgud is palpable and his appreciation warm; he understands (partly thanks to his own family background in the theatre and his own experiences as director and performer) what the job consists of, what is hard and what is easy. He unfolds the story with considerable flair and a great deal of judicious quotation, tracking his quarry into every nook and cranny of his career. Interestingly and unexpectedly, however, despite impeccable thoroughness, he ends up with an enigma, or at the very least a phenomenon, that no amount of investigation can explain. As the patient chronicle unfolds, Gielgud himself (generally referred to by Morley as John G, which rather adds to the mystery, as if he were a character in a Chekhov short story) becomes more and more inexplicable. The given circumstances are all clearly established – the cultured Anglo-Polish background (how curious that our two greatest actors should have both had such unEnglish names!) with theatre blood on both sides, but most directly on the side of his mother, Kate Terry, giving the young stage-struck boy access to his aunt Ellen Terry and her notorious son, Edward Gordon Craig (Uncle Ted); the fairly swift establishment of his career after a stumbling start, leading him to almost universal acclaim by the age of twenty-five when he played his first Hamlet at the Old Vic; his first Lear, when he was a whole year older, was accounted an almost equal success. From now on he was regarded as a paragon in classical theatre (even if, as Agate succinctly observed, 'all that goes with a bowler hat eludes him') despite the fact that he was, as he was always the first to admit, very awkward physically: many are the attempts to describe his peculiarly inexpressive physique, from Ivor Brown's famous description of him as 'niminy-piminy... scant of virility... from the waist down he looks nothing. He has the most meaningless legs imaginable', to Lynn Fontanne's (apparently approving) remarks comparing him to 'a new-born colt, and I also adore your feet, which are the youngest I have ever seen on stage'. But it was the voice, always the voice, which drew the most eloquent praise. His seemingly instinctive ability to speak verse was widely perceived to be an inherited gift ('the Terry voice'; like Ellen he spoke Shakespeare 'as if he had only just left him in the next room'); the same was said of his emotionalism ('the Terry tears'). Soon he began to direct, then to create companies within the commercial theatre, and both in his productions and in his companies he pioneered an integrated approach to the theatre which was in its way, and in its day, radical. He also constantly challenged himself by working with the greatest talents: Komisarjevsky, Harley Granville Barker, Michel Saint-Denis, Peter Brook, Noguchi, Derek Jarman, Edith Evans, the young Olivier, the young Scofield. There were ups and downs, including a period in the wilderness when he seemed to have lost his touch, only to reinvent himself in a series of plays from Brook's primitively powerful production of Seneca's *Oedipus* and Alan Bennett's *Forty Years On* to the triumphant Indian Summer partnership with Ralph Richardson in Storey's *Home* and Pinter's *No Man's Land*.

Eventually, inevitably, as he entered his tenth and final decade he began to feel a little detached from the theatre (memorably remarking, after the Globe was renamed the Gielgud, that 'at last there's a name on Shaftesbury Avenue that I can recognise'), but his contribution to the theatre and to the art of acting was universally acknowledged; even Lee Strasberg, who might have been expected to be fundamentally opposed to everything he was and stood for, noted that 'when he speaks a line you hear Shakespeare thinking'. An exemplary life in the theatre, a life of unceasing devotion to the art, of unremitting creation of extraordinary performances and exquisite productions. The theatre was his home, the centre of his being. As his mother remarked of her young son: 'When he was not acting in the theatre, going to the theatre or talking about the theatre, he was to all intents and purposes not living.' His writing about theatre (liberally quoted in *John Gielgud*) is lucid, elegant and practical; he has little time for theory, but he has a matchless gift for going to the heart of a play or a performance.

None of this quite accounts for the extraordinary impact he had. There was something about his performances which was beyond interpretation, beyond intelligence, beyond talent even. This was as true in life as it was on the stage. It is Alan Bennett who puts a name to it: a name that Gielgud would dismiss with a giggle. The word is 'saintly': 'But,' adds Bennett, 'it requires no effort. He was just born good, there has been no struggle to get there.' Perhaps the word is grace, in the theological as well as the social sense, a kind of effortless radiance stemming from some profound ground of being. Derek Granger put it in more secular terms: his acting, according to Granger, is about 'everything that is expressive of an intense inner life'. 'The poetry in John always sustains him and nurtures his spirit,' says Dudley Moore, Gielgud's co-star in the most unlikely of all his manifestations, *Arthur*. 'We all need to find what John has.' Peter Brook notes that 'submerged in each of John's performances is a core which is pure, clear, strong, simple and utterly realistic'; 'His rhetoric is impeccable,' says Lindsay Anderson, 'but his moments of pure, exposed emotion are inexpressibly touching... sheer and absolute acting genius.' And yet – and this is the paradox – this is a man who said of himself with no false modesty, 'In the theatre I have quite good taste: in my real life I'm absolutely tasteless. Outside the theatre, I'm clumsy with my hands. I'm a very bad judge of character. I'm not learned. I'm always so terribly aware of how little I know.' A man who loved to catch the occasional porn movie, who gloried in gossip, who cracked wonderfully silly schoolboy jokes. Yet to be with him was a benison, a curiously exhilarating and anarchic experience, as the lightning celerity of his thought processes took you on a kind of helter-skelter ride of surreal non sequiturs, sudden accesses of emotion and ribald asides made all the more bizarre for being uttered in those honeyed tones by the impeccably elegant gent before you. It was a personality like none other, bearing some small resemblance perhaps to the licentious monks of the Zen tradition. Certainly there was something of God about it.

John Gielgud is a very good, warm-hearted and almost comprehensive account of the man and his career, written with unmistakable affection. The story is a little repetitive, but then so was the life; essentially it was one show after another. While Olivier's life was a wild, Marlovian, *Sturm und Drang* affair of titanic ambition and cruel humiliations, Gielgud's was altogether more Mozartian, with occasional darknesses and minor-key interludes, but on a much more even keel, sparkling and sunny, pulsing with inner life. It perhaps calls for a Ronald Firbank or an E. F. Benson to do full justice to its subject's tender, frolicsome, sublime spirit, but in their absence, *John Gielgud* will do very nicely.

For an eighteen-year-old to be exposed, however much at second hand, to these huge figures, and to the processes of theatre-making at such an exalted level, was intoxicating and inspiring. I sneaked into rehearsals at the Vic whenever I could and was mesmerised by what I saw from the shadows at the back of the stalls – fascinated not so much by the occasional brilliance on show, but, on the contrary, by the slowness and the difficulty of the job, by the painstaking struggle and trial and error. This was work, *the first work I had come across that I really wanted to do. Then, and only then, was born in me the desire to become an actor. Being part of the theatre – albeit in the box office – had cured me of any illusions about the glamour of the theatre. In the canteen I had overheard enough about the frustrations and disappointments of the job to be disabused of any showbiz tosh; I had seen the toll that running the theatre was taking on Olivier; I was aware of the violent clashes of personality which could tear a theatre apart; I had observed from my eyrie in the box office how success was by no means guaranteed, even to the most talented – and there is no clearer proof of the public's unsentimentality than in the cash till. But I was excited by the thought of being part of the enterprise of putting on a play, of working – as I saw it – at the coalface of art, of grappling with all these massive and intractable problems, because the reward at the end would be to bring to life some great and complex story which might shake an audience out of its complacency or its depression, as I had seen it shaken by* The Dance of Death, *by* A Flea in Her Ear *and, shatteringly, by* Oedipus, *and perhaps change its life. I also had a pretty clear idea of the colossal amount of will involved in the process, and that one could get badly burned in action. But it was all that I wanted.*

In the box office (along with the Box Office Manager's copy of the then-banned Last Exit to Brooklyn, *which was kept in the safe), we all read a hot new theatre novel,* Next Season, *by the director Michael Blakemore. It was, one was reliably assured, not about us at the National but about the old Shakespeare Memorial Theatre. Either way, it tore the lid off the life*

*of a theatre company. We were agog. I felt that it had been written for me
personally, that I was destined to read it at exactly that moment. It may
seem improbable that a youth as theatre-obsessed as I was had not contemplated the idea of becoming an actor, but the penny had finally
dropped. Many years later, I wrote an introduction for a paperback reis-
sue of Blakemore's novel.*

When I first read *Next Season*, its jacket had been replaced with brown
paper. It was being passed around the box office and front of house at the
National Theatre like a *samizdat*. This was 1969; though no more than a
year old, it was already out of print. It was widely rumoured to be a
roman-à-clef, although no one seemed very clear as to who precisely the
characters were based on. 'Sir' (Laurence) was one of the models, said
some; Peter Hall another, according to the head usher. The events referred
to the Nottingham Playhouse, if you believed one lot; no, said a different
crowd, it was Stratford-upon-Avon. We faintly knew who Michael Blakemore was: he ran the Citizens' Theatre in Glasgow, where Albert Finney
had gone after his film *Tom Jones*; and 'Albert' (we felt we owned him)
had just opened on Broadway in Blakemore's acclaimed production of *A
Day in the Death of Joe Egg*. All I really knew was that it was about the
theatre, and it had been written by an insider. That was more than
enough for me.

The sensational aspect of the book went right over my head. I tried, from
my tiny store of theatre lore, to identify the characters, or at least
Braddington, where the novel was set. It was hopeless; but after a very
few pages, I had ceased even to try, because something far more important was coming through: this man was telling me what it was like to be
an actor. I had found what I was looking for. The other books – I'd read
them all – told you *how* to act (Stanislavsky) or (Michael Redgrave)
mused on the *meaning* of acting, but this one was about the demands and
the rewards of acting, what it takes from you, what it gives you back. Acting as work, work as passion. I cried for joy. A way of life existed which
would use my energy, my brain, my bursting heart; one which was useful and important. Somehow, never having set foot on a stage, I knew that
Sam Beresford/Michael Blakemore's experience was authentic; knew all
about his fear that his small part would be cut, his elation at finding a
characterisation that released the scene's wit and menace, his obsession

with finding and if necessary making the right kind of glasses for the part, his despair at failing to triumph when called on to take over from another actor. Above all, I knew exactly what he meant when, running through the part of Hamlet in his mind, he felt 'an absolute certainty that he could play the bloody thing, that if a stage were to materialise at that very moment, he could step on to it and astonish any audience, any-where'. He was speaking directly to the as-yet-unrealised actor in me.

Everything that I encountered when I eventually became one confirmed what Blakemore had written. Rereading the book the other day I was struck all over again by the precision and vividness of the observation; but now I saw that I had been too swept away by the revelation of acting to see what a very good novel it is. Sam Beresford, the central character, is mercilessly exposed in his emotional confusions and calculations, try-ing, in a rather cold way, to organise his sexual relationships, angry and frustrated when they don't work out. The milieu of a young actor of the late Fifties is excellently evoked, its greyness and dinginess the more sharply perceived in the light of Beresford/Blakemore's Australian back-ground. 'Grey towns drowning in lakes of smoke; hills plowed into rows of terraces that presented against the sky silhouettes as sharp and ugly as blades of rusty serrated saws.' And Braddington, the theatre and the social life of the company are all well done. But the novel's great triumph is to have placed an actor's work, his professional and creative processes, at the centre, and to have made the artistic vicissitudes of a young man who is not yet and perhaps never will be a great artist, so enthralling. The sense of uplift achieved at the end of the novel because that young man is going to continue to try to make theatre, is an exceptional achievement. Why should we care? But we do; desperately.

The conviction of ours, twenty years ago, that the book contained thinly veiled figures from the real world is not strictly true; Blakemore has transmuted his raw material into art, and conflated and refashioned his originals. If there is a *clef*, it is probably the Stratford season of 1959, in which the author played, but that legendary season in which Olivier, Robeson, and Edith Evans all appeared, was a very different affair to Braddington's. Touches of those great individuals can be seen here and there, but his major achievements of characterisation, Ivan Spears, the old classical star, and Tom Chester, the young director of the season, are so fully presented as to be archetypes rather than life-sketches. Spears, who has some traits of Charles Laughton, to whose 1959 Lear Blakemore was Knight, to whose Bottom he played Snout, distils practical wisdom to the point of genius, betraying deep understanding of the text with profound experience of realising it. 'Freddie, if you do get into difficulties, look, I think I have the trick of this scene. I think I could help you,' he says to his co-star, and we understand that the 'trick' is the master-craftsman's deep intimacy and ease with the play and the author. 'This particular play (*The Duchess of Malfi*) was Ivan's. Everything he said about it, and everything he did in his own performance, had an immediacy and a vigour which claimed the material as his own. Webster had found a spokesman, one who responded not so much to the formal qualities of his *play*, anchored in their own time, as to that enduring impulse that had led to the writing of it, and which, centuries later, in the terms of his own experience, Ivan was able to affirm. The play was his by right of talent, and he was there to turn its pages for the entire company.

In the character of Ivan, Blakemore affirms the actor's contribution both in himself ('in the terms of his own experience') and in his intuitive ability to release the play's (temporarily) frozen life – the profoundly creative coupling of the actor's inner universe with that of the play. In the context of the novel's action (the author metes him out a drastically symbolic fate), Ivan comes to embody the passing order. Tom Chester is what replaces him and his kind; Tom Chester, the prototypical directocrat, manipulator of destinies, coiner of clichés, the new man. It is a devastating portrait, bred of deep resentment. Blakemore shows the invisible processes by which the politician director, equipped with a few borrowed insights, a little oily charm and unlimited faith in his own indispensability, hijacks a complex craft from its true practitioners, replacing the living organism which was the end of their labours with a product which satisfies critics and Arts Councils and has every appearance of the real thing, but on closer examination proves to be only a plastic facsimile.

Blakemore's ear for the director-speak invented by Tom Chester and his contemporaries, part-matey, part-schoolmasterly, is flawless: 'Well, everybody, that was awful, absolutely awful. I can't tell you how bad it was. You've simply got to be better than that. And I know you can be.' And: 'This is a play about horror… we've got to create this atmosphere of darkness and cruelty, and really use the stage to suggest currents of evil moving through this enclosed Renaissance world.' More sinister, though, is Tom's power over careers and lives. In a chilling interview towards the end of the book, Tom tells Sam why he won't be in the next season: 'Talent's important, of course. Of primary importance. But talent's nothing without – well – ferocity. That's what makes it interesting. Class has gone. Race is going. You can't be above the battle any more. Which I sometimes think you try to be…? That's what I look for first in an actor. Determination is the polite word. Your trouble is you're a bit too nice.' These conversations continue to the present day; not even the script has changed. The important point, as Blakemore makes clear, is that Tom Chesterism has made the discussion of whether work is good or bad irrelevant, because the discussion is always conducted in their terms. They have won; and there will be no more Ivan Spears.

Unless…

The reprint of *Next Season* is timely, because it coincides with a resurgence of the independent spirit among actors. And this novel is the finest fictional celebration of the passionate craft of the actor. There have been remarkable novels of the theatre – from *Wilhelm Meister* to John Arden's magnificent *Silence Among the Weapons* – but no other book has so truly depicted the creative anarchic excitement of acting. Perhaps that's the real reason it was under brown-paper covers for so long.

There seemed no end to what the National Theatre at the Old Vic was able to give me. While I was there, I had also found a group of people – my colleagues in the box office – who counted as my first real friends. At school, I had had two very close friends (who eventually married each other), but workmates are a different matter. Your first job is the developing personality's first outing; you start to become the person you have been in training to be. I owe more than I can ever fully describe to those first friends: I modelled myself on some of them. They taught me how to trust other people, how to be funny, how to not let people down. Because of who they were – an amazing array of human flotsam and jetsam, with remarkable backgrounds, and in some cases real flashes of genius – we had an extraordinary time in what was really a very ordinary job; but we were all touched by the belief that we were involved in something remarkable, something that mattered. We felt part of the theatre at large – the wider community of the theatre – but specifically we were part of Olivier's empire and in some sort touched by its glory. From my personal point of view, these friends changed me immeasurably. It was with them that I did my first dining out, with them that I started to go to the movies on a regular basis, with them that I haunted theatres (and thanks to box-office connections there was no show to which I did not have access, and many shows to which I went free of charge).

On one memorable occasion, thanks to one of my box-office chums who knew him a bit, I had supper with the most jaggedly dangerous actor I have ever seen on any stage. I've described this meeting in Being an Actor; *in 1985, a year after the book appeared, he was dead, and I wrote a piece about him for the* Evening Standard *which they somewhat incongruously entitled* Farewell, Henry the Great.

Actors no doubt spend too much of their time together recounting stories which celebrate the absurdities, the perils and the glories of their profession. Inevitably, conversation turns on the great figures. We don't talk about just anyone; you have to be pretty remarkable to be discussed; either very much loved (like John Gielgud or Michael Gambon) or very much hated (like some other people); or simply phenomenal.

Into this last category falls, or rather fell, an actor little known to the public but a byword in the business, talked about wherever any of us more than thirty years old gather together. His name was Victor Henry, and he died ten days ago.

He acted mostly at the Royal Court in the late Sixties; unforgettable in the D. H. Lawrence trilogy and in a revival of *Look Back in Anger*, new-minting Jimmy Porter's rage; terrifying in Heathcote Williams's acid trip *AC/DC*; raw in the part he created in Christopher Hampton's *When Did You Last See My Mother?* He also created, magnificently, the role of Rimbaud in *Total Eclipse*; finally he gave an outrageous and ill-disciplined but quintessentially Jacobean Bosola in Peter Gill's production of *The Duchess of Malfi*. A phenomenal actor he certainly was but it was the strangeness of his destiny that made him the subject of our hushed and sombre exchanges.

Victor was a hellraiser – almost literally; not a mere roaring boy, boozing and smashing the place apart, though God knows he did enough of that, but somehow diabolically possessed. Scrawny, sandy-haired, short, his pebble glasses flashing madly away, once he had a drop of booze inside him (any time after, say, 10.30 in the morning), he set out on his lifelong quest for trouble.

If there was none readily available, he would gladly provoke it. No one was immune: innocent bystanders, the larger the better, would be urged to hit him. He didn't really much bother to offer a reason. If they refused he became very angry and would prod or punch them until the desired blow was forthcoming. Fearing that they might not like to hit a man with glasses, he'd obligingly take them off.

When, goaded beyond endurance, the victim would finally belt Victor, an expression oddly like satisfaction would suffuse his features, like an adder that's just swallowed a mongoose. If there was no one around to provoke, he'd inflict the damage on himself, taking a beer glass and eating it, for example, or knocking his head against the wall.

He could have killed himself at any moment, indeed, seemed most anxious to do so. How ironic then that he should have been stone-cold sober and completely placid when fate, in the form of a red London bus, struck. He was standing at a bus stop when the bus swerved and hit the stop, which in turn cracked down on Victor's head.

From that moment he never uttered another word. That was fourteen years ago. Since then, his mother and father have both died. His sister, who lived some distance from the hospital, visited him as often as possible, as did many friends and colleagues, all hoping that somehow he might speak again. His brain was apparently undamaged. His eyes were open and clear and expressive, sometimes seeming to be filled with rage.

From time to time he would be shown a television tape of one of his greatest performances – Gogol's *Diary of a Madman*. Nothing happened.

What makes his story particularly haunting is that all the rage and craziness of Victor's offstage personality was present in his performances, sometimes destructively as far as his fellow actors were concerned, but always at maximum intensity, terrifyingly dangerous, the stark opposite of anything routine or dull.

Dionysus is a destructive god as well as a celebratory one; Victor was his true votary.

It was an awe-inducing and deeply serious experience to see Victor act. Perhaps Kean was like that: everything Victor Henry ever did on the stage seemed to be glimpsed by lightning.

Thank God for him he is dead. Alas for us he is no more.

Greatness seemed to be everywhere at that time. Thanks to the cross-London box-office mafia, I went to dress rehearsals at Covent Garden: Joan Sutherland in Lucia di Lammermoor, *with an unknown young tenor called Luciano Pavarotti, who cracked on one of many his top Cs and in his frustration hurled his sword into the pit, where it impaled a drum; Boris Christoff in* Boris Godunov, *one of the most terrifying actors I have ever seen on any stage, in any medium, at almost Victor Henry-like levels of intensity; Geraint Evans supreme as both Falstaff and Wozzeck; Jon Vickers poleaxingly anguished as Peter Grimes. I saw ballet for the first time there, the great Russian masterpieces, all the Ashton ballets, the MacMillans; I saw Fonteyn and Nureyev. I thought him the sexiest man I had ever seen in my life; his photograph, all Tartar animal energy, adorned my bedroom wall. This is my review of Julie Kavanagh's 2007 biography of him.*

No one who was alive and conscious at the time will forget the dramatic circumstances of Rudolf Nureyev's precipitate defection to the West at the height of the Cold War, the sudden eruption of this shocking new talent into the rarefied world of classical dance and his subsequent conquest, in short order, of the great stages of Europe and America. Julie Kavanagh's magnificent and emotionally overwhelming new biography makes it clear that this was no brief dramatic interlude in his career: it was all like that, every minute of his fifty-five years on earth. From the moment of his birth on board the Trans-Siberian Railroad, Rudolf Nureyev's life was lived out in capital letters. His wartime childhood in the Bashkirian capital of Ufa was one of desperate impoverishment; his early passion for physical self-expression led to his engagement at the age of seven by a folk-dancing troupe; he was then taken up by various local ballet teachers and struggled to progress until, flagrantly defying his father, he arrived, rather late for a dancer, at the Kirov Ballet School. There – despite earlier inadequate training and physical shortcomings which he would never wholly overcome – he showed unyielding certainty about the path he intended to follow. His wilful and often unruly behaviour in class and on stage did nothing to impede his rapid and triumphant progression through the ranks of the company, leading to his ecstatic acclaim on tour with them in Paris in June of 1961 and the unpremeditated last-minute defection, straight from the pages of le Carré, at Le Bourget Airport, abandoning, it seemed for ever, his family, his fellow dancers, his teachers, his country.

But that was just the beginning. In Julie Kavanagh's scrupulously researched and supremely well-informed account, the remaining thirty-six years of his life have the trajectory of an epic novel, an exemplary tale of the artist as demiurge – a story of demonic determination, heroic immersion in life and work and ultimate, inevitable self-immolation. Kavanagh's unfolding of the story is all the more telling for its restraint, clear-eyed but properly appreciative of the uniqueness of her subject. People like Rudolf Nureyev come rarely. When they are artists, the impact is electrifying; they generally leave a trail of devastation in their wake. Nureyev was no exception. Even as a child, he was gripped by the drive, the pressure, the ruthlessness which enabled him to overcome every conceivable obstacle – including, most potently, the fierce opposition of his true-believing Stalinist father, who had spent the 1930s diligently implementing the collectivisation of farms – to reach a goal that must have seemed positively lunar in its unattainability.

His destiny was set at the age of seven when his mother smuggled him into a performance of the famous Soviet ballet *The Song of the Cranes*. 'I knew. That's it, that's my life, that will be my function. I wanted to be *everything* on stage.' Once he reached the Kirov, his Tartar pride was deeply offended by the racist scorn heaped on him ('Bashkirian pig' they called him), which confirmed his determination to show them all; by now, too, at the ripe age of seventeen, he was motivated by a lifelong compulsion to make up for lost time. He worked slavishly, in and out of class, pushing himself forward in every way, demanding the opportunity of partnering the much older female stars of the company, rejuvenating their dancing while learning from them, a pattern which would be frequently repeated over the next decade. He immersed himself in music, literature and art; a virgin at the age of twenty-one, he had an affair with his revered teacher's wife, another area in which he would soon be frantically making up for lost time, though not, for the most part, with women. Soon after, he started an affair with a male dancer; typically of Nureyev, they didn't just go to bed together: they became blood brothers. Immature, in some ways technically inadequate, poorly educated, he never doubted that his way was the right way, refusing point blank to dance choreography that displeased him, always demanding to know the meaning behind the steps. He knew the value of his Kirov training but was determined to broaden his technique, and his departure for the West was as much driven by that determination as by anything else.

Russia was simply too small for him. His ambitions were precise: he wanted to study with his idol, the Danish *danseur noble*, Erik Bruhn; and he wanted to partner Margot Fonteyn. Soon after his defection, he had met, worked with and started a passionate affair with Bruhn; not much later, he was paired with Fonteyn at the Royal Ballet. His relationship with the forty-two-year-old prima ballerina assoluta made dance history; no one who saw them together in the flesh can ever forget the overpowering sense of aliveness to each other they created, the perfection of interplay, the intimacy, tenderness and mutual inspiration they achieved. Sometimes – as in *Marguerite and Armand* – it was almost X-certificate; it made you hot under the collar. Fonteyn seemed a dancer reborn; while her young partner was simply the most thrilling performer in any medium we had seen for a long time, if ever. His physical beauty, the power of his presence and the bravura of his dancing, allied to a unique personality, half savage and half almost feminine voluptuary, created a sensation: Rudimania swept London, and soon the world.

Though he was working within strictly classical bounds, he made the prevailing external perfection of the Royal Ballet dancers seem dull. Immersed in tradition and in appearance the quintessence of romanticism, he was nonetheless intensely contemporary, rebellious, iconoclastic, moody: James Dean in tights. Kavanagh acutely observes the influence of Stanislavsky on Russian dancers: they were accustomed to think in terms of character and an emotional through-line. This in itself transformed our understanding of dance: his Bluebird was not 'prettily poised for meaningless flight' but 'tense with a strong desire to really fly away'. Not that he was a Method dancer: far from it. There was no fourth wall for him; on the contrary, he went out of his way to insist that dancing was 'a connective art'. The audience was a crucial part of the experience, and he wanted them to be aware of what it cost him. His preparation for a step was designed to signal something remarkable coming: he deliberately created tension, as Kavanagh says, in order to release it in virtuosity. He intended to dominate his audience: to make passionate love to them. In this he succeeded triumphantly; his audiences experienced a kind of collective orgasm. No wonder Mick Jagger went around London saying he wanted to be Nureyev.

Of course, there were many people both in the profession and outside of it who disapproved. The great Georgian choreographer George Balanchine had no time for him at all. At the hysterical height of his international fame, Nureyev, who idolised Balanchine, offered to join his company. 'When you're tired of playing at being a prince,' the choreographer told him, 'come back to me.' Again and again Balanchine, who figures throughout the book as a mordantly judgemental figure, rejected him. Nureyev did work with other modern choreographers (the first classical dancer to do so), learning difficult new techniques at a time when his body was beginning to wear out. He played on Broadway, bringing classical dance and new work to entirely new audiences. In addition, he was choreographing ballet after ballet – some revivals of Petipa, some his own. It was not something at which he excelled, but he was, says Kavanagh, a 'peerless pedagogue', determined to pass on what he knew, 'total body feeling in total body movement'. The design for *Cinderella*, which he made for the Paris Opéra Ballet (of which he was director), featured a huge clock; he scarcely needed to be reminded of its relentlessly advancing hands.

Inevitably death figures powerfully in the book. Once Nureyev discovered sex, there was no holding him back. In this area Kavanagh is not prurient, but not incurious, either, and she tells us what we need to know, gamely detailing the bacchanalian gay scene of the Seventies. He renounced love ('The Curse,' as he called it: 'no personal involvement. That's been abolished.') For him, apart from one or two passionate relationships, above all with Bruhn, sex was essentially a mechanical release – 'a liberation', he called it – and he was increasingly blatant about his need for it. In Paris, when he went into the back room at Le Trap, the entire bar followed him to watch him at his sport: just another performance. Before long he was buying boys by the crateload; it was inevitable that once AIDS was in circulation, he would fall prey to it. Not that he let it hamper him until almost the very end. His sense of time running out pushed him further and further, an insane schedule of performances across the globe, learning new steps, barely rehearsing them, yet somehow giving them his whole personality and all his artistry.

His body, however, was increasingly battered. 'Since 1973,' Kavanagh notes, 'Rudolf had been dancing with a permanent tear in his leg muscle; he had destroyed his Achilles tendon by years of landing badly; he had heel spurs; his bones were chipped so that even basic walking gave him pain.' His legs had turned to stone. 'It's always bandages,' observed Nureyev, philosophically, 'heel-pads for ever.' None of this deterred him. Friend after friend was dying; Erik Bruhn (unquestionably the love of his life); the critic Nigel Gosling, who had sustained him from the moment he arrived in the West; Margot Fonteyn. At this point, the book, though it remains admirably cool, starts to become unbearably harrowing. I'm glad I was at home when I read about his visit to Fonteyn in hospital to persuade her to have a leg cut off; I broke down abjectly. His attempts to start a new career as a conductor are almost equally heartbreaking.

He carried on dancing virtually to the end, on one occasion only six days after a major operation on his kidney; discharging himself from hospital, he flew to Australia and danced with a catheter in place. With perfect symbolism, his last two performances were of an Angel (in Hungary) and, in Berlin, the evil witch Carabosse in *Sleeping Beauty*. He had both of these in him. His behaviour could be disgraceful, to friend and foe alike. Kavanagh never apologises for him, nor does she try to extenuate his frequently brutal conduct. What she makes clear is that these were flaws in a titanic human being who never ceased to strain every fibre of his being to serve dance. For him there was never any comfort zone. To be a dancer, he said, was 'sacrificial work'. Violette Verdy noted that he came onto the stage as if into an arena: 'Is he going to be eaten by the lion or not?' 'Audiences come to the theatre,' he said, 'to see people obsessed with what they do.' Kavanagh's book, apart from its comprehensive and compulsively readable account of Nureyev's life and art, is an important wake-up call to the lily-livered rest of us: this is what theatre can be, but only if we give it everything: nothing less will do.

I saw all these things with my box-office colleagues, Christine and Roger and Beverley, and Joan from the bookstall. It was to them that I shyly confessed my new-found desire to be an actor, and that I was gay. Neither confession caused the slightest surprise; they had known both before I did.

I have described elsewhere how, once I had decided to become an actor, I chose to go to university rather than drama school, how I went to Queen's University in Belfast, how on the strength of my having come from the box office of the National Theatre I was given the leading male part in The Seagull *by the University Drama Society, how absolutely dreadful I knew myself to be in the part, and how that realisation gave me the determination to go to drama school to find out whether I had any talent at all. I have also written about my encounter with a man who changed my life: the great Irish actor Micheál mac Liammóir, who with his partner Hilton*

Edwards had created the Gate Theatre in Dublin, the exotic counterpoise to the Abbey: the two theatres were famously known as Sodom and Begorrah. I wangled a commission from the student newspaper Gown *to go down to Dublin to interview mac Liammóir, which I did, taking a Heath Robinson recording device with me, but on my return, rapidly tiring of the process of transcribing the tape, I switched the contraption off and relied on memory and evocation. I sent a copy of the shamelessly rewritten interview to mac Liammóir who wrote back: 'Professional journalists could learn from the wonderfully accurate account you gave of what I said.' It was the first piece of mine ever to appear in a newspaper, in March 1969.*

Harcourt Terrace, No. 4, a fine Georgian building somewhere in Dublin, that complex, vital, intermittently beautiful city full of books and flourishing theatres. The house is something of a mac Liammóir museum: prints, theatre bills, designs, line the walls. Inside the sitting room, shelves and shelves of books, with Beardsley designs on the walls. I was met by two intelligent if rather emotional Siamese cats and engaged with them till the entry, in style, of mac Liammóir himself. 'I'm infectious,' he said; perfectly true, of course, but on this occasion he meant that he had a cold. The interview began.

– Mr mac Liammóir, you are associated in the minds of most people of my generation with your brilliant and witty one-man shows, particularly *The Importance of Being Oscar*, in which your own personality comes over as strongly as the material you're presenting. Is it distressing for you when you're billed as a witty person, to have to produce a bon mot to order?

– Well do you know, I've never thought of myself as a witty person. I've never felt obliged to produce anything if I didn't want to. I've never felt on a tightrope except with certain people whom I invariably dislike and avoid as much as I possibly can. I am only productive of wit or anything at all if it comes out with a certain sympathy or is spontaneous. It is no good putting me on a tightrope because I immediately fall off with the greatest crash. As to Oscar, Oscar has never had the faintest effect on me... I regard him as an uncanny, dead friend: he's like somebody I know terribly well and like enormously; and the only thing I don't like is being – what you said just now – continually identified with him – not because of any dislike of his personality; or being coupled with somebody who was primarily in the popular mind a figure of scandal – not at all – but I dislike being coupled with anybody except myself, if you see what I mean; nobody wants to be the shadow of another man: Wilde himself said that cheap editions of great books were delightful, but cheap editions of great men were perfectly detestable.

I chose him because I feel equipped to interpret him. I've been influenced if at all by his humour more than his philosophy; his good humour more than anything else; the absurdity, the glamour and the luxury, the danger of it all. To think that he was an Irishman! And that this rather drab little country of ours should produce such a glowing peacock.

– You have devoted a great part of your life to instilling some colour through the medium of theatre into this 'drab little country'.

– Yes, though of course I didn't return to this country – when I was seventeen and after years on the London stage as a boy actor – to act; even I wasn't crazy enough to do that.

– How's that?

– Well – I've said before in print – if a London, New York, Paris, Berlin actor has a success he buys a new car, a new house, a new stair carpet, he keeps fixing himself more and more; the Irish actor if he has a success has to pack his suitcase, he has to go away and take his goods elsewhere: you run through the Irish populace like a dose of salts, do you see; there are so few of us. The entire theatrical problem in Ireland is lack of population. It has a degrading effect on the work; it drives us all to repertory and ill-prepared, there's not enough time. In a huge city you can run in a play for a year, probably soul-crushing if you don't like the part, and during the last few weeks, once you know the dates, you can start preparing your next part, slowly and in plenty of time, whereas we have two weeks to put on some great dramatic work of art. This problem of adequate rehearsal time is especially evident in Belfast.

Belfast is very tragic; a city the same size of Dublin; it is not as lucky as Dublin, but it is one of the most brilliant audiences in the world, I've found; astonishingly receptive and perceptive – what the whole of Ireland wants, North and South, it doesn't matter, is a form of specialisation; what we lack here is discrimination as a result of seeing perfect work; and perfect work is presumably only the outcome of a certain amount of specialisation. Nevertheless, there is abundant room for both amateur and professional – their feud has been exaggerated by both sides – as long as they are criticised separately as different things; I first played Hamlet in Dublin when I was twenty-eight or twenty-nine – some years ago, as you can imagine – and was received with glowing almost hysterical reviews. Then a couple of weeks later I opened the same paper, the same critic, and almost exactly the same review, for a boy of sixteen at the local grammar school! The best amateur performances are students'; the hope is that student drama will act as an incubator and that some boy or girl will go into the proper theatre. When the talent is genuine, I think it will find its way.

– There is also, with university productions, the opportunity to experiment because box-office is not the overriding consideration.

– That is a blessing – and a curse because sordid as it might seem, the box office is one side of a set of values, of a proof; it's a proof that the public is coming, that the public has been touched. The theatre at its best is essentially popular: the Greeks knew that, Shakespeare knew it, God knows.

– The opinion has been expressed that merely theatrical criteria are hopelessly ostrich-like in a situation such as we have in Ulster at the moment, and that the political situation should be used to bring people into the theatre; a production of *Oedipus* with Ian Paisley in the title role...?

– I should've thought he'd be better as Jocasta, wouldn't you? We've all done that sort of thing, or course; Hilton and I produced *Julius Caesar* once in a sort of Fascist manner – at the time when all that was current, you know – I forget which side the Fascists were on... but it was very effective and wonderful; and it brought the war home. The great error with these updated settings is the error of modern detail... Ophelia wearing a miniskirt would ruin any romance, I should think. All these girls going around thinking they look like Rosalind and in fact looking like a very bad Dick Whittington.

– Mr mac Liammóir, one thinks of you now, as I said before, almost exclusively as a performer of one-man shows.

– That reminds me of a very funny story told me by Emlyn, Emlyn Williams, a great friend of mine; he does them too, Dickens, Dylan Thomas. He was asked on one of his tours, 'Tell me, Mr Williams, do you like this better than acting?' It's the same art with a difference; it's a soloist performance. I don't miss all the things in the theatre which Emlyn misses: the fun, the gossip, the scandal, the slammed doors; I love being without all that, I love it: the privacy and the dignity of it, in a way; always...

– But is it an essentially theatrical thing for one man to hold the stage alone, displaying his own personality; does it really use the medium of the theatre?

– I think so, yes, in a different form – invented, incidentally, by a woman, Ruth Draper – and it seemed to me for a long time an essentially feminine art: she dressed up for each characterisation, and of course women can do far more with that sort of thing than we can; when John Gielgud did *The Seven Ages of Man* – which I think is wonderful (though I think it's a mistake to do those things in three parts – it gives them too long to think and discuss you and wonder what the hell you're going to do next); I thought, well, that's Shakespeare – that's different – and then Emlyn with Dickens and I never thought of being a one-man performer though I'd always suspected it in *Hamlet* because I was always so relieved when Rosencrantz and Guildenstern went away. 'I'm SO glad those little bores are going off,' I used to think... 'God be wi' ye, sir...' 'God be wi' ye... thank God.' So probably that was the beginning. It isn't necessarily that you've got to be a great actor to be a one-man performer – probably indeed the greatest actors wouldn't have done it well – it's a talent or a knack, just like having a talent for languages – just a knack of personality.

No doubt my subsequent ventures in one-man performances have been deeply influenced by Micheál's example; he was also the most completely open gay man I had encountered (though of course I never so much as hinted at it in the piece). What would I have said? There was nothing fey about him, nothing limp or nancy. The word 'outrageous' better describes him, but the most striking fact to me was simply that his homosexuality seemed to be the very foundation of his personality.

I looked after him when he came to adjudicate the Drama Festival, and then all the peacock brilliance went out of our lives and things settled down to a more regular level. For a brief while, I thought that I would stay at Queen's, seize power in the Drama Society and create dazzling theatre. I had seen a play in London which thrilled me beyond measure, The Ruling Class, *by Peter Barnes, and I had written a passionately enthusiastic letter to his agent, the legendary Peggy Ramsay, to ask for the rights. She had at first pooh-poohed me, writing to say that regional rights had to be granted first and I would have to wait my turn, dear, but the following day I got another letter from her saying that she'd sent my letter to Barnes, and that he'd told her to release the rights to me. Too late; the die was cast. I had decided to run away and become an actor. It was a sort of turning point: had I done* The Ruling Class, *and had it been a success, I suppose I would have stayed at Queen's, and finished my degree, and learned to make theatre of a sort. But my instinct to go away and subject myself to the most challenging training I could find was, I believe, the right one – indeed, the only possible one. So I must be very grateful that Peggy said no, the first of many good turns she was to do me.*

As it happens, Peter Barnes subsequently became one of my very dearest friends. I wrote this obituary for the Royal Literary Society in 2005.

When I saw *The Ruling Class* at the Piccadilly Theatre in 1968, I had no doubt whatever that I had witnessed a work of genius, an authentic modern masterpiece. Pinter and Bond were the heroes of a slightly older generation than mine: they were already established and revered and had around them an aura of profundity; their very crypticness and unknowability put them in the running to be the heirs of Beckett, and though I made the conventional obeisances in their direction, I was secretly frustrated by their lack of communicativeness. *The Ruling Class* was what I had been craving for: eloquent, anarchic, theatrical, hilarious, exhilaratingly anti-Establishment.

It was designed to get up people's noses – ten people walked out at the performance I saw – their seats thrillingly springing back 'Thunk! Thunk! Thunk!' when Jack Gurney's marriage vows commenced with the phrase 'From the bottom of my heart to the tip of my penis.' But for me when Tuck the butler confessed to having pee'd in the Thirteenth Earl's soup every day for forty years, when Jack came on for his wedding night on a tricycle singing Verdi, when the House of Lords was pushed on from either side of the wings bearing their lordships' skeletons draped across the benches, the serried ranks of corpses covered in cobwebs, I felt that as long as writers of this vitality, passion and rage continued to write for the theatre, it would live for ever. I was at university, and asked if I could do the play for the Drama Society. Against all known practice, and with minimal chance of his earning a penny, he said yes.

I didn't meet Barnes for some years, but when I did I realised that that was him all over: he didn't care about the money, he didn't even care whether the plays were done to the highest level of professional polish, he just wanted them done, wanted to be allowed to tell his hilarious 'anecdotes of destiny' (his admiration for Isak Dinesen, whose phrase that is, was absolute) – above all, he wanted to make 'em laugh. On the whole, he felt that Macbeth had got it more or less right: life was indeed a tale told by an idiot, signifying nothing, but somehow this fact – far from depressing him – gave him endless satisfaction. His own life was a perfect case in point: dozens of brilliant plays and adaptations piling up which no one who had any money would put on, though stars were queuing up to play the parts – plays crying out for the resources of the National Theatre or the Royal Shakespeare Company, whose actors and audiences would have revelled in them; while television companies simply couldn't pour enough money into his bank account for writing the screenplays he turned out before breakfast and the serious work of the day had begun. He actually tried putting up the money out of his own pocket for a production of *Clap Hands, Here Comes Charlie*, one of his most delirious and outrageous inventions, but somehow they even managed to stop him from doing that.

In his domestic life he watched his beloved first wife Charlotte slip away mentally, and would sit stoically and practically as she succumbed to paranoid delusion, reasoning with her, supporting her, feeding her, all the while behaving as if nothing out of the ordinary were happening. 'That's life,' he seemed to be feeling. Ben Jonson was his great hero, but it was the language, the energy, the invention that he loved, not Jonson's dark and bitter heart. Peter had no judgement to offer on his fellow human beings: 'We're all in it together,' was his view. 'None of it makes any sense, let's have a laugh.' He winkled out laughter from the most unlikely places: Belsen, the court of Ivan the Terrible, the bubonic plague, horrors to which the only possible human response was a joke. He was astonished, and delighted, when American companies suddenly started performing his plague play, *Red Noses, Black Death*, because they construed it as a response to AIDS. His point had simply been that purity of heart and a good belly laugh can cure the world. 'I jest, therefore I am' are the words that should be inscribed on his tombstone. When he died, I sent a card with the flowers: 'Was it something I said?' I like to think he saw the card from the great Reading Room in the sky, and let out one of his great banshee laughs.

This rare man leaves behind him a beautiful wife, four bonny babies, and a legacy of plays produced and unproduced – including his stupendous adaptations of the other Great Unperformed of dramatic literature – which could keep a theatre company going for half a century without once repeating itself. His voice is to be heard in all of them, loud, profane and clear; how we need that voice as the coalition of the correct goes about its business of extinguishing all traces of the great medieval carnival world that Peter never ceased to celebrate. Now he's swapping jokes with Rabelais, Chaucer, Marie Lloyd and Max Miller. Lucky them, poor us.

I also wrote the following paragraph for the 'Lives Remembered' column of The Times *obituary section.*

While properly jaunty, given its indestructibly jaunty subject, your fine obituary of Peter Barnes somewhat underplays the tragedy of a writer out of step with his times – or, more precisely, with fashion. Admired and indeed deeply loved by many of his fellow professionals – actors, directors, fellow writers who would gather together at his annual Christmas party – Barnes never found the sort of influential friend in high places who might have ensured productions for his plays, the only thing, apart from his wife Christy and their almost miraculously late-appearing brood, that Peter really cared about. He belonged to no discernible group, and was influenced by no one who had not been dead for four hundred years. That glorious, darkly exuberant neo-Jacobean anatomy of the English class system, *The Ruling Class*, one of the greatest of post-war plays, has never even had a significant revival. Some of us struggled vainly for years to mount one, or, more ambitiously, to stage a season of some of Barnes's numberless unproduced works (including many fine and imaginative versions of the plays of the lesser-known masters whose work he so loved), but as they were all enormous in their demands – and as often as not set in the thirteenth century – they required the resources of the National Theatre or the Royal Shakespeare Company, and recent artistic directors of both those organisations made no secret of their lack of enthusiasm for his work, which is perfectly reasonable, but rotten luck for him, and for us, audiences and actors alike. Peter and I once came very close to raising the money for an inaugural three-play season of what we only half-jokingly referred to as the Royal Barnes Company, but at the last minute, as so often, the funding melted away. Peter simply sighed, and got on with writing the next play – also unproduced. His unperformed legacy amounts to an Aladdin's Cave of glittering and hilarious dramatic audacities which it is be hoped a new generation might be allowed to see in the theatre, where they belong.

Now, with The Ruling Class *unperformed, I was liberated from academia, and I had to find a drama school. But before that, I needed to earn a living. Hearing that I was about to sign on with a cleaning agency, my old National Theatre chum Roger, who was now No. 2 at the Mermaid Theatre box office but about to return to the National, got me a job there before he left, and the great Joan Robinson, Bernard Miles's legendary Box Office Manager, found herself saddled with this overexcited aspirant actor with almost uncontrollable energy. The high point of my time there came one Monday morning in autumn 1969 when my colleague Arthur (Arfs Mincewell, I dubbed him, for fairly obvious, in fact screamingly obvious, reasons) and I, expecting a restful morning, found ourselves fighting our way through a huge and totally unforeseen queue which wound its way round the building all the way down to the river. The Prospect Theatre Company was opening at the Mermaid for a season of* Richard II *and* Edward II *with an admired but not especially famous young actor called Ian McKellen in the two title roles. There had up till now been only the mildest interest in the shows, but the day before, the* Sunday Times *had carried a review by the critic Harold Hobson of positively ecstatic fervour, acclaiming McKellen in terms that would have made the Saviour Himself blush. So, the following day, there was a queue. Arfs and I threw open the box-office window and started selling for all we were worth. We gave up putting the money in the till quite early on, so that when Joan Robinson arrived at midday, we were knee-deep in banknotes. Instead of being acclaimed as box-office heroes, as we'd fondly imagined, we were soundly berated for having let all the house seats go and told to pick up all the money and not go anywhere near the window. (Eventually poor Joan was reduced to buying back tickets from the public so that she'd have something to give the agents, on whose business she relied during leaner times.)*

Normally, things were very much quieter. There was a production of a play by William Trevor called The Old Boys, *of which the star was Sir*

Michael Redgrave. The great actor had just started to succumb to the effects of the Parkinson's disease which finally engulfed him. He couldn't remember a word of the script, so the stage management improvised a sort of walkie-talkie for him which was wired up to the prompt corner. When he needed a line – which was always – he was to tap on his chest and the text would be forthcoming. He found it hard to get the hang of it, and would quite openly ask the stage manager, via the apparatus, to repeat the line, as if he were on the telephone. This made life a little difficult for his fellow actors. A number of the audience, many of whom were almost as infirm as he was, were displeased by this, and would vent their rage at me, demanding their money back. I hope Sir Michael never knew about these complaints. The show was a pitiful spectacle, but Redgrave somehow maintained his dignity, and against all the odds, his performance was rather moving. I reviewed Alan Strachan's book about Redgrave, Secret Dreams, *for the* Guardian; *Strachan was the director of* The Old Boys.

Alan Strachan is right to point out that when John Gielgud's obituaries were written, and his place in the theatrical pantheon assessed, Michael Redgrave was inexplicably omitted from the list of Britain's greatest twentieth-century actors. The fine and judicious biography he has written does an important service in restoring a major figure to its rightful place in the theatrical landscape. It must, however, be said that, detailed as never before, both the career and the man emerge if anything somewhat more enigmatic than they were before it. Inevitably, Redgrave, whose last major creation was Jaraby in *The Old Boys* at the Mermaid in 1971, is remembered by fewer theatregoers than the other great actors who all had Indian summers well into their seventies. His distinguished body of film work – including superb performances in *The Browning Version, Dead of Night* and *The Stars Look Down* – is perhaps better known, and fortunately now includes the television film of the Chichester Festival production of *Uncle Vanya* (made for pay TV and unavailable for many years), which preserves his nonpareil performance in the title role, generally regarded as the crowning glory of his work in the theatre.

If nothing had survived but this one performance, he would on the strength of it have joined the ranks of the Immortals. For a while the complete soundtrack of the production was available on LP and even in this form the performance is both electrifying and heartbreaking from the moment he speaks his first line: the sound of a soul in anguish leaps off the vinyl grooves, all the more potent because of the graceful vocal attributes of the actor, melodious and minutely expressive of every emotional nuance. On DVD the portrait of emotional and spiritual devastation is complete: the great towering physique (6'3" – for many years he thought he was too tall to be an actor), the splendid build, the handsome face, infinitely sensitive, softly rugged, hair flopping about, beard unkempt, limbs limp and loose. The character's life is inhabited with profound complexity but also a kind of transcendent poetry: absolutely real but on an epic scale, the reality of life itself, not merely of one life. His co-star, the director of the production, is Laurence Olivier, an actor of a very different colour, no less masterful, it goes without saying; his Dr Astrov a brilliantly achieved, deeply felt performance of unique theatrical effectiveness. But Redgrave's achievement is of a different order. He does what only the very greatest acting does – he opens up the secret places of the human heart, allowing us to glimpse truths about ourselves that we can barely acknowledge, in Vanya's case the overwhelming sense of waste, the impossibility of love, the death of hope.

Michael Redgrave knew about such things. As if at destiny's behest, his early life shaped him to experience loss, disappointment, rejection. He was unique among the great actors of the twentieth century in that he was actually born into the theatre – not merely connected to it, as Gielgud was, but of it, although, paradoxically, he was the latest starter of them all. Both parents were actors, as were many of his forebears. His father, Roy, was a feckless charmer of a barnstormer who made his way to Australia, where he triumphed in outback melodramas, occasionally featuring live sheep; his mother Daisy (belonging more to the legitimate theatre) and the infant Michael joined Roy, somewhat against Roy's will, and stayed with him for a little while, during which time the boy made his stage debut, running on at the end of a sentimental monologue to cry 'Daddy!' In fact, he couldn't bring himself to utter the word and instead burst into tears, which is a very nice metaphor both for his relationship to his father (from whom they parted shortly after and whom he never saw again) and for the unusual degree of emotion he was to bring to his own work as an actor. His childhood, back in England, was as unsettled as the life of the child of a single parent who was a jobbing actress on tour could hardly fail to be, and he was constantly given over to the care of aunts (and 'aunts'), frequently depending on the kindness of landladies.

Then, quite without warning, his mother married a very respectable and comfortably off businessman and their lives changed hugely for the better – in the material sense, at least; Redgrave was plunged into the inevitable Oedipal alienation, in addition to resenting what he felt to be the bourgeois nature of their new life. He was sent to a minor public school where he was blessed by the presence of an inspired English teacher who staged plays to a high level of excellence. He also experienced the usual intense crushes on various fellow pupils; before long he had been to bed both with men and women.

Both sexes were understandably smitten by this immensely handsome, elegant, witty and endlessly vulnerable young man. At Cambridge, in the late Twenties, he had long-term love affairs with several men (among them the publisher John Lehmann), moved in Bloomsbury circles and was in touch with many of the Apostles; this was the epoch of Burgess (who designed a play for him) and Blunt (with whom he co-edited a magazine). He was confirmed in his left-wing political attitudes, though never formally a Marxist. He was not a diligent scholar, but absorbed a very wide culture, particularly during a visit to Heidelberg, where for the first time he saw the latest opera – *Rosenkavalier*, which overwhelmed him – and subsidised theatre and Expressionist cinema, all of which influenced him deeply in his vision of what the theatre and performing arts could be; he was awed by a performance by Louis Jouvet, whom he took to be the very model of what an actor should be, 'a real *homme du théâtre*', as he admiringly wrote. He had considerable ambitions as a writer (his instinctive verbal sense emerges vividly in a letter in which he describes a girl with whom he shares a dance as 'round and splodgy with an aggressive sniff and a laugh like the death rattle of a winkle') but not, as yet, as an actor. Instead he became a schoolmaster at Cranleigh, but plunged immediately into directing and acting in productions there, playing Hamlet, Lear and Samson Agonistes. By the age of twenty-six he felt strong enough to enter the professional fray, and was lucky enough to secure a place at William Armstrong's Liverpool Rep, where he played a vast range of parts in the course of a year, and met his wife, Rachel Kempson. Within a year he had been snapped up by the Old Vic and was playing Orlando opposite Edith Evans's Rosalind, one of the great romantic partnerships of the decade; a year later he was cast in the leading role in *The Lady Vanishes* for Alfred Hitchcock, his film debut. Four years into the business he was an established star in both mediums.

Despite his splendid physical and vocal equipment – the nearest thing to an *acteur noble* this country has produced – he did not quite fit into a pre-existing mould. 'What sort of actor do you want to be, Michael?' Edith Evans had asked him. 'Do you want to be like John, or Larry, or me, or Peggy Ashcroft? What sort of standards are you aiming at?' The very highest, was his immediate answer, those of Jouvet, those of his mentor the director Michel Saint-Denis (who had, said Redgrave, 'some information about life that he could tell us'). But he believed that could only really be achieved in an ensemble, in the sort of company that Gielgud was intermittently attempting in the West End, though ideally, he believed, the theatre should be nationalised. As for himself, he was genuinely not interested in stardom, and was a natural democrat, if a somewhat aloof one. He was also fascinated by Stanislavsky, always seeking to create from within; he was in fact that unheard-of phenomenon, an English leading actor who was not an extrovert. He was always in touch with his inner drama, in a way not dissimilar to Charles Laughton, an actor with whom he has surprisingly much in common, and his best work always possesses a sense of fathomless pools of complex life within. Unlike Laughton, his relationship to his own body and his face was not anguished; it is indeed very often the gap between the nobility of his appearance and the turbulence inside which gives his acting its extraordinary intensity. 'He is always at his best when called upon to undermine the effect of his tall, handsome presence with suggestions of nervous tensions amounting to terror,' wrote Frank Marcus.

His loyalty to his inner needs gave rise to an almost ungraspable complexity in his private life. He was desperately needy in his sexual and emotional demands. 'I am shallow, selfish (horribly), jealous to a torturing degree, greedy, proud and self-centred,' he wrote to John Lehmann; 'I have grasped at people's love and done vain and stupid things to get it; I am at times hideously immoral.' An early indicator is the passionate affair that he had with Edith Evans during and even after the run of *As You Like It*, starting in the seventh month of Rachel's pregnancy with her first child Vanessa, and continuing thereafter for nearly a year, an affair of which Rachel remained ignorant till the publication of Bryan Forbes's biography of Evans some forty years later. Thenceforward the affairs were with men, including at least four long-term relationships, all of which Rachel was told about to the accompaniment of copious tears, and all of which she learned to live with: indeed, she even learnt to live with the lovers themselves. He was so infatuated with Noël Coward during their brief affair that it was with him that he spent his last night before beginning his wartime naval service. Rachel was curiously tolerant, almost unnervingly so: 'I am glad all goes well with you, Darling Mike. Do you know, I envy you being always able to be with the one you love with *no* restrictions or difficulties of any sort. I don't envy you in a horrid way but I hope you feel pleased in the wonderfulness of that. It must give you calm and strength.' Of course, it gave him nothing of the kind; but it kept his inner life going. In addition to the marriage and the official lovers were unending one-night or indeed one-afternoon stands, for which purpose he had rented an office off St Martin's Lane, plus pickups in parks and stations; later – territory not covered in Strachan's book – he was to go into darker and darker realms sexually, usually fuelled by large quantities of alcohol. These lapses were always accompanied with terrible remorse and vows of renunciation, always broken, sometimes the very day of the diary entry that records them. This is something that goes well beyond mere bisexuality or simple promiscuity. It is an unshakable compulsion, driven by unshakable guilt and the constant need for affirmation. But it was inextricably bound up with his art. 'I like attempting parts of men, as it were, in invisible chains.'

The miracle is that for so much of his career, until he was stopped in his tracks by Parkinson's disease shortly after his sixtieth birthday, he remained so productive and so constantly illuminating in his work; he maintained an elegance and splendour through some of his most demanding roles and despite the unremitting intensity of his private experience. His classical roles – and in one glorious season at Stratford he played King Lear, Shylock and Antony – were absolute reinventions of the characters, but the reinvention was completely unselfconscious: he worked from profound inner promptings, his transformations organic and radical. His Antony was by all accounts a supreme account of an almost unplayable part – a man who provokes unstinting love from every other character in the play even as he destroys himself. As a director, too, he worked with exceptional taste and intelligence; and finally as a writer he wrote two of the finest books in the language about acting, and a haunting novel, about an actor and his *doppelgänger*, *The Mountebank's Tale*, the epigraph to which (by Rilke) seems to tell us something very personal about the enigmatic Redgrave himself: 'I can only come to terms with inner cataclysms; a little exterior perishing or surviving is either too hard or too easy for me. In the life of the gods… I understand nothing better than the moment they withdraw themselves; what would a god be without the protecting cloud, can you imagine a god worse for wear?'

After The Old Boys, *a tenth-anniversary production of the musical* Lock Up Your Daughters, *the show which originally opened the Mermaid, had settled in for a long run and with little now to do in the box office, I spent my days tormenting Joan with new systems for this or that, and for a month she managed to get me to join the accounting department, which was certainly an eye-opener, the miracle being that they hadn't been raided by the police. Finally, she was greatly relieved to hear of a job going in the box office of the Aldwych Theatre, then home of the Royal Shakespeare Company. Box Office Manager spoke unto Box Office Manager, and I duly started work there a week later. This was an altogether different sort of operation from Bernard Miles's inspired lunacy at Puddle Dock, where the spirit of the Elizabethan actor-managers was alive and kicking. The RSC was more like the National, in terms of quality and finish, but in atmosphere it was quite unlike. Apart from anything else, we of the front of house had no contact with the actors, or the stage management or the crew; there was no equivalent of Olivier's canteen. So the life of the front of house became the whole arena of interest. Again, in the box office I found myself part of a highly original gang of colleagues, from the manager, the sentimental, Wagner-loving John 'Puss' Ball, to the No. 2, Vera 'Lippy' Lee, a feisty cockney girl with no interest whatever in the theatre but a brilliant accounting mind, and on to Grace Turner, a former Box Office Manager now rendered unsuitable for executive activities by her staggering intake of alcohol (put to answering the phones, she could be observed slowly sliding down the wall until she was a heap on the floor, continuing all the while to converse with her customer) and Tina Adami, a spinster of a certain age with an adorable tendency to collapse in uncontrollable giggles. And the ushers were an arresting collection of gay men, mostly young and dishy, with a sprinkling of ancient grotesques, one of whom minced up to the box office on one of my first days on the window and asked me a question. I can't remember my answer but whatever it was, it caused him to turn to his colleagues and shout back to them, 'As a row of tents.'*

The RSC of the period was a particularly glorious one; Trevor Nunn, still in his twenties, was the director, and the repertory consisted, amongst other things, of his own electrifying production of The Revenger's Tragedy, *John Barton's* Troilus and Cressida *and* Twelfth Night *with Judi Dench and Donald Sinden, and a play, starring the same couple, which nobody had heard of and whose author's name no one could pronounce,* London Assurance *by Dion Boucicault. I saw all the previews of that, and saw the stupendous ensemble of that time – as well as Dench and Sinden there were Elizabeth Spriggs, Michael Williams, Barrie Ingham, Derek Smith and old Sydney Bromley – shape and edit their work as a public that had come on trust erupted in delirious laughter, all the more so for having had no idea of what to expect. During the same period, Peter Brook's* Midsummer Night's Dream *had opened in Stratford-upon-Avon. When the show came to the Aldwych, one saw that, wonderful though all those other productions were, this* Midsummer's Night's Dream *made them seem* vieux jeu. *Somehow, once again, Brook had reinvented the language of the theatre, making audiences participate in the game of theatre in a way they had forgotten how to do. That one director should have been responsible, back to back, for the National's* Oedipus *and this* Dream *was astounding – although there was a bridge in the musical satyr play Brook had tacked on to Seneca's savage ritual, in which the company danced deliriously around a huge golden phallus while the band played 'Yes! We Have No Bananas'. Brook was and is the Picasso of directors, endlessly self-reinventing. That he should also have been able to write about it with unprecedented clarity is a minor miracle:* The Empty Space *had just appeared in print and now here was the living evidence of his war on what he called in the book* Deadly Theatre. *Michael Kustow's authorised biography appeared some thirty-five years later; I reviewed it for the* Guardian.

There was an extraordinary mood among the associate directors of the RSC as they returned to London from Stratford in the spring of 1970 for one of their regular meetings. They had just seen the first night of Peter Brook's production of *A Midsummer Night's Dream*, and from my peep-hole in the box office of the Aldwych, I could see the thoughtful faces as they filed past on their way to the office upstairs. They realised, I concluded – having read that morning's reviews – that Brook had done it again: moved the goalposts for Shakespearean production, redefining himself as a director, as well as the Royal Shakespeare Company, and to some extent the Theatre itself. In his work with the actors he had set out to discover what he called 'the secret play', ignoring any realistic pointers in the text, banishing every traditional context in which the play had ever been performed, rejoicing in circus skills and crude music-hall gags while sounding the soaring lyricism of the verse at full throttle, blasting the famous Mendelssohn wedding march out of the loudspeakers and making absolutely clear the nature of Titania's attraction to her donkey lover. Through all this he somehow released, in a radically abstract white box, all the play's lewd energy, its beauty, its darkness and its light, and finally, unforgettably and heart-stoppingly, its power to heal. The acting was intensely physical, playful and passionate. Informed critics spoke of the production as Meyerholdian, and certainly what Brook had done was as fearlessly expressionistic as anything his great Russian predecessor had attempted, but it was also – though he had never done anything like it before – instantly recognisable as pure Peter Brook: rigorous, impish; theatrical, high-minded; brilliantly spontaneous, utterly achieved. It was also terribly English, and at the same time perfectly cosmopolitan.

It was the last piece of theatre Brook created as a resident of England. For the subsequent thirty-five years of his life, he has roamed the globe from his base in Paris, seeking new forms in his determination to redefine theatrical truth, aiming for a form of storytelling that transcends national cultures, tapping into the universal. In the course of these often far-flung journeys – both geographical and artistic – he has delivered a number of the key productions of the late twentieth century and provided a continuous challenge to theatrical practice. He is widely acknowledged as the greatest living director in the world today, though there are those who feel that his supreme talent – his genius, as many would have it – has been misapplied, leading the theatre not closer to its true function, but in the opposite direction, into aestheticism and, horror of horrors, mysticism. There are also those who feel he has betrayed, or at least walked away from, his particular talent. Kenneth Tynan, in his diary – not quoted in Michael Kustow's biography – cries, 'How I wish Peter would stop tackling huge philosophical issues and return to thing he can do better than any other English director – i.e. startle us with stage magic. I don't want to hear Peter on anthropology any more than I would have wanted to hear Houdini on spiritualism.' One way or the other, he has been at the heart of the never-ending debate about the purpose of the theatre, a debate which would have been infinitely more limited without him. It is Kustow's aim in this indispensable book to trace the trajectory of Brook's crucial contribution to the discussion, both in his writings and in his productions. He succeeds brilliantly, and I defy anyone to read the book and not come away thinking better of the theatre, its scope, its passion, its contribution.

It is the authorised biography, which means Kustow has had access, first of all to Brook himself, an elusive interviewee, and to a fascinating correspondence with his old childhood friend, Stephen Facey, both of which illuminate the narrative. The book is chastely free of gossip, and often omits some of the human mess that accompanies experiment of any sort, and, more surprisingly, some of the crises that Brook himself records in his autobiography *Threads of Time* (where he disarmingly tells us how close to disaster *A Midsummer Night's Dream* came). Kustow has worked with Brook, on and off, and in many capacities, for over forty years; from this perspective of easy familiarity, he has set out to lay Brook's career before us with clarity and sympathy, and in simply doing that, he offers a narrative as extraordinary as the sort of epic fable that the latter-day Brook has favoured for theatrical treatment. It is by no means a hagiography, but neither is it an intimate biography; certainly there is no attempt at psychoanalysis. In fact, the Brook Kustow presents to us, though altogether exceptional, is not especially complex; indeed, the portrait of the artist as a young man that Kustow offers is unexpectedly racy. Though he was conscious, as the son of Russian Jews, of his differentness from his fellow students first at Westminster then at Gresham's public schools, his early life was one of material comfort, intellectual stimulation and constant encouragement. He was blessed with a relationship with his father which was wholly positive (his mother cuts a slightly less engaging figure), as a result of which he knew nothing 'of the rejection of the father figure that is so much part of our time'. His intellectual precocity was encouraged (he read *War and Peace* at the age of nine) but not unduly spotlit. Stepping forth from the bosom of his family secure in his sense of being loved and wholly lacking in the typical Englishman's instinct to apologise for his very existence, he took to the theatre with easy and instant mastery; there is no hint of neurosis about him whatever, nor is he driven by anything other than an awareness of his own brilliance and a determination to do justice to it. 'For my first thirty years,' Brook says, 'I had nothing to connect with the phrase "inner life". What

83

was "inner life"? There was life. Everything was one hundred per cent extrovert.'

While at Oxford, he directed *Doctor Faustus*, tracking down the aged Aleister Crowley to advise on the magic, thinking nothing of consorting with 'the wickedest man in England'; in the absence of women he plunged with comfortable sensuality into 'every homosexual affair I could', exploring every facet of his sexual nature, until finally deciding, as he characteristically puts it, that female genitals were more congenial to him than male. No sooner had he come down from Oxford than he directed a production of Cocteau's *Infernal Machine*, hopping over to Paris without a thought for a chat with the author and France's greatest actor, Louis Jouvet. He was swiftly taken up by William Armstrong, of the Liverpool Rep, and Barry Jackson of Birmingham, where he first worked with Paul Scofield. All this before he was twenty-one. He then went to Stratford with Jackson, directing a Watteau-inspired *Love's Labour's Lost*, satisfying, as Kustow says, the post-war ache for beauty, then went on to direct Alec Guinness and Ernest Milton; he was appointed Ballet Correspondent for the *Observer*. His brutally realistic Stratford *Romeo and Juliet* brought him his first bad reviews, but it was seen by David Webster of the Royal Opera House, to whom Brook promptly wrote suggesting that they needed a Director of Productions and that he'd be just the fellow for the job: he got it. Despite a fine *Boris Godunov* (still in the repertory until the 1980s), his *Salome*, designed by Salvador Dalí, proved one provocation too many and his contract was not renewed. He was twenty-three. And so it went on: a mad whirligig, a unrelenting crescendo of success in the West End, at Stratford, in France, on Broadway, at the Metropolitan Opera House, across the whole spectrum of the theatre of the Fifties. Less successfully, he directed a film, *The Beggar's Opera*, with no less a star than Laurence Olivier.

At some point during this period, he came upon the writings of Peter Damian Ouspensky and the teaching of the Armenian avatar Gurdjieff, and found in it a view of the universe which accorded with his own understanding of himself, one based on a concept of life as the constant interplay of energies in which human personality often stood as an obstacle to experience of the real world. He absorbed this teaching into his life, submitting to its exercises and to the tough challenges of a teacher who persuaded him of 'my own essential ordinariness'. Kustow says of this commitment: 'Brook was seeking to master the maelstrom of his life.

Gurdjieff promised him a way through his hothouse of emotions. He gave him a map of his desires.' This is only partially true. Valiantly though he struggles with these difficult concepts, Kustow, the emotional rationalist, is not quite able to plug them into the main switchboard of Brook's work. The image of a river which Brook himself offers – an underground river, sustaining, informing, refreshing – is perhaps closer. As it would be for a Marxist or Buddhist, there is no question that the habits of mind this teaching has inculcated are central to Brook's life and his work, though it cannot explain it.

By his mid-thirties he started to want to break out of the theatre of which he himself had been such a supreme exponent. He had always held himself separate from his contemporaries, standing outside the mainstream post-war British tradition of his generation: the rep, the university (he had fastidiously refrained from joining OUDS), the socialist movement; he regarded the Royal Court Revolution as narrow and insular. He now permanently renounced the boulevard, and joined Peter Hall's new Royal Shakespeare Company, not without misgivings, worried that it was simply intending 'to do good things very well, the traditional target of Liberal England'. If he was to join, he must have an Experimental studio. He had after all done everything else; had had in a mere ten years what would have been an entire career for some men. His studio work, inspired by Antonin Artaud and named after his celebrated essay, Theatre of Cruelty, pushed and probed into the extremes of experience and the concomitant extremes of expression; he pushed his actors further and further, urging them to break through their limitations. They responded eagerly. (Unlike Pearl Bailey a few years earlier when he was working with her. 'We want a new Pearl Bailey,' he had told that great lady. 'Honey,' she replied, 'I ain't through with the old one yet.') The Artaud work then informed his remarkable productions for the RSC of *The Physicists* and *King Lear*, and a startling version of Seneca's *Oedipus* for the National Theatre. He also moved into the political arena with *US*, his response to the Vietnam War. The culmination of all this work was his overwhelming account of Peter Weiss's *Marat/Sade*, a tour de force of staging as well as perhaps the most advanced instance of company work ever seen in England. *A Midsummer Night's Dream* was like an enormous whoop of joy after this sustained exploration of the dark.

After *Oedipus*, a year earlier, he had written to his friend Stephen Facey, 'with the first night of the new production, with an aggressive assertive penis to boot, I saw that one whole world was over and another one would have to take its place.' Aged forty, he tells Facey that he now wants 'to face inwards rather than outwards'. A little earlier than most of us; but then his period of *enfance terrible* lasted longer than most. At least he knew it was over. It is of the subsequent years that Kustow writes most brilliantly. The book warms up enormously as it goes on – as if the early Brook, the bobby-dazzler, was a little alien to Kustow, who documents his young stardom conscientiously but without enthusiasm. It is the later search that grips Kustow, the quest for new forms, new language, new relationships with unimagined audiences: the company at the Bouffes du Nord; the treks to Africa; the engagement with epic texts from ancient cultures. Sometimes Brook would assert his genius for staging – would become again, as Richard Findlater put it after *Orghast at Persepolis*, 'the arch-magician, a self-renewing Prospero, with enough of Puck in him to change his staff in time before it is snapped by theory' – but much of his work was directed towards defining a new kind of acting: 'effortless transparency, an organic presence beyond self, mind or body such as great musicians attain when they pass beyond virtuosity'. He sought to inculcate the child's approach to play in his actors: what he calls the 'double image', where the child pretends to be a character but is always him or herself. The work he produced under this dispensation has been often ravishing, illuminating, provocative; it has also often been some-what mild in its effect. There would have been no place for an Olivier or a Scofield in these productions. The 'hell of night and darkness' that Kus-tow discerns in Brook's early and middle work seems to have dissolved, along with the 'deeply rooted aggression and anguish' in his psyche. Per-haps it is not so much that they were within him, but that he had an exceptional ability to be the conduit of what was around him. Now, in his eighties, he seems less engaged, quite understandably, with the world about him, and more concerned with distilling the essentials of what he conceives theatre to be. Tynan quotes an exchange between Henry James and Max Beerbohm on the subject of one of William Poel's 'Spartan exer-cises in Elizabethan stagecraft'. 'It's all done with great economy of means,' says Max. 'And, ah, of *effect*,' replies James.

In the 1960s, Brook had demanded a neo-Elizabethan theatre 'which passes from the world of action to the world of thought, from down-to-earth reality to the extreme of metaphysical enquiry without effort and without self-consciousness'. This is what we all long for; alas, Brook's

MY LIFE IN PIECES

own work since he formulated the demand has not been able to satisfy it. But his has been an unique and a necessary voice, reminding us that the price of a truly alive theatre is perpetual vigilance. The theatre is so unsatisfactory: its potential is limitless, but what we produce is always disappointing to us. We all long for something other than what we actually achieve. Sometimes we seem to be on the brink of something extraordinary. Brook has come closer to that something than anyone in the twentieth century. Kustow quotes a remark by John Kane, Brook's Puck, that comes as close as anything in an endlessly stimulating book to an explanation of what his contribution has been, both as artist and as elucidator: the RSC's approach, says Kane, was that they 'wanted to do things with the play'; Brook, on the other hand, 'wanted the play to do things with us'. Here, as in many places in the book, Kustow, in his quiet sober way, ushers us into the potential magnitude of theatre.

After its London season, the RSC would go off on world tours or back to Stratford, and the World Theatre Season would take its place. This annual phenomenon was somewhat dreaded by the management, partly because of the huge technical demands of the simultaneous translation system and the logistics of getting a different foreign company and its sets into the theatre every week, but mainly because it introduced into their theatre the irksome figure of the legendary one-armed impresario Peter Daubeny, who with immense flair and cunning lured the greatest theatre figures in the world (as well as some of the most obscure) to the Aldwych every year and with equal flair and cunning managed to upset them all. It may have been malice, it might have been eccentricity, or it could have been deliberate policy, but somehow – by a casual reference to a deadly rival, by a mispronounced or misremembered name, or by a conveniently forgotten financial arrangement – he kept them hopping. Press conferences were always especially prone to mishap: I once heard him introduce the great Italian actress Anna Magnani as Dame Anna Neagle, an actress of a quite different colour. Magnani looked bewildered as Peter swept on regardless. His translator-in-chief – a vital job in this theatrical Tower of Babel – was Binkie Beaumont's former secretary, the multilingual Kitty Black, who was often to be found running sobbing through the foyer after some particularly savage onslaught from Peter, who would follow her, crowing triumphantly, the empty left sleeve of his jacket, inexpertly pinned to his chest, flapping, his eyes glinting madly.

It was my job, as the box-office junior, to call him every night with the figure. Often he received the information with deep melancholy, as well he might have done – even when we were sold out, he never came close to breaking even, despite his heavy subsidy from the Observer *newspaper. But I greatly enjoyed these nocturnal telephonic confessionals, with him talking eloquently about the vicissitudes of his extraordinary life, on and off the battlefield – or perhaps one should say battlefields, military and theatrical. I rather enjoyed his raffish manners – Denholm Elliott would have played him to perfection – and from an artistic point of view (at whatever loss to his personal fortune and to the* Observer*) he was providing me and the rest of London with an unimaginable banquet of acting and stagecraft. The Moscow Art Theatre, the Comédie Française, Eduardo de Filipo's company, the Teatro Stabile di Genova, the Theatre on the Balustrade from Prague, the Schiller Theater, the Piccolo Teatro di Milano, Núria Espert, Ingmar Bergman's Royal Dramatic Theatre, the Kathakali Theatre of India, each on the other's heels – sublime productions, supreme performances. It was a seemingly unending pageant of greatness, waving a banner which said 'This is what theatre can be.'*

I was by now permanently intoxicated with theatre, out of my brain on it. I saw seven plays a week (two on Saturday) and read every book I could find on acting, being especially inspired by Stanislavsky, Edward Gordon Craig, G. H. Lewes, Eric Bentley – author of that supreme masterpiece The Life of the Drama *and editor of the still indispensable Pelican* Theory of the Modern Stage *– and Toby Cole and Helen Krich Chinoy's* Actors on Acting*. Meanwhile, I had found a drama school that I thought would suit me, the toughest one I could find, because I believed, correctly, that if I was to become an actor, some fairly significant adjustments, internal and external, needed to be made. What they were I was not sure; indeed I was not even sure what the problem was, but whatever it was that made me feel like lead when I stood on the stage of the DramSoc Hut in Belfast as Trigorin had to be identified and extirpated if I was ever to be an actor. It was from the Aldwych Theatre that I set out for the Drama Centre in Chalk Farm for my audition; what happened when I got there I've described elsewhere. The events of that day changed my life conclusively. I got in; six months later I showed up for the first day of term and for three years gave myself over wholly to its sometimes savage demands. The teaching was very much more than simply a craft training: its purpose was not simply to open us up, emotionally and physically (and God, I needed* *that) but to get our brains into our bodies. Thinking is at the heart of any art, in my view, but especially the art of acting; and the three principals, John Blatchley, Christopher Fettes and Yat Malmgren, individually brilliant and each radically different from the other, pushed us to think far harder about what we were doing or trying to do than we had ever imagined when we innocently decided that we wanted to be actors. Yat was in some ways the most extraordinary of the three. I wrote his obituary for* The Times *in 2002.*

Yat (Gert) Malmgren, who died on June 6th after a short illness, made a unique and extraordinary contribution to the training of actors in England. The school he founded in 1963 with Christopher Fettes and John Blatchley, the Drama Centre in Chalk Farm, remains one of the most influential and radical drama schools in the world, notable not only for the rigour of every aspect of its training, but also for the integration of all the varied elements involved. The pedagogic core which made this possible was provided by Malmgren's own work, Character Analysis, which is a fully worked-out theory of acting that places transformation – vocal, physical and emotional – at the heart of the acting process. He devoted his life as a teacher to conveying his profound understanding of the laws governing transformation, the means whereby the chaos of an actor's raw material is converted into the logic and focused, meaningful energy of character. His work stands with the great acting theories of the twentieth century, those of Stanislavsky, Meyerhold, and Artaud, all of which Malmgren acknowledged and admired, but – being a technique based above all on sensations – it was one less easy to put into words.

His theory was scientific and analytical, but the way he expounded it was all his own: a combination characteristic of the man, at once deeply sophisticated and apparently naïve, his creative use of the English language sometimes hilarious but more often poetic and suggestive, his approach both visionary and concrete. Above all, he was a living embodiment of his own work; his physical demonstrations were breathtaking. 'I am a peasant,' this strikingly handsome, elegant, aristocratic man would insist, 'I demand that everything must be simple.' By simple, he meant clear, and by clear, he meant specific. Generalisation was the disease, and Character Analysis was the antidote. Actors move in darkness, most of the time, hoping that intuition and inspiration will save the day; Malmgren offered a way of working which enabled the actor to understand and trust his own instrument.

He himself had been an exceptional performer in his time. Born near Stockholm in 1916, he trained first as an actor, then as a dancer. His outstanding gift was for the creation of character through movement, and he swiftly developed a career as a solo artist, taking his inspiration from the Bible but also from the political world around him. He studied continuously in Berlin and in Paris with the greatest teachers of the day, and his performances were acclaimed wherever he went. In 1940, he was honoured by an invitation to join the Ballet Jooss in exile at Dartington Hall in Devon; with them he gave performances of the great pacifist ballet *The Green Table* all over England and in America, eventually ending up in Brazil, where he stayed for seven years, performing his solo programme and teaching at his own school. At the Copacabana Club in Rio de Janeiro he sometimes appeared on the same bill as Marlene Dietrich; he later became the club's chief choreographer. He returned to Scandinavia in 1947 for more solo recitals, and in 1950, having retrained himself as a classical dancer, he joined International Ballet as a soloist, achieving particular distinction as the Baron in *La Boutique Fantasque*, under the direction of Massine himself.

This second career was cut short by injury, and he turned increasingly to teaching (though he continued to work as a choreographer, on Peter Brook's *Tempest*, for example). He was welcomed as a teacher at the English Stage Company at the Royal Court, but perhaps the most significant event in his subsequent development occurred when he was invited in the mid-Fifties to work with Rudolf Laban; shortly before his death, the great German movement theorist was evolving a system he called Movement Psychology which sought to combine the Jungian theories of William Carpenter with his own widely acclaimed approach to movement. It was this work that Laban entrusted to Malmgren, and it formed the basis of his teaching, first, at the influential Actor's Studio in West Street, Covent Garden, which he founded in 1954 with his partner, Christopher Fettes – Sean Connery, Anthony Hopkins and Diane Cilento were among the students – and subsequently at RADA, the Central School of Speech and Drama and the Drama Centre.

Malmgren never ceased evolving the work, refining and enriching it year after year. The directness of his contact with the students was crucial – he continued to take movement classes until his seventies – and his capacity to inspire them with the possibilities of the theatre and of their own talents changed the lives of all those who came into contact with him. He is survived by Christopher Fettes, another great teacher, who brought a dimension of historical and anthropological breadth to the school which complemented the depth of Malmgren's work on the expressive capacities of the actors; the Drama Centre remains the living monument of their vision, a vision not only of training, but of the place of the theatre in the world, which they both conceived of as central to the health of society. Their many distinguished students – Frances de la Tour, Jack Shepherd, Penelope Wilton, Pierce Brosnan, Geraldine James, Tara Fitzgerald – all freely acknowledge their debt.

Yat, it seemed to me, knew more about acting than any man alive. He read it with X-ray eyes; he penetrated it to the root and core. This was an intuitive gift; his life's work was to find the rationale for these astonishing aperçus of his. The Drama Centre was intensely theoretical in its approach, systematically seeking to integrate all the elements of the training – Laban, Jung, Classical Ballet, Stanislavsky. Yat was particularly enthusiastic about Stanislavsky's work because he valued logic so strongly, and he co-opted Stanislavsky's theory of actions – the idea that everything said or done in a play has a specific objective which governs the characters – as the underpinning of his own work on physical expression. Though deeply respectful of his seriousness and passion, my enthusiasm for Stanislavsky's work was not unqualified, even as a student. There was something self-flagellatory about the man that I resisted. Yet the more I read about him, the more touching I found him. His autobiography, My Life in Art, *is especially moving. Thirty-five years after my first encounter with it, I wrote an introduction to the Folio Society's new edition.*

My Life in Art was commissioned by Little, Brown & Co. in May of 1923 when the Moscow Art Theatre were on tour in America. Konstantin Sergeievich Stanislavsky, the theatre's co-founder, co-director and leading actor, was a very hot property, the focus of every artistic eye, not only because of his evident gifts as actor and director, but because of the famous System he had devised, said to be behind the exceptionally fine work that Americans were now experiencing for the first time. When the book appeared, in 1924, it was hugely popular from the start, on both sides of the Atlantic Ocean; Ellen Terry proclaimed it her constant companion. The English-speaking world wanted to know what made Stanislavsky and his actors tick.

*

Stanislavsky (1863–1938) is occasionally described as acting's Freud, its Darwin, its Marx and even – a little hysterically, perhaps – its Einstein (Lee Strasberg, in his introduction to *Masks and Faces*). The comparison with Freud is the most enlightening. Both men embarked on a lifelong study in search of the laws that govern their respective disciplines. Their findings, presented as scientific discoveries, have been immensely influential; to a large extent they have passed into the general consciousness. Both have had their disciples, who have sometimes bordered on the fanatical in their insistence that they alone have access to the truth. Both have been vulgarised, simplified and misrepresented by their own followers; the work of both has been hotly contested, both as science and as observation. In the case of Stanislavsky, there was initial dismissal (even from his own colleagues), followed by gradual acceptance and finally a more relaxed attitude from both admirers and detractors; like the Freudian revolution, the Stanislavskyan revolution has occurred, whether we like it or not. There are occasional outbursts against him: the dramatist-director David Mamet, in a recent tract, *True or False*, ringingly declares that 'the Stanislavsky "Method", and the technique of the schools derived from it, is nonsense. It is not a technique out of the practice of which one develops a skill – it is a cult'; but there are few present practitioners of the art of acting or directing who do not acknowledge that Stanislavsky's work is a source of enlightenment and inspiration, particularly, perhaps, as part of a training.

What is incontestable is that no one in the history of acting has devoted so much time and practical research to the questions which concern all actors. The theory of acting in the Western world was first adumbrated by Aristotle, in his *Poetics*, as part of his general theory of the drama; there have been very many manuals of acting, from the Elizabethans through to the present day; there have been philosophical investigations, primarily and centrally Diderot's great dialogue, *The Paradox of Acting*, which broached the eternal question of whether or not the actor actually feels the emotions that he portrays; and almost every great actor of any account has left behind a book of either memoirs or theory in which their particular approach to acting has been delineated: Irving, Coquelin, Ellen

Terry, Pierre Brasseur, Sarah Bernhardt, Sessue Hayakawa (whose auto-biography rejoices in the title *Zen Showed Me the Way*). But there is nothing in any of this to compare with the close record of his own work by one of the most distinguished actors and directors of this or any other century that Stanislavsky left us in *My Life in Art*, nor anything like his attempt, in a subsequent series starting with *An Actor Prepares*, to forge a set of exercises which, if diligently practised, would lead the actor to the Olympian heights of his profession. What made him do it? Why him?

Konstantin Stanislavsky (né Alexeyev) was a complex man, with a complex attitude to both life and art. *My Life in Art* records his unceasing struggle with, on the one hand, the dismal, corrupt Russian theatre of his youth and early manhood, and, on the other, his own unyielding self. Though his work as an actor was hugely praised, he was often deeply uncomfortable on stage. He was both blessed and cursed with a clear perception of how unsatisfactory his own performances were – of how poorly his body responded to his impulses – and how confused those impulses were. This sort of self-awareness can be quite paralysing for an actor, and there are many instances of just such paralysis in the present volume. It is a measure of Stanislavsky's doggedness, his unswerving devotion to the cause of High Art, that he persisted in his quest through appalling bouts of self-consciousness, challenging himself at every turn, never letting himself get away with a thing, until he finally achieved his goal. As Jean Benedetti remarks at the beginning of his invaluable short summary of the System, *Stanislavsky: An Introduction*, 'Had Stanislavsky been a "natural", an actor of instinctive genius, there would be no System.'

Stanislavsky's starting point was two-fold: he had been vouchsafed moments in certain of his own performances where inspiration had descended, moments which, like Shelley's Spirit of Delight, came 'rarely, rarely'; he sought to reproduce these and increase them in frequency. He had also been lucky enough to see performances by a number of great actors; he studied their work closely, striving to discover their secrets. Where had his own fitful and their great inspirations come from? There were no easy answers to his question.

His acting life had begun in 1877, when he was a mere fourteen years old. He founded a group of amateur players, the Alexeyev Circle, which performed in the front room of his wealthy parents' spacious house; the work later continued at the Moscow Society of Art and Literature. He was intelligent and tasteful, and managed, single-handed, to raise the whole level of theatrical presentation in Moscow to undreamed-of heights; both the group and he, as its leading actor, became famous. In time he met the distinguished writer and administrator Vladimir Nemirovich-Danchenko, and together, in 1898, they founded the Moscow Art and Popular Theatre, which rose to even greater heights than had the amateur circle. All this while, Stanislavsky's extraordinary gifts as a *metteur en scène* were developing apace (heavily influenced by the complex ensemble stagings of the Duke of Saxe-Meiningen's company which he had seen in Germany), and together he and Nemirovich created standards of discipline and sensitivity that were unexampled in Russian theatrical life, culminating in the production of the four mature masterpieces of Chekhov with which the theatre's name became identified.

So far, so triumphant. But at the height of his success, Stanislavsky (as he had now become known in order to protect his family name from the sullying associations of the stage) was deeply dissatisfied. He felt no closer to his goal; despite all his hard work on himself and his actors, inspiration remained intermittent. He seemed not to be able to build on his work, and depended for his effects largely on the physical production of which he was now such a virtuoso: using lighting, scenery and sound in constantly innovative ways to create unforgettable theatrical effects. All of this was meaningless to him, however, because the central element, the acting, remained earthbound, imitative, a mere *theatrical stencil*, in his evocative phrase, dimly copied from something else. It lacked, in a word, truth. This word loomed very large for Stanislavsky. He believed in the existence of an ideal truth, quite separate from mere *theatrical truth*, and he determined to track it down.

It must be stressed that at this time, his acting was universally acclaimed, admired by all, to a degree that his natural modesty, bordering on self-abnegation, prevents him from acknowledging in *My Life in Art*. In fact, there was never to be a time throughout his career when he felt entirely satisfied with his work as an actor. In 1906, at the end of the first brilliant cycle of work at the Moscow Art Theatre, he took a sabbatical in Finland to ponder these problems. He spent much of the time assessing the work of actors like the great Italians Tommaso Salvini (1829–1915) and Eleanora Duse (1858–1924), trying to fathom the source of their inspiration. He observed that they seemed to believe completely in what they were doing, and that it was this belief that gave them the capacity to be true to their inner emotion despite the public nature of the stage. Moreover, it created great relaxation: they seemed not to suffer at all from tension. At this point, Stanislavsky turned his eyes upon himself. Was he relaxed? Hardly ever. Did he believe in what he was doing? Almost never. When *had* he been relaxed? When *had* he been good? He remembered certain passages of certain performances. Why had they been remarkable? Generally, he discovered, because they were specific, rooted in either personal experience or memories of behaviour which had impressed itself on him. What if an entire role were to be constructed in this way? One would believe in every minute and relaxation would ensue, not an externally achieved relaxation, which he knew from trying made little or no difference to the performance, but a natural, spontaneous freedom. It also seemed to him that what differentiated these great actors from – well, from him, for example – was that they knew what they were doing: their characters, that is, seemed to do everything for a reason; they always seemed to want something, and every action they took was towards the achievement of this want. So there was another principle.

Armed with his discoveries, he announced them to the convened actors of the Moscow Art Theatre group. 'I have discovered the principles of Art!' he cried. 'No you haven't,' they replied, 'acting's not like that at all.' From then on Stanislavsky was something of a stranger in his own house. He eventually created a studio theatre in which to test and establish his ideas; over the remaining twenty-five years of his life he became more and more a teacher, modifying, adapting his principles, but never finally doubting the truth of those first discoveries. The founder members of the company never quite came round to them, though, and when he worked with those actors, he had to bargain with them, offering them bigger and better roles, in order to persuade them to think in terms of the strange neologised words in which he described his discoveries, some of them derived from the psychological texts he had read (by Ribot, for example), some by analogy with other sciences. The core of his approach is the idea of action: that every moment that an actor stands on stage, he or she *wants* something. The play consists of the actions the actor performs in order to get what he or she wants. He further elaborated this notion by proposing an overarching action (the super-objective) which is what the character wants in life, of which all the other actions are component parts. The actor must first identify his *wants*, then the obstacles that he faces in order to fulfil them. Of equal importance is the question of character: who is it that does the wanting? Here he devised another series of exercises which were dedicated to discovering the character within the actor, rather than imposing an external image. But before this work comes the necessary preliminary work whereby the actor learns how to access the emotions required by the part; and this, Stanislavsky determined, could only come from within oneself: the actor's *own* memories, both emotional and sensual. Only if the actor is in easy communication with his inner life and particularly with his sensual and emotional past will he have anything to bring to the role. Only if he knows what he wants in the play and what he does to get it will he know why he is on the stage. If he knows why he is on stage, the actor can never be self-conscious; and self-consciousness is the supreme evil, to be eliminated at all costs. Stanislavsky was tormented by what he called 'the terrifying black hole of the auditorium'.

The above is a simplified rendition of the first phase of Stanislavsky's work; Benedetti's book (op. cit.) gives a much more thorough, rather more technical account. There are a number of objections to the theory: firstly, it can well be objected that not all actors are afflicted by self-consciousness. There are many actors, perhaps the majority, for whom the stage is the most natural place on earth; indeed, it is almost a definition of an actor that he is someone who feels more at home on a stage in front of a thousand people than he does in his own front room. A second objection to Stanislavsky's theory is that though the actor has no point of personal contact with the character, he may be perfectly well able, from intelligence, observation and imagination, to create the character as written. Finally, it can be objected that plays are simply not written in this way; authors do not necessarily write their characters with objectives in the way that Stanislavsky describes. It is this last objection that has proved the most enduring: the Stanislavsky System can sometimes seem to be imposing something on the play that doesn't exist within it, that the *truth* that Stanislavsky so avidly sought was one of his own imagining.

This objection was first articulated by Stanislavsky's co-director Nemirovich-Danchenko, whose primary loyalty was always to the writer, and it was a contributory element to the almost ceaseless strife which existed between the two men from a very early stage in their working relationship. Nemirovich, himself a playwright and director, was a man of the widest possible literary culture, an acute and sensitive judge of plays, far more so than Stanislavsky, as the latter freely admitted; it was he who, strongly opposed by Stanislavsky, passionately urged the qualities of *The Seagull* as a candidate for inclusion in the first season, even though it had been passed over for a prize in a competition in favour of a play of Nemirovich's own. When in 1897 he and Stanislavsky had their historic first meeting at the Slaviansky Bazaar – a meeting which lasted fifteen hours – they had agreed that in their new theatre Stanislavsky would be responsible for Form, Nemirovich for Content, a tacit acknowledgement of Stanislavsky's lack of judgement in these matters. In fact, as Nemirovich gleefully points out in his somewhat feline memoirs, *My Life in the Russian Theatre* (a characteristically less high-flown title than Stanislavsky's), Stanislavsky was what we now call dyslexic, and had the greatest difficulty memorising lines or repeating them accurately. Small wonder that Stanislavsky's System places such emphasis on the physical and emotional rather than the verbal and intellectual. Interestingly, as the years went by, Stanislavsky became increasingly concerned with language, to the extent that by the end of his life he was writing (in his notes to his assistant on his late production of *Othello*; by then he was house-bound), 'To achieve the objectives (something extremely important and something actors always forget) he needs words, thoughts, i.e. the author's text. An actor above all must operate through words. On stage the only important thing is the active word.' In his earlier, logophobic days, Stanislavsky was obsessively driven by the need to take the theatre and acting out of the cerebral, mechanical area and release it into organic life, and it was this obsession that led to the new dimension in the acting of the Moscow Art Theatre; his final reconciliation with language was the culmination of his long journey towards an acting which was expressive at every level.

*

The stormy relationship with Nemirovich-Danchenko (they scarcely spoke for several years) is only lightly alluded to in *My Life in Art*, and Nemirovich is constantly praised in its pages. Despite the tensions and storms so common in theatrical partnerships (Welles and Houseman, mac Liammóir and Edwards), between them they sustained an extraordinary level of creativity and exploration over a period of some forty years, through three wars and three revolutions, encompassing the reigns of Nicholas II, Lenin and then Stalin, each of which brought its burdens. Nemirovich, with his elegant psychological acuity, is able to describe

Stanislavsky with a vividness that Stanislavsky is unable to match, but there is in Nemirovich an absence of the generosity that is so characteristic of the other man. Thus Nemirovich's account of meeting Stanislavsky for the first time: 'Stanislavsky always presented a picturesque figure. Tall, distinguished in stature, he had an energetic bearing and his movements were plastic, though he did not give the impression of giving the slightest thought to this plasticity,' he writes, affably. Then comes the stiletto: 'As a matter of fact, this apparent beautiful casualness had cost him immense labour: according to his own words, he had spent hours and years in developing his gestures before the mirror.' The more or less affectionately mocking tone is characteristic, and seems to have been a not uncommon response to Stanislavsky, with his passions and obsessions; he was known throughout the company, Nemirovich says elsewhere, as 'big baby'. Another, altogether more savage, pen-portrait of him occurs in Bulgakov's novel *Black Snow*, a naked act of revenge on Stanislavsky for the treatment that the author received at his hands during the rehearsals for his play *Molière*. In its pages Stanislavsky appears as Ivan Vasilievich, dippy, manipulative, stupid, and arrogant, and no doubt there is an element of truth in the picture. Ruled by his vision, he was not quite in the world, and thus not always capable of seeing people in their situations. Perhaps the most acute thing ever said of him was the remark of his colleague, the great actor Kachalov, that Stanislavsky always saw the artist in the person, but he didn't always see the person in the artist. Few, however, ever accused Stanislavsky of insincerity in his quest for new and vibrant life on the stage. In *My Life in Art* he presents himself as baffled, slow, obstinate, vain, foolish, sometimes even despotic, but it is hard not to love him, despite or because of this. However selective his account of the 1911 *Hamlet* which he co-directed with Edward Gordon Craig, it is clear from it that Craig ran circles round him. Stanislavsky was unable to believe that a great artist could behave unlike a great man. The innocence of his world view is a constant thread in the book, but that innocence, allied to an iron determination to pursue his quest, becomes curiously touching.

For the facts of Stanislavsky's life, Benedetti's 1988 biography is very useful, and there are whole shelves of memoirs by pupils and assistants. *My Life in Art* is not an autobiography, much less a detailed account of the Moscow Art Theatre. It is, if anything, a spiritual autobiography, an account of a seeker's stumbling path towards the mysteries, and as such has much in common with, for example, Reshad Feild's books of Sufic initiation, or the many books by the pupils of Gurdjieff. Stanislavsky's view of the art of the theatre, and specifically the art of acting, is essentially esoteric: only true adepts will gain enlightenment and know one day the bliss of arriving at the centre of their own creativity. Despite their practical and detailed nature, Stanislavsky's exercises are not unlike the exercises of certain spiritual disciplines: their purpose is refinement and concentration of the spirit, whereby the divine part of man can shine forth to the greater benefit of humankind. He is quite explicit about this: 'there is another all-powerful Artist who acts in mysteries and ways unknown to us on our superconsciousness.' It is in his later works that he attempts to describe the elements of his System; in *My Life in Art* he outlines his mission. The book is full of incidental felicities – the fine opening chapter evoking the Russia of his childhood; the brilliant descriptions of individuals, Rubinstein, Gorky, Maeterlinck, Chekhov; the detailed impressions of extraordinary performers; the gripping accounts of the creation of a great theatre company under every kind of duress. But it is above all an affirmation of the possibilities of the arts of theatre and acting and an inspiration to anyone who believes that these things really matter, and have the power seriously to influence human life.

*

From a chronological point of view, *My Life in Art* ends somewhat indeterminately with the revolution of 1917 – the Third Revolution, as Stanislavsky calls it – and the temporary break-up of the company. Physically divided by the civil war, a third of the actors were stuck in Moscow, while the rest, including Knipper, Chekhov's widow, and Kachalov (Craig's Hamlet), toured Europe. It is perhaps worth sketching in the remaining twenty-one years of Stanislavsky's life. Events both within the Moscow Art Theatre and in the outside world were unrelenting and traumatic. On a personal level, Stanislavsky was shattered by a public humiliation administered to him by Nemirovich-Danchenko. Alarmed at the amount of time taken for rehearsals of a revival of Dostoevsky's *The Village of Stepanichikovo* (one of the company's early successes), Nemirovich had, in February 1917, on the very brink of the Kerensky Revolution, taken over the play's direction. Stanislavsky, who had been co-directing with the actor Moskvin, was floundering in the part of Rostanov. Dissatisfied with his original much-acclaimed interpretation, but unable to achieve the breakthrough into something better, he was attempting to reconceive the part in terms of his new theory of the through-line, the super-objective: what was Rostanov's overall purpose? What was his goal in life? He found it hard to decide. Finally, at a dress rehearsal and in full view of the company, Nemirovich took the part away from him and handed it to another actor, telling him that he had 'failed to bring the part to life'. Stanislavsky accepted this savage treatment without demur, agreeing that it was the best decision both for the production and for the company, but he never again created a new role. The incident did nothing to improve relations between the company's two directors. Even before the *Stepanichikovo* incident (Stanislavsky had intended to write about it in *My Life in Art* under the title *The Village of Stepanichikovo: My Tragedy*, but lacked the heart to do so), they had been at loggerheads. In April 1916, Nemirovich-Danchenko had been formally ratified as sole managing director of the company. Stanislavsky thenceforth proposed to separate himself from the main theatre and focus his efforts on his studio at home in Leontievski Lane. Increasingly he saw the future of his work in a studio context.

His own financial circumstances had undergone a radical transformation with the revolution. The family business, which he had diligently maintained (he was a model and much-loved employer) was sequestrated by the authorities and turned into a cable factory. Despite the considerable hardship involved, he took it stoically. He only hung on to his apartment by the skin of his teeth, after the intervention of the cultural commissar Lunacharski. Meanwhile, he was as ever trying to secure the future of the theatre, not materially but spiritually. He maintained his lifelong vision of the theatre as one of the key custodians of the community's soul, a distinctly un-Marxist position, but one unexpectedly supported by Lenin, who was instrumental in ensuring the theatre's reopening with its traditional repertoire. Post-revolutionary cultural life had splintered into a hundred new tendencies during that glorious and short-lived epoch which threw up and actively encouraged the wildest and most stimulating of experiments. Stanislavsky's students Boleslavsky and Vakhtangov, both among the most radical of theatrical explorers, worked in the Moscow Art's Second and Third Studios. The results of their work were often to Stanislavsky's intense displeasure, but they became highly influential. Stanislavsky himself tirelessly lectured on his System and the future of the theatre. His own work focused increasingly on the opera; ironically, since in *My Life in Art* whenever he wants to denounce dead acting, he describes it as operatic: 'like a tenor', 'like a bass' (although he would equally often cite his friend Chaliapin as the ideal actor, the perfect exemplar of everything that he taught). He found, like many another director from the so-called straight theatre, that the singers were more than willing to learn from him; unlike some of his fellow actors, they had no prejudice against his System, which was instantly applicable to their work. This sustained contact with music and its essentially rhythmic and lyrical qualities made him ever more aware of that lack in his work to which he refers on many occasions in the pages of *My Life in Art*: his vocal and physical limitations, and his failure to address directly the questions of the physical manifestation of the text, its *incarnification*, as his translator quaintly but memorably puts it. This became a central preoccupation over the succeeding years, as he continued his quest in ever more surprising directions, constantly seeking the ideal definition of his art.

During this immediately post-revolutionary period, the question of whether the Moscow Art Theatre could survive at all, and if so, in what form, was widely and publicly discussed; Stanislavsky's isolation within the company and the split with Nemirovich were open secrets (particularly since Nemirovich had become a member of the Communist Party and head of all Moscow's dramatic theatres). Stanislavsky had become A Problem, widely acknowledged, even by the fiercest of young Turks, to be a great artist, a genius, perhaps, but perceived to be fettered, shackled, as they saw it, by his colleagues. His ambitious, rather operatic, production of Byron's *Cain* was something of a fiasco, but with his 1921 revival of *The Government Inspector*, he was again at the forefront of theatrical ferment. The Khlestakov of Michael Chekhov (Anton's nephew, and one of the most extraordinary talents to have emerged from the First Studio) was a startling experiment in the grotesque which violently divided audiences, some thinking it wilfully and incomprehensibly ugly, others believing it to be everything that modern acting might be: improvisatory in feeling, fantastical, poetic, dangerous. Stanislavsky aided and abetted Chekhov in his approach, and the production itself, controversial, fresh and bold, shared in all these qualities. Stanislavsky had reinvented himself.

Under intense pressure from overwhelming financial difficulties, the Moscow Art Theatre itself was by now reeling from the impact of the New Economic Plan. After a three-year gap during which the Kachalov/Knipper group had toured Europe, the company was now reunited and

Nemirovich drew up a plan for an international tour, on which the company embarked in September 1922; they did not return until August1924. The tour took in all the great European cities save only London, and entailed two separate visits to the United States, with six plays, to which were added two new productions on the road. It was as gruelling as these things invariably are, but, as we have seen, it immeasurably enhanced the already glowing reputation both of the Moscow Art Theatre and Stanislavsky himself; he was held to be the perfect paradigm of his own theories, or such of them as had filtered through to the West in publications by Stanislavsky's colleagues Boleslavsky and Komisarjevsky. Both men had left Russia before the revolution, when the System was in its first form, in which the emphasis was strongly on emotion memory – an emphasis they duly passed on to their own students, of whom the most prominent was the young Lee Strasberg, who was in time to bring it to the Group Theatre and finally to serve it up in vulgarly simplified form at the Actors Studio as The Method.

On the 1923 tour, the great and the good, the intelligentsia and the artistic community, all flocked to see the work; practically without exception, they admired it. Stanislavsky himself was offered many opportunities to teach in America; he could have earned large sums of money, but, contrary to the dark suspicions of the artistic establishment in Russia, he never had any intention of leaving his native land, to which he was passionately devoted. He was a sincere if politically naïve supporter of the revolution, and remained so despite the increasing stranglehold exercised by the authorities after Lenin's death. By 1924, when the company returned to Moscow, Stalin was Russia's master. The new political circumstances called for new plays: the Central Repertory Committee, known in the fashion of the time as Glavrepertkom, was required to approve all such works. With great difficulty and over a long period of time, Stanislavsky managed to secure approval for a production of Bulgakov's *The White Guard*, astonishing because of its sympathetic portrayal of the White Russian side in the Civil War. When it was finally performed, the play was a huge hit with the public, though violently denounced by all the critics. By one of the odder quirks of theatrical history, when some years later it was proposed to revive the production, Stalin himself demanded a private performance before agreeing to the revival. He loved it, subsequently returning to the theatre seventeen times; the reviews suddenly got better. Stanislavsky fought the official demand for politically simplistic plays with great personal courage, insisting that exposure to such work killed off the actors' talent. He continued his work in opera, and at the Art Theatre had a particular triumph with Beaumarchais' *The Marriage of Figaro*, seizing on the celerity and vigour of the play to put into practice his ever-evolving theory of physical action, establishing irresistible tempos for each section of the play, all the tempos integrated to provide an infectious sense of exhilaration. His production of *Armoured Train 14–69* satisfied the Commissariat, though two subsequent 'approved' plays flopped.

These disappointments were swallowed up in the celebrations for the Moscow Art Theatre's thirtieth anniversary: the worldwide impact that the company and Stanislavsky's teachings had made is reflected in the roll-call of congratulatory telegrams: from Chaplin, Fairbanks and Swanson in the United States, Craig in England, Reinhardt in Berlin. The latter went one further, and gave Stanislavsky a car which had cost him 30,000 DM. However, at the Gala which was the theatre's own celebration of itself, Stanislavsky, playing Vershinin in Act One of *The Three Sisters*, suffered a major heart attack. He managed to make it to the curtain call, but that was the end of his career as an actor. He was sixty-five. Thereafter, for the remaining twelve years of his life, he existed in a curious, oblique relationship to the theatre with which his name was more or less synonymous. He planned productions (including a disastrous *Othello*) from his apartment, issuing detailed production plans and guidelines for his assistants, but he rarely visited the theatre or the rehearsal room; occasionally actors would come to his apartment. The results were predictably unsatisfactory. A great deal of his time was spent on the planned six volumes in which he would describe his System: the first was to be called *A Pupil's Diary at a Drama School*. On the advice of his American friend and translator, Elisabeth Hapgood Reynolds, this was divided up into the two books now known as *An Actor Prepares* (originally, and more precisely known as *An Actor's Work on Himself Part One*) and *Building a Character* (*An Actor's Work on Himself Part Two*); they are very much part of the same text and should be seen as such. Their division has further confused an exposition of complex exercises already somewhat scuppered by the clumsy dialogue form in which Stanislavsky perhaps unwisely chose to write, though their influence has been enormous; almost all subsequent systems are a reaction to Stanislavsky's, for or against.

His health became ever more precarious; his heart condition was complicated by emphysema. When he died, in 1938, at the age of seventy-five
and surrounded by every conceivable honour, he was still trying to refine
and clarify the latest developments in his System. He had had a *rapprochement* with his old pupil Meyerhold, from whose aesthetics he had
vehemently distanced himself; it seems that near to the point of death he
began to see him as a possible successor. There was no *rapprochement*
with Nemirovich-Danchenko, who was not in Moscow when Stanislavsky
finally gave up the ghost. He had been in Stanislavsky's thoughts only
days before, however, and made an emotional oration at the memorial
service, all the more resonant for the prolonged hostilities that had prevailed between the two men. 'Immortality begins here. Enamoured and
sacrificial devotion was the pivot in the creative life of the deceased. And
when I wondered what we should adopt as our guideline in art, I decided
it was most of all his attitude to art. We may argue over the artistic issues
that we argued over when Konstantin Sergeievich was alive. But this, his
stupendous sacrificial attitude to art, is something incontestable. And
what I would like for all my comrades of the Art Theatre present here is
to make one vow beside the coffin: let us vow that we shall treat the theatre with the same profound and sacred devotion that Stanislavsky did.
Let us adopt that as the great motto left us by him. Let us vow to behave
as he behaved.'

Stanislavsky's own peroration in *My Life in Art* provides his own epitaph,
comparing himself to a gold-seeker: 'I cannot will to my heirs my labours,
my quests, my losses, my joys and my disappointments, but only the few
grains of gold that it has taken me all my life to find. May the Lord aid
me in this task!'

*How could one not love such a man? And yet, and yet. I was unable to
articulate my objection to his work until many years after I first encountered it, and when I did it was something of a revelation. The Drama
Centre's Stanislavsky training was in the hands of a remarkable, permanently gum-chewing American actress called Doreen Cannon, who was a
pupil of the actress Uta Hagen, one of many American actor-teachers to
have rebelled against Lee Strasberg's limited conception of Stanislavsky's
work and tyrannical teaching methods. I reviewed Strasberg's* A Dream
of Passion *in 1988, for the* Sunday Times.

Lee Strasberg never committed his method to print during his lifetime. He wrote a brief introduction to Diderot's *The Paradox of Acting*, and the 9,000-word entry on Acting in the *Encyclopaedia Britannica*, and there exists a transcript of some of his classes, *Strasberg at the Actors Studio* in book form. *A Dream of Passion* was to be his summa, and its working title was *What is Acting? From Stanislavsky to the Method*. Alas, he died before completing it. The book that his editors have made from the existing material is an account of his personal development. It is pleasantly, plainly, written and contains a certain amount of anecdotal biographical information, an account of several exercises (some of them hovering on the edge of primal therapy) and a central section on Stanislavsky.

Bringing a repertory of Chekhov and Gorky plays with them, the Moscow Art Theatre came to America in 1924 where they were seen by an enthusiastic audience – including the twenty-three-year-old Lee Strasberg. He immediately enrolled in the school founded by two MAT company members who had decided to stay behind. In due course, he and a couple of friends founded the Group Theatre, which, after a few glorious years, folded, whereupon Strasberg opened the Actors Studio, not a drama school in the usual sense, but a kind of forum in which his students would offer exercises to him to criticise. The Strasberg System was known as The Method.

Essentially, it consisted of Stanislavsky's formulations as found in his first book, *An Actor Prepares*. These formulations are all eminently sensible, and were obviously a useful antidote to the staginess of the contemporary Russian theatre. They are, however, the very least you can expect of an actor, a mere beginning, though admirable for drama students. Having got so far, Stanislavsky then continued to elaborate and in some cases radically alter his system, for the obvious reason that presenting a semblance of real life on the stage is not what all plays call for; in fact, very few plays fail to demand a very great deal more.

These developments, however, were ignored by Strasberg. He had discovered the true faith, which was called Emotional Truth. That was the ultimate yardstick of any performance. And who decided what was emotionally true? Why, Strasberg, of course. Despite reports coming out of Russia about Stanislavsky's revisions and his new insistence on physical action, Strasberg became, in Harold Clurman's words, 'a fanatic about emotion'. And of course, the results were often startling. A degree of emotional self-expression such as had never been seen before took the

American theatre by storm, and the material was ready to hand. A number of extraordinary performers, Dean, Monroe, Brando, passed through Strasberg's hands, some briefly, some becoming dependent on his steadying presence. Monroe could hardly act at all without either him or his wife Paula being in the vicinity. All this emotional discharge burnt up the screen, and electrified the world. Every young actor wanted to be like an American actor, wild, passionate, real and so very very NOW. Almost at a stroke, an entire tradition of American acting, articulate, witty, intelligently passionate – the tradition of Tracy and Hepburn and Cagney and Bogart – realistic but not 'real' was made to seem false, while people were expected to pay good money to watch actors working up to and away from their feelings.

There is not a word in Strasberg's book to suggest that he sees any purpose to the theatre other than watching people having emotions. The tone of the book is somewhat combative, because even at the time of his death (1982) the tide was turning. It is now fully turned. Emotion has ceased to be the ultimate goal of American actors, because it has failed to animate any but the tiniest range of plays. Strasberg's failure as a director with the legendarily bad production of *Three Sisters*, which provoked the audience to chant in unison with the mannered stumblings of Sandy Dennis when the play appeared at the Aldwych Theatre, was an early indication of this, but most recently a new and brilliant generation of American playwrights appeared with other demands to make, verbal and linguistic demands. Strasberg's book betrays what might be called logophobia: a deep distrust of words which must always result in a terrible sameness of acting; after all, there are a limited number of emotions to permutate – it is his words that make one playwright different from another. Not according to Strasberg. 'The words prepare the actor to carry out the activities desired by the author.' With the distrust of words comes an inevitable distrust of intelligence.

All great acting – Olivier's, Brando's, Laughton's, Maggie Smith's – is great because of piercing contact made with the thought processes of the character: thinking what the character thinks, hearing what the character hears, seeing what the character sees. Not according to Strasberg. 'It does not matter so much what the actor thinks,' he writes, 'but the fact that he is really thinking something that is real to him at that moment.' This technique, known as 'substitution' is a deadly practice, killing off the actor's mental responses. He describes 'the primary characteristic of the stage' as 'the non-existent reality'. But the reality *does* exist: it is the words. The most baleful result of his influence is the present widespread unresponsiveness of actors to language. No matter how brilliant the visualisation of either the character or his world, it can only fully live in the words of the play, their texture, their rhythm, above all, in their meaning.

In fairness to Strasberg, he has inherited this attitude from his Russian model. Stanislavsky was almost word-blind, and had the greatest difficulty in reading plays, preferring to work on a subtext of his own invention. (Strasberg's attempt to deny Chekhov's intense dislike of Stanislavsky's productions of his plays is feeble and patently contradicted by the writer's letters – being written in words, they are presumably not to be trusted.) A good deal of Stanislavsky's system originated in his own personal problems, like his chronic stage fright. Strasberg repeats with approval the Russian's well-known comment about the actor's dread of 'the black and remote hole of the proscenium arch': in fact, it is a wonderfully friendly aperture for most of us, its very blackness relieving us of the self-consciousness which so bedevilled Stanislavsky and his fundamentalist American disciple. In the last page of the book, Strasberg crossly rejects a trend he has discerned which is anathema to his throbbing, palpating vision of theatrical art: 'the problem of expression [is] a means of sharing one's individual way of experiencing... all human beings are in even more need of this, if life is not to deteriorate into the "playing of games", which many psychologists, and even more some theatre people, have discovered and proclaimed a way of life.' Now that Strasberg's influence has disappeared, we can drag the theatre off the psychiatrist's couch, and out of the seance parlour, and hand it back to the players.

When I arrived at the Drama Centre, though I didn't realise it, I was in a state of emotional stasis, locked, armoured, rigid. I was an ideal candidate for the emotional-memory work that is such a valuable aspect of Stanislavsky's teaching, but which Strasberg had elevated into the be-all and end-all of acting. My great emotional breakthrough came in the second year of the training; by the third year, thanks to it, I had access to an unprecedented (for me) physical and emotional freedom. But it never occurred to me for a moment that the plays of Feydeau, Caldéron, Pirandello, Ostrovsky, Max Frisch which we performed in that final year could be reduced to a series of psycho-dramas. Unlike many of my colleagues, who had been inspired to become actors by movies – especially American movies – I was absolutely focused on the theatre. I had seen so many great actors, so many devastating productions, so many towering plays, which told me that the theatre was a thing of almost infinite variety, that it was obvious to me that though emotional freedom was essential to any performance, it was only a beginning.

In order to survive financially at the Drama Centre, I had been working for the RSC (helping with the box office for their 1970 Roundhouse season) and at the Old Vic, now as an usher. I saw all the plays in what was an extremely mixed period for the National, during which the company spread across the West End, in seasons at the New and Cambridge Theatres, with a series of variably successful new productions. Olivier was seriously ill for some of this time, which sapped the company's morale in a way that suggested that the organisation was dangerously dependent on his charisma to keep it going. Extraordinary things were happening, nonetheless, including Olivier's triumphant appearance in Long Day's Journey Into Night, *whose heart-stopping first night I attended (thanks to my old box-office chums, of course). My enthusiasm for him was not shared by many of my fellow students, which puzzled me. I wrote this piece for a Festschrift celebrating his eightieth birthday; it was called* Laurence Olivier and My Generation.

When I was at drama school, the Laurence Olivier controversy raged. Was he the greatest actor who had ever lived? Or was he simply appalling, a ham, external, tricksy, unwatchable, and so on? At that time the cons seemed to be winning. It was, in fact, quite hard to find someone to say a word in his favour, among either my contemporaries or his. This being the case, I generally kept rather quiet. I was a raving fan, and frankly baffled by the inability of people to see what was as plain as the noses on their face (not to mention the nose on his face, rather larger of course, because generally made of putty): that he was the most exciting, the most daring, most interesting, the funniest, most moving person on the English stage by a mile. It's fifteen years since he was on any stage and nothing has dimmed my memory of a single moment of any performance of his. If an artist's job is to be memorable, Olivier is the supreme acting artist of my lifetime.

The sensuous impact was shocking. Most great actors operate by stealth: one's first glimpse of Ralph Richardson or John Gielgud or Alec Guinness was likely to be disappointing. Only slowly did they weave their spell, drawing you closer to them, luring you to the edge of your seat. It was quite different with Olivier. The initial image was always so clear, projected in bright sharp colours; a voice of symphonic splendour, simultaneously sumptuous and piercing; an aptness of invention; an audacity of timing, and no lack of feeling, contrary to report. In the area where he was supreme master – the tragicomic – he was desperately moving: Strindberg's Edgar, Osborne's Archie, Shylock, Richard III – all weasel men for whom at bay he found the authentic cry of pain.

Temperamentally, he was not a romantic actor, despite Heathcliff, nor a heroic one, despite Henry V. He was a Realist actor, always grounding his roles in a material, observed reality – thus diminishing them in the eyes of some of his contemporaries, who were used to acting in abstract nouns: nobility, majesty, pathos. Olivier was a very modern actor; for all his unprecedented command of the mechanics of acting, his point of reference was not the theatre, but the world. 'Acting,' he told Tynan, 'is the art of persuasion. First you've got to persuade yourself, then you've got to persuade your audience.' The all-important first half of that requirement was never forgotten, as he nagged away at making sense for himself of every moment, winkling out generalisation and banishing it. Sometimes the effect was reductive – but whatever you thought about his decision to play Othello black, instead of nobly moorish, the way in which he executed his interpretation commands absolute admiration: the observation was precise, detailed and brilliantly realised. He forged for that performance the greatest instrument any actor has ever had at his disposal. The physical, vocal and emotional flexibility of it set new standards for the rest of us to measure ourselves against. In fact, of course, none of us could begin to match those standards.

In his short film, *The Great Ecstasy of Woodcarver Steiner*, Werner Herzog shows Steiner, a skiing champion, entering so completely into communion with his sport, and jumping so far and so high, that he made nonsense of all previous records, to the degree that he was eventually barred from competing: no one else stood a chance. Laurence Olivier has approached his art like a sportsman or an athlete, and he has won the pentathlon. It was his ambition, he told Tynan, 'to fascinate the public with the art of acting in the same way that they might follow a boxer or a cricket player'. It was this that lay behind the ritual criticisms of him that I heard so often in my student years: 'I can see the wheels going round', 'it's all so calculated', 'he never moves me', and, again and again, derogatorily 'yes, it's very clever – I suppose'.

It was clever; it was meant to be. It was also, frankly, intended to annihilate the competition. It succeeded there, too. The *victor ludorum*, the glory-boy of the acting world, has, undisputedly, become the Greatest Actor Alive. But this acting that is about acting has proved sterile. It has had no issue. Othello was not the harbinger of a race of super-actors; it was an end in itself. The literalism of the interpretation remained; the giddying virtuosity of the performance flew off the edge of the globe. Nothing was left remarkable beneath the visiting moon.

Every role he played has had to be reinvented by his successors, with only middling results so far. In fact it is acting itself that needs to be reinvented. The post-Olivier vacuum yawns ominously long and large. Many good performances have been seen in the last few years, but there has been no redefinition of the actor's aim. Olivier accrued all the glory to himself; he won all the prizes. If acting is not about prizes, and not about glory, what then is it about?

Long Day's Journey *was not the only success at the National during those seasons: there was, for example, Ingmar Bergman's radical split-stage* Hedda Gabler, *with Maggie Smith supreme in the title role, and William Gaskill's superb revisiting of Farquhar with* The Beaux Stratagem. *For me, though, those years were most memorable for the brief participation of Paul Scofield in the company, first in Pirandello's* Rules of the Game, *in which he was enigmatic and compelling, and then* The Captain of Köpenick, *in which he gave a performance so extraordinary that it compelled me to rethink everything I thought I knew about acting, made me waver, indeed, in my loyalty to Olivier. They were bewilderingly different stage animals, Olivier all acting, Scofield all being. I watched him like a hawk, and was fascinated once to note the difference between a Saturday matinee and Saturday evening performance of* Köpenick; *I diligently wrote down what I noticed – it was the first writing I ever did about acting – and six years later when Scofield and I were acting together I shyly handed it to him. 'Interesting,' he said, in that dangerously veiled way of his. In it, I observed how totally in character he was, and yet how totally responsive to the audience. I've lost it now (or perhaps it just slunk away in embarrassment), but I think even at that early age, I had an inkling of the mystery of his art. He was hugely approved of by the Drama Centre as one of the few English actors who genuinely transformed. This aspect of acting interested me more than anything else, so I pondered on his work, seeing every performance in London he ever gave thereafter. Although he seemed utterly different in every role, the external changes were not signposts, as with Olivier; the change was internal, a shift of being, some ineffable realignment of his soul. When I played Pedro Crespo in* The Mayor of Zalamea *in our final-year public productions at the Drama Centre, I froze when I saw that the costume that they had borrowed for me had a label stitched to it which said 'Paul Scofield – Thomas More'. I put it on as a priest puts on his vestment.*

I watched these great ones with new admiration: now I had acted, or tried to, I knew how difficult the simplest character and the most straightforward line could be to play. But this was not daunting. Not in the least. All I felt was a sense of infinite possibility. I was filled with irrepressible excitement for the years ahead. The training had taken me deep into a new world which seemed to me to be limitless: it had instilled in me a sense of unending intellectual, emotional and physical challenge. All these stories, these characters, these visions created by our forerunners, waiting to be unleashed into the world – 'images of destiny', as Christopher Fettes so inspiringly described them. And I had felt in myself the stirrings of creativity, of power, of transcendence, which could only grow in the companies to which I felt confident I would belong for the rest of my career.

I see now that the three years I spent at the Drama Centre were the happiest years of my life. I had discovered my vocation. I had a purpose. I was alive with hope and confidence, not so much in myself as in the powerful medicine I had it in my gift to dispense: I suppose I felt like the priest I once yearned to be. I had acquired friends, who stayed friends for the rest of my life; I had had lovers, of whom the same was not true, but no hard feelings. I was ready to go, but in some odd way, I could have stayed. I had a blueprint for the rest of my life. I was filled with meaning.

The Drama Centre brokered all of this. Had I not trained there, I would have been a different actor, a different person. I went into the Drama Centre a dilettante and a clever, frightened child; I came out as an actor, and a grown-up human being. Of course, many fine actors have not trained, but I know that had I not, I would – if I'd become an actor at all – have piled on the tricks, one on top of another, and would never have created anything at all. Thirty years after graduating, I made a speech to the Association of Drama Schools. It was later printed in the Drama Centre Prospectus.

There's a well-worn story about acting which rather sums up the prevailing view. Father to son: 'What do you want to be when you grow up?' Son: 'An actor.' Father: 'You can't be both.' In fact, acting is a very grown-up job indeed. Skilled and sometimes upsetting. Hard, difficult work, underpinned by three firm foundations – example, experience and education.

The first of the foundation stones – example (or tradition) – was an ever-present factor until quite recently; a great line of succession which could be traced unbroken back to Shakespeare's actors, Burbage and Kemp. Somehow, somewhere around the 1970s and early 1980s, for a variety of reasons, the succession was broken. There were no applicants for the job of Leader of the British Theatre. The very idea seemed outmoded, undemocratic. Good actors, wonderful actors, appeared, but no one wanted to lead from the front. They left that to the directors. Actors abdicated from the position of being (the phrase is unavoidable) role models.

The second pillar of the British theatre, experience – practising the job – was, also until quite recently, widely available not only in the metropolis, with the largest number of theatres of any city in the world, but across the country in an even larger number of theatres: every town had its own, and many of them had permanent acting companies, as much a part of the town's identity as the local football team, in which the actors would develop and grow before the very eyes of the audience. There were touring companies, too, and many Theatre-in-Education groups. Thousands and thousands of opportunities for actors to consolidate their craft and to forge their individual contribution to the theatre as a whole. All this has not totally disappeared, but it is a shadow of what it was. There is no longer a training ground or a breeding ground for actors.

With the erosion of these two flagstones, the third foundation – education – has become all the more important. Until the end of the nineteenth century, the theatre was essentially a family business; actors were, in the most literal sense, born and not made. Training, a relatively recent development in England, came, at the turn of the twentieth century, out of the profession itself. Supported by all the leading actors of the day and many of its playwrights, the early drama schools boldly trumpeted the seriousness of the profession's intention of working on itself. Soon, a whole new generation of trained players emerged, which in a very short space of time brought on what is now spoken of as a golden age of actors – Olivier, Gielgud, Richardson, Guinness, Ashcroft – all of whom trained in some form of drama school. What did they have that their untrained predecessors lacked?

I would put it in a simple phrase: the possibility of going further. The old method of learning how to be an actor was built on observation and imitation; it was, essentially, an apprenticeship. You entered the profession at a lowly level, you learned how to make the most of what you'd got, you watched the leading actors like a hawk, seeing how they got their effects. You developed by doing. You formed your own ideas about what the job entailed. You discovered what worked and what didn't. Sometimes you got advice. It was a pragmatic, rough and ready, Darwinian survival-of-the-fittest sort of a business. Like anyone struggling with a language, you expressed what you were able to express – not what you wanted to say. Most people settled for what they felt comfortable with. Extraordinary talents and personalities emerged, of course, but the majority of the profession was resigned to filling in, to being a backdrop; the sense of an ensemble, of a group of people working together to create the theatrical moment, all contributing something unique, was elusive. The extraordinary ones – the geniuses – didn't need training (although it wouldn't have harmed them). It was the rest of us who did – the other 97.5 per cent.

The first and most important thing about training is that it enables an actor to work on him or herself within a controlled and protected environment. In enables you to make a fool of yourself, to expose yourself, among equally exposed and vulnerable people under the guidance of someone who knows. It enables you to develop – physically, vocally, expressively – over a period of time during which you will at first be expected to deliver nothing, to show nothing and to prove nothing. You will be learning, growing, exploring on a carefully planned journey towards certain clear goals, each stage of which is noted and built on. You will discover – we all discover – that some things come easy and some hard; you will learn which is which and how to make the most of the one and to work against the other.

You will, inevitably, find out a great deal about yourself which may at first be bewildering and unwelcome, but which will almost certainly in the end liberate you, as the truth, squarely faced, invariably does. Your time at drama school enables you to engender certain habits of mind, an approach and an analysis which enables you to delve deep into the play and character on which you may be working, to ask questions and maybe find answers about the kind of theatre that you believe in. You will learn to live with language in all its many forms in a way that the whole temper of the times denies. You will learn how to access and use parts of your body and your brain and your emotions that you scarcely knew existed. You will discover rhythm and tempo, absent for the most part from daily life. You will learn to look at life with the keen eye of someone who has to reproduce it. You will learn, as Brecht said, to drink a cup of tea in forty different ways. You will spend three years with the same group of people, watching them develop, learning how to accommodate to them and adjust to them and how to challenge them in an unthreatening way. You will discover the different responsibilities of carrying a play as the leading actor, and of providing its support and foundation in a small, perhaps wordless role. You will have to think about history, about the past, the present and the future, and you will have to ask why the theatre has been central to the life of society for more than two-and-a-half thousand years.

And at the end of it all, you will just about be able to say, 'The carriage awaits, my lord.' But if you can say it as if you meant it, in such a way that we know who you are and where you've come from and why you're there; that we have an inkling of which sort of society you belong to and what sort of play you're in; if you are able to command our interest absolutely but without drawing irrelevant attention to yourself – then you will have done brilliantly out of your three years' training.

Everything that I've said applies just as much to film acting as it does to the theatre, but not only do I entirely endorse the well-known observation that if you can act on stage, you can act on film, but by no means necessarily vice versa, I also believe that the theatre has a special importance because it is a much more democratic art than film. It is often denounced as elitist, by which people mean it costs too much (and of course it does), but it is the opposite of elitist because it is above all an interactive art. It happens live in front of an audience, whose input becomes a crucial part of the show. 'Ladies and gentlemen,' Max Wall used to say every night at the end of his show, 'you have been half.' And they are. At the very least.

The theatre offers itself up for judgement and response, and it cannot ignore either of these things. Theatre stands up on its own two feet and says: 'Look at this, ladies and gentlemen! This is what life is like!', inviting the immemorial response: 'Oh no it isn't!' But the debate has been engaged in the most vivid, the most physical terms; the model of society is flesh and blood, not mechanical.

Theatre in the West grew out of democracy, was an essential part of it. The whole city, without exception, came to see the play. It was their story. And it still is. The city demands actors who are up to its cruel demands, actors who have the stamina to offer their brilliant skills and deep human truths, in the flesh, night after night. And that is what training is for.

I left the Drama Centre a week before the end of my final term. Completely to my surprise, I had got a job, not from any of the thousand companies to whom I had sent my very attractive photo and fascinating personal particulars, nor from any of the terminally depressed directors for whom I had auditioned, but from a visiting director who had seen a second-year acting exercise I had done and had decided that I was ripe for his company, the Young Lyceum in Edinburgh. This wise, perceptive, inspired individual was Peter Farago, to whom I remain for ever indebted.

Working

My experience of the theatre proved to be quite different from anything for which my training had prepared me. In my first play, I was the front end of a horse (in Büchner's Woyzeck, *to be fair), and in the second, appeared as an extra in* The Thrie Estates *by Sir David Lindsay of the Mount, whose cast was, in effect, the entire Scottish acting profession, a formidable sight, ranged across the wide-open spaces of the Assembly Hall.*

*This was a new kind of actor to me. More than it does now, to be an actor in Scotland then meant to be multiskilled: survival was dependent on versatility. They could all – or almost all – sing, dance, do stand-up comedy, panto, blank verse, several Scots accents and standard English, direct, write, and design; and they all did all of these things in every medium known to man. Several actors in this resounding fourteenth-century allegory, dug up by Tyrone Guthrie for the first Edinburgh Festival, were huge national stars, but they all gave themselves over to it with fantastic esprit de corps. The entire Scottish profession, in fact, was a sort of company; everyone knew everyone else. At first, I felt terribly English. But the conviviality of the profession immediately asserted itself: lifelong friends were made and a lifelong love of Scotland established, despite the horrors of Calvinist cuisine circa 1973. And the varied challenges of the Rumanian avant-garde (*Woyzeck *was directed by the great Radu Penciulescu) and sprawling on the steps of the Assembly Hall with neither lines nor character, nevertheless attempting to make a contribution, were met and lessons duly learned.*

After Edinburgh, I segued into rep, which, in 1973, still existed on a nationwide basis; its subsequent decline has had dire consequences. Apart from robbing communities of their own acting team, for which they could root and whose progress they could monitor, its disappearance has denied actors a crucial complement to their training. In rep you learn to think very quickly and decisively, you discover your limitations (and your strengths), you find out how to work over a span of time with other people with whom you may very possibly have nothing in common, you figure out how to deal with directors. You lack the conditions for creating deeply meditated work, but it is astounding how much can be done under such unpropitious circumstances; and if one can get that far in those circumstances, how much farther could one not go with just a little more time, a little more money, a slightly bigger cast? Yet when the pressure is off, somehow the focus diffuses. I'm not sure whether 'focus' is quite the word for what we had in Lincoln, but we did keep the show on the road. Just. This piece was written for the Guardian *in 2004.*

Christmas of 1973/'74: it was the best of times; it was the worst of times. On the one hand, it was a freezing winter in the midst of the miners' strike and Edward Heath's three-day week; on the other, I was twenty-four years old and in hog heaven, theatrically speaking. I was a leading actor at the Theatre Royal Lincoln, only three months after leaving drama school, and had already played major part after major part. Business had been so-so; astonishing, really, in the economic circumstances, that it had held up at all. But now, in December, we were about to embark on the shows which would justify our existence in the town and make it possible for the company to survive for the rest of the year: *A Christmas Carol*, playing mostly to parties of schoolchildren, and *Aladdin*, playing to families. *A Christmas Carol* went with a swing in rehearsal, mingling pity and terror with low comedy. The latter was my particular contribution: I was playing Bob Cratchit and Mr Fezziwig and countless other larger-than-life characters and romped through it all with the naked energy and shameless exhibitionism of extreme youth. We shrieked our way through rehearsals; Chris Ryan (later of *The Young Ones* on television) was playing Scrooge and we vied with each other in outrageous invention. We soon learned that to catch each other in the eye was fatal – so of course we caught each other in the eye as much as possible. Getting on stage and dealing with the set sobered us up a bit. It was a beautiful, complex piece of work – miraculous, considering the budget – an affair of lifts and traps and moving scenery, wonderful in action, but it took some negotiating.

Snow drifts were achieved by scattering crumbled polystyrene from the flies overhead. At the dress rehearsal, as I joyously raised my voice to belt out 'Hark the Herald Angels Sing', I sucked in a mouthful of the stuff, inhaling more up my nostrils, and was suddenly unable to breathe. Young audiences may have been somewhat shocked by the sight of the kindly Bob Cratchit ramming his fingers down his throat and vigorously emitting projectile vomit into the wings, rather in the manner, some years later, of Linda Blair in *The Exorcist*, but we had no time for niceties of etiquette; the show must go on, whatever.

On another occasion, during the party at the Fezziwigs' house, just as Mrs Fezziwig (Thea Ranft) and I riotously led the assembled company round the stage in a brisk cotillion, we suddenly found ourselves hurtling some fifteen feet through the floor. The stage trap had given way under us. An awful silence fell on stage. Thea and I reassured each other in our pit that we were not dead and then became aware of ten horrified faces staring gingerly into the trap. 'Down in the wine cellar, again, Mr Fezziwig, ho ho?' one of the actors gamely ventured, while another, her face frozen in a rictus of reassuring delight, signalled desperately to the stage manager to bring the curtain in, but he too was paralysed with disbelief. Fuelled by adrenalin, Thea and I briskly shinned up the ladder pinned to the side of the understage and shortly appeared, bleeding and blinking. The little ones in the audience must have been baffled because the figure that now appeared from the hole in the stage was not Mr Fezziwig, but, unmistakably, Bob Cratchit, since the only things which had distinguished the one character from the other – the wig, side-whiskers and spectacles – had come off in the fall. Regardless, I assumed with demented vivacity the bent posture and wheezing vocals of dear old Fezziwig and vigorously launched into 'God Rest Ye Merry, Gentlemen', cotillioning madly offstage, where Thea and I could finally collapse in painful laughter.

There was worse. The day before Christmas Eve I arrived at the theatre at nine o'clock in the morning for the first of that day's three performances, to be greeted by the director with the news that Chris had a fever of 103° and no voice: either the little ones must be sent away, bitterly disappointed, their Christmas outing ruined, or I must go on for him as

Scrooge. I was aghast. I barely knew my own parts, let alone his. For a minute and a half I allowed myself and everyone else to believe that the little ones would indeed be disappointed, could, in fact, sod themselves as far as I was concerned; seconds later I was being bundled into the character's padding, nightshirt and heavy Victorian suit. Before I knew it I was staggering about the stage, inventing Dickensian dialogue, being pushed in and out of the light by the director, who had come on stage with me as an Angel. The experience of acting a scene with another actor playing Bob Cratchit, saying the very lines to me I had myself said only the day before, and me answering him in the lines that until yesterday someone else had been saying to me, was severely hallucinatory; it must have been even weirder for him: the poor chap had been roped in that morning while passing through, visiting his girlfriend.

I lost half a stone that day. Fortunately there was only one more day to go, Christmas Eve, and after the performances we could do the technical rehearsal of the pantomime and then go home to our Christmas beds and our Christmas Day off. We would have done, too, had not the designer, overwhelmed by the scale of his task, panicked and decamped (the *mot juste*, I think). This exotic young man, known as Diane – his name was Moshe – had spent the budget on a flimsy physical structure he had knocked up in the workshop before setting off back to London, never to return, and a great deal of luminous paint, glue, glitter, and gilded seer-sucker fabric, which we found, hidden at the back of the set. There was nothing for it but to start decorating, which we did, until we dropped (having already given three *Christmas Carols* that day) at about four in the morning. We crawled home, and then did our best to pretend that it was Christmas. I was sharing my flat with an actress who was, much to the dismay of her young son, macrobiotic: roast tofu with all the trimmings was our distinctly unDickensian repast.

Edward Heath did the rest. Television came to an end at ten o'clock, and a post-tofu walk down Lincoln High Street only deepened the gloom, since the Christmas lights which had been hung up were never lit, thanks to the fuel restrictions. At about six o'clock in the evening, we'd gone into the theatre and done a few hours on the set, and this, in its way, was the high spot of the day, inspired by the Dunkirk spirit, and a certain amount – a large amount – of other spirits, too. The next day, Boxing Day, we crawled into the theatre at 9 a.m. and finished the job off, discreetly adjusting the perhaps somewhat exuberant execution of the day before.

It all sort of fell into place. I was on first as Abanazar – 'Ha! Ha! Ha! HA! By the Ninth Book of the Nephritic Pentacles, I summon the genie! Ha! Ha!' – and so on, *ad libitum*. This was accompanied by a flash of flame from something called flash wool. Needless to say, the designer had omitted to order it, and the young stagehand in charge of it had improvised something. It was his job to light it, then beat a hasty retreat as the curtain rose. On this first performance, he duly lit it. There was an enormous explosion which rooted him to the spot, at the same time brilliantly lighting his soot-covered hands and face. 'Oh fook!' he cried. This was thus the opening line of *Aladdin* in Lincoln, Christmas 1973. 'Oh fook,' indeed.

For me the great thing about Lincoln was that I had found my director. Or rather, he had found me. Robert Walker, who had been running the Close, the studio space of the Glasgow Citizens' Theatre, and before that had been electrifying the citizens of Watford with his work at the Palace Theatre, had, like Peter Farago, seen me at the Drama Centre and invited me to be in his opening season at Lincoln in September 1973, immediately after the Edinburgh Festival.

The directors I had had in Edinburgh were as different from each other as they could possibly have been: Bill Bryden, sharp, smart and Scottish, had handled his somewhat unruly gang ('No, no, Bill, Sir Tyrone always had me move right *here') with aplomb and energy, but there was no time for nuance and personal touches; Radu Penciulescu was an intellectual and a teacher and an experimentalist, and very very clear about what he wanted, though he spoke no English and communicated his observations in French, which I, the new boy in the company, translated for him.*

Robert Walker was something altogether different, a huge, rather beautiful man with the physique of a rugby player, in love with language, exceptionally well-read and entirely on top of all the theories of drama, wildly, surreally funny and playful to the point of anarchy. Above all he wanted the theatre to be alive with a crazy, reckless sensuality; sex had to be at the back of everything, for him, which led to some unusual departures when we were doing Aladdin. *The inventiveness and audacity of his rehearsals were thrilling and liberating. He was utterly and totally actor-struck – actor-struck as opposed to stage-struck. Everything he did – the design , the music, the staging – flowed out of what the actors were doing.*

And we dared recklessly for him, carried along by his joy in our work. He was the best audience any actor could ever hope for, agog at what we came up with, ruthless at editing it. He was not without rigour of a sort – a poetic rigour, which demanded perpetual spontaneity and heightened awareness. He would countenance anything except what was wooden and mechanical; he also had a hatred of what is usually called beauty. Beauty to him was whatever was smudged, raw, naked. Finish and polish were hateful to him. This was a wholly new concept to me: I was a homosexual aesthete, after all. But I trusted him and came to see that this sawn-off beauty of his was indeed poetry of a different order. He himself was polymorphously perverse, like some magnificently articulate baby, endlessly stretching out and touching, all appetite and no inhibition, and his theatre was like that, too. Swept on by his enthusiasm and permissiveness, I soared. It seemed impossible for me to displease him. I managed, just about, to hang on to the logic and discipline of what I had learned at the Drama Centre, while taking more and more risks.

The panto (see above) might have been a risk too far. The audience openly rebelled at times. Things were looking a bit rocky at Lincoln by then. Business – apart from the Christmas shows – had not been good; Howard Brenton's rewritten Measure for Measure, *with the Duke as Harold Macmillan, Angelo as Enoch Powell and a black Isabella, had emptied the place, and the local council was asking for more familiar fare, done more normally. Robert was deflated and enraged, as he often was, by being required to be realistic. So when Peter Farago of the Young Lyceum, my first boss, asked me to go back to Edinburgh, Robert told me to go; a couple of months later he threw in the towel too. Lincoln was my only real experience of rep; it was probably enough, but it was a wonderful time, absurdly overworked, but bursting with camaraderie and good humour and broken hearts and discovery. One of the great discoveries of that time for me, an extra-curricular one, was Max Wall. I came face to face with the music-hall tradition which was, so to speak, in my blood, but of which till then I had had no direct experience. I wrote this for the Max Wall Society's organ,* Wallpaper.

Was there ever a time that one didn't know what Max Wall looked like or how he sounded? And yet, growing up in the Sixties, I can't recollect seeing him on television or hearing him on radio. But that image of a professorial sort of chimpanzee was so familiar, so deeply rooted. Like the greatest clowns, he seemed to come from deep in the collective memory, from some unknown past of the race, and the very sight of him stirred not only instant laughter but also some other emotion, a disturbance of the soul, a touch of pity and terror. I was a young actor at the Lincoln Theatre Royal when it was announced that he was playing at the local working men's club, and the whole acting company immediately booked tickets, running in our make-up direct from the theatre, where we were doing *A Taste of Honey*, to sit excitedly in the back row, just managing to squeeze in.

It was a small space and his appearance in it was somehow shocking: the moment he walked on the stage he seemed in close-up, in extreme close-up, in fact, as he leered at us like an ape in a cage, his arms swinging loosely at his side, his undershot jaw hanging slackly. He was underway without warning, before the chatter had subsided, precise, rhythmic, with slight intimations of a cleft palate, his eyes glinting like the Ancient Mariner's. 'Max Wall, Max Wall, I come from a long line of walls, my grandfather was the Great Wall of China, my father was a marvellous man, he had a long hair growing out of his left nostril, when he sneezed, it cracked like a whip, one day he caught the flu and he flogged hisself to death.' A bit of fancy footwork, a shudder, lips curled strangely, and he was off again. The actors were beside themselves with joy. It wasn't until about five minutes in that we realised that no one else was laughing. At all. Stony resentful silence was all around us, and finally defeated us. We smiled idiotically in his direction. He carried on regardless, indifferent to the indifference. He sat at the keyboard. Each arm proved longer than the other; a cowed actor let out a gurgle of pleasure but couldn't sustain a full laugh against the waves of circumambient disapproval.

On Max went. Lifting up the strut of the piano lid, he said, hollow-voiced: 'Brings back memories.' At the end of the forty minutes or whatever it was of distilled comic genius, we cheered, a few members of the audience applauded, and the auditorium emptied. 'Last time 'e ever comes back 'ere.' ''E's 'ad it.' 'Load of old rubbish.' It was shocking for us stripling actors to hear. A few months later, he was announced for the Garrick Theatre in London. He performed exactly, to the comma, to the flare of the nostril, the act he'd played in Lincoln. This time, however, it lasted twice as long because of the laughter which threatened at times to become uncontrollable. 'Ladies and gentlemen,' he said at the curtain call, 'you have been half.' He'd said the same thing in Lincoln, but it hadn't been true. He had done it all. After that Garrick season, he could never have had the bird again, though no doubt, after long and bitter experience, he never ruled out the possibility.

Back in Edinburgh, Narrow Road to the Deep North *and* The Fantasticks *(on tour across Scotland for the Young Lyceum) were differently delightful; then I joined Mike Ockrent at the Traverse Theatre. He was attempting to create a company there again, and for a year we did a staggering amount of work, starting with a play which I had seen in Ingmar Bergman's pared-down version at the World Theatre Season with no less artists than Harriet Andersson and Max von Sydow,* Dream Play *by Strindberg; we went on to do Brecht and the Israeli writer Hanoch Levin. Another play in the Traverse season,* Schippel, *tamed by C. P. Taylor from Carl Sternheim's savage German original and rendered anarchically hilarious in a particularly British way, turned into a runaway success, as it was when we revived the whole season for the Edinburgh Festival. We were invited to take it to Belfast, in 1975, when we played to a soundtrack of distant and sometimes not-so-distant exploding bombs and machine-gun rattles so alarming that one of the actresses was unable to suppress her fearful farts, which only added to the soundtrack of explosions, as well as eliciting some spontaneous re-blocking of the play to avoid wiping out the rest of the cast. Then on to London, to the Open Space Theatre, my first experience of the London Fringe. There the play was seen by that sweet Goon, Harry Secombe, who took it (and me) into the West End, under the name of* The Plumber's Progress; *all too predictably, it flopped, Harry's fans failing to see the point of it. I then appeared at Verity Bargate's Soho Poly in* The Soul of the White Ant, *an extraordinary and visionary one-act play by Snoo Wilson, which soon after became a full-length play and transferred to the Bush; later we took it on a tour of Holland, playing every night to standing ovations of up to ten people. West End stardom (my name had actually been up in lights at the Prince of Wales Theatre, however briefly) gave way to an extended period in the Fringe, then at its first great peak. Thirty-five years later, in a piece for the* Guardian *written when I was doing a play at the Southwark Playhouse, I looked back on the period with great tenderness.*

For those of us starting out as actors in 1973, as I did, the theatre was a house of many mansions. Or perhaps an estate of many dwellings, with the Big Houses – the RSC and the National Theatre and the West End – at the centre and innumerable smaller places elsewhere in the grounds. Foremost, there was rep: over a dozen theatres each with its own year-round company; many of the actors retained for two or three or more years. Most reps also had studio theatres and Theatre-in-Education units. Then there were touring companies, some also with an educational bias, others with political or community or other philosophical programmes; there were arts centres, with budgets to stage plays; there were a few club theatres (notably Hampstead). And there was the Fringe.

For many of us, the Fringe was where our theatrical hearts lay. The disciplines of rep and TIE were clearly invaluable and helped to build our vocal and physical instruments; the touring companies were character (and muscle) building – the actors generally unloaded and erected the sets with the stage management, and took them down again afterwards – and the work was inarguably important. We were aware, too, of the rather distant goals of the National and the RSC and the (to us, then) somewhat suspect lure of the West End. Theatres like the Glasgow Citizens', the Theatre Royal Stratford East and the Royal Court were all inspirations in their radically different ways.

But the Fringe belonged to us. It was our laboratory, our playground; it was where we made our statement, where our voices were heard. It was experimental by definition, in production and in writing and in acting. You had an idea for a play or for a production and you simply put it on. At the Soho Poly, for example, the wittily provocative Verity Bargate had the courage to be undiscriminating. If a new writer with a spark of life in him or her had thrown something lively onto the page, Verity would run it up the flagpole and find out what was there – a real play, or just a sketch; a flair for dialogue or a weird take on life. Either way, a writer was given a chance to learn, in the only way that matters. With an almost non-existent budget, Verity would whip together a brilliant cast at a moment's notice from actors between jobs, or even doing jobs. It was a lunchtime theatre, to begin with. A director and a designer with nothing to lose and a fiver to spend would transform the tiny space, and someone's passing inspiration would come to life. Out of just such a process emerged, for example, Barrie Keeffe, one of the key writers of the post-war period, whose humanist rage and surreally fantastic humour were first seen in the trilogy he wrote for the Soho Poly; his energy and inventiveness seem to sit unhappily in the institutional theatre, though he is as close to what we mean by a radical popular dramatist as we have had since the glory days of Joan Littlewood.

The Almost Free Theatre was run by Ed Berman, a burly, bearded American maverick whose company was based on a tiny farm located in his back garden in Kentish Town; they also, inexplicably, had a West End base in Rupert Street, off Piccadilly, where they gave space to, amongst other things, the Gay Sweatshop company, which staged a rapidly convened season including, amongst many other plays, *Passing By*, the first of Martin Sherman's to be seen in England, and *Kennedy's Children* by Robert Patrick; the performers included mainstream actors like Antony Sher and me as well as the core Sweatshop company who, on a shoestring, transformed lives and attitudes and generated some remarkably innovative work. I vividly recall going along to Ed's farm to meet Drew Griffiths, the director of *Passing By*, and reading, as the cow mooed and the goats bleated, the simple boy-meets-boy/boy-loves-boy/boy-leaves-boy romantic story, stunned with disbelief: this was the story of my life, but I had never for a moment expected to see it represented on stage, much less to be performing it. For me personally, I have to confess, it was far more radical than anything that the Royal Court was offering. I tremblingly agreed to do it, half believing that I was destroying my career; if I'd had more time to think about it, I might have said no. As it was, a mere couple of weeks after that first meeting, we were up and doing it in the little theatre in Rupert Street, and those lunchtime audiences were as moved and shaken by it as I had been at first reading. And I continued working.

Was it art? Most certainly. The imaginative contrivances with which we responded to the limitations of budget and space were as stimulating as anything that might have been achieved by chequebook designing. By some paradox, it is easier to go further with a style or an idiom on slender resources than it is with a fat Lottery grant. When I took Buddy Dalton – another stage-struck eccentric who, after converting the old morgue at New End into a theatre, founded the even smaller Offstage Theatre in Chalk Farm – an odd, haunting little play called *The Passport* which didn't seem to make any sense except as a nightmare, I told her that I wanted to do it like *The Cabinet of Dr Caligari*, and without comment she gave my designer Bruno Santini a hundred pounds from which he conjured the most thoroughgoing Expressionist set I have ever seen or worked with. Equally, when I devised a one-man play called *Nicolson Fights Croydon* for Angus Mackay (about the patrician diarist's election campaign as a Labour MP), we had an even smaller budget, and lit it without any theatre lamps at all, using only the electric lights in the room in which he was supposedly staying, creating a Joseph Wright of Derby effect of striking beauty, which would have been impossible in a larger space.

Freedom, spontaneity, risk, imaginative challenge: all these things were central to the experience of the Fringe. They are all notably elusive in the other available theatrical environments. It's true that since those reckless days of the early Seventies, the Fringe has itself become a house of many mansions. Theatres like the Bush and Hampstead now constitute a sort of Higher Fringe, with production values not unlike those of the national theatres and the West End. This is an inevitable and by no means negative development: people and organisations must always move forward. Faking innocence is both offensive and doomed.

But for me it was very exciting when the Southwark Playhouse, a relatively young organisation with a dazzling recent track record, and blessed with a playing space of exceptional character and inspiring limitations, decided it wanted to do Franz Xaver Kroetz's 1975 play *Through the Leaves*. The way it came to their attention was this: the young American director Daniel Kramer had been looking for a play which would enable him to work with that superb actress Ann Mitchell, whose recent performance in *Tantalus* had been so overwhelming for critics and public. *Through the Leaves* stirred her deeply, and merely as a matter of interest Daniel let me read it. I felt then exactly what I felt twelve years before when by chance I read Manuel Puig's *Kiss of the Spiderwoman*. I knew that I was reading a masterpiece which had something utterly original to say about the human arrangement, and that within the confines of its relatively short duration and its two-character cast, it achieved an epic image of the struggle to find some sort of truth in a seemingly doomed relationship.

I asked if I could be in it. And Dan said yes, though Otto the alcoholic steelworker would have seemed to most people rather further out of my natural range than had the hot-pant wearing little queen in Puig's play. Just as I had approached the Bush all those years ago with *Spiderwoman* and after a single reading of it they had said yes, Dan approached Thea Sharrock, the artistic director of the Southwark Playhouse, and by a miracle they had a slot in their schedule when Ann and I were both free, and gave it an immediate thumbs-up. There was money to be raised – sums that would have seemed surreal to us back in the Seventies – and there was a full team to be assembled, twice the size of what we would have used at the Poly. But what happened is essentially the same: we fell in love with this play, the theatre fell in love with it too *et voilà, tout*.

At the end of his life, Orson Welles said that the fun had gone out of movie-making because the gap between the impulse to do something and its realisation had become so enormous. In this case, in Cromwell's wonderful phrase, we are not merely striking while the iron is hot but making it hot by striking it. The rehearsal room is like a boiler room, bursting with violent energy and excitement as we engage with the dark theatrical world of Kroetz, Ann and I and our young, daring colleagues trying to find the most fearless way in which we can put it on stage. I feel as if I've lost thirty years.

Not long after the West End production of Schippel *had folded, in 1975, I had gone back to the Open Space Theatre, a remarkable organisation (long gone, of course) situated on the Tottenham Court Road next to a couple of 'adult' cinemas. Thelma Holt, an excellent actress, had created the circumstances at the Open Space to enable the maverick American director Charles Marowitz, Peter Brook's quondam assistant, to stage a succession of provocative pieces – collages of Shakespeare, pastiches of Oscar Wilde, Picasso's great play* Four Little Girls, *new work by Peter Barnes and Trevor Griffiths – which were like nothing else that was being done at the time, literate but deeply radical. They presented plays at lunchtime, too, and in that slot Thelma and Charles decided to do* Down Red Lane, *a horribly prophetic piece by B. S. Johnson about a diner eating himself to death in a restaurant (Johnson met his own death by striding out into the sea after having eaten as much Indian food as he could cram down his gullet). In the play, I was the waiter and Martin Coveney, brother of the critic, played the diner's stomach. The diner himself was played by Timothy West, then one of the best-known actors in the country (Edward VII had just been on television, and he was currently playing Judge Brack to Glenda Jackson's Hedda at the Aldwych for the RSC); this was typical of the fringe of the time, where the most famous and distinguished actors were only too delighted to do a quick run of a play. But it was also typical of Tim, who quite unselfconsciously treated the two unknown young actors he was working with as his equals, simply colleagues.*

After Down Red Lane, *I did a play by John Antrobus at the Royal Court (with a cast that now exists mainly as obituaries: Richard Beckinsale, Ian Charleson, Philip Stone, Patience Collier, as well as the happily still living Denis Lawson, Beth Morris and Cheryl Cooke) and then a starry revival, with a now equally melancholy cast list: Derek Godfrey, James Villiers, Nigel Hawthorne, of* The Doctor's Dilemma *at one of my Alma Maters, the Mermaid. It wasn't an altogether happy production: Derek, the dazzling original Earl of Gurney, as it happens, in Peter Barnes's* The Ruling Class, *was subdued, already suffering from the cancer that killed him, while Jimmy Villiers was very put out about working on Good Friday. 'I'm sorry, Jimmy,' said Robert Chetwyn, the director, 'I'd no idea you were religious.' 'Fuck religion, darling,' said Villiers, 'it's the races.' But Nigel Hawthorne, on the brink of national fame in* Yes, Minister, *gave an exquisite performance as Cutler Walpole. This is my 2002 review for the* Daily Mail *of his posthumously published autobiography* Straight Face.

There is in the public mind some idea of what actors are like. I suppose it is summed up by the loathed phrase 'luvvie': bombastic, over-the-top, compulsive, shallow, gushing, posturing, self-promoting, raffish, promiscuous, loudly laughing, uncontrollably weeping, always 'on'. There may indeed be actors who fall within the parameters of this unlovely image – perhaps some of us see it staring back at us when we look into the mirror – but one who most certainly did not was Nigel Hawthorne, an actor as far from the popular conception as could be imagined. Slow, shy, thoughtful, stubborn, principled, middle-class and proud of it, he deviated from the norm in only two ways: he was an actor, and he was gay. Nothing in his background or his upbringing encouraged or accounted for these uncommon proclivities, but, typically, he accepted his destiny in both departments and doggedly tried to make a go of it. In both areas, it was a tough journey, with a slow start, until he achieved simultaneous glory in both, at the age of fifty, when he became famous as an actor and met the true love of his life.

His story, as told by him, is a curious, in some ways a sad one. The words 'disappointment', 'disappointing', 'disappointed' chime through the book like a tolling bell, as do, only slightly less frequently, two others: 'guilt' and 'guilty'. His early struggle as an actor does not tell the usual rackety but romantic tale of wild indulgence, the sowing of wild oats, artistically and amorously: it is a terrible stop-go affair of small breaks leading nowhere and crushes which were unexpressed or unfulfilled. He seems plagued with ill-luck and wrong choices. After a messy and failed one-night stand with a scenic designer when he is in rep in Northampton, he decides to move in with the man, and stays with him for twenty-seven years in a relationship devoid of sex and fraught with social difficulty. As an actor, he is told, even before he becomes a professional, that it will take him years before he will make his mark; and it does – decades of mere subsistence. Then, by sheer dint of sticking at it, the actor and the parts find each other, and the talent that had never been in question finds its outlet, and overnight he is one of the most admired, best-loved performers in the country. And at almost exactly the same time, he meets the drop-dead gorgeous Trevor Bentham, who, to Nigel's disbelief, falls in love with him, and he finds the thing he has dreamed of all his life – domestic bliss. And then he dies.

The tenacity is astonishing. Never was there such a story of persistence rewarded. The sadness that pervades the book comes from a nagging sense that it all should have happened much, much earlier. Those of us who remember his work from the mid-Sixties were never in any doubt that he was an exceptionally fine actor. He felt underused – stuck in character roles of no consequence – but already there was about his acting a sort of inner pressure, an emotional rage behind the comedy, which singled him out as an original. In life, even in those days, he was cautious and respectable and slightly crusty, but just beneath the surface there was a certain element of anarchy, determination and need warring with each other, which produced the tension that any remarkable performance must have, a pull in opposite directions. This quality led to what I continue to think of as his greatest performance (though there is some competition): Major Flack in *Privates on Parade*, where he endowed the erratic field commander with a touch of madness which was both hilarious and touching, and ascended at times almost to tragic proportions: he made us deeply pity the absurd man. In a way, it was the King Lear he didn't quite manage to give when he finally came to play it.

Perhaps the most affecting but also the saddest moment in the book is contained in his last few lines: after he and Bentham were crudely and pointlessly outed by the press, 'we both believed the world would be looking at us with disgust and that our lives had been irrevocably changed. Things did change – but for the better. We no longer felt the need to pretend. The "Straight Face" we'd worn through the years was no longer necessary. Everybody knew. We'd been liberated.' All those years of hiding, of feeling ashamed, and guilty: wasted. Nobody minded. He was loved, not for pretending to be straight but because he was a wonderful actor. If only he'd known that earlier.

The book is deeply honest without being in any way sensational. There are some very funny and very moving sections (his emotional breakdown when he came to act the climax of *Shadowlands*), and his doggedness is sometimes unintentionally funny; a latent tetchiness keeps breaking through. There is no attempt to conceal it. The author's self-portrait is superbly complemented by Trevor Bentham's epilogue (the best writing in the book), in which he tells us, utterly convincingly, what an enchantingly contradictory man Nigel was, and why he provoked the love that he did, in Trevor and in the great public. A most unusual account of a most unusual actor.

Nigel belonged to a generation that had good reason to fear being identified as gay. By the time I became an actor, the Labouchère Amendment had been repealed for a good six years, and life was loosening up for gay people. I had never concealed my homosexuality from anyone (apart from my mother, fearing an absolute cataclysm). I had told everyone about it at school – though my sexuality was theoretical at that point, since I had not had sex with anyone of any gender – and had made a full and free confession of it to my chums at the National (though still a virgin). The same candour had applied in Belfast, at university, though I was now the oldest homosexual virgin in the land, and at the Drama Centre, where I finally (phew!) lost my cherry. At the Vic, everyone knew who the gay actors were, though none – apart from John Gielgud, for obvious reasons – was publicly identified as such. It never occurred to me to conceal my proclivities. When I became an actor, the same was true. But there was now no danger, no disadvantage: as far as I know, there was no director who would fail to hire you because you were gay. On the other hand, there was, as far as I knew, no well-known actor who had admitted to being gay in an interview. Anxiety hedged the subject. When I was asked to appear in Martin Sherman's Passing By, *for Gay Sweatshop at the Almost*

Free Theatre (you paid what you could afford), I paused for a moment, wondering what the consequences might be for my relationship with my mother. I had no other anxiety: although scarcely what you might call a political animal, I could see that this was an important, useful venture; besides, it was a great part – young and in love with a beautiful young man: I could relate to that. By no means all the actors who worked for Gay Sweatshop were gay, so it wasn't a public admission of homosexuality; but there would be newspaper coverage, reviews and so on, which my mother might well see. Very well, I thought. Destiny has forced my hand, and I set off to break the glad tidings. 'If you're anything like your father,' she responded, when I told her, 'you'll be a sexual beast, and since there were no women, there must have been men.' I took this as a blessing, and went on my way. I would cross the next bridge – being interviewed – when I came to it. If I came to it.

Passing By *was my first experience of political theatre. Though in essence a very sweet account of a passing love affair between two young men, it was utterly radical in offering no apology or explanation for the affair – it was just an affair, like any other. The effect on the predominantly gay audience was sensational – they wept, not because it was sad, but because it was the first time they'd seen their own lives represented on stage without inverted commas, with neither remorse nor disgust. Mart Crowley's* Boys in the Band *– 'Show me a happy homosexual and I'll show you a gay corpse' – had been packing them in, gay and straight, in the West End only a couple of years before: the acceptable face of homosexuality – brittle, anguished, self-loathing.* Passing By *was the antidote to this seductive but poisonous brew. I was shaken by the effect the play had on the audience. I knew all about political theatre – I had seen the best (7:84) and the worst (7:84) – and was properly electrified, when it was good, by its rousing, invigorating quality.* Passing By *was none of these. It provoked in its audience a huge collective sigh, as if sloughing off a centuries-old interdict. The defensive, the reflexive, the self-protective mask was shed, and shy, tender, loving emotion flowed gently round the tiny auditorium. The slight play had the power, like a great popular song, of speaking directly not only to, but for, its auditors.*

Not much later, I became a company member of another explicitly political theatre group, Joint Stock. Here the relationship with the audience was very different, and indeed those of us putting on the plays had a very different relationship to each other. Gay Sweatshop's objectives, initially, at any rate, were very simple: to put gay life on stage from a gay point of view, for the benefit of other gay people. The problem with Joint Stock, an organisation which produced a great deal of remarkable theatre, was that nobody ever articulated the precise political position that we were sup-posed to be taking. The success of David Hare's Fanshen, *created before I joined the company, had convinced the company that its outlook was essentially Maoist, but it wasn't (though our starry-eyed uncritical embrace of Communist China is a little embarrassing in retrospect). Very good work was done nonetheless, especially – during my time with the company – Barrie Keeffe's superb* A Mad World My Masters, *one of the few really successful large-scale social comedies of the period.*

It was David Hare who had brought me into the company. His brilliant self-assurance, his incisive wit and his extreme displeasure at being crit-icised sometimes mask his compassion and generosity, his delicious sense of fun and his deep personal vulnerability. Our lives have run parallel without ever really interlinking since those early Joint Stock days, but I have always been astonished by his fearlessness about moving into terri-tory of maximum personal challenge. I wrote this in my Diary column in the Independent *after seeing his play* Via Dolorosa *in 1998.*

Theatre: what is it? Definition is elusive and finally, perhaps, impossible. Theatre, you might say, is whatever takes place on a stage and is com-pelling. It is clear that plays as such are not the *sine qua non* of theatre. Among the most extraordinary pieces of theatre I have ever seen, a per-formance entitled *Milva Canta Brecht*, staged by Giorgio Strehler, springs to mind. The great Italian cabaret singer with her Titian-red hair, dressed in black, stood alone next to a grand piano. Her hair was up to start with; at a certain point, it came down like a copper gash across her shoulder. We gasped. The light changed. She sat down; she stood in profile; she sang with her back to us. Nothing more happened, or could happen. Her con-nection with what she was singing, her characterisation, her engagement with the text, creating action out of the emotional narrative, made for a theatrical event of extraordinary purity.

Even starker in means was another event which I would rank among the supreme theatrical experiences of my life: a lecture by A. J. P. Taylor at the National Film Theatre on Hitler and film. The small bespectacled fig-ure, raffishly bow-tied, stood in the darkened auditorium, brilliantly illuminated in a single spot from which never moved. His argument developed with buoyant lucidity, the lines of thought arching and converging in the dark, a sort of mental callisthenics, pentathlon of the intellect, until with perfect command, he finally brought us past the final tape, all the threads of his discourse firmly in his hand. A cheer went up as the spotlight faded. What is the common element here? Performance, of course, the drama of watching a lone person justify his or her moment in the spotlight, the stage as high wire. Acting is not necessarily indispensable to theatre.

Take David Hare's *Via Dolorosa*, of which the writer gives the last performance tonight. Hare is reporting on an actual personal experience, his trip to Israel and Palestine, but also – and this is crucial – on himself. He offers himself up for examination: this is what happens to a person, he says, when he or she goes to Israel. This is what you find, and this is how it affects you. In the very act of his standing on a stage, without even so much as a lectern, he offers himself up for examination, for contemplation. Unlike Taylor, Hare has not spent a lifetime of lecturing in public, honing his act. He is an intensely engaging speaker, witty, penetrating and often emotional, but he is not a pro in this area; much less has he acted in plays, like Harold Pinter and Wally Shawn. He walks with jagged self-consciousness onto the stage; his body jackknifes as he speaks; words and phrases come accompanied with superfluous or sometimes contradictory gestures. He lacks the actor's whorish skill of making it seem as if he was saying all this for the first time. It's definitely a text. Nor does he shape the material particularly well, paragraph by paragraph. It is possible to imagine the text better delivered.

All of this is beside the point. The point is that it's him telling us about what happened to him, and in that sense the event is similar to the experience of hearing a poet read his own verse. The sense of authenticity is somehow the greater for the lack of finesse in the delivery. The same is true of the characters whom he describes: Mike Yarwood he ain't, but you get a remarkably vivid impression of the tone, the personality, of these people and – this is the crucial point – what he thinks about them.

What he has to say about Israel and Palestine is naturally of deep interest, acute and informative. What is perhaps unexpected is how moving it is. The Israeli experience becomes cumulatively heartbreaking, and Hare the performer seems to sag under the weight of it. He pauses, sits at a table, sips water. What he has witnessed seems to pass before his eyes.

The powerlessness of passion, of intelligence, of kindness, all seems to bear him down. He wanders about the set, contemplates the impressive model of Jerusalem that rises up and hovers in mid-air like a spaceship. He looks at these things, but he does not seem to see them. An actor would relate to the set, to his surroundings, with a conscious effort of focus, but Hare is elsewhere, playing over his memories on a mental screen. When the show is over, he seems to see us for the first time, bows almost absent-mindedly and then walks all the way to the back of the stage, leaves, and then walks all the way back again.

It is as haunting as anything by Beckett. The event has become a metaphor, and *that* is what the theatre must never fail to be.

I was with Joint Stock for two highly argumentative years. My next job after leaving the company was to play Titus Andronicus at the Bristol Old Vic, my first Shakespeare and the first of the director, Adrian Noble. Although I had been passionate about the plays since my childish spout-ings from Dr Dibelius's edition, my only actual contact with the work had been the brief and unsatisfactory experience of playing Friar Laurence at drama school in my first year, when it was hard to tell who knew less about what they were doing, the teacher or me. The Drama Centre had a deep bias against Shakespeare, preferring as a matter of policy to pro-mote other Elizabethans and particularly the Jacobeans. So I had played Cocledemoy in The Dutch Courtesan, *and Adam Overdo in* Bartholomew Fair, *but no Shakespeare. Adrian, who was my contemporary at the Drama Centre, may have suffered in the same way, though needless to say he has made up for it since, as, to a lesser extent, have I. Titus was a bracing experience, a wonderful place to begin my journey through Shakespeare, since it is very early Shakespeare: in a sense we were start-ing together, the writer and I. As he learned to write, I learned to act. This was a contribution for the Globe Theatre's magazine* Around the Globe *in 1997.*

I was just twenty-seven when I played Titus Andronicus, and it was, need-less to say, the hardest thing I had ever done to that date. I suspect that it is one of the hardest parts in the canon. At that green age, though, it nearly finished me off altogether as an actor. It's a very long part, but stamina was not a problem of mine. The difficulty is in the length and extent of the journey that the character undergoes, from triumph to tragedy to madness to revenge, and in the evolution in style which Shakespeare himself seems to have undergone as he wrote the play. As Titus is put through more and more of Destiny's hoops, his language passes from bombast and fustian to a sort of heroic but still formal grieving, until it breaks up completely as his mind gives under the weight of all his woes – or does it? By the end of the play he is thinking with startling clarity and focused purpose, and the language too expresses this.

The latter part of the play is in fact wonderfully easy to act; everything the actor, even the twenty-seven-year-old actor, needs is there. Who could not rise to the extraordinary pathos and indeed realism of Titus's scenes with Lavinia, tongueless, handless, ravished:

> Wound it with sighing, girl, kill it with groans;
> Or get some little knife between thy teeth,
> And just against thy heart make thou a hole,
> That all the tears that thy poor eyes let fall
> May run into that sink, and soaking in,
> Drown the lamenting fool in sea-salt tears.

Or:

> Speechless complainer, I will learn thy thought;
> In thy dumb action will I be as perfect
> As begging hermits in their holy prayers:
> Thou shalt not sigh, nor hold thy stumps to heaven,
> Nor wink, nor nod, nor kneel, nor make a sign,
> But I of these will wrest an alphabet,
> And by still practice learn to know thy meaning.

And the extraordinary exchanges over the fly that Titus's brother Marcus kills:

MARCUS. Alas, my lord, I have but kill'd a fly.

TITUS. 'But'? How if that fly had a father and a mother?
> How would he hang his slender gilded wings,
> And buzz lamenting doings in the air!
> Poor harmless fly,
> That with his pretty buzzing melody
> Came here to make us merry, and thou hast kill'd him.

The scene in which Titus madly fires off arrows with letters attached to them to the gods has a weird jazzy energy to it that spits off the page. Told by his bewildered nephew that Pluto has urged him to wait, he cries:

> He doth me wrong to feed me with delays.
> I'll dive into the burning lake below
> And pull her out of Acheron by the heels.
> Marcus, we are but shrubs, no cedars we;
> No big-bon'd men framed of the Cyclops' size;
> But metal, Marcus, steel to the very back,
> Yet wrung with wrongs more than our backs can bear:
> And sith there's no justice in earth nor hell,
> We will solicit heaven and move the gods
> To send down justice for to wreak our wrongs.

All of this is perfectly recognisable human behaviour (given the extremity of the situations), expressed in a flexible, varied and inventive form. Here Shakespeare seems to have left his Senecan models completely behind; it is entirely individual in music and in thought, and Titus's character is embodied in his verse.

The beginning of the play – or rather Titus's beginning in it – is another matter, although it is arguable that here the expression also reflects the man and his circumstances: the war-weary hero, supreme commander, doughty warrior, servant of the state, for whom he has sacrificed many sons on the field of war: his utterance is long-breathed, rhetorical, pompous, though not without deep feeling. It is the speech of someone who is used to being listened to:

> Hail, Rome, victorious in thy mourning weeds!
> Lo, as the bark that hath discharg'd her fraught
> Returns with precious lading to the bay
> From whence at first she weigh'd her anchorage,
> Cometh Andronicus, bound with laurel boughs,
> To re-salute his country with his tears,
> Tears of true joy for his return to Rome.

It was a hard note for a young actor to hit, that tone of weary authority, that easy massiveness. It is critical that the character makes his first entrance at the absolute height of his power and dignity if those humiliations which Saturninus heaps on him in quick succession are to register. In fact, his decline is vertiginous, quicker by far than that of Lear; it happens with comic-book speed. Within minutes, he has slain one of his own sons who defies him, is spurned by the Emperor whom he has just endorsed, sees the Queen of the Goths whom he has just beaten in battle become the Emperor's consort, and endures seeing two of his other sons falsely accused of murder. That is a mere prelude to what then happens: his daughter is raped and mutilated; he hacks off his own hand, in exchange for the return of his sons; and he takes delivery of those sons' heads severed.

One damn thing after another. And Titus is heroically eloquent in his distress. Tynan's wonderful phrase, 'a concerto of grief' (a concerto for left hand, in this instance), precisely expresses the musical quality of the lamentation, and it needed an actor with far greater range than I then had to find the variations within the grieving. The imagery is all watery, of tears and the sea, and in my mind's ear I heard *The Flying Dutchman* and the waters of the Rhine, and I hurled myself at these great arias, forcing the emotional stakes higher and higher, pushing my vocal resources to breaking point. The text is conventional; neither in imagery nor in phrasing does it begin to express the individual who is grieving.

> I am the sea. Hark how her sighs do blow;
> She is the weeping welkin, I the earth:
> Then must my sea be moved with her sighs;
> Then must my earth with her continual tears
> Become a deluge, overflow'd and drown'd;
> For why my bowels cannot hide her woes,
> But like a drunkard must I vomit them.

The impersonality, is, of course, part of the point: the actor needs to become a conduit for these torrential, primal emotions. How I longed for lungs of brass, a throat of steel. I wanted a *Heldentenor*'s ability to ride a hundred-piece orchestra. Knocking myself out with a sort of Method approach to the emotions, and killing myself with absurd vocal challenges, I rendered myself voiceless after three performances. Restored to some sort of audibility with dubious potions brewed by the notorious and sorely missed laryngologist Norman Punt, I had to learn to husband such feeble resources as I now had. By the end of the run, I had learned a number of invaluable lessons about Shakespeare and about myself, and was giving a reasonable lightweight account of the impossible part. I was a shrub, no cedar, I, but it was true and clear enough. I was never happier, though, than when I was mad, a state into which I sank at each performance with deep relief.

After Titus *I was obsessed by Shakespeare and his work. In a way, it was and probably always will be an outsider's obsession because I started acting his plays late and never had the complete immersion in his work that membership of the Royal Shakespeare Company has brought to so many British actors. This has not stopped me from seeing the plays on every possible occasion, and from greedily consuming books about him. But I am aware that actors are still, in 2010, judged by their Shakespearean achievements, and mine – by comparison with my friend Tony Sher, for example – have been occasional and somewhat erratic.*

With Titus, *I celebrated five years of acting professionally, long enough for some of my pigeons to start coming home to roost. My first two employers reappeared in my life and each offered me something wonderful: Peter Farago, now associate director at Birmingham, asked me to play Eddie, the psychiatrist in David Edgar's play* Mary Barnes, *and Robert Walker, now running the Half Moon Theatre in the East End of London, offered me the title role in Brecht's anti-Nazi, pseudo-Shakespearean comic strip,* Arturo Ui. *The latter caused a real sensation. Robert's dangerous, sawn-off production transformed the old synagogue in Alie Street into a metal jungle of the cities, and, as before, he encouraged me to go further than I could possibly have imagined. Brecht offers every opportunity; I created a Frankenstein's monster, put together from spare parts – my wig discovered in the dustbins of the Royal Opera House, my nose and Hitler moustache from a joke shop, tied on with the thread plainly visible, my body an ape's. Underlying it all was the soul of a malevolent clown (some genetic influence there, perhaps). It was, I admit, a stab at Great Acting, something which had preoccupied me for a long time, though it was a very unfashionable notion: the very words were poison in, for example, Joint Stock. I determined to do something people would never forget. I'm not sure whether that happened or not, but it certainly attracted attention.* Mary Barnes *was a huge success, too, both in Birmingham and in London at the Royal Court. It certainly had a great performance at its centre, but it wasn't mine. It was Patti Love's in the title role, an account of such unsparing emotional truthfulness that it threatened to unhinge the actress; for my part, no acting was required – I simply responded to her. Ironically, however, it was this performance, in* Mary Barnes, *and not my* Arturo Ui, *that led to the biggest break I ever had professionally. I wrote the following for the* Guardian *in conjunction with a revival of the play in question in 2007.*

I'm sitting in my tiny bedsit in Hampstead in the sweltering summer of 1978 thinking about Zen Buddhism. The phone rings. 'Callow?' a voice growls. 'Dexter. Listen. Ruby Shaffer's written a play about Mozart and you're going to play Mozart so you'd better get your fucking Köchel numbers together, hadn't you?' 'I suppose I had,' I say. And he rings off. Now, there were a number of remarkable aspects to this conversation, not least the fact that John Dexter, Head of Productions at the Metropolitan Opera House in New York, original director of *The Royal Hunt of the Sun*, *Equus* and the legendary production of *Othello* in which Laurence Olivier had played the title role, was one of the most powerful directors in the world, I was a relatively unknown, relatively young, relatively new actor (I was twenty-nine and I'd only been acting for five years), and he had never seen me act in any medium. I'd met him once, it's true, in conjunction with another play – he'd given me kippers at the Savoy and we'd got on splendidly – but the play had never happened, and I had heard no more from him. Now here he was barking down the line at me and telling me that Peter Shaffer had written a play about Mozart. I knew enough about the business to know that this was a piece of theatre history in the making. The team was perfect: a play about Mozart, good. A play by Shaffer, very good. But a play *about* Mozart *by* Shaffer (and directed by John Dexter): a dream ticket, as we hadn't yet learned to say. But how would he write it? What was the story?

The play was on my doormat later that afternoon – the first script I'd ever had biked to me – and I found that I already knew the central situation. By obscure chance, being a bit of a classical music trainspotter, I had heard Rimsky-Korsakov's one-act opera *Mozart and Salieri*, a setting of Pushkin's little drama of the same name inspired by the notion that Joseph II's Court Composer Salieri had poisoned Mozart; the story had first appeared in the conversation books of Salieri's former pupil, Beethoven, by then so deaf that he could only hear with his eyes. Pushkin's play is brief, dark, chilling, a simple and haunting tale of envy and rivalry. Shaffer, I discovered, had taken this grim anecdote as a starting point for a vast meditation on the relationship between genius and talent, postulating a Salieri who was industrious, skilful and pious, driven to frenzy and ultimately homicide by a Mozart who was foul-mouthed, feckless, infantile and effortlessly inspired. Salieri, in Shaffer's play, was the one person in eighteenth-century Vienna who fully grasped the extent and implication of Mozart's genius, and was thus the one most savagely wounded by what he saw as a cruel joke perpetrated by the God he worshipped: the vessel chosen to receive the greatest music ever written was the least worthy of His creatures, all Salieri's piety, diligence, good taste and talent passed over in favour of a repulsive little nerd. The cosmic insult thus delivered, reasoned Shaffer's Salieri, was a snub to virtue everywhere. What was the point of living morally and decently if the only thing that really mattered – to Salieri, at any rate – was quite independent of decency and morality? The only way to silence those intolerable questions was to snuff out the source of them: to erase Mozart.

I was not yet thirty and on the brink of a promising career, but I could understand that. Who has not felt dully foolish as they diligently plough their furrow, doing the best they can with what they've got, only to see someone else who has some ability, some quality for nothing, for *absolutely nothing* – a face, a voice, a body, a brain – surge forward effortlessly to claim the golden prizes? It's not even necessarily a question of the prizes: it's the ability to do or be in some way extraordinary, beyond the reach of mere work or application or even talent. If one can't be or do that, what's the point? As I sat in my bedsit, one of a handful of people in the world ever to have read the play, I knew that before long the typed manuscript in my hand was going to be part of the lives of hundreds of thousands of people all over the world. Shaffer had touched a nerve, had dramatised an idea which would reach out to the collective inner experience of an audience in a way in which few plays – *Equus* and *The Royal Hunt of the Sun* among them, as it happens – ever do. 'Mediocrities!' Salieri addresses us, claiming to be our patron saint, and scarcely a person in the theatre feels that he might be talking about someone else. (One night at the Olivier Theatre, a year or two later, one individual sat in her seat, bolt upright, keenly focused on the stage. The rest of the auditorium was keenly focused on her. Did Margaret Thatcher, that night, allow her eyebrow to rise ever so slightly at being included in Salieri's mocking embrace? She hadn't liked the play, she said afterwards: it was dirty.)

A question formed in my mind: was it true? Not did Salieri kill Mozart, but was Mozart really so immature, so unthinking, so unstable? Could he really have been Pete from *Big Brother*? Shaffer had mined Mozart's letters – especially the ones written to his cousin Maria Anna Thekla in Basel – for scatological baby-talk, to rub Salieri's nose in Mozart's dirt. He had recycled certain myths (about Mozart never making a correction in his scores, for example). He had simplified his personal relationships. He had omitted Mozart the endlessly adaptable craftsman. He had done, in other words, what a dramatist does: he had left things out if they were not germane to his purpose. He had written a Mozart, Mozart glimpsed by lightning, true, as far as it went, but not the truth, the whole truth and nothing but the truth. We were in a theatre, not a court of law. As for Salieri: here Shaffer was free to make up a great deal, since so little was known of the private man. Above all, what he had done was to make the story not merely dramatic, but theatrical. The answer to my question – to all my questions – was provided by the dramaturgy, by the framing device: everything that happens in the play is told to us by Salieri. The stage directions were very clear on this point. Not merely are we to understand that Mozart's character and his actions as we see them are filtered through the memory of a very old and distinctly eccentric man: so is his music. Shaffer's dazzling idea was for us only to hear what Salieri could remember – fragments, sometimes exactly what Mozart wrote, often a mere approximation, on occasions a distortion.

Whatever I saw or didn't see on that first reading – those first feverish readings, one after another – I knew that I had just been handed (without audition, without interview, without discussion) the part of a lifetime. Salieri was on stage for much, much longer than Mozart – perhaps twice, maybe three times as long – but every time Mozart appeared it was to dazzling effect, and when he wasn't there, he was being talked about. He strutted, preened, shrieked, farted; he rutted, he burbled, he dreamed; and finally, after a long and frightening scene with a masked figure whom he took to be the messenger of death and whom he abjectly begged to reprieve him, he died. As imagined by Shaffer, this Mozart contradicted everything that his music seemed to be. The audience would be in a constant state of uproar, but in the end, they would be won over, their every preconception overturned. And this would be done by theatrical means, not literary ones.

I had been an ardent fan of Shaffer's from my youth: for my A-level English paper I had written about his plays, which in the published editions come complete with descriptions of the first productions, and was thus deeply excited to see on the page, the virgin page, how essentially geared to performance *Amadeus* was at its core. One scene above all struck me as pure theatre: Salieri welcomes Mozart with a charming little march of his own composition to the Court of Joseph II where he is Kapellmeister. When the Imperial entourage has departed, and the two composers are left alone, Mozart thanks Salieri for his march but – wouldn't it be interesting, he says, running over to the keyboard, if you changed this phrase here? altered the rhythm a little? used this harmony? – and in a minute and a half, he has turned the Italian's anonymous exercise in note-spinning into what the world will soon know as 'Non più andrai' from *Le Nozze di Figaro*. The whole dynamic of the play was there, in that single scene, mediocrity mocked by genius. For an actor it was, to borrow a phrase, pure theatrical Viagra.

And I was that actor. Who, however, would play the central role, Salieri himself? Dexter invited me to lunch at the Savoy, scene of our one previous meeting, and introduced me to Peter Shaffer, quizzical, feline, funny, above all modest, and anxious about the destiny of his play. Dexter was in rampant form, like a Tartar warlord, dividing up kingdoms, making demands, devising strategy. He *might* do the play at the National, but only when Jocelyn Herbert, the designer of his choice, was free, which could be three years from now. He would insist on twelve weeks' rehearsal, which ruled out a commercial production. He would get Michael Tippett to write the incidental music. And who, I asked, who would play Salieri? Dexter hadn't made his mind up. It should be Larry, but Larry was frail. John was too nice. Ralph too mad. Burton? Drunk. Christopher Plummer? Not Italian enough. Paul Scofield? suggested Peter, timidly. My heart skipped a beat. Scofield, the master of human complexity, his body all circumflex angles, with his witchy ability to sound every subtle resonance in a phrase, finding echoes and reverberations that opened up doors into unknown cavities in the human soul. Yes! 'So much – gravitas,' I said, suddenly doubting whether that was a very smart thing to have said. 'Too much fucking gravitas, dear. We'll have to knock that out of Mrs Scofield if we cast her.' 'Right,' I said, 'we will.' He signed for lunch and was gone. Peter sighed deeply. 'You see?' he said. I did. It was wildly exciting.

We chatted for a while and I went back to my bed-sittingroom and heard nothing. Nothing at all, for months. Once or twice in the foyer of some theatre I would bump into Shaffer, who seemed to be sick at heart. 'This can't go on,' he moaned. 'It won't. I know my plays. They have to be done when they have to be done. *Amadeus* has to be done now.'

More months elapsed. I was deeply unemployed. I turned thirty. That day I spent my last few pounds on hiring a dinner jacket to go to a party, knowing that the following day I would have to think seriously about finding another profession. Next morning there was a call from my agent.

John Dexter wanted me to play Orlando for him at the National Theatre. Oh, and they also wanted me to play Mozart in a play called – was it? – *Amadeus*, directed by Peter Hall. Paul Scofield would be playing Salieri. And so it came to pass. Dexter and Shaffer had finally fallen out over a matter of royalties: Dexter wanted to be paid every time the play was done, whether in his production or not. That was pretty shocking. But it went deeper. Peter had been rolling on the carpet every night during their discussions, whimpering and sobbing. He could no longer endure John's view of a play as a piece of crude raw material for him to shape. Dexter thought he was playing out the scene at the piano between Mozart and Salieri in real life, and there were no prizes for guessing which one he thought he was in that relationship. What I had read – the supposedly crude, raw material – told me otherwise.

While we were doing *As You Like It*, John's thoughts were only bitter, and the production of that sunniest of plays was infused with his rage and resentment. *Amadeus*, on the other hand, was as open and even a rehearsal as I can recollect, Shaffer ever-willing to change, rewrite, reshape, Hall amiable, always loyal to Mozart, Felicity Kendal superb as Constanze, cheeky, shrewd, sexy, with a core of obsidian right down the centre, Scofield slowly, quietly marinating the huge role in some profound personal essence, filling it with those notes which are his alone to command. The first preview brought an eruption of passion from the audience which continued unfalteringly for the two years we played it at the National (except of course for the night Margaret Thatcher paid her visit and withheld her compliments).

A few years later, I directed the play at the Theatre Clwyd in Mold. I had some pretty smart ideas about the piece. I wanted to set it in a lunatic asylum during the Napoleonic bombardment of Vienna in 1809. The inmates – all musicians, among them Salieri – would play out the story against that backdrop; they would make music with whatever came to hand, trying to evoke Mozart's work on saucepans, bottles, washboards. Inexplicably, Shaffer was a little resistant, so I devised another scenario, one where the action came to life in an abandoned theatre. There was a High German Romantic, an E. T. A. Hoffmann, quality to the piece that I was trying to nail, and with the young Rupert Graves at the height of his youthful beauty and brilliance as Mozart, we finally found it. During rehearsals, though, I had sat watching the play I knew so well and despairing. It seemed so flat, so thin. The moment the technical rehearsals began and we had the costumes and the lights and the effects and the music, the old magic began to assert itself, and when the audience arrived, they were as enraptured, as disturbed, as moved as spectators at the National Theatre had been the first time round. Shaffer has constructed a piece of theatre which can be staged in a multitude of ways; only one which denies its theatricality can fail.

I was now back at the National, as a Leading Man, ten years after leaving it as an 'umble box-office clerk. Of course, it was a very different National: Denys Lasdun's vast Theatropolis on the South Bank was a thousand times better equipped than the Vic, and though the backstage areas were charmless and functional, the whole operation was superbly organised and efficient. The canteen was slick and practical, dispensing a million meals a day, and commanded superb views of the Thames, but it lacked the sweaty, steamy intimacy of the Vic's underground cubby-hole, with its temperamental little chef. There was a Green Room (the actors' bar, actually), which the Vic never had, and there were veritable armies of actors, among them some friendly faces from the Old Days (Anna Carteret and Mike Gambon and, indeed, dear old Boddington). In the Green Room I was greeted by the lovely Scottish actor James Grant, who had remembered me from The Thrie Estates *in Edinburgh (how? He was the King and I was sprawling on the steps). 'Hi, Simon,' he said, 'Welcome to the Green Room. See that hole over there, in the carpet? That's where Derek Newark falls.' This was an allusion to the tall, notoriously bibulous actor who was one of the key members of Bill Bryden's company at the Cottlesloe. And there was John Dexter, never a comfortable presence anywhere, and inextricably associated with the idea of Olivier's National Theatre, who was the whole reason for my being there. This monstrous but perversely lovable figure wrote an interesting if involuted autobiography,* The Honourable Beast, *but the most vivid account of him is to be found in the pages of* The Birth of Shylock, the Death of Zero Mostel, *by the writer with whose early work he had been so closely involved, Arnold Wesker. Their relationship was nothing if not challenging – but every relationship with Dexter was challenging. (Taunted by Dexter's constantly referring to him as Ruby, Peter Shaffer had one day said, 'Now, look here, Rose – ' 'Rose?' 'Yes: as in "rose, thou art sick".') I reviewed Wesker's book in 1997 in the* Sunday Times.

At the time of the almost unanimous critical drubbing for my production of *Les Enfants du Paradis* for the RSC, I determined to write an essay called *Anatomy of a Flop*, describing the love, energy, imagination and hard work that had gone into the making of the show, and attempting to answer the critics' question, sometimes explicit, sometimes implicit, of how such a – to them – palpable catastrophe had ever been allowed to happen. With the publication of Arnold Wesker's wonderful new book, which describes the 1977 Broadway production of his play *Shylock*, my essay is redundant. There has never been such a complete account of how frighteningly touch-and-go is the business of bringing a play, particularly a new one, to the stage, even in the hands of a master director.

Wesker describes *Shylock*'s genesis: how his violent reaction as a Jewish man against Laurence Olivier's interpretation of the most famous Jew in dramatic literature resolved him to write a work of his own in which he would try to understand the actions of Shakespeare's character, and offer an alternative image of him as intelligent, compassionate and deeply moral. Despite the encouragement of friends, producers failed to show any interest; Peter Hall turned it down for the National Theatre. At that point John Dexter, director of Wesker's greatest successes but somewhat distant since their falling-out over *The Old Ones*, read it and immediately set up a New York production backed by the Shuberts, with Zero Mostel in the leading role.

The play opened in Washington. After the first preview Mostel fell ill; within days he was dead. The understudy took over, the production resumed and eventually opened on Broadway. Despite wild excitement from the preview audiences, the New York critics, especially the *Times*, were unenthusiastic, and the play closed at the end of the week. All this Wesker recorded, minute by minute, in his journal, and it is this, with a few letters and pages of notes appended, which comprises the present volume. It is his *Anatomy of a Flop*.

It is also a great deal more than that. First, it is a book about work in the theatre. Wesker is a deeply, even desperately serious man who believes passionately in the importance of his job and of the theatre itself, and every page of the book celebrates that belief. He describes the endeavour of a large group of people to create a theatrical event of power and substance in language that might be used to describe a love affair, or an illness, both of which it closely resembles. In the 'making of' genre, it is a masterpiece, the best of its kind, a detailed study of group dynamics, of

145

collective enterprise and of the nature of leadership. More than that, it is a poignant and sometimes distressing account of a friendship gone wrong. Finally, it offers a full-length portrait of one of the most terrible and wonderful individuals ever to devote himself to the stage, the director John Dexter.

Wesker has lately become a prophet without honour in his own profession, that most unhappy figure, the unfashionable dramatist. For what is an unperformed playwright? The plays accumulate in his drawer, unseen, or seen briefly and obscurely. Once, though, Wesker was the man of the moment, who put the world of working people and indeed their work itself, on stage. Unlike his contemporary, John Osborne, who expressed their rage, and his own, in torrentially rhetorical language, Wesker addressed the aspirations and frustrations of the post-Second World War generation in detailed and concrete terms in a number of strong, sober pieces posited on robust socialist humanist principles.

He had the supreme good luck to find an interpreter who was able to offer his work what it needed: a fanatical commitment to realism, and an uncommon gift for choreographing complex action for maximum theatrical impact. John Dexter, a sometime actor seeking to establish himself as a director, seized on the plays that came to be known collectively as the Wesker trilogy, and staged them first in Coventry, then later at the Royal Court Theatre, with the young Joan Plowright as Beatie Bryant creating an unforgettably radiant image of aspiring, intelligent youth. More plays followed in quick succession: *Chips with Everything* and *The Kitchen*, both directed by Dexter, both highly successful. Then things started to go wrong.

Wesker was now being superseded by a new wave of radical writers, more pessimistic, more overtly revolutionary and more experimental theatrically. The era of the well-made left-wing play, it appeared, was over. After two egregious disasters (*The Journalists*, at the RSC, which was withdrawn when the actors refused to perform it, and *The Friends*, sabotaged from within by the leading actor), he was beginning to feel out on a limb. It was then that he wrote *Shylock*. Re-enter John Dexter.

Nobody who worked with Dexter, who died, pointlessly young, in 1990, is likely to forget him. He brought to the stage some of the most memorable productions since the war: apart from Wesker's plays, and Peter Shaffer's, he was responsible for the musical *Half a Sixpence*, Olivier's *Othello* at the National Theatre, a glittering *Misanthrope*, *M. Butterfly*, and innumerable triumphs on the operatic stage at the Met and else-where. His heyday was at Olivier's National, where he helped form a uniquely flexible acting company, mentally and physically brilliant. He was funny, exciting, and a master of his craft, but he could also be savage, castratingly rude, and as capable of draining the life out of a piece as releasing it.

Dexter had been afflicted with polio in his youth, been tarred and feath-ered by the women in the factory where he worked in Derby, endured bullying during his War Service and terrible hostility when he went to prison (for the alleged abuse of a minor, who was in fact blackmailing him). All these experiences convinced him of the need to assert himself decisively over both people and materials. He had to believe in himself as an absolute master; when belief faltered, he would attack those who seemed to threaten his success. Most often they would be actors whom he felt were not up to the job that he had unthinkingly given them because they were pretty or nice, or because he was in the giving vein that day; when they fell out of favour, he would attack them again and again in excruciatingly personal terms, generally to little positive effect.

This was not directing: it was spite. He would turn on authors, too, accus-ing them of not understanding their own plays, of being lazy or of not being able to write. A famous sally of his, understandably not quoted by the author in the present volume, was hurled at him during rehearsals of *The Kitchen*: 'Shut up, Wesker, or I'll direct the scene the way you wrote it!' He came to believe that he alone was responsible for his great successes. He was also quite capable of being kind, illuminating, witty and even humble. He worked staggeringly hard – fuelled by booze, sex, drugs – willing himself to great heights of scholarship (becoming far more learned than the university-educated colleagues whom he so despised); he could be the best fun, too, but you never knew which mood would prevail, or why. Eventually he alienated almost all of his friends; the exchange of letters between Wesker and Dexter at the end of the pro-duction of *Shylock* in which he formally suspends their friendship, is particularly painful to read.

Artistically, his judgement of plays and actors became increasingly er-ratic, and the productions themselves seemed oddly punitive, austere and cold, as if he now wanted to dominate and bully the audience, too, to get them to shut up and listen properly and stop fidgeting. There were no concessions; all the old sensuality and sweep were gone.

Despite all this, I and many other people loved him deeply – a love he roughly brushed aside – and mourn him to this day. He is here in Wesker's pages in all his complexity, angel and demon, tyrant and inspiration; the book alerts us, too, to the existence of a big play with big themes that cries out for a proper production at one of our great subsidised theatres. Meanwhile, read Wesker's book. It is a totally authentic and powerfully moving account of how plays are made – or broken.

This was the man I was about to work with. I knew enough of his reputation to tremble; but in the event he was only kind to me.

Olivier, of course, was the great absentee from the National – his personal touch, his leadership from the front, on stage, at the head of his gallant band, his eye on every single detail of the organisation, all absent. The current director Peter Hall, whom I had yet to meet, could scarcely duplicate that. But who could? Not even Olivier, as it happens, not even at his height. The place was simply too big. This was not to say that wonderful work couldn't be done – it was being done, and it would be done, again and again. But the missing element was the one which Oliver had brought to the enterprise: gallantry – an odd word, perhaps, for a gang of thesps, but one which, for me, characterises the theatrical enterprise at its best: a spirit of struggling against the odds, with mingled courage and insouciance, in a great and noble cause. And it is hard to feel that camaraderie across a whole army. Loyalty is to battalion, to regiment.

There were, of course, great actors in the company, and they created a living link with the older tradition that Olivier had so vividly represented: Peggy Ashcroft (once Juliet to Olivier's Mercutio and Romeo, in alternation with John Gielgud) had been the great beating heart of Peter Hall's first RSC seasons; Ralph Richardson had run the Old Vic company in tandem with Olivier, until Tyrone Guthrie manoeuvred them out of the job. Sir Ralph was by now an extraordinary presence, like a more or less benevolent dinosaur, stealthily padding through the theatre, his eyes madly blazing. I wrote this brief profile to accompany a splendid photograph of him by Roddy McDowall (who was a great photographer as well as a good actor and an incomparable friend) in his 1989 book Double Exposure.

'Cup of coffee, Sir Ralph?' asked one of the younger actors in the National Theatre canteen during a break in rehearsals. There was an electric silence as the great man, head gently shaking, eyes gleaming strangely, contemplated the question. 'I'd rather have,' he said, 'a cup of hemlock.' This last word was pronounced Hem Lock, which somehow made it all the more real and terrible. And, of course, funny. He was always an alarming presence, on stage and off, never merely avuncular or dotty, as he might so easily have appeared. Anarchy and potential violence never lay far behind the drolleries. In the trial scene of *The Merchant of Venice*, his Shylock suddenly produced, with a frightening flash of steel, a huge knife from his belt, and moved with superhuman speed across the stage, missing Antonio's proffered breast by the merest millimetre. Only the prompt intervention of his Portia stood between the actor playing Antonio and certain death. Her intervention produced an audible gasp of relief from the audience. Had she missed her cue, Sir Ralph, I have no doubt, would have been a homicide.

In addition to this physical danger he had an earthly spirituality, a quality a million miles removed from that of his friend, John Gielgud. That much mimicked voice, a sort of drunken gargle, could speak of life and death with startling actuality. Though it was not his last, his performance of John Gabriel Borkman remains in memory as a glorious leave-taking. Like many of his performances it was disorientatingly original. He seemed to play the second act in a sort of trance. The third act was piercingly urgent, and his last act among the greatest things I have ever seen on a stage. At the moment when Borkman stands high above the city, gazing down on the industrial world below, Richardson, who somehow conveyed in his performance a sense of the great height of the mountain and the terrible teeming world at his feet, emitted a mysterious sound: three hoots. 'Hoo hoo hoo.' Shortly after, Borkman dies. The sound was heart-stopping, unforgettable. I ran home to find Ibsen's stage direction. Nothing.

A couple of years later I asked Peter Hall, who had directed the play, how it had come about, how the actor had discovered the exact sound of a soul leaving the body. 'He just did it,' said Hall, 'and we all knew that it was right. No one ever mentioned it.'

When he had arrived at the National Theatre, Richardson insisted that there should be a ceremony of some sort to mark the first performance of a new show. Accordingly, he set off a rocket for the very first night, and thereafter, on every first night, rockets cleaved the sky above Waterloo Bridge. These are his memorials: dazzling, dangerous fireworks and those strange other-worldly hoots.

Inevitably, the fireworks were suspended after a couple of years owing to Health and Safety considerations: not considerations that the whisky-swigging, motorbike-riding Sir Ralph ever took into account (the leather jacket he wore on his bike carried the legend Hall's Angels). *His old chum and sparring partner John Gielgud played a season at the Olivier, too, giving his Julius Caesar and Sir Politick-Would-Be in Peter Hall's production of* Volpone. *He and Richardson did not, alas, appear together at the new National, which was a shame after their knock-down brilliant turns in* No Man's Land *and* Home; *what wonderful Broker's Men they would have made in a panto, or perhaps Ugly Sisters. I wrote this piece about the sales of their respective effects for the* Daily Telegraph.

By curious chance, the collections of two of the last century's greatest actors have come up for sale at more or less the same time. They were utterly different both as men and as actors, but in later years they became fast friends and – in plays by David Storey and Harold Pinter – members of one of the greatest double acts the British theatre has ever known. Their performances, together and separately, left indelible impressions on all who saw them, but off the stage, their private personalities were every bit as memorable. At Monday's Private View of the Gielgud Collection, the great and the good of the acting profession turned up in large numbers, more, one felt, to immerse themselves again in the great man's aura than specifically to buy his effects, which, beyond the superb theatrical memorabilia, and an enormous number of gifts from friends and admirers, consist largely of domestic items – elegant furniture, carpets, china statues, paintings of varying quality (a superb Nicholson, a Lely and a fine Dufy, alongside others with specifically theatrical significance) – that attest to the conventionally tasteful taste of Gielgud's partner of some thirty years, Martin Hensler, with whom he had lived in comfortable splendour in Wotton Underwood near Aylesbury. All of the items have charm; but a sixteenth-century Buddha head and two ravishing alabaster busts of the Emperor Hadrian's boyfriend Antinöos are striking, and somehow unexpected. Their London house, in Cowley Street, had been given up some years before: 'Nobody gives parties any more,' Gielgud proclaimed, not altogether accurately, in the mid-Seventies when they made the move. What he meant was that nobody gave parties that he wanted to go to any more. 'So nice to see you,' he once told Gyles Brandreth, 'because all my real friends are dead.'

In a sense, he had outlived his age. The world of theatre to which he had devoted himself had changed out of all recognition, although, paradoxically, he seemed, when he died at the age of ninety-six, younger than ever, a constantly witty figure, perennially fresh and alive. His countenance, once noble and Roman, had become softer, pinker and rounder, the face of the bonniest baby imaginable. Always appreciated, generally admired, he was by now universally loved, even by those who had never set foot in a theatre.

At Sotheby's the distinguished guests, including many a knight and a dame of the British Empire, were decidedly of the theatre theatrical, and they were to be observed scattered around the room in anecdotal clusters, telling and retelling their favourite Gielgud stories, all attempting with greater or lesser accuracy the readily imitable voice, with its unique music, starting with a husky warble, oscillating legato around a couple of notes before ending with a characteristic descending fifth. Most of the stories devolved on the failure of his self-censorship mechanism, leading him to blurt out his inner thoughts at the most unfortunate moments. 'We've been working like blacks,' he said in the presence of the West Indian actor Tommy Baptiste. 'Not your kind of black, of course, Tommy.' The solecism was always the more delicious because so felicitously expressed, as if he suffered from a sort of epigrammatic Tourette's syndrome or as if, perhaps, his subconscious had been scripted by Congreve. Although capable of the silliest of puns, the most direct of Anglo-Saxon expletives and the naughtiest of suggestions, his delight in his own sallies was always so complete and so infectious, and the delivery so impeccable, that one was swept away on a small tidal wave of merriment. 'Poor Laughton!' he said to me once, 'he was so ill at the end, they had to have lorry drivers shipped in for him from the East Coast!' and then laughed till he almost wept, as did I.

Equally, he could suddenly be moved to tears of sadness by the memory of something which suddenly struck him. It was all part of the lightning speed of his mind, his instant responsiveness to thought. His heart and his mind were as one. In no sense was he, nor would he have claimed to be, an intellectual, but his active intelligence, the rapidity with which one thought succeeded another, was palpable, visible and in the air like an electrical storm. Congratulated on his consummately quirky performance in *No Man's Land* at the Old Vic during Olivier's regime, he famously remarked 'Oh, do you think so? I don't know why I got the part, really, I think it's only because Larry's dead – I mean dying – I mean much much better.' This celerity of brain was at the core of his acting, that and the great openness of his heart. His particular genius for Shakespeare and the writers of the Restoration period derived from his instinctive sense of their rhythm and melody, which formed a conduit for the lightning transitions of thought and emotion he matchlessly purveyed. He spoke the words of these writers as if it was the most natural – the only – way in which to speak, and indeed, being with him one felt as if one was oneself in a play by one of these masters; until, that is, one opened one's own mouth and spoke.

He was an all-consuming reader, and his library is one of the glories of the collection at Sotheby's, including an exquisite edition of *Hamlet* with Gordon Craig illustrations. He devoured books, his swift brain racing through their pages and delivering instant and often very funny judgements on the contents. He was, too, a tireless correspondent, always replying in person and by hand to letters in which he simply transferred his conversation to the page, bubbling over with gossip, some of it fifty years old, full of non sequiturs, but always faultlessly composed. The letters' appearance on the page was as distinctive as everything else about him, the left hand margin drifting inexorably to the right, so that the last couple of lines on the page would consist of no more than two or three words.

In his long career and life, he had had many failures, and no one spoke more openly about them than he, but they were never failures of courage or taste. This was perhaps one of the points of common ground that he and Ralph Richardson may have found when they eventually came to be close friends. They were never rivals – as Olivier and Gielgud had been, though in truth the rivalry in that case mostly came from Olivier – and scarcely played the same line of parts, but, as Richardson later admitted, the odd-looking, powerfully built, vigorously heterosexual fellow with a mad twinkle in his eye, struggling initially to find his niche on the stage, felt nervous in the company of the thoroughbred homosexual aesthete upon whom favour seemed to descend as of divine right from the gods of theatre. From the beginning Gielgud had the manners and the looks of a matinee idol; Richardson was cut of coarser cloth. While Gielgud made Shakespearean role after role his own – Hamlet, Richard II, Romeo, Prospero, Lear, Leontes – Richardson never seemed comfortable with the great heroes. His stupendous Falstaff (a prose role, of course) was a rare success for him in an Elizabethan play; instead he was able to conquer the great outsiders: Peer Gynt, Cyrano de Bergerac. J. B. Priestley wrote a number of plays for him which exploited the unique prose poetry of his acting, the visionaries, the battered romantics, the men of mystery, of which the supreme example was his Inspector Goole in the original production of *An Inspector Calls*.

He had within him a divine spark all the more extraordinary for the rough-hewn exterior. He had access, as an actor, to profound darkness and an ability to convey the numinous denied any of his contemporaries. He was capable of an exquisite sentimental tenderness, too, but somewhere underneath the surface there was always a latent power, bordering on violence. When Peter Shaffer told Gielgud in the late Fifties that he was writing a play about an axe murderer, Gielgud told him without a moment's hesitation 'Oh, you must get Ralph.' He became ever more eccentric, or perhaps one should simply say he became ever more himself. His mania for fast cars and then large Harley Davidson motorbikes persisted well into his late seventies; he was famous for the parrot that perched on his shoulder when he was at home in Regent's Park, where he sat in his study at the top of the house, sipping Scotch, brooding over his scripts. In the evening when he and his second wife Meriel – the Lady Mu, as he called her – dined alone together, they both wore full formal dress (it is the Lady Mu's recent demise which has occasioned the sale of the present collection). Richardson's conversation, too, bordered on the gnomic. Asked to appear in an Amnesty Gala for Imprisoned Writers, he said, 'I don't think so. You see, I think all writers should be put in prison.'

In life and in his performances he came to resemble a Zen Master, transcending all conventional notions of behaviour or of thought, cutting through to deeper and more surprising truths. His voice, like his bearing, was interior sprung, an astonishingly unnatural instrument in which vowels of no known geographical provenance were rolled on the tongue like a fine dry sherry, but the end result was expressive, true and always surprising. The tremble from the mild Parkinson's disease from which he latterly suffered added to the sense of otherness, but it was a very earthy,

153

a very English otherness, the strangeness of Herne the Hunter, a figure from ancient folklore. There was nothing fey about Sir Ralph.

His taste in clothes, in furnishings and in art was equally original but equally grounded, as the catalogue of his collection reveals. Like Gielgud, he had trained as a painter, but while Gielgud's instinct was towards the beautiful surface, Richardson sought things of solid craftsmanship and profound significance. There is a feeling about his possessions that he could have made any of them; Gielgud is simply a collector. There is in Richardson's catalogue a magnificent mahogany folio stand of 1825, a fine creation of struts and hinges, at once practical and beautiful, that is particularly expressive of its former owner. There are timepieces of many sorts; each painting and drawing has an individual power. The William Nicholsons are especially fine, but there are watercolours by Rodin and Wilson Steer, drawings by Lear and Gaudier-Brzeska. The Egyptian figures are exquisite and powerful. Gielgud surrounded himself with charming things, but Richardson's seem to be part of him.

In both cases, a rich and complex human being is revealed by these collections. Both men, in their entirely different ways, were English eccentrics in the grand tradition, but in both, the spirit, burning so bright within them, transcended affectation. We tell stories about them, not because they were cards, or even because they were exceptionally talented, though God knows they were both both of those things, but because they filtered life through the medium of their souls to create new and rich variations on the human condition: they lived their art to the fullest extent possible. Of whom shall we be telling stories now?

There were, in those days, still companies at the National. Each auditorium had one, with a director of its own: the Cottesloe, under Bill Bryden (to which James Grant and the so frequently horizontal Derek Newark belonged); the Lyttelton, under Michael Rudman; and the Olivier, under Christopher Morahan, to which I was proud to belong because of the name. I was 'an Olivier actor'. Actors didn't move from one stage to another, and there was a certain jokey rivalry between us. Dexter quickly mastered the vast and wide-open Olivier stage, although his bleak and wintry As You Like It, *in which, to everyone's amazement, I played Orlando, pleased few critics (though audiences took to it well enough). But the play moved me deeply, the perfection of its music, the freshness of its discovery of love. I became aware of something I had not quite experienced on* Titus *(perhaps because Shakespeare hadn't yet, either): the absolute naturalness of the writing, transforming you into the character even as you speak the lines.*

No sooner was As You Like It *up and running than rehearsals for* Amadeus *started. The play was now being directed – to John Dexter's intense and unconcealed disgust – by Peter Hall. It arrived at a critical moment in the fortunes of the National Theatre on the South Bank, which was just recovering from its traumatic early birth pangs: the uncomfortable takeover by Hall from Olivier, the industrial action which threatened its very existence, and a number of very public failures. The theatre deeply needed a smash hit. It got it. It was such an extraordinary event for all of us that I think it worth printing another, rather different piece about it, written in 2009 for* Gramophone *magazine.*

Amadeus is thirty years old. If that makes you feel a little long in the tooth, think what it's doing to me. Peter Hall who directed it and Peter Shaffer who wrote it and I who first played the role of Mozart assembled the other day on the stage of the Olivier Theatre at the Royal National Theatre where it was first performed, and chewed the fat. Or was it the cud? In fact, having us all together there (for the first time since the play opened, as it happens) only reminded us of how electric and risky it all seemed at the time. Not that we ever doubted that the play was going to be a success. In fact, it was already – as Oscar Wilde might have said – the most enormous success, before a single customer had crossed the foyer. The moment it was announced, the combination of Shaffer, Scofield and Mozart led to a box-office siege. This, of course, made it all the more nerve-racking for those of us who assembled in Rehearsal Room One at the National some eight weeks before the first night to read the play for the first time. Could we possibly satisfy expectations? What Peter had written was deeply provocative. It offered a portrait of the composer that was profoundly at odds with the public perception of him. Students of Otto Jahn's three-volume *Life* and Otto Deutsch's *Documentary Biography* (and indeed of Emily Andersen's translation of the – very carefully – *Selected Letters*) were aware that Mozart was, at the very least, a complex figure, but the general view, the view of music lovers everywhere, was of a rococo manikin, sweetly childlike, tragically early death casting a halo over him.

So there was tension in the air. Without being competitive in the anxiety stakes, I think I can safely say that I was more nervous than anyone else. Neither Paul Scofield, nor Peter Shaffer, nor Peter Hall, had ever seen me act. I had been cast by John Dexter, who was originally slated to direct the play, but he had left the production amid sparks of vituperation and recrimination, like the Queen of the Night. Not that he'd seen me act, either. I had, thank God, acted with Felicity Kendal, but I had much to prove. I was also nervous because it was a very difficult part. It was Mozart seen through Salieri's eyes, vindictively and selectively; even the music was misremembered through his distorting ears.

Mozart makes his first appearance as a pussycat, chasing his wife; there is some seriously smutty talk, after which, uproariously cachinnating, he disappears. He then reappears variously as arrogant, silly, pugnacious and jealous. Shaffer allows him one or two brief moments to speak seriously about music, and then he's back to his Tourette's syndrome self. There's a magnificent long speech to the masked man he thinks is God, but is in fact Salieri, then he relapses into childishness and oblivion in his wife's arms. All wonderful acting opportunities, but fraught with danger. At the reading, I gave it my best shot. Perhaps rather better than my best shot. In fact, I may have shot my bolt, giggling, shrieking, sobbing. I feared the worst when Peter Hall put an arm round my shoulder and said, 'That was a very brave performance.' What he said next, however, transformed my work (and probably my career): 'But I have to believe at all times that he wrote the Overture to *The Marriage of Figaro*.' That became my task for the next few weeks. Meanwhile, Paul Scofield was quietly getting on with his towering performance and we began tentatively to engage in the play's dance of death.

The first preview was astonishing. It was as if the audience had been waiting for the play for years. They ate it up greedily and the ovation at the end was like the roar of the ocean. I had never and have never quite experienced anything like it. And it was like that every time we did the play. Many factors were responsible, not least Scofield at his most complexly, sexily dangerous, and the play's theme – successful mediocrity and its revenge on genius – rang bells with many people. But in the end I believe that what it was all about was music: music as the expression of the spirit, music, one might say, as God's voice. Shaffer and Hall unerringly chose moments from Mozart's output – the adagio of the great Wind Serenade, the Masonic Funeral music, the finale of *Figaro*, the

Requiem, of course – which expressed the sublime. This was the hunger that the play fed, for something beyond the realm of compromised life, for the absolute. And Shaffer's brilliantly melodramatic edifice superbly stage-managed those moments. It was that which sent shivers round the auditorium for every single night over the course of the two years that we played the play, and it was that which transformed Mozart from being a hugely admired composer into being the idol of millions. The film clinched it. I can think of no other instance of a work in one medium so deeply affecting the perception of another.

Shaffer had done it again. There is something uncanny about Shaffer's ability to hit the nail on the head quite so resoundingly, a knack not possessed by any other dramatist of the twentieth century. I wrote this piece about Peter Shaffer for the Daily Telegraph *to commemorate an auspicious (if rather overdue) event.*

It seems only the other day that Milton Shulman was complaining that while actors and directors routinely received knighthoods, playwrights – without whom there would be no theatre – seldom or never did. Someone up there must be unexpectedly responsive to the testy old Canadian, because there has since been a positive rush to the Palace, with Ayckbourn, Stoppard and Hare all bending a knee within the last couple of years; Pinter conspicuously remains a commoner, presumably from choice. One curious omission will be rectified later this month when Peter Shaffer is shoulder-tapped by Her Majesty. A unique and often controversial figure among modern dramatists, for three decades he produced a series of massively successful plays which tackled huge themes in a spectacularly theatrical manner, making him the playwright who forced the mainstream audience to think about the big ideas of their times. In a series of large-scale public plays from the mid-Sixties to the mid-Nineties – *The Royal Hunt of the Sun, Equus, Amadeus, Lettice and Lovage, The Mask of the Gorgon* – he put these ideas into general currency in a way that only the theatre can, being, as John Osborne famously remarked, a minority art with a majority influence. Imperialism, psychiatry, creativity, terrorism, modern architecture: these were all dramatised and debated in his plays at the National Theatre, on Broadway and in the West End, but not drily, not dialectically.

Not for him the intensely focused intellectual argument of a Frayn or the severe and savage historical analysis of a Bond or a Hare. His background is liberal humanistic; his concern is the dilemma of the individual faced with the loss of certainty in the world, sometimes in the form of ritual lament – the death of the Sun God in *The Royal Hunt of the Sun* – sometimes tragedy – Salieri's increasing conviction that his God is not a benevolent one – sometimes farce: Lettice and Lovage's declaration of war on modern architecture. His dramatic method is frankly one of seduction: he loves, and has always loved, since childhood in Manchester, the theatre theatrical: music hall, pantomime, opera, melodrama. He loves language, especially rhetorical language. Although as far from Brecht politically as could be, he has been very happy to use Brecht's theatrical practice, the outward forms of the Epic Theatre. He loves actors and has written some of the most challenging and rewarding roles of the twentieth century. He especially relishes a theatre duel, allowing Atahuallpa and Pizarro, Strang and Dysart, Mozart and Salieri, Lettice and Lovage, to slug it out to the great excitement of the crowd. Above all he has a genius for crystallising his themes into theatre imagery which tells the story unforgettably and in a way which could only happen on a stage (with the single exception of *Amadeus,* radically rewritten with its director Milos Forman, Shaffer's plays have proved irredeemably uncinematic). Atahuallpa appearing metamorphosed in the great golden sun; Alan Strang, riding his horse (impersonated by an actor in silver hooves, with a head of wrought metal); Mozart at the piano turning Salieri's feeble march into *Figaro*'s 'Non più andrai'. They constitute pure theatre, as, sublimely, does *Black Comedy,* its action played out in the dark: the audience can see the characters, though they cannot see each other.

It's worth noting that his plays, apart, perhaps, from the early *Five Finger Exercise,* are not at all autobiographical. In person Sir Peter – who celebrates his seventy-fifth birthday this week, too – has very little of the epic about him. Consummately urbane, he is one of the most wickedly amusing conversationalists on either side of the Atlantic, and brings an atmosphere of contagious hilarity with him wherever he goes. His circle of friendship, across the globe, is enormous; his audiences – also enormous – love him too, sensing, quite rightly, that he loves them, which is by no means always the case with dramatists, knighted or otherwise.

Shaffer's plays (Amadeus was no exception) normally leave the public stunned. He plans his last lines very carefully, shocking and satisfying the audience in equal measure. There is a silence, and then the roar of approval begins. I had never, up to that point (and not all that much since, alas) been exposed to quite so much sheer volume of applause. It was of course entirely delightful, but it took some adjusting to. The Guardian *asked me to write this piece, which they called* Darling, We Were Wonderful, *in 2008.*

One of the most universally held beliefs about the theatre is that performers are applause junkies, living for that moment at the end of the evening when they step down to the footlights and gratefully accept their reward. My own experience – and, I think, that of many of my colleagues – has been rather different. Most of us do not view the curtain call with relish. What matters much more is what has passed between us and the audience over the course of the evening – especially if it's a musical – but even then, it's the minute-by-minute interplay (as often as not silent) that really counts, the sense of communication, the engagement with an audience. It is generally the case that an audience who have laughed and applauded a great deal during the show will be less forthcoming at the curtain call: they've done their bit, and the final bringing together of hands is more a formality than anything else. An audience who have sat silently through a show often burst into vivacious applause at the end – a great relief, though baffling. What was holding them back?

The chemistry of a thousand people sitting together in a room, watching a play, is endlessly fascinating – the way they sometimes react as one from the beginning, or stubbornly refuse to come together, or respond only to a show's broad physical comedy, or sometimes to nothing at all, beginning, middle or end. But the fact is, something needs to happen at the conclusion of the show: we all need closure. What form this should take is a delicate question. Both the cast and director rather dread the day when the curtain call is set. Partly this is to do with the niceties of hierarchy within the cast, those unspoken but very real gradations of fame and distinction balanced against the size of a role and its impact in the show. The complexities of these protocols are infinite and can lead to tears when the procedure is announced, generally with a promise that it is merely temporary and will be refined before the press night (this is rarely true). Should Sir X or Dame Y, with their distinguished cameos, have precedence over Miss Z, who just left drama school last month but whose part is three times the length of theirs put together? Should the three supporting actors take their calls together even though only one of them is getting all the laughs? There is an element of ego in this, of course, but also the consideration that the audience wants a chance to show their enthusiasm for an actor who has particularly dazzled or who is dear to their hearts. (It can sometimes work the other way. On one production I directed, after a fraught technical period and the cancellation of a number of previews, I nipped into the leading actor's dressing room to give a quick account of a rough curtain call that would, of course, be only temporary. 'X comes on here, Y comes on there and then you come straight down the centre stage,' I said. 'Why,' this immensely distinguished artist enquired, 'should I carry the can for this pile of shit?')

In the 1970s, I acted with the theatre group Joint Stock. We were performing, among other things, David Hare's austere play *Fanshen*, which examined a radical realignment of society – one which, the play suggested, might be worthy of imitation. It seemed inappropriate, after thus throwing down the gauntlet, to come on to our hopefully chastened bourgeois audience all beams and bashfulness, so we experimented with various different ways of ending the evening. The first was to come on and stand in front of the audience – not bowing, not grateful, just standing there, in a sombre row. Resembling as we did a line-up of dangerous criminals in a police identification parade, we soon cowed the audience into silence, then shuffled moodily off. Next we attempted the Russian method of applauding the audience ourselves. The result was that the audience felt deprived of their one moment of self-expression, and stopped clapping. Our final innovation was the most radical: we just didn't come on at all. That shut 'em up pretty damn quick. In the end, we just did what everyone does: we came on and took our applause.

For some actors, there is an awkwardness about appearing in front of the audience as themselves rather than in character: many actors who appear to be gloriously free spirits during the performance suddenly become crippled with self-consciousness at the curtain call. Some actually remain in character, or take on another character, which is them-as-faithful-servant-of-the-public; in the days when leading actors used to make speeches after every performance, they created a persona in which to address their public, giving another performance. For others, there is a residual resentment about seeming to ask for approval, some race memory of a servant–master relationship between actors and audience that outrages their democratic souls and leads them to stare balefully out into the stalls, as if they were inmates in a prisoner of war camp who had just been forced to perform in front of the Gestapo.

For tragedy, or plays about child abuse and Third World debt, a demeanour of some dignity is appropriate. An actor who has just played Richard III or Mother Courage may legitimately betray some symptoms of exhaustion – Sir Donald Wolfit liked to emphasise this by hanging on to the curtain – though playing the lead in a light comedy can be just as draining. There, sweat-free urbanity is expected, as if giving the show had been, as it was for the audience, a mere prelude to supper. In the end, the curtain call is a sort of good manners, like not rolling off and falling asleep after making love. It says, on both sides, 'Goodnight, lovely seeing you, thanks so much, see you again.'

As an actor, you only think about applause if it doesn't happen. My first play in the West End was with Harry Secombe. Every night when he got home, his wife, Myra, would ask him: 'Did you get your claps tonight?' But it's a faulty kind of index. Rather than thinking, 'What a wonderful reception I got tonight,' you'll be thinking, 'Why wasn't it as good as the night before? What are we doing wrong?' And there is, too, a danger that the public will feel disappointed if they haven't cheered and clapped enough. American audiences tend to perform themselves much more than British ones. There the true orgasmic fulfilment of the evening tends to be at the curtain call, rather than during the performance. When I've worked as a director in the US, I've often received friendly advice on how to engineer a standing ovation – the Holy Grail of performance Stateside. 'Get the guys to hold hands, Simon, and then run down to the audience and then, on a count, fling their arms right up in the air. It works, perfect, every time.' I regret to report that it does.

In my view standing ovations should be reserved for something utterly out of the ordinary. I was lucky enough (as an usher at the Old Vic) to see Laurence Olivier on stage many times. He never once got a standing ovation. Maggie Smith once did get a standing ovation for her Hedda Gabler, but that was because the whole of the Swedish Embassy had booked the front row. Needing to get to dinner very quickly, they had stood up as a man, and the rest of the audience simply followed suit.

Still, a performance needs a formal ending of the contract between audience and actors – a handshake, as it were. In *A Midsummer Night's Dream*, Puck says to the audience: 'Give me your hands, if we be friends / And Robin shall restore amends.' In Peter Brook's sublime production, the actors did just that: they left the stage, came into the auditorium and grasped the audience's hands. It was the most perfect resolution to an evening's theatre I ever saw.

Amadeus was a hit of a rare order. Even people who never went to the theatre, politicians, for example, felt they had to have been able to say that they'd seen it. Although the reviews were decidedly mixed, for all of us – and some of them were downright abusive about my performance – we were the talk of the town. At the next word run-through of As You Like It, *Greg Hicks, who was playing Silvius, said to me, by no means enviously, 'So you're famous now, I suppose?' It was nothing but the truth. We were all cheered, every night, but the ovation that greeted Scofield was extraordinary, an expression of fealty, or primitive, almost tribal, acclaim; he took it superbly, with a half-smile followed by a sharp, small bow followed by a graceful extension outwards of his arms, opening out the palms of his extraordinarily expressive hands in a gesture of benison. The public felt embraced and blessed. Contact with him on stage, night after night, was enriching in ways that even now I find hard to analyse. His death, thirty years later, hit me harder than I could possibly have imagined. I was touring in* Equus, *sitting in a taxi heading for the station to take me to Milton Keynes, the next venue on the road, when a text message from a friend appeared on my phone saying: 'So sorry about Scofield.' I felt as if I'd been punched in the stomach. Then the phone rang: it was BBC News wanting a reaction. I gave one, an inadequate, numbed one, then I called the* Guardian *and asked if I could write something more considered about him. They said I had two hours to write it. I did it on the train heading for Milton Keynes, and immediately emailed it from my dressing room in the theatre.*

Paul Scofield was the last of the theatrical Titans, a late flowering of that astonishing generation which included Olivier, Gielgud, Ashcroft, Evans, Redgrave and Richardson, and his death on Wednesday leaves the stage immeasurably impoverished. I say the stage, because, despite his Oscar for *A Man for All Seasons* and much distinguished work in other films and on television, he was above all a creature of the theatre, and no one who saw him treading the boards will ever forget it. He was such an uncommon physical phenomenon: tall and powerful, a fine figure of a man, but complex, even physically. Every inch of him seemed to be expressing contradictory things. His face was sensationally handsome – as a youth he would have been called beautiful – but there too there were contradictions: the soft sensuousness of his mouth denied by the sharp precision of his nose, his eyes often veiled, his brow imperious, his eyebrows endlessly mobile. His skin was astonishingly smooth and soft.

Perhaps the most extraordinary of his physical gifts, though, was his voice, an instrument like none other – an organ with limitless stops, from the mightiest of bass rumbles, through light tenorial lyricism, to falsetto pipings; he seemed to be able to sound several notes at once, creating chords which resonated to the most remarkable effect, stirring strange emotions. He would swoop effortlessly up and down the register, but always for expressive purpose, never for mere virtuosity. Given this exotic physical endowment, it is surprising that he was able to transform himself so completely. His Uncle Vanya and his King Lear within a few years of each other scarcely seemed to come from the same planet; and could it be the same actor playing the gloriously shabby, bedraggled Wilhelm Voigt in *The Captain of Köpenick* who would appear a few seasons later in the role of Oberon, all made of air and silver? Equally he had access to a kind of deeply human nobility best exemplified in his Thomas More. These transformations were of great virtuosity, but they never drew attention to themselves. He was unusual among English actors in that, however exuberant his assumptions might sometimes be, he was not an extrovert. Whatever he did had a profound charge of interiority within it. His performances owed nothing to any influence but were entirely original, many-layered and complex. With him, the inner workings of the character were made flesh. In the early 1970s I was an usher at the Old Vic and saw his Wilhelm Voigt night after night. I found myself deeply nourished by the performance. It was like gazing at a great painting and finding more and more in it: endless detail, sudden vistas of great depth, marvels of technique producing immense emotion.

In the light of all this, it may be imagined that I approached the prospect of acting with him with a kind of bliss mingled with dread. The play was *Amadeus*; he of course was playing the machinating Salieri, I was to be

Mozart. I was thirty, in the grip of almost uncontrollable energy which I scarcely knew what to do with, on stage or off. He was fifty-seven, two years younger than I am today, but giving a good impression of the Ancient of Days, with his magnificent silver head of hair and noble mien; the only bohemian element – the only clue that he might be an actor rather than a king, say, or a Nobel prize-winner – was his penchant for pastel-coloured shirts. In person, he was sweet, courteous, without any side whatever. He laughed easily, but it was evident that he was very shy, socially. He wore country clothes and smoked his pipe whenever he could. Once the formalities were over, we swiftly got on with rehearsing the play. He said very little, and was evidently wrestling with a very long part which was being constantly rewritten. I, on the other hand, seemed to be suffering from Tourette's syndrome, busily offering suggestions on every subject, including his performance. Scofield eyed me warily from behind his high-backed chair. In other words our relationship was pretty well that of the characters in the play, with the difference that I was play-ing a genius, while he actually was one.

I noted that his approach was to seem to sketch the performance in quite lightly, and then suddenly plunge in deeper, like an aqua-diver. He would emerge from these sudden immersions with another important new note in the character, which would then be incorporated into the role. How-ever it was that Paul contacted his inner life, it had nothing to do with the Method or any conscious seriousness of purpose. He simply sent the character for a swim in his own secret streams, the deeply hidden pools of emotion and fantasy deep within which I suspect even he knew noth-ing about. As the older Salieri, he had invented an extraordinary old geezer, wheezing and leering, a doddery comic fuss-budget, who then disappeared in the twinkling of an eye when the young Salieri stepped forward and the action of the play commenced. I was rather shocked by how much he seemed to be enjoying playing old Salieri – there was almost a quality of music hall about it. Acting with him in the rehearsal room was inspiring and paralysing in equal measure. I was desperately nervous and overcompensated by being too emphatic, shrieking and gig-gling over his lines. He bore it with great patience.

What he could not endure was the constant rewriting. One day, Peter Hall, who was directing, told me that he and Peter Shaffer had realised that there were a couple of lines necessary in a certain sequence in one of his scenes with me, and that they were going to give them to Paul.

During a break, the four of us gathered round the piano in the middle of the rehearsal room while the other actors sat around, chatting, having tea and so on, well out of earshot of our little group. Hall said, 'Paul, Peter has a small rewrite which – ' He never finished the sentence. Scofield said in a voice that was barely audible but of unimaginable intensity, 'I'm not. Learning. Another. Line.' Suddenly the whole room fell silent and the temperature turned to ice. Hall immediately said he was sure it wasn't really necessary, Shaffer started gibbering and I offered to say all the new lines myself. End of discussion. The veil of courtesy had been pulled away for a minute and one saw the massive power that lay behind the affable exterior. It was this power that underpinned every performance he gave. On another occasion, I was as usual solving the play's problems, as I saw it, and said, 'It just needs a line here,' and Paul roared, 'Not from me, baby!' And then he turned to me and added, 'You monster!', the word hurled at me like a thunderbolt. I felt duly pulverised, was actually shaking physically, but had the good sense after a suitable interval to go over to him as he fumed behind his high-backed chair and say, 'I've just got a few rewrites for tomorrow, Paul,' and he laughed and explained his anxieties and we started to know each other properly from that moment.

When we left the rehearsal room and got into the theatre, I felt him stretching and prowling like a panther in the jungle, sniffing the space out. He seemed, even during technical rehearsals, to be expanding. He started getting taller. When the audience arrived at the first preview, he seemed like a giant. I was physically shocked by the intensity of the public's response to him. They ached for him, they wanted to consume him entirely, every delicious morsel. I had no experience of this sort of thing and foolishly tried to tug him back into the relationship we had had in the rehearsal room. He would not tolerate it. He and the audience were making love and woe betide anyone who came between them. When I finally got the hang of it and attempted a little gentle lovemaking with them myself, he changed completely. He was more than happy to encourage a *ménage à trois*. From then on, for the remainder of the two years during which we did the play, there was a deep twinkle in his eyes, as we played the great game together in close communion with the audience. He plumbed the depths and soared to the heights of Salieri's tormented soul, but behind it all, somewhere, was that twinkle.

We got on wonderfully well without ever really spending any time together. Our relationship was unspoken, until one night on the stairs on the way back from the stage, he suddenly told me that he would never play Salieri with anyone but me. I swore the same to him. We remained faithful to our vows. I would see him from time to time, we wrote to each other, we did the play on the radio. He had no small talk, but then he had no big talk either. He did not live the usual semi-public life of an actor. When he wasn't acting, he retreated to the home where he lived in perfect domestic equilibrium with his beloved wife Joy. He didn't much like to leave the country, except to go to the Isle of Mull where, as everywhere else, he read and thought and nurtured his inner life. After a triumphant *John Gabriel Borkman* at the National Theatre, he seemed to have quietly retired. And then, about eight years ago, I asked him to take part in a gala I was directing at the Palace Theatre one Sunday night, and he duly stepped forward at the end of the evening, slightly frail, a little smaller than he had been, but still in majestic command of his great vocal instrument and his adoring audience. It was Prospero's farewell, and he filled that large auditorium with his unique music:

> But release me from my bands
> With the help of your good hands.
> Gentle breath of yours my sails
> Must fill or else my project fails,
> Which was to please. Now I want
> Spirits to enforce, art to enchant,
> And my ending is despair,
> Unless I be reliev'd in prayer,
> Which pierces so that it assaults
> Mercy itself, and frees all faults.
> As you from crimes would pardon'd be,
> Let your indulgence set me free.

I and everyone in the cast and all the stage managers and the stagehands surrendered to his spell. Perfect silence fell. And now that great voice is silent. It is hard to imagine another such voice being heard in our lifetime.

After Amadeus, *John Dexter, still breathing fire and spitting venom, was back at the National with one of the greatest triumphs of his career, which further confirmed his absolute mastery of the Olivier auditorium. But* Galileo *was a triumph for everyone, not least Michael Gambon, who suddenly emerged, as people sometimes do, overnight, as a major classi-cal actor. I had known him since 1969, when I was in the box office of the Mermaid Theatre, and he was the shy, sexy, funny boyfriend of the Pro-duction Manager's secretary, Lyn Haill. He dressed oddly: in a safari jacket, with a silk scarf tied round his neck, and his huge long feet encased in suede shoes. We used to pass the time of day together: he laughed so charmingly and naughtily and told the tallest stories. I was a rather self-conscious twenty-year-old who thought he knew everything and who knew nothing, but Michael talked to me as if I was the person he most enjoyed talking to in the whole world. When he became famous, he refused to give interviews. American* Vogue *was desperate to do a piece on him: they contacted me and offered me a lot of money to write it, so I phoned Mike and told him that I'd give him half. He agreed. A month later, I found that he'd cashed the cheque in favour of his son.*

He is known throughout the English theatre as, simply, 'Gambon'. Sir Ralph Richardson referred to him as 'The Great Gambon' – as if he were a circus act, Michael Gambon believes. The appellation declares both high esteem and familiarity. Within his own profession, he is the most loved actor of his generation. Love is not easily earned in a world as competi-tive and critical as that of the theatre, but he has it and has had it for as long as I can remember.

His public acclaim was clinched on a night in 1980 when his perform-ance in the title role in Brecht's *Galileo* brought the audience – including several critics – to its feet. This is still rare enough in the English theatre to have warranted a mention on the front page of *The Times*. The reviews repeated the standing ovation verbally. More than one of them contained the phrase 'a star is born', though they might more accurately have said 'recognised', since they had been acclaiming him, quietly, for a good ten years.

At the curtain call that first night, Gambon himself seemed distant, uninvolved. He clung to his fellow actors (I was one of them), until, inevitably, he had to take a solo call. He shuffled forward, nodded a slight acknowledgement, smiled his characteristic awkward grin, then shuffled back to the security of the line-up. We all trailed off back to our dressing rooms, which at the National Theatre give onto an inner well. Gambon appeared at the window of his dressing room. Suddenly every dressing-room window was open, and we all hung out of them and clapped and cheered him. He wept, not surprisingly.

In twenty years in the theatre, I've never seen anything like it. It was not, to repeat, very English. More than a great tribute to his performance, it was an expression of love for the man. And it was private. Actors sometimes applaud each other in public to show what good chaps they are, but this was different. Here, there was no audience.

On the face of it, both the love and the admiration are a little surprising. Gambon is a shy man, not a great socialite. He has charm and is a supreme raconteur, but he takes no pains to dominate a conversation, to dazzle. He reveals little of himself, and when he does, he is so startling ('the thing about me is I hate a lot of people') that one hesitates to investigate any further. He once told me that he needed advice on a very sensitive subject: would I come round his place for supper to talk it over? I arrived only to find half a dozen other people there. The subject, whatever it might have been, was never mentioned.

Despite the veils drawn over his most private self, there are many, probably countless, people who consider themselves Gambon's friend. He is most at ease with his fellow actors, and however large or central his role in a play, he always remains part of the group. He refuses to play at being a star, never makes public announcements, and hardly ever attends the award ceremonies at which he is so regularly honoured. Asked if he would ever like to run a company, his 'no' is instant and unnegotiable.

He genuinely dislikes fame. It has rendered him incapable of passing unnoticed in a pub or a restaurant. Not long ago he could go to the half-dozen pubs in his neighbourhood, visiting each one in a different persona, using a different voice – Scots in one, Welsh in another – telling a different story about himself. Not any more. Like it or not, he is very famous indeed, both from the astonishing succession of brilliant stage performances he has given since that *Galileo* and from his television performances – above all *The Singing Detective*, where, bedridden, his aching, flaking presence dominated the series that kept the nation, from palace to pub, glued to its sets.

He is more astonished by all this than anyone. Not that his career has been difficult: while training as an engineer, he spent every spare moment in amateur dramatics until, on an impulse, he answered an advertisement for the famous Dublin Gate Theatre run by the great Irish actor Micheál mac Liammóir – the man who had given Orson Welles his start. Gambon played a season with them before coming back to London, where he worked as a stage manager on Spike Milligan's surreal comedy *The Bed-Sitting Room*. Then, only a year after becoming an actor – and despite having audaciously auditioned in front of Olivier with a speech from *Richard III* – he became a founding member of Olivier's National Theatre Company. His fellow spear carriers included Derek Jacobi, Michael York and Anthony Hopkins. He progressed slowly through the ranks, acting in all the productions in that golden period of the English theatre, until, knowing that he must cut his teeth on a great role, he found himself in Birmingham playing Othello. It was then that some of his extraordinary qualities began to make people sit up: his massive stamina, a huge and apparently indestructible voice, and sudden and exquisite lyrical delicacy.

But he didn't return to the classics for some time, becoming instead the supreme interpreter of Alan Ayckbourn's bourgeois tragicomedies. He is not built quite the way classical actors are supposed to be. Though not short – 5'11" – his body lacks regularity. His great box of a chest – 'as deep as it is wide', in his own words – sits on top of legs whose shortness is belied by long tapering feet. His hands, too, are immense, with extremely long, delicate fingers. The contrasts thus afforded – massive weight and elegant, almost dainty precision – are perfectly embodied in a face that is big and open, but whose eyes and mouth are constantly expressing myriad intermediate emotions. The whole impact is of a humorous and subtle warrior, a giant who chooses to tease. A word from his mouth confirms the impression. Strong enough to ride Lear's storm twice a day on matinee days, or to take Galileo through his four-hour decline eight times a week in the most vocally hazardous auditorium in the country, his voice can have the same consistency as Ralph Richardson's: a kind of *mille-feuille* lightness that is almost literally delicious. And when this big man makes love, his voice is strangely affecting. At the end of the first production of Pinter's *Betrayal*, Gambon gave the final declaration of love a lyrical urgency, an almost Puccini-like golden melodiousness that hasn't been heard in the English theatre for many years. It wasn't until *Galileo*, in which he was an unexpectedly cast by the great actor-trainer John Dexter, that the range of the tragic was opened up to him. The danger, the anger, and the big shout that dwell deep inside him, fuelled his performances, which have redefined those heroes for the Eighties.

He has no imitators. Like Katharine Hepburn, what he does works only because it is he who is doing it. His rhythms, his inflections are so unusual that they would be thought mannered were it not that they come, not from a desire to impress, but from inner certainty. He was born in Dublin, and an occasional Irish vowel sound will seep into his speech, but he owes no more to his Celtic background than to anything else. He claims to hate the Irish – 'low, crafty, grasping people' – but as he says it, there's something sly at the corner of his eyes that makes you wonder whether you or perhaps the whole idea of national differences are being sent up. It's impossible to pin down why he should have endowed Eddie Carbone, in his triumphant revival of *A View from the Bridge*, with a kind of balletic grace, but somehow it made the final tragedy doubly affecting. He just felt it that way.

He seems, too, to owe nothing to any other actors. Laurence Olivier is the subject of some of his best stories, but if Gambon acquired the trumpets in his voice from Olivier, the orchestration is so different that you'd never notice. He speaks with awe of Brando and De Niro, but what he has taken from them is summed up in his dictum that 'You've got to be brave, haven't you?'

And brave, above all, is what he is – whether in the cockpit of the plane he flies in his spare time ('I like the power, the authority') or on the stage. I caught his Uncle Vanya in the last week of its run. I was startled by something he did in the third-act confrontation. At the height of his tirade against Serebriakov, he fell to the floor, apparently in the throes of a heart attack. Pumping his arm, he dragged himself to his feet and retired to the corner of the stage. I rushed back to see him and asked why? And how? 'I did it for the first time tonight,' he said. 'The scene needed it.' Chekhov doesn't ask for it, I don't know how one would ever think of it, but it was perfectly right, and at the same time was the single most audacious piece of theatrical invention I've ever seen.

He is the great original of our theatre.

Michael's naughtiness is well-known. It is of the same order as Paul Scofield's, the playfulness of someone who is so in command of what he is doing, that he is able to maintain his performance with perfect intensity while at the same time attempting to amuse his fellow players. In Galileo,

I played the Little Monk, a fiendish part, in that it's fully ninety minutes into the play before the character comes on, and then for only two unspeaking minutes, to reappear shortly after with a huge ten-minute aria of a speech. Dexter had told me that when I spoke, it must be as if I hadn't spoken for five years, a wonderful note which I could never convincingly fulfil; in fact, I always had a sense of failure in the part. It's a very exposed speech, containing the only persuasive counter-argument to Galileo's, and it needed tremendous focus. Galileo simply listens. As I started the speech on the first preview, and out of the corner of my eye, I noticed one of Gambon's famously long fingers slowly, over the whole course of the speech, unfurl itself until it was, by the end of it, erect, in an unmistakably obscene gesture. On the first night I gave him, as a present, a large matchbox, in which I had concealed a plastic hand, bought in a joke shop, filled with water and the fingers strapped down all except for one, which, as he opened the matchbox, emerged and stood erect. He always mentions this whenever we meet.

Gambon apart, one of the abiding memories I have of Galileo *is of that fine actor Andrew Cruickshank – in his time one of the great Ibsen actors, as well as Claudius to Olivier's Hamlet at the Old Vic, and later a national figure on television as Dr Cameron in* Dr Finlay's Casebook *– playing the small role of one of the grandees of the Church in the opening scenes of the play. Then, instead of going home, as he had every right to do (if you're finished in the first half you don't have to stay for the curtain call), he retired to his dressing room with a bottle of Glenmorangie and his favourite Kierkegaard text. Four and a half hours later, at the end of the play, he would emerge, to take his bow, but somehow – all that Kierkegaard, no doubt – he never quite got to the stage in time, meeting us all in the corridor on our way back to our dressing rooms, and not minding at all, just happy to be part of the company and in a theatre, working.*

I also acted in Ayckbourn's Sisterly Feelings, *again with Gambon, and Stephen Moore, Penelope Wilton, Anna Carteret, Greg Hicks, Michael Bryant, and Cruickshank: a real ensemble play, which also took full advantage of the Olivier stage, including a genuinely alarming moment in which I cycled down a steep grass hill at full pelt, generally knocking Anna Carteret into the front row. The possibilities for collective hysteria were all too many, and rather too frequently indulged. The staff director, that genial and deeply serious man Kenneth Mackintosh (Olivier's understudy* as Othello at the Old Vic and a fine actor in his own right), was livid: 'Sir Laurence would never have allowed it!' he would furiously tell us. And he was right. Something about the clockwork perfection of Ayckbourn's comic mechanism, with its perfectly plotted and infallible laughs, seemed to create a mood of anarchy among us, and all it would need was for Andrew to be facing the wrong way when the lights came up at the beginning of the play (easily done: it is very hard to get on in a blackout on the Olivier stage), and we were all on the brink of hysterical laughter. I like to believe that the audience never noticed. Michael Bryant was the worst offender, because his facial mask never cracked. In the picnic scene he would pour a glass of orange juice for me and say, perfectly audibly, I felt, though there was never any audience reaction, 'Hand that to the pervert.' This was the same Michael Bryant who, during rehearsals for As You Like It, when Sara Kestelman was getting into her stride, would hold up a large piece of paper with the words 'Too Jewish' on it. When it was my turn, the piece of paper would say, 'Too camp.' And when I performed all one hundred and fifty-four of Shakespeare's Sonnets one afternoon at the Olivier Theatre, there was Bryant in the wings, in his underpants, for some reason, with a placard saying '1/2'. No doubt he was right.

For many years, the Sonnets became my main connection to Shakespeare. That extraordinary event at the Olivier was a one-off, never to be repeated by anyone in his or her right mind. But they remain not only one of the most remarkable collections of poems ever published, but also one of the greatest accounts in the language, perhaps in any language, of amour fou. I have performed them across the world in various combinations, always essentially based on the highly controversial sequence by Dr John Padel (father of Ruth); I have recorded them, twice; I have broadcast them for the BBC, twice (one in the 1609 printed sequence, the other in Padel's); and in 2008 I did a shortened version – a mere eighty-four of them – in an event called There Reigns Love, commissioned by the Shakespeare Festival at Stratford, Ontario. The more I perform them, the less important it seems to me whether they tell us anything about Shakespeare himself, and the more remarkable they seem to me in their account of the psychopathology of love. Audiences in Stratford were astounded by their intensity of feeling, so powerful that in certain poems – towards the end of the cycle, in Padel's sequence – the verse, as in many of the later plays, threatens to break down completely. I performed them entirely from memory, this time – at the Olivier I had a book in front of me – and this also *had a transforming effect on my performance: as I said of* As You Like It, *in a sense, very little acting is required. The verse tells you everything, does it all for you.*

I wrote a piece for the Guardian *on the occasion of the BBC broadcast of the Padel version.*

Michael Kustow, then Associate Director of the National Theatre, telephoned me one day, nearly fifteen years ago, to ask if I'd be interested in performing a new version of Shakespeare's Sonnets. It was one, he said, which not only revealed an extraordinary, complex background story which seemed to account for some of the mysterious, half-submerged allusions in the verse, but – more importantly – made more sense of the poems as poems than any previous reordering. My head reeled, not just from excitement (these were sensational claims) but from ignorance. I scarcely knew more than half a dozen sonnets, and to be truthful, no more than the first lines, which seemed somehow to make up a sort of ghostly sonnet on their own:

> When I do count the clock that tells the time,
> Shall I compare thee to a summer's day?
> When most I wink then do mine eyes best see;
> My mistress' eyes are nothing like the sun.

They sat there, those one hundred and fifty-four poems, in their own separate volume, seeming to have little to do with the man who wrote the plays that are for me and every English actor the unavoidable mine down which we all must go sooner or later if we are to come to terms with our language, our craft and ourselves. But we know so very little about that man. Kustow's call offered the chance of dispelling some of that ignorance – maybe of meeting the man Shakespeare face to face.

I set to reading all one hundred and fifty-four poems as printed in the poet's lifetime, and emerged with some confusion, a confusion I shared with virtually everyone who has read the Sonnets through. To whom are they addressed? To two people at least. What is the betrayal spoken of in a number of them? Whence this overwhelming sense of rejection? What is the marriage so ardently desired?

It's impossible not to feel that somewhere behind these, for the most part unconnected, poems is some experience, a hidden story involving the young man to whom the majority of them are addressed, the woman to whom a smaller number belong, and the poet himself.

The young man and the woman are vividly characterised: he aloof, glacial, young, beautiful, aristocratic; she earthy, passionate, teasing, tormenting, dark-haired, dark-eyed. There is an interesting difference in the descriptions: though desired, she is excoriated for her temperament, her behaviour ('forbear to turn thine eyes aside'), even her face. He, on the other hand, is uncritically adored. Set down as a paragon, possessing every virtue, physical, intellectual, moral, he is never described, except, significantly, in the famous elliptical sonnet 'They that have power to hurt and will do none', in which his face is said to be inexpressive, his thinking inscrutable.

The person who jumps out at you from the pages is The Poet himself: feeling himself to be old, ugly, unloved, unworthy of love, tormented by base desires and crucified by ecstatic aspiration, passing through almost pathological states of emotional experience, to positions of defiance, resignation and, finally, tranquillity. All this glimpsed by flashes of lightning in a fog of confusion produced by impossible juxtapositions, impenetrable syntax, contemporary references and even, on rare occasions, very poor verse.

The sequence that Kustow had been sent was devised by a psychoanalyst and teacher of classics, Dr John Padel. Hypnotised, like so many before him, by the enigma presented by the 1609 edition, he became convinced that there had to be some unifying matrix, a way of looking at the poems that made a sensible whole. He started to find patterns in the separate poems, subtle unities of resonance, common metaphors. As if playing with pieces of mosaic, then standing back to look at the whole pattern, Padel saw not merely a general pattern, but a precise organisation of units within the collection.

It seemed that almost without exception the Sonnets had been written in groups of either three or four, and that these they made up single poems, to be spoken as one. The four-sonnet poems and three-sonnet poems were part of larger patterns – the first seventeen poems are four groups of four plus an epilogue; the 'Dark Lady' poems a sort of prologue of one group of three sonnets, followed by six groups of three, eighteen sonnets in all. And so on. Elizabethan fascination with numerology is well attested, but no one suspected it here. So what? Apart from antiquarian interest, what does it matter?

Firstly, Padel's sequence made sense of the poems from a poetic perspective; the groups hung together, illuminating each other. He had in effect discovered, as he claimed in the title of his book on the subject, *New Poems By Shakespeare*. Secondly, they enabled Padel to reconstruct the background story. Like others before him he identified Mr W. H. as William Herbert, eldest son of the Earl of Pembroke, and postulated a sequence of events whereby Shakespeare was commissioned by the young man's mother, the sister of the poet and soldier Sir Philip Sidney, to write a series of poems for the young man encouraging him to get married. From this commission grew a relationship, essentially that of poet and patron, which furthered the Countess of Pembroke's project of getting her son married, but also developed an intense dynamic of its own: the poet introduces his patron to his mistress, the so-called Dark Lady, and the two of them, to the poet's despair, have an affair. When this burns out, the poet and the patron resume their relationship; finally, it cools, but over a number of years Shakespeare continues to send Pembroke (as he now was) sequences of sonnets in which the central event becomes the war waged by the poet against time. His verse, he claims, will defy time's ravages. He was right.

Padel's work is an extraordinary illumination of a corner of the Elizabethan world: the relationship of poet to patron, and of verse to life. Only another scholar could refute or confirm it as a definitive context for the sonnets. For me as an actor, the order, right or wrong, offers two things: firstly, an astonishing dramatic text, previously only perceived as a series of lyrical or philosophical meditations; secondly, an insight into Shakespeare's creativity.

What started out as a commission, conventionally conceived and executed, became a personal experience of an overwhelming kind, in which art and life were in constant dialectical interplay. Shakespeare invents the young man, and reinvents himself, the 'I' of the poems. These creations then begin to lead an independent life, and the drama of Shakespeare's relationship with W. H., touching from point to point the actual but different reality, was worked out to its conclusion. Shakespeare found himself entering irresistibly into an imagined experience which brought him close to the very nature of beauty and love, probing – inevitably – the questions of time and self posed by love's simultaneous intimation of infinity and mortality. The poems celebrate this paradox and resolve it: they commemorate the experienced beauty and are themselves beautiful and enduring: they defy time and transcend self.

In all this, one sees the relation of the poet to reality. It seems characteristic of Shakespeare's art that he is able to empathise, to enter the mind
and heart of his creations to the extent that he almost obliterates himself.
It is an actor's method and the Sonnets – in this new version – reveal it
in its purest form.

*I had a powerfully personal response to the emotional states described.
What Shakespeare feels for the young man addressed in so many of the
poems was an uncannily precise rendition of the intense and often self-
lacerating feelings I had entertained for various unattainable young men
over the years. Intuitively, my view was that Shakespeare and Mr W. H.
never had sex with each other (they so often speak of distance, and of
inequality). But the poems chart an emotional experience that encom-
passes a great deal that is instantly recognisable to a gay man. I wrote
the following for the* Evening Standard, *which at the time (1990) seemed
to see me as their unofficial correspondent on gay matters.*

Was Shakespeare gay? This simple – if, until very recently, unthinkable
– proposition begs two large questions: what do we mean by 'gay', and
what do we mean by 'Shakespeare'?

Shakespeare is the unassailable fortress of our culture. Around his name
grew up, first, on a modest scale in the eighteenth, then, comprehensively
in the nineteenth centuries, an aura of godlike genius. All the splendour,
the grandeur, the despair and the exultation of human life seem to be
there. It was only the moral tone which was found wanting. No matter!
Here is Dr Thomas Bowdler, ready with his blue pencil, to delete the
offending phrases. There is, it is found, altogether too much of the sexual
element in the plays. This is suppressed, and pageant supplied in its place.

There is always, thank God, the love poetry, the exquisite, tender, and
largely chaste verse, guaranteed to bring no more than a slight blush to a
maiden's cheek. The Sonnets, for example, with their unforgettable first
lines: 'When I do count the clock that tells the time', 'When to the ses-
sions of sweet silent thought', 'Let me not to the marriage of true minds
admit impediments', 'O thou my lovely boy – ' Hold on. What's this? O
thou my lovely *boy?* These love poems seem – it's pretty unavoidable, in
fact – to be addressed, for at least two-thirds of the volume, to a young

man, in terms of growing passion. 'Lord of my love, to whom in vassalage.' 'A woman's face... hast thou, the master-mistress of my passion.' And the young man in question is being addressed directly, personally by The Poet – W. S. – the Swan of Avon – the Bard. Unnatural vice in the master-poet-philosopher of all time? Outrageous suggestion! Ignore it, as beneath contempt; or, better still, change the pronouns. He for she, her for him. Of course! It was all a terrible typographical error.

But of course it wasn't. And it's the only document we have that seems to be in any way autobiographical. 'With this key,' said Wordsworth, 'Shakespeare unlocked his heart.'

There is no doubt of the intensity of his feelings for the young man. The playful admiration, growing infatuation, anguished sense of unworthiness; pain of betrayal and final renunciation ('Farewell – thou art too dear for my possessing') chart the typical trajectory of the state of being hopelessly in love. The hopelessness comes, not from the fact that they are both men, but from differences in their circumstances: the object of the poet's passion young, beautiful, well-connected; the poet himself old (he was all of thirty-seven!), unlovely and a member of a despised profession: he was an *actor*, for God's sake!

However, we have to tread carefully before we make any categorical assumptions. Intense – cauterising – though the emotions may be, and focused so strongly on the physical beauty of the young man, do they really speak of sexual love? A large number of the remaining third of the sequence are addressed to Shakespeare's mistress, the famous and equally unknown Dark Lady, and the nature of these poems is quite different. They reek of sex, and the mixed emotions, mingling desire and disgust, which intense carnality so often brings. At a certain point in the (deliberately?) complicated sequence, it seems that Mr W. H. and Shakespeare's mistress have been to bed together, affording the poet some sort of masochistic pleasure. He forgives them both. This story, enigmatic though in some ways it seems, is the stuff of modern life: it could be the subject of a novel by Iris Murdoch.

But it still leaves unanswered the question: was Shakespeare gay? What we want to know, I suppose, is: did Shakespeare go to bed with men? Once again, we need to tread cautiously. The past, as L. P. Hartley famously observed, is another country: they do things differently there. Which brings us to the other question: what do we mean by 'gay'?

In the last twenty years, a great deal more research has been conducted into the nature of the Elizabethans' sex lives. One thing is clear: the idea of exclusive homosexuality, men or women who only have sex with their own kind, was completely unknown. If anything, desire of one man for another (there are few accounts of women desiring women) was regarded as a surplus, an overflow, of sexuality. Not content with women alone, some over-sexed men, Elizabethans believed, found it necessary to work out their libidos on other men and, indeed, boys, and this excessive appetite was understood and dealt with quite leniently. Sodomy was a capital offence, but the legal records of the time reveal very few instances of the law's penalty being exacted.

The romantic love of a man for man, or a boy, was something else altogether. Saturated as educated Elizabethans were in Greek literature, Plato and Homer, in the stories of the love of warriors like Achilles and Hercules for Patroclus and Hylas, of the god Jove's love for Ganymede or the philosopher Socrates for Alcibiades, they were acutely aware of the power of men's love for each other. This was part of life, part of human nature, and the myths defined and idealised this love, which is certainly a part, a large part, of gay love as we understand it. Was sex part of it too, as it is for us? The jury of scholars is still out on this. Maybe; maybe not. We just don't know.

Certainly the Elizabethan ideal of male beauty was very far from ours. The miniatures of Hilliard and Oliver reveal the softness, the flowing lines of men's clothes, emphasising their fine calves, their slim waists, their broad graceful shoulders. Codpieces glamorise their manly parts. Tumbling ringlets adorn their brows, earrings hang in their ears; they stand gracefully, pliantly. A feeling of androgyny hovers over them. But these men were soldiers, politicians, statesmen. The women, by contrast, have all their natural lineaments contradicted. Their breasts are flattened, their nether regions hidden under vast tents of dresses, their faces blocked out with make-up, their eyebrows plucked, their foreheads huge under the severe line of their wigs. No, the men were the romantic figures, without a question, and they responded to each other accordingly, in terms courtly and chivalrous, easily addressing each other as 'lover'.

And yet: this still doesn't mean that we should assume that they were 'gay' – involved in physical-emotional relationships with each other. A sense of each other's beauty is no guarantee that they had sex together. What it did mean was that sex was not compartmentalised, rigidly defined; it was all around them. And Shakespeare responded, as he responded to every impulse he ever had, with a dramatist's vividness. Like the Roman playwright Terence, nothing human was alien to him, and thus throughout the plays we find passages (Antonio in *Twelfth Night*, for example) where the love of a man for another man is given noble and powerful expression. The Victorians were right: Shakespeare's work contains the whole world. But, as Hamlet remarked, there are more things in Heaven and Earth than their philosophy dreamed of.

A Shakespearean leading role at the National beckoned for a moment. John Wood was playing Richard III, and when he had to leave the company to fulfil another engagement there was talk of my taking over from him. Olivier's film performance was still burned on my consciousness, but of course I longed to have a go at it. For one reason or another, the run of the play ended when John left, and the world was deprived of my Richard. Later I played the part on radio – an interesting challenge: how do you convey the hump? The experience taught me that I have nothing interesting to say on the subject of psychopathic regicides, but I also learned something about the nature of my own ambition. You can't even begin to play Richard unless you intend to throw down the gauntlet and demand attention. It's a part for someone who intends to be a contender. I found myself oddly reluctant to enter the ring.

Towards the end of 1980, my contract at the National was coming to an end. Elijah Moshinsky was directing All's Well That Ends Well *for BBC television; he asked me to play Parolles. This was irresistible. I knew, though, that they intended to keep* Amadeus *in the repertory at the National, and that I would have to talk to Peter Hall about it. Elijah gave me a piece of advice: 'Go in wanting nothing,' he said, then added: 'Don't try and play chess with Peter. If you think you're six moves ahead, he's twenty.'*

I had always had a very pleasant relationship with Peter, often visiting him in his office for little chats, in the course of which he had spoken with extraordinary candour about his work and his life. Once, he had asked me to play Montano in Othello. *'Who?' I had said. 'Indeed,' he had replied. 'And when your friends come to see the play, they will say, "Why did you take the part?" And the only answer you will be able to give them will be, "Because Peter Hall asked me to do it".' I asked for an hour or so to think about it, then phoned and said no. 'Ah well,' sighed the great pragmatist,*

'I had to try, didn't I?' I was sure our little chat about Parolles would be just the same. I booked an appointment with Peter, breezed in and told him that I'd been offered the job and that I'd like to go, please.

What happened next took me aback. A large tear rolled down his cheek. 'My dear friend,' he said. 'We must have failed you very badly. I thought you were happy here?' 'Yes, very happy, but – ' I spluttered. 'No, you have to go. Of course you do. But – may I give you some advice? – not till you've done a play-carrying part in the Olivier. Then you can go. Then you must go. But not before. How ironic, though, that you should come to see me at this very moment.' 'In what way?' 'I was talking to Tom Stoppard just before you came in. I've just put the phone down, in fact. I was asking him to adapt a play by Nestroy for you – you know who Nestroy is?' 'Yes, yes, he wrote Einen Jux will er sich machen. Thornton Wilder based The Matchmaker on it, didn't he?' 'Of course, I knew I could rely on you to know this wonderful writer. Well, I have just asked Tom to do a version of the play for you. To be done in the Olivier, with you finally carrying a play in this auditorium you have so made your own. In – let me see – ' he consulted his calendar – 'yes, in six months' time.' 'Peter,' I said, barely able to speak from excitement, 'this changes everything.' 'Does that mean you'll stay?' he said with a charming smile, sunshine breaking through clouds. 'Of course, of course. Of COURSE.' I skipped out, and a week or so later we signed the extension of my contract. Shortly after that, I had a very nice card from Stoppard saying that he'd seen As You Like It, and much enjoyed it, and I wrote back to him and said how much I was looking forward to the Nestroy. A week after that, I bumped into him at the Evening Standard Awards, and he said, 'Who's Nestroy?'

Which, of course, is why Peter Hall is such a genius at running theatres. The Nestroy adaptation turned up a year later as On the Razzle, with Felicity Kendal in my part (don't ask). I carried on with Sisterly Feelings and Galileo and, of course, Amadeus. And then, finally, I left, to play Verlaine in Hampton's Total Eclipse at the Lyric Theatre in Hammersmith, a play neither critics nor audiences seem to like very much, but which actors, directors and writers adore, and so it proved on this occasion. After that, I played the epically brilliant part of Lord Are in the world premiere of Edward Bond's Restoration at the Royal Court. And then I did J. P. Donleavy's own adaptation of his novel, The Beastly Beatitudes of Balthazar B, at the Duke of York's Theatre, in St Martin's Lane. This was my first play in the West End since The Plumber's Progress in 1975 with Harry

Secombe, and it felt like a triumphant return. Until the reviews appeared, that is. Business was not good (though there are people who think my Beefy was the apogee of my achievements as an actor, and who am I to quarrel with them?). So, inspired by a very elegant article Ian McKellen had written for the Evening Standard, *I suggested to the press office, as a way of whipping up business, that the paper might like a piece from me. Unexpectedly, they agreed. It was my very first piece for a newspaper. I had a rare old time writing it and took it with high spirits to my new friend Peggy Ramsay, the famous play agent. She read it, tut-tutting the while. Soon she came to a phrase in which I said that Donleavy was 'a bit of a Ming vase'. 'Have you ever SEEN a Ming vase?' she asked. 'They're very heavy. Is that what you meant?' I submitted a soberer, more considered version to her, and the* Standard *printed it without changing a word. I felt immensely proud, though now I look at it, it seems oddly naïve. I give it as it appeared on the page, headlines and all.*

HOW BEEFY AND BALTHAZAR BURST ON TO THE BOARDS

Actor Simon Callow reveals the enterprising story of how J. P. Donleavy's The Beastly Beatitudes of Balthazar B *came to be launched in the West End.*

The whole thing started one day in January when Patrick Ryecart – whom I'd never met – phoned me to say that he'd bought the rights of *The Beastly Beatitudes of Balthazar B* by J. P. Donleavy and would I like to play Beefy?

A friend of his, also an actor, was going to direct, and he'd said, independently, that I should play it.

I laughed, because five years previously John Dexter had asked me to play the same part, in a production which fell though. I'd never read the play – only the novel; but I thought that if the role was anything like as funny and outrageous as the character in the book, I wanted to play it more than any part I'd ever clapped eyes on.

So I said yes, of course. It turned out that Patrick had been cast as Balthazar in a later production which had fallen through too. Like me, he'd gone crazy for the character and the book. It's a lovely funny sad thing, as riotous, as bawdy, as ebullient as *The Ginger Man* but with a deep tender thread of melancholy running through it.

Pat had been deeply disappointed by the collapse of the production and when he heard that the rights had reverted to the author, he determined to get hold of them himself. Nothing was going to stop him playing that part. So he wrote to Donleavy.

Donleavy doesn't have an agent. If you want to do one of his plays, you have to get hold of him – which is easier said than done, because he lives in isolation on his farm in Mullingar, in the west of Ireland. The first letter was met with silence. Others followed over the next six months, all unanswered.

Pat nearly gave up hope. Then one morning, out of the blue – he was in his bath – the phone rang and he heard for the first time the halting but exact Anglo-American tones of the writer, suggesting tea at Fortnum's – not the first place one would expect to meet the creator of *The Ginger Man*, or the only begetter of Beefy (who would surely be more at home in some murky dive off Piccadilly about perhaps to start his third bottle of Glenlivet). But in fact, your man is a different creature altogether; delicate, courtly, fragile. Fortnum's was just the place.

Donleavy was enchanted by Patrick and agreed to sell the rights to him. It was an incredible coup. Patrick had bought the rights to a world premiere by one of the top-selling authors in the world. He was that unheard-of thing; an actor who owns a play.

But the idea of setting something up from scratch was daunting. Isn't that an awful lot of money? I asked. Peanuts, Pat said, it's a marvellous play, they'll be falling over each other to put it on.

Developments were astonishing. He'd tried several West End managers, who were rather cool. Coolness wouldn't do. It had to be passion and love. So he went to someone who'd never put on a play before, Naim Atallah, head of Quartet Books and Financial Director of Asprey's.

Atallah read the play, fell in love with it – and put up £100,000. Pat then went to Capital Radio, who own the Duke of York's Theatre. John Whitney and his board all turned out to be Donleavy buffs and welcomed the play with open arms. Now having the backing and the theatre, he went to an old friend, the producer Howard Panter, and asked him to manage the show. All systems go.

Then a big black cloud came into view. The director was obliged to pull out. Suddenly we were without the key person in the whole operation.

For the first time, I saw Pat daunted. There was no point in just getting the play on. It had to be done with love and imagination. And time was running out. We couldn't keep putting the Duke of York's off, and Pat and I couldn't keep ourselves available indefinitely. It was ridiculous. We had everything but this one detail – the most important of all. Then, that week, *A Midsummer Night's Dream* opened at Stratford to rave reviews for its director, Ron Daniels. They spoke of its magic, beauty and earthy laughter. Exactly what we needed.

We'd assumed that Ron wouldn't be available because of his heavy RSC schedule, but we checked nonetheless. He was. He came down overnight, having read the play and the novel, and loving both. Everything he said about the project delighted us. We signed him up and packed him off to Donleavy. Together they produced a version of the play which was quite different to the one we'd had all these months: richer, funnier, bolder – truer to the novel.

Ron had ten days to do everything: to work on the script, to cast the play, to work with the designer. When we started rehearsing, we had half a cast and half a script. The designers were working round the clock. The whole cast only got together to read the play a week after rehearsals started. Bits of script arrived daily, completely new scenes were put in, new characters introduced. It was a crazy time. Buoyed along by Daniels's good humour and sureness of touch, it was also creative in a way that rehearsals often aren't.

When Pat first said to me would I like to play Beefy, I said, if anyone else plays him, I'll picket the theatre. And I would.

Patrick was and is an uncommonly optimistic fellow. He was convinced that something would turn up and that the play would become an overnight success. He shared this view with Naim Atallah, who devised a dozen schemes to lure into the theatre what he thought was the play's core audience: yuppies. Nothing worked. But Patrick's conviction never wavered. He was sustained by his belief that one day Prince Andrew – the Duke of York – would come to the Duke of York's, and that somehow, magically, this would reverse our fortunes. It is true that the people who did come – by no means only yuppies – fell in love with the characters and were swept away by the language, which has a real champagne quality, and often came back for second and third helpings, but there were never enough of them. From time to time, Donleavy – Mike to us, by now – would come to see the show, dryly noting the divergences from the text ('I recognised a phrase or two from time to time and seemed to remember having written something like it once upon a time'). One night, on Patrick's insistence, the three of us went to a dubious club in Mayfair, where we were greeted at the door by mammiferous lovelies, naked from the waist up; downstairs, even more lightly clad maidens were romping around on all fours, pursued by middle-aged gents in their shorts. Patrick called for madder music and for stronger wine, I nervously sipped my Campari and soda, and Donleavy surveyed the scene, which could have come from any one of his novels, with fastidious interest, as he sipped cocoa, Patrick roaring his encouragement at the romping couples at our feet. This excursion cheered him up no end, and kept him going through another month of empty houses.

Eventually, Patrick's dream came true. Naim invited Billy Connolly to see the show, and Billy expressed an interest in taking over from me, which he did. I did not picket the theatre. Every penny that the management had lost during the ten months of my playing the role was recovered during Billy's eight weeks' tenure.

Among the very charming cast of the show my special friend was Sylvia Coleridge. When she died in 1986, the Evening Standard *allowed me to write a memoir of her:*

When people talk about the richness of English acting, they probably mean the brilliant young men and women, the wonderful character actors, the aged knights. But there is another layer of actors and actresses who are quite as glorious, those actors of marked individuality who never play a leading part, but who illuminate what they do with unique truth and distinction. One of these, Sylvia Coleridge, has just died. I am proud to have been her friend for the last few years of her life, and proud to have acted with her.

We met when we worked together in *The Beastly Beatitudes of Balthazar B*. It was a typical Sylvia Coleridge role: nothing, or next to nothing, on the page; but she made something so remarkable of it, that were she not as generous in her acting as she was in her self, one might have found oneself seriously upstaged by it. She played a dowager in Harrods, over-hearing the scandalous conversation of Beefy and Balthazar. She expressed her outrage by a roll (well, several rolls, actually) of those uniquely expressive eyes and much pantomime with a copy of *The Times*. In due course, Balthazar leaves the stage, and I, as Beefy, saunter over, in my navvy's boots, to her chair, where, in a few well-chosen phrases, I melt her into sunshine smiles. The smiles were something rather extraor-dinary. She had the great actress's gift of releasing radiance in increasing bursts of delight; her voice, a somewhat unpredictable instrument, was likewise able to strike a word with a shout of pleasure or a quite unex-pected growl.

She was always alive and full of play. One afternoon, she appeared on stage wearing a hitherto unglimpsed fox stole. Cheekily I said, 'May I say, madam, how much I admire that animal on your shoulder?' 'Oh do you like it?' Sylvia replied without hesitation: 'My husband shot it in the Scilly Isles.'

She used to pop down to my dressing room for a quick cig, or a glass of wine, or a vigorous discussion on the merits of the new Proust transla-tion. Her vocabulary was not without the occasional growled four-letter word, which somehow coexisted quite happily with the rest of her impeccable syntax and phrasing.

Bit by bit I picked up details of her life and background. Everything, it seemed, had happened 'a million years ago – before you were even thought of'. She was born in India, where her father was a general. She came to England when she was twenty, determined to be an actress, knowing no one except Norman Hartnell, who couldn't help her at all, of course, but who gave her a dozen dresses, and on the strength of those, she never stopped working for the first few years in rep (although, she claimed, she was always being sacked).

Her career was a bit of a mystery. I had seen her in various roles for as long as I could remember, but every time I mentioned one, the eyes would roll, and despair would set in. Nothing, it seemed, had ever been any good. Her acting days were over, she insisted, and every job was the last, but scripts arrived with gratifying regularity. In the last few years, she gave performances as etched and true as anything she had ever done: Mme Pernelle in *Tartuffe*, and the aunt in *Waste*, for the RSC; perhaps best of all was her wonderful performance on television in *Bleak House*.

The last time I saw her for any length of time was last year, when I took her with some friends to Cheltenham, where I was reading some poems of Coleridge. We had often talked about him – he was her ancestor by direct descent. In fact, I had agreed to do the recital because I hoped she'd be able to come. Though quite deaf by now, she followed with the keenest attention and her usual passionate engagement. Afterwards, we wept a little together; and then laughed a great deal as always.

I cannot doubt that in the nirvana to which – as an unofficial Buddhist – she aspired, she is weeping and laughing and delighting her fellow spirits; as always.

Sylvia was even more extraordinary than I was able at the time to write. She loathed the actress Elspeth March, with whom she was obliged to share a dressing room in The Beastly Beatitudes. *They had been girls together in India, and were great chums. But when they came to England at more or less the same time, Elspeth, being very pretty, was taken up by the beau monde, while Sylvia trudged around the provinces with her Hartnell trousseau; whenever they happened to meet, Elspeth would snub her. So when we told her with a triumphant flourish that Lally Bowers was leaving the cast due to ill-health but that her role would be taken over by Elspeth, she was unable to conceal her dismay. Stoically, however, she accepted that they must share a dressing room. The once exquisitely soignée Elspeth, now the size of a small cottage, brought a small, spiteful dog with her and a television set, which she watched throughout the show, while Sylvia struggled to keep half an ear on the play as it was being relayed over the Tannoy, at the same time working her way through the new Proust. Her visits to me in my dressing room were mostly to howl with rage against her portly new room-mate. We kept in touch after the show closed; our encounters were always rather heightened. Once over supper she told me that she had a technique for cheering herself up if she was ever low, and pulled a photograph of me as Beefy from her wallet. Quite soon after the show closed, she received a phone call from a hospital casualty department: an elderly gentleman claiming to be her husband had had an accident, but was now about to be discharged, and had given her as his next of kin, would she please come and collect him? She had left him fully forty years before, and they had barely been in touch since, but she dutifully went to collect him, installing him in her house in Notting*

Hill Gate, where she nursed him till his death two years later. They barely spoke to each other, she said. She herself died not long after. As a Buddhist, she asked to be cremated and to have her ashes scattered to the wind. We performed the little ceremony, and as we did so, a great gust of wind threw the ashes up into the upper leaves of a tree in the garden. We all went in to raise a glass to her, and as we were remembering her, her daughter's boyfriend, who had taken it on himself to hose down the tree so that the ashes descended, put his head round the door. 'Kate,' he said, 'the dogs are drinking your mother.' How Sylvia would have relished that detail.

Despite the bad houses for Balthazar, *my ten months at the Duke of York's had many incidental charms. In a way, it's like having a pied-à-terre in the centre of town: the stage door is permanently manned, and one can drop in with parcels or read a script or, indeed, write one. Inevitably, given the proximity of the theatres in the West End, one sees a lot of one's fellow actors, in coffee shops, on the street, in the theatre restaurants – Joe Allen and Orso, Le Caprice, Sheekey's, the Ivy, now (but not then) the Wolseley. During the run of* Balthazar, *I spent a lot of time with the very young Rupert Everett. He still is the very young Rupert Everett, though now fifty. I reviewed his autobiography,* Red Carpets and Other Banana Skins, *in the* Guardian *in 2006.*

The other day I bumped into Rupert Everett in the street. We had a cordial chat and promised to meet again, but we didn't. Since the heyday of our friendship we have become those well-known personages, 'Rupert Everett' and 'Simon Callow'. Twenty-something years ago we were Ru and Si, still in the throes of becoming. I am ten years older than he is, and when we first met, I was on the crest of a wave, theatrically speaking, while he barely had his toe in the water. Despite my advantage over him in terms of age and professional experience, he made all the running. He had failed to get the part of Rimbaud in a production of *Total Eclipse* in which I was to play Verlaine ('too queer,' the producer somewhat surprisingly said), and I'd run into him later and told him that it was only a matter of time, which was not particularly brilliant of me: he was extravagantly beautiful and possessed of a unique quality, both boyish and regal, which, though scarcely fashionable in the early Eighties, was too striking not to be snatched up somehow, for something, sooner or later.

187

It happened almost immediately, in fact, and when he triumphantly arrived in the West End with *Another Country*, which might have been written with his DNA in mind, he phoned me in my dressing room at the Duke of York's, just round the corner from his theatre, and we went out for some tea, and suddenly we were inseparable. It wasn't sex, though sex was the subject of most of our conversations; it was a very sweet relationship, based on the idea of us as young bloods in the West End, both given to romantic infatuations and excessive behaviour, a love of gossip, some mutual friends, and boundless *joie de vivre*. I realised early on that he was dangerously imperious by nature, and also that for a twenty-five-year-old he had had a rich and varied experience of life that made mine – which had not been without its colourful interludes – seem like a vicar's tea party.

Well, I didn't know the half of it. Our friendship arrives on p. 120 of *Red Carpets*, by which time he has already played Titania and Elvira, walked out of his public school aged sixteen, become a regular on the Earls Court gay scene, received the reasonably well-paid sexual favours of various kerb-crawlers, developed a nice little heroin habit, decamped to Paris where he has become best friends with Delphine the Brazilian transexual ruler of the Bois ('hers was a famous erection'), bopped with Nureyev, shagged Ian McKellen, been thrown out of Central School of Speech and Drama and found his true theatrical home at the Citizens' Theatre in Glasgow. I knew some of this, as much as he chose to vouchsafe, but Ru was not one for dwelling in the past: it was the future he was focused on – fame, fortune (up to a point), fucking and fun. Above all fun. Laughter was and is the music of his life, even more than applause or the whisk and thud of paparazzi bulbs; he has an almost fanatical loyalty to the concept of enjoyment, to the detriment, it might be argued, of his art, though to the great enrichment of his being; and for Rupert, as he makes clear in this continuously brilliant memoir, the best theatrical autobiography since Noël Coward's *Present Indicative*, acting is being.

It is a startling self-portrait – unapologetic but not in the least confessional, not analytical but in-depth – of a man, now middle-aged, who has done exactly what he has wanted when he has wanted to, and to hell with the cost. He asks neither for admiration nor condemnation; he did it his way. In the end, no doubt, it was that that doomed our friendship, his and mine. He did behave so very badly. Up to a point, bad behaviour is exhilarating, though I used to wince when he cast the unwanted cream from the chilli con carne we used regularly to have on matinee days onto the St Martin's Lane pavement, causing pedestrians to swerve and slip; it is when the bad behaviour is turned against oneself that it becomes right-eously unacceptable: after him begging me to come for breakfast after a long and very late dinner, and as I sat bleary-eyed in his front room at eight in the morning, it was something of a slap in the face to hear him answer the phone 'No, nothing at all – there's no one here and I'm bored to death.' His behaviour brought to mind the admiring comment about Alfred Douglas made to André Gide by Oscar Wilde: *'Aoa! Comme il est terrible!'* He has brought the same personal ruthlessness to his profes-sional life – 'I was a terrible monster', 'I behaved like a cunt', 'I was impossible' – but he is unrepentant: the film or play in question was no longer fun, or never was fun, and what is the point if it isn't fun?

Us goody-goodies are inclined to believe that it is the audience's fun that matters more than the performer's, but Rupert's commitment to his posi-tion is absolute and principled: in the end, for him, all that matters is that the actor should blaze with unfettered charisma. The moment he saw the film of *Mary Poppins*, a 'giant and deranged ego was born', and he knew, he says, that he must find a new personality to express it. Actually, it seems that his personality was fully present at least from the font; his grandmother pronounced him, from her deathbed, to be 'musical'. Whatever measures his hapless mother might take to counteract his latent tendencies only confirmed them: the Catholic Abbey of Ampleforth intro-duced him to drugs, sex and acting; a spell in Paris to learn the language led him to Delphine and the delights of the Bois, where he picked up, he says, only a rudimentary French sex vocabulary. Bent on 'world domina-tion', he then took himself to the Central School of Speech and Drama, hoping that they would teach him to act like Garbo; finding that he already knew how to do that, he left, and soon found his spiritual home at the Citizens' Theatre in Glasgow, where Philip Prowse conjured up Fellini-like visions in the Gorbals. The screen, however, was where he was inevitably headed, and much of *Red Carpets* is taken up by his adven-tures in Hollywoodland. But here too, he is ruthlessly uncompromising, refusing to make any of the concessions upon which that place is founded. By the time he came to make the British film *Dance with a Stranger* he had become 'a fully fledged diva in a frosty land where that crazy bird had become extinct'. He proceeded as if he were Elizabeth Taylor or Bette Davis. 'These people,' he says of a Hollywood funeral, 'were the symbols I adored, everything I loved about my job.' He immersed himself in their world and those who created the enchanted spaces in which they could move. For him Andy Warhol embodied 'the very essence of his time'. So it must have seemed as one bobbed along on the waves of excitement engendered by crystal meth and disco beat.

What no one could possibly have imagined was that this witty, wicked waif apparently off his trolley was observing it all, and remembering everything; nor that when he came to write it all down he would prove to have a dazzling gift for evocation and a witheringly sharp perspective on those lives he so admired and emulated. His two novels revealed a brilliant writer, but there, as he says, he was in Capote mode: here he is in more elegiac vein, with an inexhaustible Proustian fascination with the monstrous minutiae of his chosen universe and a deep nostalgic sense of loss. In perfectly etched vignette after vignette, he conjures up the lives and deaths of those of all ages and persuasions (many of them 'now forgotten') to whom he has been drawn, *monstres sacrés* for the most part, whom he bathes in affection and approval. He writes with moving restraint about the great love of his life, his dog, Mo. He is only forty-seven but he writes of a disappearing world of character and classiness; one to which, by implication, he belongs and from which he is now dispossessed. He is an acute social commentator, though politically somewhat conventionally apocalyptic. His idiom is the conscious stylisation of a Firbank; the highest of high camp. As is his life, though he is quite capable of enduring a celibate and hard-working year filming in Russia, or of visiting Africa and seeing through the charity cant to the real horror of what is happening. He is like one of those queens – his word for himself, brandished defiantly – who astonish everyone by fighting fierce and gallant wars: like them, he has lived his life on the front line, albeit in his case a front line awash with poppers and irradiated with glamour. *Red Carpets* is his despatch; shot through with a sense of his own absurdity, it is a superb and unexpectedly inspiring achievement.

Another Country *changed Rupert's life; he and it were the toast of the town. Balthazar, which had its passionate devotees, had no such impact on my life or my career. It was utterly at odds with the temper of the times, both bawdy and beatific as the title suggests, as well as being anarchic and nostalgic, in a way that I fully see could be thought to be reactionary*

– an exaltation of aristocracy and wealth. It was nakedly sexist, full of buxom tarts and lurid fantasies. From a dramatic point of view, the play was unquestionably imperfect, but the characters and the language were rich and joyous in a way that few characters and little language was in the early 1980s, and the deep and heartfelt vein of melancholy in the writing moved me greatly.

But I could hardly wait to go. For me Balthazar was the end of something. I had finally managed, after nine years of pretty well continuous acting, to exhaust my addiction to it. I simply had to stop. When I left the play in the summer of 1982, I felt liberated, not just from the eight shows a week – though I was beginning to go ever so slightly but quite seriously demented as we played night after night to a hundred or so desperately self-conscious individuals huddled in the stalls – but from my driven need to create another part, strut my stuff again, earn approval. There was, I knew, a life elsewhere. It seemed symbolic and right that to find it I should brush the dust of England off my feet, which I accordingly did.

Expanding

It was to America I went, with a small group of actors from the National Theatre, to be part of the initial season of the British American Theatre Institute (which lived with its rather silly acronym for a couple of years before becoming the British American Drama Academy, which still lives and thrives). We went to Santa Fe, still then an altogether uncommon place, not yet part of the extended mall which the American South West has now become. The light, the bald mountains, the mystical associations as well as the somewhat sinister proximity of Los Alamos, site of the first nuclear tests, took one as far away from the West End and the South Bank and the whole working world of the theatre as humanly possible. For the first time in my life I taught and directed, both of which activities forced me to stand outside of myself and think about what I had been up to for the last nine years. Greer Garson lived there, and all our work was done in the theatre named after her. (I had occasion while I was there to write to Gore Vidal, but got no reply; when I saw him later in London he apologised, saying that he couldn't bring himself to write to the Mrs Miniver Theatre.) After I had been in Santa Fe for a week or so, I had a letter from Peggy Ramsay telling me that Nick Hern had commissioned me to write a book. I shook when I got the letter, and I admit that I wept a little, too, then ran round telling everybody to whom the information would mean anything at all, as well as a baffled few to whom it meant nothing. This, far more than anything that had happened to me in my acting career, was genuinely beyond my most unbridled fantasies. Hern was head of theatre books at Methuen, one of the best drama publishers in the country at the time. I celebrated by going up in a balloon at dawn in Albuquerque and hung in the air, at that eerie and soundless moment when they switch off the engine and two currents of air hold you suspended over the world, and reflected that life could hardly get any better.

When you come down from the balloon ride, you end up in the town dog dump (DUMP DEAD DOGS HERE, a sign says). They then baptise you in champagne, a symbolism I greatly liked. For a while it seemed that I might stay in Santa Fe and form a company based on some of my very talented students. A millionaire was found to pay for it, but his enthusiasm drifted, our season ended, and no more was ever said about it. Back in Britain, I set to work on the first series of a deliciously original television sitcom, Chance in a Million, in which I appeared with Brenda Blethyn. Then I wrote the book, in a frenzy, in three separate weeks, one in France, one in Switzerland and one in Brighton, and gave it to Nick Hern, who encouraged me to cut the first three pages (imperishable prose about my family) so that it opened with the words, 'When I was eighteen I wrote a letter to Laurence Olivier', and then printed the book pretty well unchanged. When Being an Actor appeared, it caused a small scandal by opposing, in its last pages, the stranglehold of directors over the theatre. I knew that I was taking a risk when I wrote the book, first by making no secret of my homosexuality, and secondly by challenging what I called the 'directocracy'. No one even blinked at my coming out, but my polemic against directocracy caused a bit of a sensation. Michael Billington, in the Guardian, thought the supposed attack on directors was 'tragically misguided'; but the following day, in the same newspaper, Ian McKellen rode up like a knight in shining armour, to defend me and the book. The actor Dinsdale Lansden wrote a review in Plays and Players which feared for my future; and I got hundreds, literally hundreds, of letters from actors who felt that I had, as I hoped I would, spoken for them. The idea of actors reclaiming some autonomy was in the air; very soon afterwards, Kenneth Branagh started up a company of his own, as did Mark Rylance. As it happens, my purpose had never been to denounce directors. It was to remind actors that they were not just pawns in the hands of the grand-masters of the theatre, but artists in their own right, whose contribution – imaginatively, emotionally, intellectually – was essential to the process. They were the ones, after all, who made the word flesh, up there on the stage, or in front of the camera: their bodies, their hearts, their brains, their creative energies were the heart and soul of the enterprise. My war cry was not about doing down directors: it was to encourage actors to *raise their own game, be ambitious for their art, and not allow anyone tell them to shut up, as many directors, in those dark days, quite literally did.*

Publication of the book had many unforeseen outcomes. One day, I came home late at night to find a letter on my mat whose envelope was written in a highly distinctive semi-italic hand. It was from Sir Alec Guinness. I reviewed Garry O'Connor's biography of him, The Unknown Alec Guinness, *in 2002, in the* Guardian.

Knowing Alec Guinness – I have to stop right there. I didn't know Alec Guinness. We had a sustained and very rewarding acquaintance which was curiously complex and in some ways surprisingly intimate, but I would never dream of claiming that I knew him. Garry O'Connor's new account of his life implies that no one ever did, least of all his biographer, now making his second attempt to wrestle the old shape-shifter to the ground. The title of the book is exact – Guinness is and remains unknown; any suggestion that this book reveals him for what he was is misleading. But O'Connor's biographical inquiry is nonetheless deeply rewarding and entertaining for all that.

My own encounter with Guinness is a fairly typical one, but it shows some of what O'Connor has been up against. Like everyone else, I had been enchanted and astonished by his film performances, from *Great Expectations* and *Oliver Twist* on to the Ealing comedies and *The Bridge on the River Kwai* and *Tunes of Glory,* awed by his transformations and conscious of a curious intensity, an interior quality irradiating his work. From the late Sixties, I saw his work in the theatre – Sir Henry Harcourt-Reilly in *The Cocktail Party,* an Ivy Compton-Burnett curiosity called *A House and its Heritage,* and two plays by Alan Bennett – and here I was surprised, a little baffled, by his impact. A militant fan of Laurence Olivier, I was initially disappointed by the absence of visceral energy in Guinness's work; having recently discovered John Gielgud for myself, missed that great actor's mercurial thought processes. But I soon succumbed. The measured gravity, the detachment, the faint air of whimsicality should all have produced a muted impression, but they were, on the contrary, curiously compelling. The physical transformations in every case were complete, but not conspicuous: they did not draw attention to themselves, which had seemed to me to be the whole fun of the thing when Olivier did it – Guinness seemed to change alchemically, his metal altered in the crucible of his imagination rather than painted from a make-up box.

Vocally, too, there was an evenness of production, a careful turning of phrases, an ability to let thoughts hang in the air, which compelled in a very different way both from the great Romantic orchestral effects of Olivier – the trumpets, the violins, the cymbal crashes with which he coloured his voice – and the Mozartian babbling brook of Gielgud. There was nothing to excite the ear, but one found oneself listening very deeply. And then, most surprising of all, he would take you to some very strange place, a zone of the soul rather than any emotional or sensual or even mental place, and on these occasions the temperature in the auditorium would change palpably. In Bennett's *The Old Country*, a civilised meditation on loyalty and national identity, Guinness as a Philby-like defector to Moscow purred his way intelligently and interestingly, if a little soporifically, through the play, assessing the unexpected and unsought offer of a pardon and repatriation. Finally understanding that he had no choice, that he was being used as a bargaining coin in a diplomatic manoeuvre and that he must go home, he was left alone for a moment on stage, opened a drawer, took out a gun, looked at it, put it back in the drawer and left the stage. That's all. But the moment the gun was produced, something impossible to explain happened. The theatre was suddenly engulfed with dark energy, as if the wings of the Angel of Death had passed over us all. It became for a moment hard to breathe; one's stomach muscles tightened; the heart beat uncomfortably rapidly. Then Guinness put the gun back and left the stage, and everything went back to normal. (I know that this was not merely an overexcited extrapolation of my own because a couple of years later, when I first met that least mystical of men, John Dexter, we talked of Guinness and I mentioned *The Old Country* and before I said another word Dexter said 'I know what you're going to say: the moment with the gun. Terrifying.')

This sort of juju happened in *Habeas Corpus*, too, in Dr Arthur Wicksteed's final dance, a moment created entirely by the actor, against the express wishes, O'Connor tells us, of the author. It was a kind of Dance of Death, an odd deconstructed death-haunted music-hall shuffle which rounded off Bennett's brilliant play on a note of almost Expressionist ghoulishness that took the evening to a different level of theatrical poetry. Here was a formidable operator, attempting things that no other actor I had seen seemed capable of, or interested in; and yet he seemed outside the mainstream, unlike his friend Ralph Richardson, who also seemed to function on a somewhat mystical plane but who was more recognisably actorly. Beneath his demure exterior, Guinness seemed to be involved in the black arts; there was something priestly about his procedure, as if he were practising a ritual which would result in a moment of contact with strange powers. This was even true in the Compton-Burnett, where the affable character he played seemed to carry with him, behind the seraphic smiles and jaunty Edwardian manners, a curious and in some ways an inappropriate force. By now, of course, he was Obi-Wan Kenobi, though nothing that George Lucas's special-effects division could conjure up came within a mile of what the actor could manage by his own efforts on a stage.

In the summer of 1984 I received a card from Guinness (how had he got my address?). He had, he said, read the just-published *Being an Actor*, and he wanted to thank me for writing it, because it had made him feel that it might after all be worth carrying on as an actor. This card did not, he said, require a reply. It got one, of course, and from then on until his death sixteen years later, we were in fairly regular correspondence, and I doubt whether a month went by during all that time when I didn't get some communication or other in the unmistakable hand, each line shorter than the one before, like a surrealist poem, culminating in the final *Alec* (he unknighted himself for me at our very first meeting). My letters to him were on writing paper which was all the colours of the rainbow, which he seemed to find charming. Soon he came to see plays that I was in or which I had directed, and we had a number of meals, always at the Connaught ('when I have a little money,' he would say), generally in his room, though there was one alarming occasion when we dined in the Grill with Victor Bannerjee (Aziz in Lean's *A Passage to India*) and his wife. Mrs Bannerjee was full of nervous energy and obviously determined not to be daunted by the wood-panelled hush of the famous restaurant, or by the gravity of her host, and talked her way loudly through the menu, advising on what would be wise to avoid because of the season. 'I think you'll find,' said Alec, mildly, 'that all the food at the Connaught is edible,' but the atmosphere this remark created was anything but mild. Again, the Force was with us, and a locked, unbreakable silence of many minutes ensued until Bannerjee managed to find some item of small talk that got us going again, though the meal never fully recovered.

Generally, though, supper was in his room. He alerted me to the delicious fact that the room-service waiter, a Spaniard, had never been able 'properly to pronounce one's name' and that when he was entertaining guests, they would be surprised to hear the waiter ask 'Eberytin to your sassisfaction, Sir Alice?' At the first meal I had with Alec, the waiter obligingly asked this question, and as he did, Guinness caught my eye with a look of the deepest and most complicit hilarity. His smile was something extraordinary, a zygomatic manoeuvre of such perfect control that he was able to increase it continuously over minutes until he became all smile, a perfect mask of sublime amusement, in which his other features seemed to disappear. He was able to talk through this immense grin, which suggested that he had remarkable control of the muscles in his mouth. Control is the word that is unavoidable in speaking of Alec Guinness.

These dorm bean-feasts at the Connaught were substantial, many-coursed affairs, and the amount of alcohol consumed was prodigious, starting with cocktails, proceeding to wine, several bottles of it, red and white, continuing with Armagnac, then resuming with more wine, and finally, at about three in the morning, he would pad over to the fridge to produce a bottle of beer for the road. Throughout, Alec would puff away at cigarettes and talk in his measured way about his life. He did so with unexpected freedom, revealing deep hatreds (of Laurence Olivier, for example, or his mother) and profound loves – of poetry, mostly. He never spoke to me directly of any of the celebrated crushes to which he was prey, though occasionally he would write to ask if I knew how to get in touch with *X* or *Y* whom he had just seen in a play; these were invariably the tough, straight guys to whom (it was common knowledge) he was always drawn. I never knew whether he got in touch with any of them; he never referred to them again.

He spoke most beautifully and illuminatingly about other actors, in particular Charles Laughton; he knew from *Being an Actor* that I had an almost idolatrous admiration for Laughton which he shared. He told me details of their personal friendship in the Thirties, and then, when I told him a few things about Laughton's sex life (I was beginning to research his life for a biography I was writing) he astonished me by quite casually telling me that he, too, had engaged in sexual relations with men, but 'then one married and gave up all that sort of thing'. He received information about my emotional life, elicited by his polite enquiries, with

interest but without comment, though now and then he allowed his eyebrows to rise a highly expressive millimetre or two. He liked to talk about
people's sex lives, not in a salacious way, but more in a spirit of gossip,
though there was never any suggestion that he himself any longer had
anything to do with sex. Nor was there ever the tiniest suggestion that he
might have found me attractive; it was my vitality and my idealism about
the theatre that he liked, which brought out a certain tenderness in him,
as if anxious that I might be hurt and disappointed. But sex was definitely
not in the air.

Once, though, he described an occasion when as a very young actor he
had gone to stay with John Gielgud for the weekend; Olivier and his first
wife, Jill Esmond, were the other house guests, and the Oliviers had
decided to go back to London on the Sunday night. They offered Alec a
lift which, since he was not working till the following night, he declined,
and he saw a look pass between the Oliviers which meant only one thing,
which outraged him because, as he said, 'even when one was very young
and sort of pretty, John never so much as put a finger on one's knee.' After
the Oliviers had gone, Gielgud and he had another bottle of wine, and
went to their separate beds. The following night, Alec was standing in the
wings as Osric, and Olivier – Hamlet – sidled up behind him and whis-
pered into his ear 'So did Johnny put his thing up you or did you put
yours up him?' As he told me this, his rage, nurtured over fifty years,
almost shook him physically. 'He was vulgar beyond belief,' he said. He
didn't have much time for Olivier's acting, either: after any of his performances, 'one would rush back to the text because some line, some
perfectly unimportant line that one had never really been aware of, had
been given such prominence that one doubted one's ears. It was meaningless.' Interestingly, when he delivered the oration at Olivier's Memorial
Service, he cited that habit as characteristic of Olivier's genius.

Over our meals he gave me advice about film-acting ('When one briefly
had a certain power, one would always insist on a full-length shot in one's
first scene to establish the general statement one was making, and then
one could focus on detail') and toyed with thoughts of roles that he might
yet play on stage. There was a kind of part that he longed to play but
which seemed not to exist: fantastical creations, like the Abel Drugger
with which he had had such a success at the Vic in the Thirties, but also
poetic, moonstruck. 'One had a sort of gift, a rather small gift, for clown-
ish parts, for innocents. There haven't been any possibilities in that line

lately.' It was hard to envisage the seriously stout gentleman opposite me, brimful of alcohol with a fag hanging from his lips, undertaking any such light-footed role, but then he would make a moment's mental contact with the image in his mind and there it would be, on his face, in his body, in the room with us – his harlequin, an exquisite creation as light as a dragonfly's wing. But then he would lose contact and the vision was gone, and he and his body sank heavily back to earth. On several occasions I tried to interest him in roles – Tiresias in *La Machine Infernale*, Dr Knock, the crazy old drama teacher – female – in Penelope Fitzgerald's *At Freddie's* – but he gracefully deflected them all. Then one day he left a message on the answer machine asking me to direct him in *A Walk in the Woods* but I didn't get back to him till twenty-four hours later, when he told me rather airily that he'd got someone else. This, as may be imagined, is fairly high on a list of regrets of a lifetime; but the swiftness of his withdrawal of the proffered possibility was absolute.

That was one of the occasions on which a silence fell between us – that dreaded silence known to everyone who ever had any dealings with Alec. Letters went unanswered; one could never get him on the phone. The silence was broken, typically, by the completely unconnected gift of something – on this occasion, an original cartoon done by Gary Cooper when he was in the trenches during the First World War. Or it might be a confidence suddenly vouchsafed, as when he wrote to me to tell me that he had just seen *A Passage to India*, and that as the lights had come up he had vomited in shame at his own performance as Professor Godbole. There were two seriously difficult moments in our relationship: once, in a moment of emotional and physical exhaustion, I wrote asking him to recommend a retreat. He wrote back a twenty-page letter, a sort of Good Monk Guide, with detailed and witty observations about the sort of spiritual service one could expect in each establishment, which monks liked to talk too much, where the food was excessively spartan. It was a positively Epicurean approach to the spiritual life, which gave perhaps a small clue to that side of Alec's existence. Needless to say, I did nothing about it, emotional and physical circumstances having changed, and there was another long silence. The other problem was when he invited me down to Petersfield to write the book I was about to embark on. I would never see him or Merula, he said, there was a little cabin at the bottom of the garden where I could write, meals would appear invisibly on the doorstep and only if I should ever feel in need of companionship would I ever meet them at all.

It was impossibly daunting. I should never for a second have been able to forget that mighty presence at the other end of the garden path, and I declined, feeling rather feeble. I had a sense of having been tested, and having failed. From that moment on there was a diminution of our friendship, though he never ceased to come to see my performances and occasionally dropped me a card. I sent him a present for his eightieth birthday, which he acknowledged, but not too warmly. (That was partly, too, because he loathed receiving anything.) But I *had* failed him; I was alarmed at the thought of taking our relationship deeper, of coming too close to his orbit, of being under his control. Another bar to its development was my general horror of the telephone, a medium of which he was a supreme master. He intensely disliked the answer machine, and mine was never off, and that was against the rules. At an early age, it seems, he had created an elaborate code of conduct by which he led his life, as arcane as the rules of Versailles or the sixteenth-century Spanish code of honour; its provisions were known only to him, but woe betide anyone who unknowingly transgressed them.

One card from him contained a request not to cooperate in any way with Garry O'Connor when he came to write his first biography of Alec. I obeyed. The book, when it appeared, was a broken-backed affair, but one could see why. O'Connor is the author of one of the very best theatrical biographies ever written – that of Ralph Richardson – but here his hands were tied; his heart seemed not to be in it. When he came back for a second attempt, I talked to him, as did many other people who had not been helpful while Alec was alive. He has woven these oral testimonies together in a way that lends the book a very interesting texture: he is in constant dialogue with others, with the facts, with theories, trying to make sense of this peculiarly elusive phenomenon, both as man and as artist. As in his Richardson book, though without the personal encounters with his subject which made that book so electrifying, he has let his quest dictate the form of the book. He is in a constant state of discovery, Det Supt O'Connor, Head of the Theatrical Unsolved Crimes Division, in pursuit of the thespian Moriarty, whose diabolic (or in this case, perhaps, divine) cunning makes him so hard to pin down. He has uncovered some fascinating new material – particularly about Guinness's war, in which he fought under his mother's maiden name, assuming, as O'Connor would have it, yet another new persona – but the thrust of his inquiry centres on two matters which are in fact one: sex and identity. He is determined to prove that Guinness was actively gay, and that he was not what he appeared to be.

As far as the sex is concerned, it is perfectly reasonable to assume – as he told me – that he was homosexually orientated, but that he decided not to live his life that way. There were probably lapses, and his feelings found other forms of expression, sometimes rather foolish ones: supper *à deux* as a substitute for, or a sublimation of, sex. It is the readily recognisable situation of a repressed gay man of a certain epoch. But O'Connor's problem is that there is no evidence whatever of any actual sexual activity. There is a rumour about an arrest in the 1940s, when Guinness allegedly gave his name to the Police as Herbert Pocket; and Angela Fox reports her husband Robin having got Alec off the hook some time in the 1950s. Neither is authenticated. Otherwise, nothing whatever. O'Connor talks a great deal about Alec's double life, but since he knows nothing about the hidden side of it, it becomes both repetitive and unenlightening to bang on about it. It would indeed be fascinating to know what Alec did and with whom, but we don't, and there's an end to it. Except there is no end to it in the book. (I am inclined to think Christopher Good is quite right when he says, in the book, that Alec enjoyed being speculated about sexually; perhaps it gave him a sort of vicarious sex life.) The issue of personality, which is of great interest in any biography, but inevitably central in that of an actor, especially one so multiphrenic as Guinness, is pursued with equal doggedness, as if to have a public face were a lie, as if we didn't all conceal our innermost desires and impulses behind the carapace – consciously fashioned or not – of personality. 'Constructive deceits,' O'Connor calls Guinness's manoeuvres, feeling that he has somehow found him out.

However, despite this aggressive line of questioning, a good deal else is thrown up of great interest in which Guinness's real originality is made manifest. His background, so powerfully described in his first volume of autobiography, *Blessings in Disguise*, is considered at length, in all its Dickensian detail – the terrifying stepfather, the solicitor dispensing the monthly allowance from an unnamed benefactor, the doubts as to the identity of the real father, the louche and drunken mother. The very particular nature of the young actor is well evoked (although analysis of performances tends to predominate over description or evocation, which pushes us a little in the direction of the semi-semiotic, where everything signifies something, and nothing ever simply is anything). But O'Connor

201

is keenly aware of the nature of the acting enterprise that Guinness was slowly identifying for himself, his unusual sense of character, his uncommonly economical transformations (I was in the dressing room with him on the last night of his *Merchant of Venice*, which provoked one of his most remarkable physicalisations, and watched him dismantle his Shylock by removing two pieces of Blu-Tack from behind his ears – 'Jumbo ears,' he said – and wiping off a little eyeliner). Above all he identifies Guinness's thrilling capacity to embody thought: to harness mental power.

'An actor needs a slightly mystical approach to the stage,' he said at a relatively early period in his career, 'you can't force yourself on the character.' O'Connor very skilfully shows how his personal confidence grew and grew during the war when, as Commander Cuff, he had charge of a ship; at the same time, he was adapting *The Brothers Karamazov*, which reveals the depth of his literary enthusiasms, and indeed his aspirations as a writer himself. It was clear after the egregious disaster of his second, post-war Hamlet that 'the specifically English challenge of being a classical stage actor' was not going to be his path (though there were yet to come Richard III, Shylock, Macbeth); instead he was working towards a sense of character which, as O'Connor says, had more to do with being than with doing. In a wonderful phrase, *Time* magazine's anonymous profile-writer said that Guinness's 'essential gift is not for creating characters but existences'. His characterisations seemed to transform him to the very marrow, altering his chemistry. Much later, George Lucas, watching rushes in which Guinness had been accidentally socked on the jaw, saw his face pass through a series of different characters, 'all in a split second, starting with Obi-Wan Kenobi and ending with Alec, with about a half-dozen completely different characters in-between'. This is, to coin a paradox, assumption from within.

His talent was perfectly suited to film and in an astonishingly short period of time, he was widely spoken of, by the mid-Fifties, as the most famous British actor in the world, and possibly the most famous actor in the world full stop. That cannot last of course; as with Laughton, star character actors always peak quickly. The more brilliant, the more diverse they are, the sooner they dwindle into supporting actors. By the mid-Sixties he seemed to have started the slow withdrawal from acting that lasted until his death in his early eighties; he increasingly took on roles because he thought he should, and then at the end he seemed relieved not to have to do it any more. He wrote to me crowingly about taking hols, and then more hols after the hols.

Did he enjoy his life, one wonders? Can you enjoy life if your life's task is one long working-out of the dilemma posed by your childhood, a process which demands a supreme and continual exercise of will? Alec certainly took pleasure in things and people, but the forces of rage and resentment and shame which were held bottled up inside him with the lid tightly screwed on must have constantly threatened his peace – hence the structure he created for himself with his wife Merula at its centre. It is a sad consequence of his self-denigration that he felt impelled to denigrate what was his, which meant that both Merula and his son Matthew were often publicly put down; but the extraordinarily tender note that he left for her to be read after his death is incontrovertible proof both of his love for her and his awareness of how heavily he had dealt with her. Her ache to join him as soon as possible after his death is eloquent testimony to her profound connection to him.

Guinness's very publicly affirmed religion has always been a source of fascination and some merriment – 'a certain very holy person', wags called him – with a suspicion of some faint hypocrisy somewhere. But it seems to me, and it seems to O'Connor, that he was fighting a lifelong struggle for mastery of his soul, and that Catholicism helped him in that struggle. Not many actors engage with that battle. Whether organised religion is a useful way of working on the inner spirit is not for me or for anyone to say, but at least Guinness acknowledged that his immortal soul was the very stuff of his acting. The translucency of so many of his performances is evidence of it, but his awareness of the dark, the engulfing dark within him, is equally responsible for the crushing power that he so often brought to his work. Garry O'Connor's openness to this aspect of Guinness has resulted in a theatrical biography which goes far beyond the reach of most such books, and is his best book so far.

Another unexpected outcome of the publication of Being an Actor *was that I was asked by Claire Tomalin, who had just read the book, if I'd like to review books for her at the* Sunday Times. *I said I would; and I've reviewed books more or less uninterruptedly since then (1984). The second one I did for her was a book by Simon Gray,* An Unnatural Pursuit, *in 1985.*

Simon Gray is one of those writers whose popular image bears little resemblance to his work. One goes to the theatre expecting a Simon Gray Play, urbane, incestuously bitchy, with a central star role which knocks everyone else into the ground. Instead one gets extraordinarily complex ensemble pieces full of surreal humour and devastating visions of loneliness, defeat and despair. It is true that the social world and the overall tone of the pieces, with a couple of exceptions, remain the same from play to play, though no more and no less than those of Chekhov – with whom his finest play, *Quartermaine's Terms*, can well stand comparison. In the same manner, and almost equally fine, is his latest play, *The Common Pursuit*, whose production by Harold Pinter is the ostensible subject of the present volume. In fact, the lasting impression of *An Unnatural Pursuit* is of the author himself, with a brilliant cameo portrait of Pinter, and a number of sharp and savage observations about the business of putting on a play thrown in as a bonus.

The bulk of the book is a work-journal. He starts with the completion of the play ('I numbered the pages, packed and shaped them into a completed-looking pile, toasted myself with a further gulp of whisky and a few more cigarettes, gloated. This, for me, is the only moment of pure happiness I ever experience in the playwriting business…'), then follows its career through the stages of casting, rehearsal, performance, failure to transfer, and closure. It's a vivid picture of those particular horrors, the sad series of compromises as you decline from your initial bright dream of the play: not being able to get this theatre, that actor, those dates; the mysterious failure of companies to gel, of rhythms to quite take hold; the wilful blindness of certain critics and the regrettable tendency of the public to listen to them; the terrible brevity of the run if the play doesn't transfer – so much talent and work and passion squandered. All this is accurately and wittily described. But the book is more remarkable than mere reportage. For one thing, the playwright's-eye view is a unique and inherently frustrating vantage point; second, the playwright in question is Simon Gray. By the end of the book we come to know him very well indeed.

'Actually, he's not nearly such a pain as his self-portrait would have you believe,' says Pinter in his Foreword. No indeed, but *pain* is nevertheless exactly the word: not that inflicted on others, that undergone by himself. The wildly funny accounts he offers of his paranoia, power-mania, anxiety and doubt simply heighten one's sense of it. Smoking like a beagle, his veins throbbing with booze, he pours his nightly confessions into the tape recorder, a haunted, haggard, positively Dostoevskian figure. *En passant*, he offers much lucid analysis of his play and the processes that are leading to its realisation. But at any moment, in the midnight stillness of his study, speculation is liable to run riot: why are his actors behaving like talentless buffoons and/or obstreperous Marxists? Why does Harold Pinter wish to exclude only *his* photograph from the programme? 'I do actually feel very passionately that the play was written by me, I am the author, and yet the only people who are going to appear in the programme are the actors and the director, with the author, the only begetter, not visible.' After a restless night, he becomes convinced that one of the actors has acquired a lisp. 'I formed a plan to watch Nick Le Prevost's lips like a hawk, and the moment I saw or heard the lisp, to alert Harold to it. He could take it from there... I do think the chap who plays Stuart shouldn't have a lisp. Or a club foot or a hunchback. At least without giving me a chance to rewrite the text.' This is madness, of course, but it is the divine madness that makes the author of *Butley, Otherwise Engaged* and *Quartermaine's Terms* an infinitely darker, more passionate, less rational artist than the waspish boulevardier of the critics' report.

There are two areas of legitimate interest to which the book doesn't address itself: the actual writing of the play; and why, given an excellent cast and a masterly director, it didn't quite work. Mysteries, both, no doubt. What you do get is the lowdown on the playwright's relation to the production, and a full-length soul-sketch of one of the best living practitioners of that art: in the second section of the book, the Gray of the work-journal is supplemented by the even darker Gray of *My Cambridge*, one of the occasional pieces reprinted in the present volume. (The other pieces are the classically hilarious *Flops and Other Fragments*; an appreciation of Leavis; and two pieces about cricket, upon which I am neither qualified nor about to comment, except to be duly awed by the figure of Lopez, the infant off-spin bowling wizard.)

My Cambridge is an astonishingly bleak account of the author's academic career, culminating in his years at Cambridge, where his ambition, triumphantly achieved on his own admission, was to be the very thing his harshest critic might accuse him of, 'a fluent fraud'. Every anguished and hilarious word of this piece and indeed the whole book refutes that accusation. Death and demons swarm over its pages, held off by fags and booze and love and many, many wonderful jokes. But the sombre note echoes through: even Lopez killed himself, in the end.

When I wrote the review, I had just met Simon, and that was another result of the publication of Being an Actor. *I wrote about our friendship in the* Guardian *after his death in 2008.*

It seemed to many of us who loved Simon Gray – and perhaps it even seemed to him – that he might perhaps be indestructible. God knows, he had tried hard enough to destroy himself, but his body survived savage assault after savage assault as he returned, reckless and debonair, to the attack. When I saw him a couple of weeks ago for what I now know with infinite sadness to have been the last supper (rather a good title for a Gray diary, come to think of it), he looked as well as I've ever seen him look: bonny, clear-skinned, relaxed, with a little Greek sun still sitting on him. Some years ago, when he had just emerged from intensive and very much touch-and-go multiple surgery, we had dined together at his then favourite restaurant – there was always a favourite restaurant, adhered to with passionate loyalty, until it fell, as inevitably it must, from favour – and there he sat, at the exact table, in fact, where he had so recently collapsed after taking the sip of champagne that his doctor had expressly forbidden and from which he had been rushed to hospital. Some few weeks of intensive care and several near-death experiences later, he looked wonderfully well and fresh and youthful, and I had commented on this. 'Where it really shows is in your eyes,' I said. 'You mean you can see them now,' he replied, and surrendered to wheezy paroxysms of yelping laughter.

Those were the days, of course, of unbridled smoking, an activity out of which a great deal was now demanded, now, that is, that drinking was off the menu. As far as I know, he never once touched a drop of alcohol after the operations on his kidney and liver: the connection between drinking and mortality had been vividly demonstrated to him, and he had no desire to die. But like some mad scientist, he refused to believe in the destructiveness of anything until he had seen its results with his own eyes, proved it beyond a shadow of a doubt. And I'm not sure that he ever fully believed that cigarettes were his undoing. His relationship to them, so well and hilariously documented in the diaries, was not sensuous, like Ken Tynan's, nor emotional, like Pinter's, but somehow intellectual. Popping the cigarette in and out of his mouth, he seemed to be having a querulous conversation with it, testing it, challenging it: like many of the conversations we had over the years, where he would pick at some proposition one had lightly advanced, prodding it, probing it, becoming exasperated, outraged, appalled, before eventually collapsing into helpless hilarity in which all controversy dissolved and disappeared.

In earlier years, when he was still fuelled by unimaginable levels of alcohol – mostly champagne, but after a certain point all comers were welcome – the laughter didn't always materialise. Ignition point could be very low. At our very first meeting, after he had written me a disarmingly generous letter about my first book, I had ordered the wine before he arrived, and said that I hoped that Gamay would do. 'No it will NOT do,' he said, with alarming force, 'as it happens I think Gamay is the most disgusting, repulsive wine in existence. I loathe Gamay.' After this thorny matter had been settled, with some difficulty, he immediately became funny, generous, easy. But it was a sticky moment. On another, much later occasion, after an out-of-town preview of his own production of one of his plays, we had supper with our mutual friend, the play's producer. Simon was not happy because an important cue had gone wrong in the first scene of the play, after which he had repaired to the house manager's office to brood and smoke and drink (and write: a new play, in fact), so supper afterwards was somewhat electric. He asked for comments, which both the producer and I were careful to pad with entirely genuine praise, slipping in the odd reservation like a Bob Martin's tablet embedded in a pound of steak for a dog. There was a sex scene which was not going too well. We both commented on this, and I wondered whether this or that or the other might not be tried. 'There's no point, because the actor has no sexuality.' I questioned this, at which he snarled, 'We all know about *your* sexuality – all too fucking much about it, in fact.' I stammered that I intended no sort of criticism, that the show was, in fact, quite brilliant, but in certain small ways – unimportant ways – it could, perhaps, be better. 'Everything could be better,' he raged. '*King Lear* could fucking well be better.' At which he said he had had enough, and abruptly left the restaurant, to be driven furiously off to London. The next morning he called and said that he thought he might have been a little intemperate the night before and that, by the way, there was a screenplay in the post with a role in it that he'd like me to play.

It turned out to be that television masterpiece *Old Flames*, in which Stephen Fry played a father-to-be hallucinating, as he waited for the birth of his child, about a school contemporary (me) whom he had once bullied. Though it was not at the time seen as typical of his output, the weirdly morphing screenplay was quintessential Simon Gray. He was thought of, especially in the 1980s, as a sort of high-level boulevardier, the Marc Camoletti of the Common Room. But though he was indeed a master of sophisticated dialogue (in life as much as in his plays), the phantasmagoric held a central place in his life and in his work. This propensity was, initially, perhaps liberated and even exacerbated by alcohol, but it outlived the alcohol, and in fact came triumphantly to centre stage in his great sequence of diaries, which reveal his almost Dostoevskian capacity to descend at an instant into delusion and paranoia: except that of course, Simon being Simon, the nightmare, though hatefully real, is always wildly comic. It was the phantasmagoric element in his idol Dickens that he valued above all others, the endlessly transmogrifying metaphors, the fantastical distortions, the elements of the grotesque, all underpinned by a great central humanity: and this was what characterised so much of Simon's work – in a different key, of course, from Dickens's, and on a different scale, but still recognisably the same. It was what we both loved in Dickens, and what I loved above all in Simon and his work. Conversation with him was often free-associatingly surreal, hilarious and slightly dangerous.

It was this dimension that was so rarely explored in productions of his work. Of course, there were in his output straightforwardly well-made plays, but many more of them were predicated on an awareness of the oddity of things when viewed from another angle. Dickens had a word for it: 'mooreeffoc', which is simply 'coffee room' seen from the other side of a glazed door. I believe I introduced Simon to this coinage, but he jumped on it: it was what he was about. His sense of the sheer strangeness of things was acute; perhaps the greatest character he ever created, Quartermaine, so sublimely incarnated by Edward Fox in the original production, is a kind of Holy Fool, hardly able to connect with the outer world. Often this perception lent a dark dimension to his thinking. Insanity often beckons his characters. I acted in his play *The Holy Terror*, which is the most extreme example of dislocation in his work, in which not only the protagonist but the play itself seems to be having a nervous breakdown; it was universally detested by critics, though it still seems to me to be a fearlessly exploratory and deeply felt work.

The other side of his disorientation was his acute sense of wonder at simple things, which is again a common thread in the diaries, some of whose most remarkable pages stem from loving, even enraptured contemplation of the ordinary, culminating so movingly at the end of the last one in his joy at being given an extension of life by his surgeon. Though outwardly a typical, cricket-loving, somewhat fogeyish, doggedly non-PC middle-class Englishman of his generation, he never quite felt himself to be entirely part of the normal, the ordinary world. Before that first meeting of ours, describing himself as a 'topographical imbecile', he had asked for a map of where we dining. The restaurant in question was in New Row, off St Martin's Lane, in the very centre of the West End where so many of his plays had been triumphantly performed, but despite the map he had the greatest difficulty in finding it. In truth, he entirely lacked a map for the world in which he worked, and was never a member of any of the unofficial clubs which are the central organising principle of British society. He had no skill at self-promotion. He raged against this, but he was resigned to it.

Friendship was his mainstay, and his life was genuinely blighted by the loss, at regular intervals, of some of his greatest friends, many of them well before their allotted span. The early death of Alan Bates grieved him profoundly. Alan was his thespian alter ego, and they adored each other; often at the end of a meal I was having with Simon, Alan would drop in for coffee or a brandy just for the sheer pleasure of spending a few extra minutes with him, and it was extraordinary to hear the two men in duo-logue, like a man's conversation with himself. Though Simon was not necessarily the first person you'd go to if you were in trouble, he was unstinting in his interest, enthusiasm, appreciation and advice about any professional matter, always the first person to read anything I ever wrote, likewise sending me everything he ever wrote, draft after draft, charac-teristically typed with triple spaces, manuscripts monstrous to handle, but irresistible to read. His last dramatic masterpiece, *Little Nell*, about Dick-ens and Ellen Ternan, was given short shrift by the critics, but it will come back and be properly recognised, in all its dark, nightmarish complexity, its sense of things falling apart and the centre not holding, as will his as yet unproduced but entirely extraordinary Dionysian fantasia *Hullabaloo*, and then perhaps he will at last be understood for the truly original fig-ure that he was, both in life and in art.

The last and most completely unpredictable result of publishing my anti-directorial jeremiad (as it was now perceived), Being an Actor, *was an invitation to direct an opera,* Così Fan Tutte, *in Luzern. I had already directed in the theatre: it started more or less by accident in 1983 when my old friend Snoo Wilson (whose play* The Soul of the White Ant *I had acted in at the Bush, as described elsewhere) lost the director for his latest play,* Loving Reno, *also at the Bush. He suggested that he might direct it himself, but for some reason this made them nervous, so I proposed that we co-direct it, which we did, with very happy results (we were nominated by the* Sunday Times *critic James Fenton as the Best New Directors of the Year). As it happens, it was virtually the end of Snoo's career as a director, and the beginning of mine. It was apparent that he had no appetite for the multiple roles that a director has to perform – sergeant major, psychoanalyst, perfect audience, problem-solver, team leader, cheerleader, seminar-leader,* leader *– and he gradually sat back in the trance-like state adopted by most writers in rehearsals (half reliving the writing of it, half longing for it to be the way they imagined it would be, impatient of and bewildered by its present transitional stage), while I got on with it. It was the beginning of a long working relationship between us, which I described in an article in the* Sunday Telegraph *on the occasion of the first night of my production of Snoo's play* HRH *in the summer of 1997.*

Snoo Wilson is one of the great unregarded originals of the British theatre. His work is rarely, too rarely, seen in the great subsidised theatres, though it is often epic in scale and richly deserves an outing; audiences there don't know what they're missing. Ideas and history are his territory, and he takes them several rounds in the ring. If Tom Stoppard is the intellectual ping-pong champion of the world, Wilson plays rugby football with the mind. He is quite incapable of writing an ordinary play. (Or an ordinary novel. *I, Crowley,* his latest, is a piece of brilliant self-deconstruction, the Great Beast explaining himself in lapel-grabbing prose; it comes complete with goat's tail dangling from the book's spine.) He is the least autobiographical of writers; or if he is, I'd rather not be his psychiatrist. It could be said of all his plays that whatever their nominal location, they really take place inside the skull of the human race.

There the conscious and the unconscious intermingle, and time itself exists in simultaneous strata, crackling across the synapses. Historical figures – Aleister Crowley, John Dee, Conan Doyle – co-mingle with ancient Babylonian gods and blokes who've come to fix the plumbing. He has no interest in imitating the surface of life; instead the work grows out of his restless pursuit of history and ideas. Historical personages rise up before him, blocking his path. Dodging nimbly about, he throws his net over them, finally encaging them, kicking and shouting, within one of the idiosyncratic structures that he calls his plots. There they are debriefed of their ancient wisdom and forced to confess their wickedness; often they are confronted with similar creatures from another age or culture.

The spectacle can be terrifying and pitiful. It is always very funny. And it is wholly novel, always challenging the limitations of what can be attempted in a play. For this reason his work has not, till now, anyway, entered the mainstream. He has not been fashionable. His plays do not express the Zeitgeist, they do not present recognisable mirror images of our life and times. To their critics, they are tales told by an idiot, full of sound and fury (plus a few jokes), signifying nothing.

To those of us who love them, they are magical mystery journeys, laced with wisdom and poetry, deeply farcical, releasing wild laughter and sometimes tears; through them stride strange mutant figures, crazed, amorous monsters, puffed up with vanity, abject with desire. They are the creations of a man who has gone burrowing into some pretty odd tunnels, and come back, covered in mud, with golden nuggets between his teeth. They come from the Other Side. Snoo is the fully paid-up shaman of the Theatre Writers' Union. I first met him in 1975 when I was cast in his play *The Soul of the White Ant*. I had been doing a West End show called *The Plumber's Progress* with Harry Secombe; the moment I read Snoo's play, tasteless, recklessly imaginative, essentially theatrical, I knew it was the perfect antidote. But it wasn't just outrageous. Somewhere, behind the ribaldry, was a huge and rather moving compassion.

The central character of the play, Mabel, played by a young and brilliant Lynda Marchal (now Lynda La Plante, world-beating author of *Prime Suspect*), had killed her houseboy, with whom she had been having a somewhat unusual affair: thinking it wrong to consummate with a married man, she has had him relieve himself on the other side of the room into Tupperware containers which she has been dutifully storing in the fridge behind the bar.

Enter Eugene Marais, the famous South African anthropologist (and author of, *inter alia*, *The Soul of the White Ant*), long dead, but now resurrected into this obscure bar, a walking cadaver, covered in mud, eyes staring out of their sockets, worms wiggling out of his pockets and ears. He makes for the jukebox, which bursts into a spontaneous rendition of Fats Domino's 'Blueberry Hill', after which, somewhat revived, the corpse sits down at the bar and engages in largely incomprehensible conversation with the phrenology-obsessed journalist Pieter de Groot. He disappears, and the murder of the houseboy is covered up, but meanwhile the girlfriends of de Groot and his police chum Van der Merwe, having taken a dip in the river at the very point where the men have emptied the semeniferous Tupperware, have fallen pregnant. Re-enter Marais, now impeccable in a white suit. As before he makes for the jukebox; again 'Blueberry Hill' sings out. As Marais passes the girls, he touches their stomachs. Their periods start. Curtain. It was hilariously, outrageously amusing; but it was also full of mystery and tenderness and a most unexpected sense of pain. Once seen, it was not easily forgotten.

The author, on acquaintance, was perfectly normal to look at, though there was something odd about him. Tall, but seemingly planned on an even larger scale, he had the look of someone on whom a hod of celestial bricks had fallen at an early age, and he was still trying to work out what had happened. His hair was green, red and yellow. In physiognomy almost Ancient Roman, heroic in profile, his handsome features betrayed, as they still habitually betray, an expression of intense attention to inner voices speaking in strange tongues. This rapt concentration on aetheric communications was broken from time to time by explosions of nearly orgasmic mirth, wave on wave of spluttering delight. 'What? What?' he would gasp as the joy spread. Our relationship was informed, at that time, by mutual wonder: neither of us could believe that the other had gone quite so far out on a limb in our respective arts. His writing and my acting fitted each other like a glove; we were both then intent on exploring the wilder reaches of the human condition.

I started my career as a director seven years later with his play *Loving Reno*, a saga of Chilean incest and bad magic. We co-directed it, though after a while he lost interest in the mechanics of staging and the processes of actors and contented himself with offering guidance and inspiration. It was a wonderful partnership, and we dubbed ourselves not co-directors but Co-Optimists (after the great end-of-pier troupe of the Twenties). The latest Co-Optimistic venture is *HRH, or, David and Wallis in the Bahamas*, an account, scurrilous but scrupulously researched, of the wartime misadventures and Nazi fraternisation of the ex-King and his American bride, events which have until very recently been suppressed; it is at the same time a deconstruction of the Greatest Love Story of the Century, and a hellish vision of two people trapped in a sort of time-lock with nowhere to go and nothing to be. It is wickedly funny and somewhat tragic and as tight as a drum, Snoo in Racinian mode, strictly adhering to the unities, Aristotle meets Agatha Christie. It addresses, as everything he has ever written does, history, in this case a particularly murky moment in the story of our times, and indeed that of the House of Windsor. This is Co-Optimism at its world-beating best and will, I believe, at last introduce Wilson to the wider world.

Alas, HRH *didn't quite hit the jackpot, despite the witty elegance of Amanda Donohoe as Wallis Simpson and a bagpipe-playing, ukelele-strumming Corin Redgrave as the Dook. (In my account of Snoo, I omitted to mention his thespian gifts: he gave a definitive performance as the Dolphin in Virginia Woolf's* Freshwater, *in which the other roles were played by Eugène Ionesco, Alain Robbe-Grillet and Nathalie Sarraute. Snoo was effortlessly at ease with this group.) At the time of* Reno, *I was conscious of the cynical smile on people's faces when I announced my new career as a director, so much so that when I returned to the fray, at the Offstage Theatre in Chalk Farm, in 1985, I felt obliged to explain myself. The piece is rather innocent, my first excited impressions of directing.*

I never said we could do without directors. Honest, I never did. In *Being an Actor* I wrote, rather movingly, I thought, about what one demands from the director, how much one needs him, and how little he can expect in return. It was his power that I denounced, the structure – which I called the directocracy – that places him at the summit of the theatrical process, and ensures that the art of the theatre becomes, by means sometimes subtle and sometimes naked, the execution of his will. Everything would be different, quoth I, if the economic relationship were to change, and the actors hired him rather than the other way round.

And so it comes about that I am directing *The Passport* by Pierre Bourgeade at Buddy Dalton's Offstage Theatre. My friend, the gifted actress Anna Korwin, came to me with the play, we sent it to Buddy, and then we set about casting the other role (and luckily got the quite remarkable Peter Bayliss). I then gave an account of what I thought the play was. In a sense, I auditioned for the actors. Had they not agreed with me about the nature of the play we would have parted: that is to say, I would have gone. In the event, they bought my vision, which was not exactly what leapt off the page. Most people who read the play have been critical of certain aspects of it: what I proposed was that – as seems to me not infrequently to be the case – the apparent weaknesses of the piece were actually its essence and its chief attraction.

All too often, directors, it appears to me, go to great lengths to achieve unity where diversity is the very nature of the work, or to rationalise what is essentially non-consequential. In brief, I felt that the play was a kind of nightmare: the characters are trapped in the twists and turns of a capricious plot. To realise this view of the play, an excursion into the murky realms of Symbolism and maybe even Expressionism (dread thought!) was required. Expressionism is a word which brings a prayer to the lips of the pious and has become merely pejorative. It takes fearless actors rich of resource and bold of means to bring it off; Anna and Peter were two such.

I hope the foregoing absolves me of apostasy, as if the Pope were suddenly to start selling contraceptives. I have, in any case, directed before, in tandem with my friend and co-optimist, Snoo Wilson, at the Bush Theatre, and very enjoyable it was. But different. One so quickly forgets what it felt like to be on the other side, in much the same way that to drivers the world is plagued with pesky pedestrians who deliberately try to prevent one from simply getting from A to B, to the benefit of all, until they leave their cars at home and become themselves pedestrians, at which point the world becomes a nightmarish place swarming with four-wheeled macho brutes hell-bent on killing every human thing in sight in their crazed desire to get from one unimportant place to another. Why don't the actors know their lines? I find myself asking. Why are they systematically misinflecting every phrase? How can they allow themselves to stand THERE, where they can't be seen? Above all, why can't they remember their own inspired inventions from yesterday?

The thing one forgets is just the sheer bloody difficulty of acting, the paraplegia which overcomes the actor as he strives to recompose his psychic structure. As a director you gaze on the proceedings with a mixture of pity and helplessness until you begin to consider what help you can offer. Simple things, first. Good humour, energy, unfailing interest. Then a kind of osmosis can start to occur, whereby you feel what the actor is going towards, and can either put in words for him what it is he's beginning to do, or even suggest a shape that might lead to a sensation that might release something. You develop a sense of the kinetic energy that the stage can liberate. If the actor moves two inches to his left, he becomes vibrantly present; two inches to his right, he disappears. So, by suggestion, you can offer the actor short cuts to his destination.

But the greatest task of the director is in the articulation of the style. One of the most remarkable directors I ever worked with was Jean Jourdheuil, who created *Melancholy Jacques*, a piece about Rousseau I did a year ago. Only after the production had opened and he'd gone back to France did I realise that he'd never given me a note, as such, never suggested I do this or that. He had simply defined the intention of the production over and over again, in a hundred various ways: what the play was, how it worked, what we were hoping to release in the audience. The moment I grasped those things all problems simply became problems of execution. In the same way, on this play, *The Passport*, I'm trying to express to the actors the organic principle of the piece, and to some extent the organic principle of the characters, but in such a way that those principles, and not my impositions, dictate everything that they do: so that their work is their own, and so that my work, the actual staging of the piece, can constantly be challenged by reference to this objective thing, the principle of the production.

Once that has been established, we can behave how we like, I can leap up and show them what I mean, give them line readings – do everything you're supposed not to, because they can shout me down when I transgress the production's principle. And oh the joy, the joy unconfined, when that organic connection is made, and the acting starts to flow, a live and dangerous substance. When that happens, it's both moving and wild, the anarchy of creation itself, when the actors burst the integument of their own personalities and become the conduit of great forces.

The most cherished compliment I received at the time of *Loving Reno*, Snoo Wilson's play, was from the author and co-director. He said, 'I didn't know you could ask so much of actors.'

There is no limit.

The late Peter Bayliss, who played the customs officer in The Passport, *was one of the grand eccentrics of the British theatre. Stories about him were lovingly circulated by his fellow actors. Cameron Mackintosh wanted him to play Doolittle in a revival of* My Fair Lady. *Peter had no agent, and suggested to Cameron that they might meet and have the discussion at the Soda Fountain at Fortnum and Mason's. He said that he went there often, and that he would as usual be bringing his dog. When he arrived, he had no dog, but when he ordered, he asked for a bowl of water for the dog. The waitress asked where the dog was; Cameron told her just to bring the water, which she did. Cameron opened negotiations. '£1,000 a week,' he said. 'Sounds very good to me,' said Peter, 'but I'll have to ask the dog.' Which he did. 'I'm afraid the dog says no,' he said after a while. By the time they left, he'd got Cameron up to £5,000. When he and I met to talk about* The Passport, *he told me how much he admired* Being an Actor, *his favourite book of all time, he said. I asked him how he liked to work. 'Oh, I like to be directed,' he said: Tyrone Guthrie, that genius of blocking, was his idol. So when we started rehearsing, I explained my interpretation and gave him detailed moves. 'What are you doing?' he said. 'You're taking my performance away from me.' I apologised and said that I was only too willing to incorporate any suggestions he might have. What would he like to do? 'I dunno,' he said, 'you're the director.' Somehow we escaped from this vicious circle and got on with doing the play, but not before he told me that he was going straight from the theatre to Waterstone's, where he would move all the copies of* Being an Actor *from the non-fiction to the fiction shelves. 'You're terrible, you are,' he said. 'Who do you think you are? Max Reinhardt?' He tortured Anna Korwin with similar mad mind games, but every day he developed more and more exactly in the quite extreme direction I was keen to explore. We opened, and his extraordinary performance was rightly acclaimed: huge, dense, very Russian, very disturbing, everything I had hoped for. Eventually Pierre Bourgeade, the author, came to see this mad production of his little play. He adored it, he said, the design, the lighting, the production, everything. As for Bayliss, he was astounded by his performance – 'bouleversant' – and begged to be allowed to meet this great actor, this genius. I took him to the dressing room, which I found to be locked. I knocked, calling out Peter's name. 'M. Bourgeade LOVED the show, Peter. He wants to congratulate you.' Eventually from deep within, Peter said that he didn't want to meet the author. He wanted to go home. I cajoled, I begged, I shouted, with no effect. 'At least let Anna out, Peter.' She had translated the play, as well as having given a very good performance herself. At last, as if we were under siege in Beirut, the key was turned in the lock and the door opened long enough for Anna to be ejected, then the door was locked again. He never did meet Bourgeade. After supper I was walking home, and bumped into him. 'I wouldn't have known what to say,' he said, amiably. He kept working almost to the day he died; in his will he left instructions that his ashes were to be flushed down the lavatory.*

Peter was the second replacement in the role in The Passport. *The first actor was Vladek Sheybal, who had been wonderful in Wajda's early films. He was, in his own Polish way, a match for Bayliss in the eccentricity stakes. He put in an urgent call to me while I was in the dress rehearsal of a play that I was acting in just before starting on* The Passport. *I rushed to the phone: 'Yes, Vladek?' 'Simon, you know our play? I've been thinking about it. Don't you think it's rather thin?' 'In some ways, Vladek, but I believe that by doing it the way I've proposed to you it won't seem so.' 'Hm. I still think it will seem thin. Do you know Chekhov's play,* The Three Sisters?' *'I do, Vladek.' 'You know the big scene between Masha and Vershinin?' 'I do.' 'Don't you think we could just slip it into our play?' 'Don't you think someone might notice?' 'Oh, we change the names, of course. Do you like my idea?' 'Vladek, I have no time to discuss it, but no, I don't think it would work and I don't think it's necessary.' 'Ugh!' It was as if I had stabbed him. 'Very well, I see you're going to be difficult. I think we should terminate our relationship now. Goodnight.' The second actor was my friend Vernon Dobtcheff who discovered at the end of the first read-through that for tax reasons he had to leave the country that very evening. And so we got Peter.*

The play whose dress rehearsal Vladek had interrupted was Manuel Puig's Kiss of the Spider Woman, *which remains almost my favourite experience in the theatre. This masterpiece is a two-hander: my fellow actor was Mark Rylance, fresh from his definitive Peter Pan at the Barbican. We played at the Bush Theatre – my last appearance there, in fact. This piece was written in 1997 to celebrate the theatre's twenty-fifth anniversary.*

My debut at the Bush was in a transfer from the old Soho Poly of Snoo Wilson's *The Soul of the White Ant*, expanded to full length with the addition of a lurid scene by the roadside during which I was required to quaff a cocktail in which a variety of salads and a small umbrella floated in a liquid looking and indeed tasting very much like calamine lotion; it was called a Pink Flamingo (or 'Punk Flamungo' as my character, the knobble-knee'd Jo'burg journalist Pieter de Groot, would have said). The play was full of the rough magic for which the author is so justly famous, and it was my introduction both to the Fringe – of which I was flatteringly held eventually to become, for a while, the King – and to the Bush, which became my spiritual home, theatrically speaking, for some years. At that time, the theatre was at the beginning of the long journey from high-spirited chaos to ruthless efficiency and matchless production values at which it has now arrived. Though the journey was right and inevitable, there was a certain charm to the chaos, to the informality, of those early days, and it was still then possible for me to wander into the office with a play in my hand and ask to be allowed to do it and a month later we would be on.

The first time I did that was with Richard Quick's one-man show called *Juvenalia*, in which the right-wing Roman satirist was supposed to have slipped through the time warp to harangue the audience for some seventy-five minutes in a DJ, in verse, under a revolving glitter ball on a stage made up to resemble a seaside cinema. Strange to relate, the show worked, both artistically and commercially. As part of the deal, I had agreed – my arm hardly needed to be twisted – to play Princess Anne in David Edgar's parody of *Equus* (*Hippos*, it was called) as part of *Blood Sports*, a collection of four short plays on politico-sportive themes. This also worked. One that didn't work was my Charles Bukowski show, *Ejaculations*. It would have been wonderful, I have always believed – the original politically incorrect man, Bukowski wrote like an angel, a sort of hobo Jeffrey Bernard. We had tried valiantly to get hold of the author for permission, but on the first day of rehearsal the director Rob Walker walked in with a telegram in his hand which simply read: 'Absolutely not. Bukowski.' We never found out why. This was perplexing, and also vexing, but only mildly. We just moved quickly along to the next thing.

Matters were beginning to get rather more serious by 1982. Simon Stokes, Jenny Topper and Nicky Pallot now formed a directorial triumvirate, and were slowly transforming the place into what it has since become. Everything at the Bush was still done on a shoestring, but it was a shoestring of infinitely expandable dimensions. For *Loving Reno*, Grant Hicks designed an ambitious set which was simultaneously an airport lounge, an amphitheatre and the inside of a cranium. It was hugely complicated and strange, fashioned out of materials begged, borrowed but very rarely bought. It was installed to an impressively high level of finish – as it had to be; sets at the Bush were inevitably submitted to very close scrutiny, with the audience only inches away from the stage. There was no question, in those days, of any limitation on the hours that the actors or the theatre staff would work; as a production came close to opening, all outside life, any attempt at regular meals or sleep, was abandoned, and an increasingly hag-ridden team, sustained largely by roll-ups and pints from the pub below, would doggedly ensure that the latest vision was realised in that tiny little black room above the pub.

The pub itself really was, in those days, a pub, run by stout Irish Tommy and his incomputably large family. He and indeed all of them were robustly indifferent to what was actually going on in the room above, though perfectly friendly and delightful to all of us who worked there. The local clientele of the pub, equally oblivious of the dubious goings-on upstairs, were less tolerant of the influx of poncey theatre buffs and puffs coming between them and the next pint at around eight o'clock. The lavatories were properly pungent and awash with misdirected urine; no concessions to West End standards there. Of course it was vexing for the theatre lot to be artificially yoked to this counter-culture, but it was also healthy, in its way. A certain roughness in the experience prevented it from drifting away from life altogether. Backstage, conditions were on the primitive side of rough. The dressing rooms were on the other side of the auditorium from the stage; a small cupboard, modestly divided into male and female with a curtain held up by gaffer tape. During *The Soul of the White Ant*, Clive Merrison had first to cover himself with soil, then to wash himself spotless, in this cupboard, with all the rest of us dancing around him. No matter how large or small your part, you had to sit there from beginning to end of the show – although it was possible to get round to the other entrance, the one by the door, by going down the back stairs and running, in costume and make-up, down the Goldhawk Road and back through the pub, forcing one's way through the mystified regulars, by now on their fourth or fifth round of the evening. Nightly I made my entrance as Princess Anne by this route, with ponytail and jodhpurs, to much rubbing of eyes.

The stage manager for a large portion of my time at the Bush was the charismatic Dutchman, Bart Cossee, the shy focus of many fantasies, no whit discouraged by his habit of wearing black string vests through which his rippling musculature was sharply visible. He was of that breed of stage manager who, having had a maximum of two hours of sleep and half a sandwich, risk life and limb twenty times a day, wiring up live fittings, swinging from the rafters, heaving vast skips around, and then quietly and nonchalantly sipping a pint at two o'clock in the morning. Heroes, they are, and the Bush somehow found an inexhaustible supply of them.

After *Loving Reno*, I had two last stints at the Bush, both as a performer: the first was in another obscure one-man show, *Melancholy Jacques*, this time about the philosopher Rousseau, a sublimely cryptic meditation in which the audience were made to feel as if they were overhearing – barely – an almost incomprehensible private monologue on the subjects of art and love. Again, astonishingly, this seemed to work, and cast a considerable spell. One night the tent in which I was supposed to be spending the night, brewing my Nescaff, burst into flames; neither I nor the audience were at all animated by this, as I placidly doused the flames with Evian water, not interrupting my meditation for a minute. The second show was even more incendiary, though not quite so literally. It was *Kiss of the Spider Woman*, which, again, I had brought to the Bush, and which it had taken Jenny and Simon and Nicky exactly half an hour to decide to do. A genuine masterpiece – oddly neglected – by the novelist Manuel Puig, it was given an exquisite production by Simon Stokes, with Robin Don's masterly set, which converted the auditorium into the interior of an Argentine jail, the textures scrupulously and perfectly realistically painted by the great team of Gordon Stewart and Andrew Wood, now both dead.

Mark Rylance and I enacted the story of the improbable and tender romance that blossoms between Molina, the camp little queen, and Valentin, the determinedly heterosexual revolutionary hero, incarcerated in the same cell, and despite indifferent or non-existent notices (it was widely ignored by the broadsheets), it played to bursting houses, in an atmosphere of emotional intensity that I have never before, and alas, never since, encountered in any performance of which I was a part. The Bush is able to generate, given the right play, and the right production, a mood which is like none another, not even in comparable theatres; despite the least comfortable seats in London – perhaps the world – and an odd L-shaped configuration, and primitive air conditioning, and the roar of the Goldhawk Road's traffic, and the occasional throb of a distant rock band, there is a complicity between performers and audience which is both intimate and epic, which somehow fans the actors into blazing life, and which has informed an astonishing range and scale of work. There was talk at the time of transferring *Kiss of the Spider Woman* to another theatre, but much as I loved the piece, I was glad it never happened. The experience that Mark and I and the few hundred people who saw the show that sultry summer had was unique, and uniquely right, pure Bush. There's nothing quite like it.

Life was joyously expanding in every direction, it seemed. In reality, 1984, as I have written elsewhere, exceeded, for me, Orwell's worst projections: my adored friend Peggy Ramsay was found to have cancer of the breast, at the age of seventy-five no picnic; she overcame it, but her struggle against it seemed to me to have hastened the onset of Alzheimer's disease in her. And hard on the heels of that, my partner Aziz Yehia, a beautiful, brilliantly gifted and personally enchanting man, exhausted by the depredations of his bipolar condition, did away with himself.

I was acting in a play at the time, On the Spot *by Edgar Wallace. I found great strength in the age-old imperatives of the profession to keep going at all costs. The play was a dark and joyless one; thank God. I don't think I could have faked the inner blitheness demanded by comedy. I wrote a note on the play for the programme.*

On the Spot is a play which bursts with naked power and sexual passion – a wholly credible evocation of the world of Prohibition Chicago, at its centre the Capone-inspired figure of Tony Perelli, ruthless and half-crazed with power and lust.

Who was the Englishman who wrote this? A very remarkable one indeed as it turned out. Of course I knew his name from a hundred book spines and from the opening titles of a series of British B-movies of the Fifties and Sixties in which his apparently dead body, a cigarette clenched between his teeth, revolved, swathed in smoke, in lurid black-and-white while an electric guitar pounded out chords of suspense and danger. I had no inkling then of the astonishing life and prodigious output of the man, his powers of invention or the popularity and widespread love which attended him, both as man and writer. He was a phenomenon:

221

poet, journalist, novelist, short-story writer (seven hundred of these alone), playwright, screenwriter, stage director, film director, racehorse owner, bon viveur, chronic bankrupt; what he crammed into his fifty-seven years almost defies belief. Most remarkable of all, a great deal of what he wrote is of very high quality, including a clutch of works which have passed into the cultural subconscious: *The Four Just Men, Sanders of the River*, and the work on which he was engaged just before he died, *King Kong*. But the finest thing he ever did was *On the Spot*.

Its genesis is unusual. Invited across the Atlantic by his American publishers (he was as famous in the States as in England – during the trip he signed 1,250 autographs), the greatest crime-writer in the world was drawn irresistibly to the city of crime, Chicago. He made a special detour. Twenty-four hours was all he could spare, but he spent every minute of it being shown the notorious sites of gangsterdom: the garage of the St Valentine's Day Massacre, O'Bannion's flower shop, the morgue. His guides were the Commissioner and Deputy Commissioner of the Chicago Police Department, and it was to them that he dedicated his play. He left the city laden with pictures and clippings of Capone, the homicidal grandee who now filled his imagination. The five-day journey back to England on the *Berengaria* found him brooding and silent. As soon as he docked he summoned his secretary, Jenia Reissar, and started, at midnight, to dictate. Within three days, the play was finished. Within weeks it was in production, with Charles Laughton as Tony Perelli. It was the biggest theatrical success of either man's career.

The vividness and accuracy of the master-journalist, combined with the master-showman's timing and manipulation of effect, have given the play an electric charge which is as powerful now as fifty years ago – but its authenticity is astonishing. *This happened.* Wallace's play is a front-line report. Its truth and urgency is not dulled by the clichés of the genre, because he was inventing the genre. It was the first gangster play, and appeared before any of the contemporary gangster films were released. It presents an almost Jacobean vision: a world writhing with energy and desire but terminally corrupt. The judiciary, the police, the senate – all are corrupt. One cop struggles against an entire system – and when he finally gets his man, it's by a bitter irony – a miscarriage of justice. The play's vision is at once harsh and vital, horrible and exciting. Webster or Ford would have understood these people; Machiavelli would have recognised their world.

I knew of the play because of Charles Laughton's involvement in the orig-
inal production, of which a wonderful account is given in Emlyn
Williams's autobiography. (Williams came to our first night at the Albery
Theatre, fifty-four years after appearing in that first production, just
round the corner at Wyndham's. By now, he couldn't remember a thing
about it.) I wanted to know more about Laughton's theatre acting – more
about him. For the most part, though, I found precious little of value in the
extant books. Charles Higham's biography was written under the aegis of
Elsa Lanchester, who was intent on revenging herself on her late husband;
Higham later told me hair-raising stories about how she had set private
detectives on to Laughton, and wanted the biographer to print the photo-
graphs they had taken of him in flagrante delicto. *The other biographies*
were cobbled together from press cuttings and, worse, press releases. None
of them had anything to say about his acting, so I decided to fill the gap;
this was to be my second book, again for Nick Hern. I have no idea what
occasion provoked this piece, or when I wrote it; as far as I know it was
never printed. It is called Looking for Laughton *and describes my first fal-*
tering foray into biography.

For the last two years I have been, more or less single-handedly, the
Charles Laughton Industry: I have written a biography of him, recorded
a documentary about him for radio and filmed one for television, and
next Monday I deliver the *Guardian* lecture on him at the National Film
Theatre. The curious thing is that all this has come not from obsession,
still less identification, but from the clear realisation in the spring of
1984 that I was not him. I was doing a play that he had made famous in
1930, *On the Spot*, and I was unable to make it work, which caused me
to ponder how he had managed it. Most of us draw our performances
from what is written on the page: he had brought an altogether extra
dimension to a character that is essentially a lurid stereotype. He had
made people believe in him, to a frightening degree. He had taken the
outline Edgar Wallace handed him and filled it with truth – in this case,
a very ugly truth. This was an act of creation: of what order, I wanted to
know.

He was, I should say, among the half-dozen most fascinating actors of the
century, and a handful of his performances have a power and a scale that
demand comparison with the work of painters and poets. It was clear that

his life in art was a kind of quest which took him into unusual areas for an actor.

I was an egregiously amateur explorer into those areas. I had an idea of the kind of book I wanted to write. It was Laughton's acting I was concerned with; and it was acting itself I wanted to write about, with only as much about the actor's life as would illuminate that. I had no truck with those biographies that concerned themselves only with their subjects' careers or with the occupants of their beds. I *read* them, of course, and not without pleasure. My objection to them was simply that they contributed nothing to an understanding of acting as either craft or art. That was what had led me to want to write the book in the first place.

My first book, *Being an Actor*, was about the actor as Everyman, and attempted to delineate the common experience of actors by looking at the professional experience of one average young actor – me. In the Laughton book I set out to look at the work of a genius – to see what heights might be scaled with acting, what the conditions were for that sort of greatness. Laughton was, in my view, one of the very greatest actors who lived; even Laurence Olivier, who hated him, described him as a genius.

When I was trying to play Tony Perelli in *On the Spot*, I turned to the only available biography, and to Laughton's wife's autobiography, and there was virtually nothing in either about the performance as such, or about how he'd achieved it – let alone what he was trying to achieve in general. The best book I know about any actor as an artist is Parker Tyler's *Chaplin: Last of the Clowns*, and I modelled myself on him, hoping to emulate something of the searching analysis and openness to resonance of his work. I would like to have written in his deliciously fancy-pants prose, too, but I wisely refrained from even trying. Another influence was Robin Lane Fox's *Alexander the Great*, which eschews any attempt at novelish continuity or authorial omniscience and instead stops the flow again and again to say: what does such and such bare fact mean? What is its context? In doing so, it opens doors on history which no seamless narrative could hope for. Those were my models – but actually doing the work was something else.

I knew nothing about research, where to go, how to look, how to take notes. I had help: the publisher provided me with a hundred man-hours of it. The man whose hours I was given was a very agreeable and thorough Canadian who, at my behest, found the cast list and credits of every picture and play Laughton had been involved with, marked those who were still living in one colour ink, those who had written books in another. Then he located as many reviews as he could find; and then it was over to me. I read every word anybody had ever written about Laughton; I read every play he'd ever performed, and every original source from which any of his films had been drawn. Then I went to America; Laughton had lived half of his adult life there. I had a clutch of introductions and – which I was sure would impress any potential interviewees – the imprimatur of the BBC, who had asked me to make a radio documentary for them. I went out and bought the most expensive Sony recorder I could find, and sometimes it worked, though not too well, alas, when I spoke to Billy Wilder. I was so awed at eating bagels with the director of *Sunset Boulevard* and *Some Like it Hot* that I never asked him to stop swivelling round in his chair like that and could he possibly close the window? But he had astonishing things to say, and made me laugh again and again. What was wonderful about our conversation was his unreserved enthusiasm for Laughton, and his certainty that not only was he a great actor but a great intellect, too: 'He was a renaissance man,' Wilder said, and it rejoiced my heart.

I interviewed over fifty people, and learned to develop photographic hearing for the times (one out of two) when the tape recorder failed me. If it wasn't batteries, it was the mike; if it wasn't the mike, it was the tape; and if it was neither of those, I'd just forget to switch the thing on. On one occasion (the director Michael Blakemore it was) everything was perfect, bar one tiny detail: I'd left the microphone at home. I pretended that there was a built-in microphone, and switched on regardless, even checking the batteries at periodic intervals. I spoke to an astonishing range of people, some famous, some not. I spoke to Stewart Granger ('To know Charles was *not* to love him'); to Belita, the ice-skater whom Laughton had taken under his wing when she tried to become an actress, and who said he was 'the sexiest man alive'; to Benita Armstrong, who had seen me on a television programme talking about writing the book, and who invited me to tea to talk about her late husband who had designed Laughton's season at the Old Vic and his flat in Bloomsbury; to Robert Mitchum, who chose to answer me only in monosyllables: it was like trying to make small talk with Mount Rushmore. I tried to speak to Christopher Isherwood, who refused, most courteously. He died not long afterwards – I realise now that he didn't want to talk about someone who had died of the same disease that was killing him – but not before I had dropped a copy of my first book through his letter box. A year later I phoned his partner Don Bachardy to see whether he might have something to say. He declined, saying that 'Charles was an enthusiasm of Chris's that I didn't share.' Instead, he said, would I care to let him draw my portrait. When he'd finished the drawing, he showed it to me: it was an extraordinary thing, half me and half Laughton. And when he'd shown me the picture, it somehow released him to talk about Laughton: and what he said provided me with some of the most acute insights of anyone I spoke to.

I spoke to Laughton's family. The two female cousins with whom he had been brought up in Scarborough now lived together in London. I had been warned in advance that one was manic-depressive and that the other had recently had an unreliable set of dentures installed. Exactly as predicted, the younger of the two started out vivaciously but quickly sank into gloom and finally deep silence, while the other talked wittily and sharply about Laughton as a boy to a castanet obbligato from the new teeth. His brother Tom's widow thrilled me by telling me that she had a tape of a family gathering at one of Charles's visits back home on which not only Charles but both his brothers and his mother speak. When we sat down to listen to it, nothing but a soft hiss came out of the speakers. She had played it that morning, she wailed, and it had been fine. She had obviously pressed the record button while playing it back. Meanwhile, her new husband, a Scottish doctor, helpfully informed me that Laughton was sexually insatiable: 'He was homosexual, and your homosexual is invariably promiscuous: it's in his nature.'

Eventually, I had amassed sufficient evidence to begin writing, when Nick Gray from Yorkshire TV called and suggested that it might be interesting to do a TV documentary as well. Quite apart from the intrinsic interest, this was a tremendous bonus because it meant that I could reach certain people that neither a book nor a radio documentary would lure (Robert Mitchum, for example); and a big organisation could provide further facilities for research, particularly in the celluloid sphere, and so it proved. Helen McGee, a genius cinema sleuth, tracked down extraordinary things, like a Movietone News sequence of Laughton making up as Perelli in his dressing room at Wyndham's. We filmed the documentary as I was writing the book, so new discoveries could be fed from the one into the other. I wrote the book quickly, and, taking the proofs with me,

I found myself in Los Angeles dining next to a nice chatty fellow. When I told him about the book he said, 'Find anything interesting in the Archive at UCLA?' I looked at him aghast, my mouth working but no words coming out. Finally I croaked, with an insouciant little laugh: 'Archive?' 'You know,' he said, 'the Laughton archive.' I laughed my pearly laugh again and beat a rapid retreat. The next day, I got a cab to UCLA's leafy campus, ran into the library, and breathlessly demanded the Laughton archive. I sat in a somewhat clinical room waiting for it, cold sweat forming on my brow. The door opened and three trolleys were wheeled in containing the twenty-six boxes of the archive. A feverish search of the boxes revealed to my almost lachrymose relief that twenty-five of them contained screenplays Laughton had rejected. The twenty-sixth box contained pure gold – letters from Brecht, Orson Welles, sketches for pieces he was writing, an annotated script for his production of *John Brown's Body*. I made my notes, asked for my photocopies, and ran for dear life. I had warned Nick Hern to hold the press; I was able to rewrite sufficiently quickly to accommodate what I had just discovered. Saved by the bell.

Meanwhile, I had ventured into Laughton's territory: film. In 1985, I wrote a piece for the Guardian, *about my first film as an actor. They called it* Acting Netcheral.

Milos Forman was at the first preview of *Amadeus* at the National. We learned this from Peter Hall at a note session. Forman, it seemed, had loved the play, saying, 'It's just like Hollywood in the Thirties: Joseph II bought up all the available talent so no one else could have it, but then he didn't know what to do with it.' A good thought: and his approval of the production was encouraging and just what we needed. What we didn't know was that Milos had decided there and then that *Amadeus* was to be his next film. His and Peter Shaffer's agent, Robbie Lantz, was at the same performance, and immediately put the wheels in motion.

We had other things on our minds: the press opening, the gratifying controversy, the unprecedented popularity of the play, the even more extraordinary reception of the play in New York. Of course a film would be made, but what kind of a film? Starring whom? In London there had been a steady procession of megastars hovering hungrily around like

227

legacy hunters at a sickbed. Dustin Hoffman, Robert Redford, Robert De Niro all passed through. Any or all of them seemed likely candidates.

When, eventually, Milos Forman's name was announced to direct it, that broadened the field. Forman was known to favour unknowns but now a new question entered our minds: were we sufficiently unknown?

It was pleasant to read in *Screen International* that Forman had cast Ian McKellen and me in the roles that we'd played on stage, Ian as Salieri in New York, me as Mozart in London. But neither we nor our agents had been informed, which seemed extremely forgetful at the very least. A call to the producer established that no casting had occurred, but there was every possibility that one would be playing the role. In the fullness of time, one would be informed.

Rumours started. Every week, it seemed, a new cast was announced. Hottest tip for Mozart was Dudley Moore. Why not, one wondered, revive the *Arthur* team, and cast John Gielgud as Salieri with Liza Minnelli as Constanze? Further calls to the producer met increasingly ominous vagueness.

Peter Shaffer was ensconced with Milos Forman, wrestling with the screenplay. He claimed casting was the last of their concerns. They weren't even thinking about it till the script was right, which, as far as he could see, would be never. 'What's Forman like?' I asked. Peter replied with a long feeling look, such as men use to tell of terrible wartime experiences at the hands of the Japanese. 'It's coming along,' he'd say through a tightened jaw.

Then one day a friend told me he'd been asked to screen test for the part of Mozart. I began to hear of more and more actors who'd been asked to screen test for the role. I became mildly bitter. Only mildly because everything one had heard or experienced of movies taught one that their makers believe themselves to be Nietzschean figures beyond the codes of ordinary human decency. It was a surprise, then, to get a call from the producer saying that Mr Forman would like to meet me. 'Meet me?' I said. 'He wants to screen test every other actor in London, but he wants to MEET me? Well, I'm sure I'd love to MEET Mr Forman. I'm sure he's a very interesting man.' And in this captious spirit, I made off for the Connaught Hotel.

When I got to Forman's suite my worst fears were confirmed. The room seemed to contain every actor under the age of thirty who had had a good review in the last ten years. We stared at each other balefully. Then Richard Griffiths arrived – surely not to play Mozart, one thought. We got chatting. After a few minutes, the door flew open and everyone's idea of a Hollywood director strode in, chewing a very large cigar and bellowing in an unfathomable Central European accent. He flung his arms round some of Richard Griffiths.

Richard introduced me: 'Milos, do you know Simon Callow?' He sprang back. '*Ah!* YOU are Simon Callow. I wanted to look at you. Come in, come in,' and ushered Richard and me into another room, which also contained Saul Zaentz, the producer, looking like a superannuated Santa Claus from Macy's. We made small talk for a minute or two, but this is not Milos's forte, and his eyes began to wander. The trickle of anecdotes ran dry.

He said to me, 'I want to tell you something. I have seen ten Mozarts, and you were by far the best. Everyone else was either great at being an asshole or great at being a genius. You are the only one who combined the two. Yes, a really fantastic performance. Brilliant. No, really, great.' He tailed off, deep in thought.

'I wonder,' he said, his brows furrowed, '*What* could you play in our film?' He then started to search the cast list. Up and down the list his eyes went, but nothing seemed to suggest itself to him. 'What?' he asked me. 'I really can't imagine,' I replied. 'What kind of actor are you looking for?' 'A little one,' he said, 'like a *bird* – ' he vividly impersonated a bird – 'and also a brilliant actor. Tell me,' he looked at me accusingly, 'where will I find such an actor?' 'I – I don't know,' I apologised. He grunted. He looked again at the cast list. 'Well, we must think of something for you to do. I shall think about it.'

Two days later I was lunching at the Tate Gallery when the waitress came to my table and said, 'You're to phone a Mr Forman at the Connaught Hotel.' To my great surprise, the telephone was answered by Forman himself.

'I was a fool,' the bass-baritone growl admitted. 'Of course I shall test you for Mozart.' Accordingly, a day or two later I found myself in a studio being directed for the first time by Milos. He was incisive, concentrated, sparing of words. He demonstrated what he wanted by acting out the emotion in question in a style that would not have surprised the audience at a Kabuki play but which was rather alarming at close quarters. 'Mozart is happy,' he would say, showing what the word meant by manipulating his mouth into a grin that extended to the corner of his eyes, which were themselves gleaming with maniacal delight. 'You see? Netcheral.'

I heard nothing. One day, it was discovered that the part of Mozart had indeed been cast, but there was interest in my playing something else in the film 'Schumacher? Schickelbart?' 'Schikaneder,' I prompted. 'Yes, yes, *Schikaneder.*' Who on earth is he? my agent wanted to know. Was he in the play?

I knew all about the wonderfully ripe Schikaneder, librettist of *The Magic Flute*, the first Papageno, the leading actor-manager of his day, and the first man to play Hamlet in German. He had ended up in a lunatic asylum having provided the Viennese public with increasingly surreal and incoherent entertainments, a kind of Marx Brothers mayhem *avant la lettre*. But the role in the film was slender. More important, could I bear to watch some unknown Yank becoming world famous in my part? Anyway nothing apparently came of it. Until suddenly, and as always, panic. 'They do want you for Schillerkrantz, darling, and you have to go to Abbey Road Studios on Friday to record a couple of arias and a duet with the Academy of Saint Martin-in-the-Fields under Neville Marriner.'

'But I've not agreed to play the part. And there's *singing*. I daren't even sing in my bath, let alone in front of Neville bloody Marriner. Just tell them thank you very much, but no thanks.' Which she did. The effect was most gratifying. When I reached home, four messages had been left on my answering machine — one from Peter Shaffer, one from Saul Zaentz, and two from Milos Forman. I called them, the latter first, and was again amazed to get straight through to the man himself. Normally in the film world, anybody important is screened by layer upon layer of sidekicks. 'I'm delighted you're doing the movie,' he said. 'I understand there's some problem with the singing, don't worry, don't worry, if necessary we'll dub it. Of course, it would be *nice* if you could but don't worry' 'Oh, okay,' I said, 'fine.' Apparently everything was settled. Not so. 'We'd better meet to make sure we feel the same way about the part. Then we can go ahead.'

Back to the dear old Connaught. The door was opened by Milos himself, all alone, again strangely bereft of lieutenants. 'Schikaneder!' he cried, and I saw his point. Quite by chance, I had turned up wearing my usual winter costume: a sweeping black fedora, an ankle-length black overcoat, and a bright red carnation in my buttonhole. We sat down and read a couple of scenes. Any attempt at characterisation was stamped on. 'No, no, simple, simple. Be netcheral!' I felt I had a lot to contribute in terms of the psyche of the actor-manager. Milos was having none of it. 'It's you! I want you.'

Nevertheless, he cast me. 'Very good, very good. Perfect. Only one problem: can you ride whores? 'Good God,' I thought, 'he's auditioning my sexuality.' 'Whores?' I said weakly. 'Yes, whores, whores, clip-clop, clip-clop…' 'Oh, *horse*, yes, yes, of course, I mean, no, but I can learn easily.' 'Very good. See you next week. And remember – *NO ACTING*. I wish I could change the name of the character to Simon Callows.'

Things were looking up. The latest version of the script contained a much augmented role for Schikaneder, and I finally discovered that Mozart was to be Tom Hulce, whom I'd met in New York two years before – delightful, funny, and good – one of the Alan Strangs in the Broadway production of *Equus*, so we had John Dexter in common. We re-met at Abbey Road, and from that moment, I never experienced the slightest pang.

We began, as usual with Milos, *in medias res*. Singing arias was bad enough but there was a scene (Mozart, Schikaneder and three of his actresses standing round the piano improvising tunes from *The Magic Flute*) which could only be a nightmare. So of course we started with that. Milos gave a vivid impression of how he imagined the scene: wild anarchy, raspberries blown and belches belched, Schikaneder, thumping the keyboard, Mozart, giggling insanely – and all within the framework of tunes being played, tossed around, transformed, stood on their head. 'Okay?' said Milos, and went, taking Shaffer with him.

Eventually we did concoct something which satisfied him. Of its nature, though, it was almost impossible to repeat; and sustaining that level of crazy ebullience for a sound recording is a desperate task. 'I know,' said Shaffer, and disappeared, returning a minute later with two bottles of champagne. So it came about that the rather surprised walls of Studio One, Abbey Road, where some of the great classical recordings of the century had been made, witnessed a performance of certain tunes of Mozart by a gaggle of drunken actors shrieking and farting and hitting a priceless instrument.

My aria was another matter. 'It's a shame,' I said to Milos, 'and I'm very sorry, but if I don't have to worry about the singing it'll be better for my acting.' 'Acting?' Milos's eyes narrowed. 'Acting? There will be *NO*

ACTING in my film.' 'But, Milos,' I said, 'he's on a stage, in a theatre, acting.' A dark and terrible pause. 'Yes. Okay.' Another pause. 'But this will be the *only* acting in my film!'

A month later, I was in Prague, to rehearse all my scenes in one day. Tom and Meg Tilly (Constanze) had tottered off their planes, having been on them for sixteen hours. The set was built, and the moment we all arrived, Milos plunged in. He said nothing about the scenes, simply gave us our physical movements, and then told us to start. Within seconds, he would be on his feet, protesting. 'No, no, no, no. Simple. Please. Not like this – ' a not entirely complimentary impersonation of one's physical and vocal attributes ensued – 'like this – ' a cartoon of the desired performance was now indicated, with many a grimace and grunt.

'Don't worry,' I said to Tom. 'We are graduates of the John Dexter school of acting. Nothing this man says can harm us.' I was wrong. 'No, no, no, no, NO!' he would cry, time and again. It was as if he couldn't believe the perversity of what we were presenting to him. How could we not be playing the scene the way he had envisaged it? Faced with the offensive performance, his technique was to destroy it by brute force. As far as one could judge, it was nothing personal: simply that this piece of wrong acting had to be expunged from the world. With mad energy Milos would assault it, raining insults, parodistic impersonations, reproaches upon its head, until, inevitably, it succumbed.

Basically, netcheralness was the goal; but Milos's definition of what was *netcheral* was quite arbitrary. What it amounted to was that the way Milos saw it was netcheral — any other way, not. Moreover, 'Remember that I have a camera here and this light is here so it would help me very much if you will keep your head low here and turn only thirty degrees this way.' *Netcheral* was a relative term, and one that became irksome. We found an antidote. During the interminable hours of piano practice I endured in order to play a twenty-second fragment for a scene, I remembered that in Germany the note B natural is called H. Thus whenever Milos would cry, 'Be natural!' I would murmur, 'H.' This was oddly consoling.

Over supper that night, Milos further expounded his theories of film technique. 'Stage actors are wonderful, big, generous. But they can't use film, always *acting*, always *doing something*. On film, you must BE. And you must *be yourself*, I cast you to be you. Otherwise I cast someone else.'

'But Milos,' said a slightly uneasy Murray Abraham, playing Salieri, 'if you cast everyone to be themselves, well, Salieri's a very nasty man.' Milos stared at him for a long time. 'Murray,' he said, 'you think too much.'

Over the next six months I took fifty-seven planes in and out of Czechoslovakia, staying at the Panorama Hotel (the panorama being like a building site in Luton) and working at the urine-infested Barrandov Studios. There, where Milos had begun his career, he was the absolute centre of operations, exerting his massive concentration on the whole huge team. The shot would be set up without him, he would emerge from his room, and the scene would proceed.

If the shot was good, 'Very good, very good, very good,' he would say, and withdraw back to his room to sleep while the next shot was set up. *If not* – if not, he would descend like the cavalry to root out imperfection. Sarcasm was the principal weapon. 'Not bad, not bad. In your speech there were two or three lines where you sounded *almost* like a human being. This is very good, I like this.'

His preferred method of demonstration would sometimes conflict with what he was saying. 'You come into the room, you open the door, you say "*HELLO!!!!*" lightly, like that.' Praise was implied rather than stated, but, when it came, the sun certainly shone. One day, after rushes, he said to me, 'What we shot with you yesterday was wonderful, strong, true, netcheral,' then added, quite without malice, almost as if to himself, 'I wasn't sure it would be, but it was.'

The scene he was speaking about had been achieved only by dint of violent explosions and uncomprehending abuse – not really at me, but at the inexplicably wrong things I was doing – things I had no way of knowing about, because he hadn't explained them to me. Why should he? he must have thought. They were so *obvious.*

When this piece came out – on the day of the British premiere of the film – I was loitering in the cinema foyer when Milos, with thunder on his brow, came over to me. 'I rrread your piece in the Gwaaaaaarrrrdian,' he said. 'I'm happy to have it. I just rrrran out of toilet paper.' But he was amused. Later, he asked me to share his cab on the way to the reception, and I told him that I was directing a play by his old friend Milan Kundera in Los Angeles. 'Very good. I will come to see it. And I will review it for the GWARRRRRRRRRRDIAN.' *If* Amadeus *was a gruelling film to make, my next film,* A Room with a View, *directed by James Ivory and produced by Ismail Merchant, was pure balm, from beginning to end. This account of it was written for the* Sunday Telegraph *magazine in 1986, and it charts the beginning of my fascination with the world of film-making.*

Last May in Florence broke all records for rain. The sky was black, the grass was wet. For two days we could do nothing. On the third day a glint of sunlight made shooting possible, though not perfect. Eventually we had to shoot what we could regardless (Time is Money). If the light is good, it's surprising how much rain you can have without it showing on the film. Mud is a different matter, however, and the first day's shooting chiefly concentrated on the progress of two carriages through the Fiesole countryside. Denholm Elliott, Judi Dench and I shared a carriage. Our horse, Giacomo, had an unfortunate inclination to collapse from time to time. There was, moreover, the matter of the falling tree.

This marvel of mechanical engineering was designed to smash across our path, frightening the ladies and giving the men a chance to take command of the situation. It had to fall late enough to look menacing but early enough to avoid the horses. Every time it fell wrongly, we had to ascend the little hill again, walking through the mud to give the horses a break, clutching our skirts or gaiters. So there we are in our carriage, chattering away, and finally the tree is right. A good take at last. But we need another to be safe. Suddenly Maggie Smith, seconded by Judi Dench, protests. The Florence Fire Brigade has been in the bushes, simulating a sudden downpour that's needed for the scene. The water has been bearing down on the horses' heads. They've been shying away in fear. For the last take, then, the water, is, as they say, cheated to fall yards ahead of them. The effect is almost identical.

All this has taken over eight hours to shoot – we were on location at seven – and will result in under a minute of film. A brilliant minute, as it happens. About ten minutes out of those eight hours was spent in front of the cameras.

And so it goes for every day. Encamped in our villa at Fiesole, which is playing the role of Forster's *pension* in the film, we are squeezed into our costumes, and gummed into our hairpieces, and our blemishes are painted out by the make-up artists. My motorcycling scar is a much-loved challenge. After five minutes' assiduous application, it's invisible. Then, like souls in hell, we wait to be called. Unending supplies of coffee and biscuits and sandwiches appear at regular intervals and then lunch and tea and eventually supper. The Edwardian costumes have a way of making everyone look cross or at the very least severe, uptight, in corsets and waistcoats. Reading is difficult, writing impossible. All you can do is talk, smoke and eat. The talk becomes more and more abstract. Starting with theatrical anecdotes, by the end of a shoot you're on to Zen Buddhism and the meaning of life. The most intimate and terrible secrets have been vouchsafed and friendships have been born, flowered, declined and died. As in Buñuel's *Exterminating Angel,* or the plays of Chekhov, we are stranded together, cut off from the world, pawns of a capricious and inscrutable destiny: the director, the weather, the cameraman.

Life becomes real again when you work. Best of all is unremitting hard work, a thirteen-hour slog. Not only is it good to be at it, but you feel your existence is justified. You're part of things, and of course from a solipsistic angle, you become the focus of the whole enterprise.

No one on the set looks more worried than Jim. It is as if we were filming a documentary on Hiroshima instead of an Edwardian comedy. He shouts 'Cut.' 'Was that all right for you?' he asks the cameraman. 'I was a little worried about the shadow on X's face, but if it didn't worry you, it doesn't worry me'. 'How about the acting?' one of us asks. 'It was all right.' 'All right?' I demand. 'By which I mean sublime, of course,' says Jim.

On the stage, you project. In film, it's different: instead of offering yourself, you admit the camera into your aura. This is a little like being X-rayed. More like dreaming. At the end of a long session, you can feel absolutely transparent, as if the camera had passed through your veins and organs. Very exhilarating.

Denholm Elliott puts it another way. 'I mean – ' he does the look he describes as his angry caterpillar look. 'It's only dressing up for Mummy and Daddy, after all.' But he's swallowed the camera lock, stock and barrel, if anyone ever has.

At the far corner of the set, concentrating harder than anyone, is Ismail. He's willing the scene to be good, for reasons both financial and artistic; but he's also wondering whether he can't have another party soon. His therapy is culinary. The fatigue, fraughtness and fragility of filming has one remedy: food. He will commandeer any unlikely space to throw a party. Up to a point, this is because cooking is therapeutic for him; but also it's a very personal and charming hand-holding with all of us. And such is the excellence of his cooking that everybody's good nature is restored. The phrase 'to curry favour' might have been invented for Ismail.

Louche dives are a necessary diversion from film acting. Somewhere to blow out steam, fall down, jump about. The work is concentrated and not usually very sustained. It is, in fact, not unlike very bad sex; it's all over in thirty seconds, and it's an hour before you can do it again.

So some sort of antidote is called for. In the case of Florence, and for the few hardy spirits who could brave it, it was a club magnificently called Chez Rudy GoGo, a transvestite discotheque much frequented by gay German dwarfs and immensely tall, five o'clock-shadowed, bulging-calved Italian men in natty little off-the-shoulder numbers. The feeling of the place was as of a tepid tribute to Weimar Berlin; but it was a relief from Edward Morgan Forster and the dog collar. Very friendly, everyone was, with no pressure of any kind. Julian Sands and I would weave a drunken path back to the Excelsior through the moonlit statues and arcades of Florence, after which I would retire to translate a few pages of a French play. This was another lifeline to sanity; something to show for one's time.

It's as well to have done something else by the end of filming. Judi Dench does embroidery, very beautifully. It was, I suppose, tactless of me to enquire if the reason it was called petit point was because there's so little point to it; tactless – and wrong. She was making first-night presents for her next show.

We transferred to Kent after a month in Tuscany, and were plagued by the wettest summer that county had ever known. These climatic vagaries apart, the film continued on the even keel Jim and Ismail skilfully maintain; but the atmosphere is quite different when you're within twenty minutes of London; it becomes more like an ordinary job. But there was a spectacular finale; the scene in the 'Sacred Lake', in which Mr Beebe and the two young men of the story, George and Lucy's brother, take an impulsive dip, only to be surprised by the ladies. By now it was July. A pool had been dug and at the very least lukewarm water was promised. At the very most, as it happened. For three days we stood disconsolately around, the lads flexing their pectorals, I morbidly gazing at my Michelin Man contours, waiting at a moment's notice and with the hint of the tiniest sunbeam to plunge into the arctic waters of Sevenoaks.

Water, one way and another, had dominated our lives; so it was witty of Ismail to hire a pleasure boat for our end-of-film 'wrap' party. It was a Dionysian affair – I speak for myself. Fabia Drake may have a different tale to tell. But near the end of it, Jim, in his soft voice and with his sharp brains, said, 'I'm so glad you played Mr Beebe for us. It could have been so fuddy-duddy and... boring... and well... it isn't.' That's as handsome a compliment as I ever expect to receive.

It was on A Room with a View *that I first met Denholm Elliott; I became deeply fond of him, though he could be very peppery. Once, filming in Kent, Jim had said to him, 'Could you do a little... less, Denholm?' and I, perhaps presuming too much on our fairly new friendship, had said, 'What does that word "less" mean, Denholm?', intending to implicate myself in the sin of overacting too. 'Fuck off,' he roared at me. 'Fuck off! Who do you think you are? Only your second film and you're teaching me how to act.' We repaired the rift soon enough, and thereafter spent hours talking – about sex and acting, mostly. He was very dismissive of his own acting: 'If you look very carefully you'll see that all my work is based on the Muppets.' This concealed a deep and romantic love of acting. His only criterion for accepting a part, he once said to me, was whether it made him cry or not. This is a review from the* Mail on Sunday *of his wife Susan's biography of him,* The Quest for Love *(1994), published shortly after his absurdly early death from AIDS.*

There are actors who seem to change with each performance. They take their cue from the author's style, from the period in which the play or the film is set, from clues in the writing. Others remain more or less the same from role to role. The best of these actors bring something to the part, something mysterious of their own, filling it with a depth of experience hard to analyse. Denholm Elliott was one of the greatest of these; once he had found himself as an actor (in early middle age) he brought to everything he did, regardless of the quality of the writing, a richness, complexity, depth and meaning quite out of the ordinary.

Where did this inner life come from? Susan Elliott's book answers the question. Denholm was a quite unusual human being, an oddball, both reckless and driven – but not by ambition or a desire for glory. His goals were equally out of the ordinary; they are very well summed up in the book's title: *The Quest for Love*. He wasn't interested in technique or interpretation – he just did it; or rather, he just was it. He brought all the pain, confusion, doubt and occasional beauty of his life to his work; life and art met up there on the stage or the screen with remarkable intensity.

The first part of Susan Elliott's book gives the background: the shy and virginal schoolboy, the drama-school reject, thrust into the war barely out of his teens, first as a member of a bomber air crew, then as a prisoner of war for three long, lean years in STALAG VIII B, an experience which seems to have taught him what's real and what's not, what matters and what doesn't, and gave him his sense that life was too short to waste on anything less than absolute fulfilment. This fulfilment was a long time coming; the second part of the book records his early success, and then sudden failure, the eventual triumph of his career, the marriage, the children, and increasingly, the secret love life. He wanted it all; but it was never enough.

I did not know Denholm well (did anyone?) but over the years we had a number of sharp, passionate conversations in which – as in his performances – he laid his life bare. He told me once that his children had given him a birthday present, for which he had thanked them, but that he knew there was something more that they wanted. 'They wanted me to tell them how much I loved them – but I can't – I haven't got enough love for myself.' He fought desperately hard to escape the shell of reserve, of inhibition; the unequal struggle brought unique intensity and pressure to his work. In the end it brought him death.

There can be no one who does not know that Denholm died of AIDS, a casualty of the increasing promiscuity which did not end until he was diagnosed HIV-positive in his late sixties. Susan knew when she married him that Denholm was bisexual; as the years went on he became increasingly interested only in sex with men, literally roaming the globe in search of ever more intense experiences with them. This was not the outcome of an excess of hormones, nor even a desire for mere sensual indulgence. It was, in its own curious way, highly romantic, a quest, indeed, for love, but one doomed to failure because in the end Denholm could never believe that the love he got could be enough. He received a great deal of it – in every shape and form, from men, women and his own children – but, as Susan Elliott says in an acute perception, one of many: 'Denholm's constant need for bolstering was ill-matched with his inability to give much in return.' It is a very common predicament of English men, which is why he was so wonderfully good at portraying us. Susan Elliott's compulsively readable book lovingly and forgivingly records the life and work of one of our most remarkable actors.

Ismail Merchant, the producer of A Room with a View, *was like no one else in the film industry, or anywhere else, come to that. It recently occurred to me that the historical personage whom he most resembled was the great Russian impresario, Sergei Diaghilev, a similarly outsize character, also motivated by great passion for his native land and its art, similarly given to apocalyptic rages, equally gifted at bringing together extraordinary people, every bit as imaginative in his financial arrangements. Both died far too young; both wrought their wonders by sheer force of personality. I acted in six films for Ismail and Jim, and mad though the process of making each and every one of them was, they were deeply exhilarating. Diaghilev's friend and collaborator Alexandre Benois said of him: 'he had a gift for creating a romantic working climate, and with him all work had the charm of a risky escapade', which was exactly true of Ismail, whose* modus operandi *is perfectly encapsulated by another phrase of Benois's: 'the psychology of the hectic'. I wrote this piece for the* Daily Mail *after Ismail's death in 2005; when he died, I was in India, which he had always promised to show me one day.*

Ismail Merchant, the producer who brought the world such delicious films as *Heat and Dust, The Bostonians, A Room with a View, Howards End* and *The Remains of the Day,* is dead. Impossible to believe that I'll never find myself on another movie location with the director James Ivory calmly pursuing his objectives while Ismail passes through like a tornado, hassling, jostling, exhorting, soothing, denouncing, and above all feeding, his troops. A sudden image of him comes to me from the *Jefferson in Paris* shoot in 1994. He was doing his usual thing, ablaze with impatience and urgent advice, only this time he was dressed as a Maharajah, a role he had somewhat absent-mindedly agreed to play, without realising that he would be encumbered by turbans and false whiskers and pantaloons and confined to one place. Restricted for the purposes of a particular shot to his Royal Circle box in the reconstructed theatre, and looking like a malicious caricature of himself – the Maharajah of All the

Rushes – he hurled instructions at functionaries on ground level like some crazed potentate. Or impotentate, in this case: nothing seemed to happen. Jim was obliviously involved in the lace on someone's costume, while Ismail, raging like an ogre from *The Arabian Nights*, stood up to scream at the top of his voice, 'Shoot, Jim, SHOOT!' It was just another day in the life of Merchant Ivory.

This man was larger than life, to put it mildly. He swept one up. He swept me up the moment I met him twenty-five years ago, after a performance of *Amadeus* at the National Theatre. His old friend Felicity Kendal, star of that early Merchant Ivory masterpiece *Shakespeare Wallah* (1965), introduced us, and there and then I became, unquestioningly and uncon-ditionally, part of Ismail's extended family. From that moment on it was a round of suppers, teas, lunches, and the immediate offer of a part in *Heat and Dust*, which they were about to make. I had never acted in a film, and was thrilled at the prospect. In the event I couldn't do it, stuck in a West End run; I clearly was family, however, because one day Ismail phoned me and said, 'How is your mother?' He had never met her, but after I had reassured him about the state of her health, he said, 'Would she like to come to India to be in a film? I need some very elegant older ladies to visit the harem.' She was family too, it appeared.

A few months later he called me again, this time to tell me I would be playing the lead in *A Room with a View*, a film, he said, that they were making especially for me. I marvelled at their imagination and generos-ity in casting me as the romantic lead, George, and immediately planned to lose weight, visit the gymnasium, start a running regime (in the novel there was, after all, a rather famous nude scene in a pond). Only when my agent told me that the part they had in mind was the role of the portly fifty-year-old vicar, the Reverend Arthur Beebe, did I wake from my dream, and, feeling very foolish at my self-delusion, immediately told my agent to say no. But 'no' was to Ismail only the opening gambit in a long game, and blandishments followed on a daily basis, with Ismail always calmly ending the conversation by saying that they wouldn't make the film unless I played the Rev in it. Finally, he threw a large party with many distinguished guests, at the climax of which he introduced me as 'Simon Callow, who is playing the Reverend Beebe for us'. I said, 'Oh no he isn't,' but I knew the game was up, and settled down, to general con-gratulations from the other guests, to one of those sumptuous banquets of Indian food that Ismail used to rustle up apparently out of nowhere and in minutes. And of course, it was one of the most enjoyable parts I have ever played. The day before I left for the airport to go to Florence, there was another, slightly more sheepish, call asking if I wouldn't mind accepting half the agreed wage: some faint-hearted investor had pulled out. And naturally I, like everyone else on the film, said yes. That was what you did with Ismail.

He was the most generous of men in every way, a wonderful host and an utterly supportive friend, but when he had his producer's turban on, it was a different matter. Then the negotiations were horrible, nightmarish, and it was touch and go whether you would ever get what was finally agreed on. He would do anything for the film, to realise it exactly as they had envisaged, and that generally meant getting everybody to work for as close to nothing as possible. His and Jim's tempestuous relationship was predicated on an absolute loyalty to the film, which must be realised to perfection in every detail exactly as they had conceived it. In the end, they didn't really care whether anyone else liked it, as long as they did. What they offered those of us who worked for them was a chance to participate in an undiluted vision.

Ismail liked to surround himself in myth. A Muslim, he was, he used to claim, conceived in a Hindu temple on the banks of the Ganges, and was born – he *said* – on Christmas Day in Mumbai in 1936. His businessman father sent him to New York to study business administration, but his passion was always for film: he was Oscar-nominated for his first short, *The Creation of a Woman*, but he discovered his real destiny as a film-maker when he met James Ivory, another aspiring director, in 1962.

They were wildly different as individuals, but instantly formed the potent personal and creative relationship that lasted over forty years. Their early films were made in India; when they started making films in America, their first hit was *The Europeans* (1979). It was a slow journey to success, but they were both absolutely certain about the sort of films that they wanted to make: literate, visually ravishing, exquisitely acted. Jim, in particular, had a fascination with the minutiae of social behaviour; Ismail had had an opportunity to study the Raj and its manners at close quarters. In some ways, they found their perfect subject in the Edwardian English middle classes, in Ishiguro's *Remains of the Day*, of course, but above all in the novels of E. M. Forster, whose concern with connecting decency and order with true passion was what Merchant Ivory were all about.

241

And they took extraordinary risks. I had never expressed to Ismail or any-one the slightest desire to direct a film. But he had decided that it was time that *The Ballad of the Sad Café* should be shot, and that I, as one of his extended family, was the man for the job. And so, eighteen months or so later, Ismail and I found ourselves standing in front of a screen in Berlin after the first showing of the film. We were being booed. Now, there is no booing quite like German booing; it's so thorough. But Ismail beamed broadly, as if he were receiving a standing ovation, and went off in triumph to supper, where he expressed nothing but optimism for the film's success. As it happens, it was never really liked, a strange film from a strange book, about the love of a giantess for a dwarf, but to the end Ismail expressed genuine and admiring affection for it, as he did for all Merchant Ivory films, by definition.

Glamorous, immensely handsome (as a young man he was voted among the five most handsome men in India), exquisite in his manners and passionate in his enthusiasms, he longed all his life to connect all the things and all the people he loved. My final memory of him is of a golden, dusty twilight in Austin, Texas, on the set of *The Ballad of the Sad Café*. He had somehow brought to that dry, isolated place a consort of superb Indian musicians, who sat on the verandah of Miss Amelia's broken-down café, joyously improvising their glittering ragas, and Ismail, seated in the front row, turned round to beam at the little audience of actors – Vanessa Redgrave and Rod Steiger and Keith Carradine – of extras and crew and designers and me, all of us woven together in perfect happiness, any thought of financial injustice or temperamental harassment banished. That was Ismail's genius, bringing together cultures and individuals, different worlds and philosophies, the British and the Indian; the English and the Italian; the American and the European; the Schlegels and the Wilcoxes; the dwarf and the giantess; himself and Jim: always connecting.

The Ballad of the Sad Café *was shot in 1989. But already in 1986, my career as a director seemed to be taking over from my life as an actor. After* The Passport *I directed my old friend Angus Mackay in an oddly haunting little play called* Nicolson Fights Croydon, *which we put together from Harold Nicolson's diaries and letters. It concerned his unexpected but successful candidature for the seat of Croydon East on a Labour Party ticket, done in a theatre so small that we were able to do it without using any stage lights at all, using only local light on the set – a table lamp, the light in the wardrobe, the shaving light and so on. It resulted in a kind of hyper-realism, and cast a curious spell, helping to make Angus uncannily convincing as Nicolson: his son Nigel came to see the play and said that he had felt unnervingly as if he were in his father's presence again. (Nicolson's old friend James Lees-Milne came too. 'V. well done,' he wrote in his grumpy diary. 'Resemblance to H not bad, though he was too smartly dressed and unable to catch H's slurry voice.') Having now directed three small-scale plays (plus* Amadeus *in Mold), I took a very deep breath and took on* The Infernal Machine *at the Lyric Hammersmith with Maggie Smith as Jocasta. Robert Eddison played Tiresias, Lambert Wilson Oedipus. I had translated the play while acting in* A Room with a View *in Florence, happily immersing myself in the work of a desperately unfashionable writer for whom I feel great affinity. The following is a piece I wrote about Cocteau for the programme of Sean Mathias's very successful production of* Les Parents Terribles.

Jean Cocteau is one of those few creative artists who seem more substantial after his lifetime than during it. Now that the noise of his tireless self-advertisement has died away, he can be seen to be both more impressive than, but also quite different to, the star of a thousand photo-calls who alternately vexed and charmed his contemporaries. Never was a writer more omnipresently public (unless it be George Bernard Shaw, who in some unexpected ways he rather resembles): Cocteau talking about his work, Cocteau writing about his work, Cocteau posing in front of his work, Cocteau, like a Zelig of the arts, present at all the important events of the twentieth century, clinging proprietorially to the great man or woman at the centre of them. We know, it seems, everything about him: his views, his vices, his romantic passions, his religious aspirations, his sexual fantasies. He concealed nothing; he made art out of his impulses and his experiences almost as they were happening, clothing them in gorgeous verbal garments which were nonetheless quite transparent. He is everywhere in evidence in his own work, which, like Goethe's, consists of autobiographical fragments, barely transmuted. He was perfectly frank about this: Yvonne in *Les Parents Terribles*, he said at the time, was an amalgam of his mother and Jean Marais'. Not only do we know all about him, we are on first-name terms with him, too: his signature – that spindly 'Jean', with a star dancing above it, or beneath it, sometimes trailing behind – is written all over the work, quite literally, as often as not. And yet, by a paradox that he loved to enunciate, the more we know of him, the more invisible he becomes. 'Jean' was, of course, a mask, or rather a series of masks, designed to liberate his impersonality. It was a means of making himself a vehicle for inspiration. 'Acute individualism is the highest form of collaboration.' He was curiously available to being taken over completely by a more potent individual, whether a lover or a fellow artist. He was compulsively drawn towards great creative figures; in their presence he became an unashamed groupie. His offerings to them – the scenario of *Parade* for Picasso and Satie; the text of *Oedipus Rex* for Stravinsky; numerous scenarios for Diaghilev – were naked attempts to ingratiate himself with them, but equally to allow himself to be suffused with the source of their inspiration. The somewhat equivocal response of these great ones to his advances did not faze him in the least. 'To admire is to efface yourself. To put yourself in someone else's place. Unfortunately so few people know how to get outside themselves,' he wrote in his journal. 'In the presence of certain performances, I no longer exist. To be what I see and hear.'

Aesthete and dandy though he seemed, the supremely sophisticated master of the calculated pose, he worked desperately hard at preserving his spontaneity, his amateur's love of the medium. This enthusiastic innocence is at the heart of everything he ever did, a sort of dazzlingly complex naïveté, mingling grave myth with fun and nonsense. It is the work of a wise and witty adolescent determined to reveal his insights and himself in as many ingenious ways as possible, expressing his relatively simple experience polysyllabically, prestidigitatiously, and sometimes preposterously, but never failing to bring an affectionate smile to our lips, while what he says somehow sticks in our minds. The innocence is partly a side effect of his spontaneity: for all its self-consciousness, both his writing and his drawing are instinctive and unrevised: 'If tempted in the least to think, to try to make a correction with the aid of his reason – he was sure that his drawing would be a failure, that it would not live that life of its own without which a work of art is not a success,' wrote Edouard Dermit of his graphic work. Entirely untrained in any medium, Cocteau made himself into a uniquely responsive conduit: 'Only intensity matters. Talent – either you have it or you don't. Intensity must be our one study.' He even dismissed his own cleverness. 'Intelligence has been granted to me in the form of intuition and sudden flashes. Which makes me seem intelligent though I am no such thing. Which gives me the disadvantages of intelligence without the advantages. I am not bright enough and I have the reputation of being too bright.' His acting out his life as a piece of theatre proved to be a cunning diversionary tactic: all the while, he was consciously shaping himself to receive messages from the unconscious. Stopped dead in his poetasting youth by Diaghilev with the fierce command '*étonne-moi*' – 'astonish me' – he accepted that it was an artist's task to disturb, not merely to divert. *Parade, Le Boeuf sur le toît, Le Potomak,* accordingly outraged and baffled contemporary audiences. He became the personification of the avant-garde. It was another jolt, this time from his young lover and protégé Raymond Radiguet, that taught him that the systematic pursuit of novelty was as deadly as stale repetition, and that existing forms were apter vehicles for poetic truth. It was Radiguet's sudden death from typhoid at the age of twenty which gave Cocteau's life as an artist one final decisive new direction: he became an opium addict, nearly killing himself but at the same time putting him directly in touch with the deepest levels of his subconscious. Under its influence he created many of his most characteristic works: *Orphée, Le Sang d'un Poète, La Machine Infernale, Opium* (of course) and *Les Parents Terribles,* which was written in eight drugged days.

The surprise is that Cocteau's work itself proves on examination to be filled not only with invention, fantasy, paradox and pain, but above all with innocence, and its concomitant, mystery. It is typically Coctelian that he should see his opium habit as a route to innocence. 'Children carry a natural drug within them... all children possess a magic power of *changing* themselves into whatever they want. Poets, in whom childhood is prolonged, suffer greatly from the loss of this power. This, no doubt, is one reason poets resort to the use of opium.' Perhaps, as Maurois suggested when welcoming him to the ranks of the Académie Française, Cocteau's *personnage* had protected his *personne*. The bobby-dazzling style was not meant to distract from a lack of content, as it had often seemed at the time, but to lure the audience into an intuitive state where they might experience awe and deep tenderness. The torrent of language is a sort of cataract out of which springs a rainbow. The language itself rarely tells us what he is saying. Another paradox: the great manipulator of words, stringing them together dexterously like beads on a necklace, was only interested, finally, in the ineffable. It is the final and cleverest cleverness of this very clever man that behind the glittering surface of his work was nothing; or rather, nothing that could be expressed in words. 'Often young foreigners write to poets apologising for reading them so badly, for knowing our language so poorly. I apologise for writing a language instead of simple signs capable of provoking love.' On another occasion, striking the same suddenly grave note, he defined poetry as 'a machine for manufacturing love'.

'From the age of fifteen,' he said, 'I've never stopped,' and it is this sense of *perpetuum mobile* that is the overwhelming impression made by his life and work. He turned his hand to every conceivable form: plays, films, novels, verse, philosophy, theology, drawings, sculpture, murals, paintings, fashion design, stage design, opera libretti, ballet scenarios, masks. He described all this vast output with one word: poetry. It was poetry of film, poetry of painting, poetry of theatre. Not poetry in the theatre; poetry *of* the theatre, Cocteau insisted. Nor did he speak of texts, but of *pretexts*: the structure of words, characters and situations was merely a device, like Eliot's bone which the burglar gives the dog while he opens the safe, to occupy the conscious mind and facilitate the release of the unconscious. It was natural that he should reach for myth in trying to engage with those secret areas of the human heart, but for him myth was not confined to the Olympian gods (though they fascinated him too); there were divine creatures nearer to hand. It may be said of Cocteau that if he reduced the gods to boulevardiers, he made up for it by apotheosising the boulevard.

He was in love with the theatre from the earliest age, with an almost morbid sense of its power and splendour: 'Since childhood and the departure of my mother and father for the theatre, I have had red-and-gold sickness. I've never got used to it... as time goes by, the theatre in which I work loses none of its prestige for me. I respect it. It intimidates me. It fascinates me. I split in two when I am there. I live there, and I become the child that the ushers admit to Hell... the theatre is a furnace. Anyone who doubts that will be consumed by it in the end, or go up in smoke on the spot.' His view of the denizens of the stage was essentially heroic; heroically childish. 'I see the actor or actress exhaust himself for us and lose – like an animal fatally wounded by destiny – this pale blood of the boards, lose it and hold it with full hands, hold it in and "hold" until the final bow on which the curtain falls, each evening, like the guillotine. The crowd adores them, hates them and longs for them to stumble, and to enjoy them, it is necessary to cultivate and rediscover the childhood that poets prolong to their death and that grown-ups in the town boast of having lost.' His sacred monsters, with whom he wished to be associated in life and whom he delighted to depict, were equally heroic: 'the thing that distinguishes them from others, that makes them stars, derives less from any striving for uniqueness than for a struggle against death, and that pathetic struggle gives them greatness – differentiates them from simple caricatures to just the same degree that that gentleman over there, carrying a parasol and walking along with tiny footsteps, is different from an acrobat who does exactly the same thing on a high wire.' Cocteau could scarcely have invented a more precise image of himself, though perhaps his essentially paradoxical existence, in which nothing is as it seems, is even better summed up by a little aphoristic tale he called *Surprise at the Court of God*: 'A little girl steals some cherries. Her whole long life is spent making up for this fault with prayers. The devout old woman dies and goes to heaven. GOD: You have been chosen because you stole cherries.'

As I looked round the extremely colourful cast of The Infernal Machine *on the first read-through, I had an odd premonition that it was going to be a nightmare, but that it would be worth it. Right on both counts. Rehearsals, technical rehearsals and previews were riven with problems from beginning to end, but, as in backstage movies, everything came wonderfully right on the first night. The reviews were splendid, Bruno Santini's superb sets, which had been such a source of despair to the technicians, finally worked triumphantly and Maggie gave a masterly performance which in the last act ascended to the sublime. Even Cocteau came out of it very well, though Lambert Wilson's father, the late Georges Wilson, French actor and director, wondered when he came to see the show whether it was a good idea to have a homosexual production of a homosexual play. Whether it was or not, on the strength of it, the producer Bob Swash, by one of those leaps of imagination that are rarer and rarer in today's theatre, asked me to direct the West End premiere of Willy Russell's masterpiece,* Shirley Valentine, *the best one-person play I know of, its greatness consisting precisely in its being a play and not merely a show. Pauline Collins inhabited Shirley to the last wrinkle of her nose. But it was by no means a foregone conclusion: at the last run-through in the rehearsal room Willy had said, 'She's good, but she's not Shirley.' I said: 'Wait till we get into the theatre, Willy.' At the technical rehearsal, it was immediately apparent that Pauline was no longer playing Shirley; Shirley was playing Pauline. After the first night in London, it was impossible to get through the foyer because of the queue of very distinguished ladies waiting to get into the loo so they could repair their make-up. When we did the play on Broadway, women openly broke down in the stalls, while their husbands turned sternly away, lips aquiver.*

I had been away from acting for some time, so, as if to make up for it, I took on a part for which vast amounts of the stuff were required: Goethe's Faust. *All of it. This piece, written at the time (1988), focuses heavily on the physical demands of the part, no doubt precisely because I had not acted for so long.*

I haven't been on stage for two and a half years, since *Kiss of the Spider Woman* at the Bush. I am rediscovering how relentlessly physical it is. By contrast directing, writing and acting in front of cameras, which have occupied the last couple of years, are all quite unhealthy. Writing, apart from the pacing up and down and long walks to clear the mind, keeps you hunched in front of the typewriter, with fingers bleeding – the only two I use, anyway – and vice-like tension in the shoulders and upper arms. Directing breeds apoplexy. I used to think that people became directors because of the power. I have since discovered that the essential experience of directing is impotence. To sit through a performance at which things are going wrong is crucifixion. When lights, machinery or actors fail, you want to stand up and scream, but you must sit through it all motionlessly, digging holes into your palms, eyes rolling, as strangulated moans escape your lips. It was this sort of thing that gave me a hiatus hernia earlier in the year. As for movie acting, the early hours, the hazards of the location, and famously, the waiting, interminable hours of just sitting around, turn you into a greedy zombie, forever snooping around the catering van, snaffling cakes and biccies, and drinking yourself into your early bed. Acting in the theatre, by contrast, demands, and gives, health. A part like Faust – what am I saying? There are no parts like Faust – demands the tone and stamina of an athlete, and you learn to handle yourself as carefully as an athlete does.

It's very hard to get the day right. A daily visit to the gymnasium is vital, and the earlier you take it, the more good it does you. So, painfully, you crawl there at ten, and then there's the question of lunch. It must be protein-packed but not heavy, because you'll need another meal nearer the show. This little meal, taken at about six to allow an hour and a half for it to work its way through your system, is a poser. You're eating it to get you through the second half of the play, but it mustn't weigh you down for the first half. Joan Littlewood once remarked that if, before a show, you feel on top of the world, raring to go and awash with adrenalin, you should eat a pork pie. Adrenalin is indeed a dangerous ally, but then, after the first few performances, it disappears. Simple energy becomes the problem. Two weeks ago, I solved my six o'clock problem. An organisation named Spud-U-Like peddles baked potatoes. One of these, filled with chilli con carne, offers exactly three hours and thirty-five minutes of sustained energy; after which, at the end of the show, I drink three glasses of wine. Three! That's it. I, a three-bottle-a-day man, can hardly believe my self-control, but the play needs every single brain cell, and the self-disgust at missing even a beat out of the play is too high a price to pay for an hour or two's happy oblivion.

Playing one of these parts is like having a rare disease. Like most of those it involves a lot of giving up. I gave up coffee, of which I drank upwards of fifteen cups, often espresso, a day, because I felt as if I was going to fall over on stage. I gave up cheese because it was coating my vocal chords. Sex must be taken sparingly. It would seem that Maurice Chevalier's great dictum remains true: 'Every time you walk on stage, you must make love to the audience – but you must live like a MONK.' All of this has, of course, had a highly beneficial effect on my health. I have lost a stone in weight, my complexion has improved and my body is as streamlined as it ever will be. I am thinking of publishing my findings in *The Faust Diet* (*Parts One & Two*).

Finally, the words. There are many, many thousands of these. When I first ran my part to myself it lasted four hours. In order to be ahead of this seemingly unending stream of image, conceit and apostrophe, the words must bubble up of their own accord, not be separately drilled for. That means running through most of it before every performance, getting it into the teeth and tongue, hearing it afresh. The best place for doing this is in the street, and so, like a priest at his breviary, I wander Hammersmith, muttering my divine office. The other night, as I was invoking the earth spirit, or lauding Helen of Troy's beauty, or something, a merry party, red of cheek and white of beard, accosted me. 'You're himself, aren't you?' he said, pointing to a nearby poster of the play. 'I'm no one

– I'm just an old Welsh twit, I'm a bit pissed, too – but I just wanted to say one thing; don't ever stop being an eccentric.' And he was off. On the whole I think he was right: this job of acting is, like all performing arts, and perhaps all arts by definition, an unnatural activity.

Goethe, needless to say, is one of the greatest of all writers, and, more surprisingly, a loveable one. But he crammed Faust *full to bursting point: he wrote it over the whole of his life, and it contains everything he knew. Rehearsing it was like wrestling an octopus. I began to feel seriously out of my depth, despite the three arduous months of work we had done on it. The night before we started technical rehearsals (a week of those) at the Lyric Hammersmith, I slipped off down the road to see a company I barely knew of, the Maly Theatre of St Petersburg (or Leningrad, as it then was), and saw them do a rather ordinary play called* Stars in the Morning Sky. *Even as my brain was telling me how ordinary the play was, my guts and my groin and my soul were in turmoil. This was the greatest piece of collective acting I had ever seen: an ensemble, at last! This was it, the* ignis fatuus, *the hopeless dream, the doomed vision, the thing wiseacres said could never exist. Never, not in all World Theatre Seasons nor anywhere else, had I seen such depth of character from every player on the stage, and the relationships, between the characters and the actors, were palpable, visible, a living tissue. I literally shook throughout the performance, and walked to the station sobbing heavily. There was nothing sentimental about my reaction: I was in a state of physical shock, like being in a car crash. So* that *is what the theatre can be, I thought. That* is *what it should be. Always. I crept into the Lyric the next day feeling very small. Subsequently, I became somewhat obsessed by the Maly; some ten years after first seeing its work, I reviewed – for the* Guardian – Journey Without End *by the director of the company, Lev Dodin. The books editor decided not to print it, saying that it was more like a manifesto than a review. I see her point.*

'After a performance an instant of experience remains,' writes the great Russian director Lev Dodin in this new book of reflections on the theatre; 'that is the moment when something inside us remembered God.' Immediately, we know that we are involved in a very different kind of discourse about the theatre. Dodin is the artistic director of the Maly Theatre of St

Petersburg, unquestionably the greatest ensemble of actors in the world, so it is worth paying attention when he speaks. The company frequently visits Britain; their remarkable *Uncle Vanya* has just toured the country, and their overwhelming version of Chekhov's *Platonov* was seen here some six years ago. This last was astounding in every way: in richness of imagination, in emotional power, in freedom of expression, in depth of conception. It was, frankly, rather shaming: where on the British stage could one see such work?

Every one of the actors brought lives of startling fullness and complexity onto the stage, performing, with exquisite precision, without the slightest self-consciousness and no demand whatever for applause, feats of great physical and emotional virtuosity which emerged quite naturally out of the action; the narrative focus, despite frequently having the large company all on stage together at any one time, was crystal clear. It was a whole world on stage: a world of experience and of expression, taking us deep into the very core of the layered lives of these people in their time, a kind of MRI scan of their souls. One was scarcely aware of a directorial hand, scarcely conscious of a style of performance: one was too busy intimately sharing the complex crisis in the lives of a community of thirty or so fellow human beings. The production spoke directly and overpoweringly, and left those of who were there at the Barbican Theatre that night astonished, moved, enlightened, and ravenous for more.

How is it done? How do these artists achieve such miracles? The answers to these questions are to be found in this collection of transcripts, essays and observations by Lev Dodin, and they may be a bit hair-raising for British actors and directors. The book includes a revealing short study on *The Making of Platonov* by Anna Ogibina, describing the elaborate and lengthy process by which that miraculous production came about. The initial impulse to work on the play came in the late 1980s; in 1990 the company steadily worked on some *études*, or exploratory exercises, which they continued for five years, while playing and even rehearsing other plays. At the end of this period, in 1995, the play was provisionally cast and the process of reading and analysing it began. Actual rehearsals started nine months later, the actors pushing further and further into the lives of the characters and their forms of expression. Different actors tried different roles; they kept going back to the table to read the play throughout rehearsals. Meanwhile the entire auditorium was gutted, the stage completely reconstructed to install the set, which included a pond, a house, and riverbanks; there were run-throughs of the play on the set, after which Dodin made various further casting changes. It was now mid-1996.

The company returned to the rehearsal room for a further six months, during which time everyone was immersed in music classes, since the decision had been taken – *Dodin* had taken the decision – that music would be played live on stage and that every actor would play an instrument; they rehearsed over a hundred musical numbers. Dodin then felt that the play's offstage dinner party should be part of the action, while the play as written was going on in parallel: to that end a large table was placed on stage and an elaborate dinner sequence was devised and integrated; the production was reimagined in its entirety. In April 1997, the company went back on stage; in June of that year one of the leading characters was cut from the play, then reinstated, then permanently cut. The first public performances finally took place in July 1997, some ten years after the initial impulse to do the play. It has changed innumerable times in the subsequent seven years and remains in the repertory, in a state of constant development. Dodin can see no reason to cease playing a production. 'Theatre is already an ephemeral occupation, so how could we plan our baby's death?'

Now, most British actors or directors reading the above will be filled with either scorn or dread. I doubt that there is an actor in the country who would not be inspired and made somewhat envious by the work of the Maly actors, but few, very few of us would submit to the process which produces it. For a start, Dodin is an unqualified autarch: he is the *fons et origo* of the whole enterprise. Most of the actors are his students, he is responsible for the choice of play, the casting, the physical production, the method of rehearsal. In *Journey Without End* he makes it very clear that he is not a *régisseur*, however, on the Max Reinhardt, Tyrone Guthrie, or Franco Zeffirelli model, devising the staging in advance in detail and transmitting it to his actors on the floor. Dodin's process is entirely different, because his conception of theatre is not a mechanical one. To his newly enrolled pupils he says: 'Together we will study a theatre that doesn't yet and may never exist, a theatre that we won't ever be able to master. We will train our ourselves in a dream,' sternly exhorting them to remind themselves that 'the apprentices in Andrei Rublev's workshop had to fast for several days just to start mixing the colours for the great icon painter'.

He makes no claim to omniscience. To begin with, he admits to not knowing how long it will take to achieve the production. Rehearsals simply take as long as they need. Solving this scene or that is neither here nor there: the scene as written is merely the tip of the iceberg. Where does the remaining ninety per cent come from? From the actor. 'Nothing,' he says, 'is more important than human substance... when rehearsing, we try to learn something about ourselves. We try to produce work which concerns us deeply, which we feel very deeply.' For this, the actors need to feel at ease, uninhibited. They need to develop trust in each other, and real understanding. Nor must they be forced. 'Interference in people's spiritual lives is a tyranny,' he says. It is 'a despicable lie to impose a false sense of community... enormous inner culture, discipline, and tact are needed.' This is a slow process: 'It takes ages to develop quality in art.' And theatre, for him, is supremely an art: 'The idea of a commercial enterprise in the theatre is alien for me... the theatre of the one-off show is almost always a theatre factory... if I knew my production would only last for a few weeks I am not sure I would want to do it.'

The seeming modesty of his discourse, innocent but searching, is typically Russian, simultaneously naïve and hugely sophisticated, and it enables him to ask the largest questions in the most direct way. His view of life is essentially tragic. Utterly repudiating 'the vile revolution' of 1917, he admiringly recounts how his mentor refused to interrupt rehearsals as the Kremlin was attacked. 'Only later did I understand that [he] was one of the very few people who were, on that day in 1917, engaged in something worthwhile.' He is equally despairing of both the present and the future. 'I am sure there is something ghastly in human nature, an inbuilt desire to destroy others similar to us.' But he believes that the theatre offers hope. 'Troubles help create an artistic impulse in us... I believe that the only thing which will prevent a general collapse in human relations is a constant effort at self-knowledge and a struggle to retain our values.' Civilisation is only a flimsy veneer – 'that's why every manifestation of civilisation is so important. Theatre is still a sign of civilisation even if an inadequate one.' Only the prospect of self-knowledge, he insists, can bring people to the theatre and keep them there. The more tragic and hopeless the action on stage, the more shocked and ultimately redeemed both the spectator and the actor feel. By rousing an audience's compassion for someone else, 'they learn to be compassionate towards themselves.'

Such unabashed idealism is uncommon in writing about the theatre. It is not simply fine talk: it irradiates every moment of the work produced by his company. Many British actors and directors subscribe equally whole-heartedly to Dodin's convictions, but to no avail, given the prevailing circumstances of production in this country. His genius is to have evolved a process which makes his glorious sentiments flesh. It costs a great deal of money, and a massive commitment of time, energy and, as he says, 'human substance' on the part of the company. Its existence is already threatened in Putin's Russia. But *Journey Without End* shows what can be done in the right conditions. The first half of the book is a classic of the twentieth century. The second half, his close analysis of *Platonov*, is specialised and, frankly, a little dull; it might perhaps have been better to publish the first half on its own as a slim volume of major importance, which without question it is.

As it happens, the reviews for Faust *were rather good, as was business, especially for those days when we did both* Part One *and* Part Two, *seven hours in all. Whatever my reservations about the unplumbed depths of the play, it was a revelation for many people to see the work so central to European intellectual history laid out as a whole before them. (Of course we cut large chunks of it: when Peter Stein did the whole text a decade later, it lasted twenty-four hours.) Simon Rattle came to see our version, and at supper afterwards he said, 'Now I know how to conduct Beethoven.' He also started conducting Mahler's Eighth Symphony, the second part of which is, of course, a setting of the end of* Part Two *of the play. My personal notices were on the whole good, though – such is the morbid oversensitivity of actors – I can remember only one of them, Michael Billington's in the* Guardian: *in his review of* Part One *(a mere three hours), during which I started at the age of a hundred, suddenly became twenty-five, engaged in a savage sword fight, plunged into a vast cistern of water, leaped all over a climbing frame and swung on ropes with a lot of witches, all the while haemorrhaging rhyming couplets, he observed of my performance: 'Simon Callow, as Faust, neatly manages the transition from age to youth'. And that was ALL.*

My parallel career as an all-purpose director, meanwhile, continued to bowl joyously along. I went to the Los Angeles Theatre Center in down-town Los Angeles to direct my translation of Jacques and his Master *by*

Milan Kundera (he wrote it in French, I hasten to say), and was given a superb cast among whose number were a Caribbean black actress, a Chinese-American one, an African-American actor, a blond mid-Westerner of Lutheran stock, a Jewish comedian from the Bronx and Irving Thalberg's great-niece. They embraced Kundera/Diderot's eighteenth-century world with joy and wit, learned that melancholy and depression weren't the same thing, and collaborated with me on amending the script, which I had translated with slavish accuracy to the French original, but with British inflexions. Having heard them read it, I suggested that we should only change it where strictly necessary – where a choice of words might be actually confusing to an American audience. One of the more important such changes was made in a line which troubled one member of the cast (the Bronx comedian). 'It says here, "That night I got assholed." How did he feel about that?' 'Fine,' I said, 'it was great.' 'Huh. Just "great"? I mean, did it hurt?' 'Not at all. Not at the time. The next morning he might have had a hangover.' 'A hangover?' 'Well, yes, if you get drunk, you get hungover, don't you?' 'Yes, but, even if he was drunk, if a guy puts his – you know – his schlong up – ' Suddenly I saw. I explained what arseholed meant to a Briton. 'But what should we say instead?' I asked. 'Pissed.' 'Plastered.' Too genteel I said. Then the Chinese-American woman spoke: 'I got it: shit-faced.' 'Shit-faced?' I said, aghast. 'Yeah, shit-faced. That's what we say. That's what it's like, isn't it?' 'Well,' I said, 'it's obvious you and I go to very different parties.' So shit-faced it was. Big laugh.

Back home, Scottish Opera asked me to do Die Fledermaus, *one of those many musical masterpieces of the operatic stage saddled with an almost impossible book. What I wanted to do – what I always want to do with the plays I direct – was to reproduce in the audience the feelings that the first-night audience at the very first performance would have had, when the piece was unknown. In this case, they would have seen themselves being wickedly sent up. I accordingly transposed the piece to contemporary Glasgow, with which the parallels with the Vienna of 1874 were striking: a newly rich entrepreneurial class (yuppies, in 1989), a country without political power but considerable economic clout, a pervasive culture of hedonism. Kit Hesketh-Harvey of Kit and the Widow wrote the outrageously funny book and lyrics, and the singers (among them the sublime Amy Burton as Adèle and Omar Ebrahim, fabulously decadent as Prince Orlovsky) took to it with gusto, except for the tenor, the fragrantly named Justin Lavender, who thought it was 'crap, really', as he explained* to me one afternoon, but he got his laughs just the same, and clearly enjoyed them. The leading soprano in the revival was something else. She rehearsed with abandon. Then, when we came to the dress rehearsal, for each act she found a place on the stage in which she was comfortable and stood there, stock still, and released her golden tone into the auditorium (actually it was made of rather baser metal). Afterwards I said, 'What happened, Cynthia?' [Not her real name] 'Oh,' she said, 'rehearsals were fun, but this is the performance. Now my loyalty is to – ' here, imitating an action I had been longing to perform all evening, she placed her hands round her neck – 'la voce.'

While I was doing Faust at Hammersmith, the National Theatre had asked me to direct Alan Bennett's new play, which was a double bill called Spy Stories, consisting of An Englishman Abroad, his classic television play about Guy Burgess and Coral Browne in Moscow, lightly adapted for the stage, and a new play, A Question of Attribution, about Anthony Blunt and a character called HMQ. I was to play Burgess and direct A Question of Attribution, while Alan would direct Englishman Abroad and play Blunt. This offer did not require deep reflection on my part.

The National additionally wondered whether I had any ideas for a title, because the present one seemed uninspired. I pulled the Penguin Book of Quotations off the shelf, turned to Shakespeare, found Hamlet, and there the new title was, staring at me in the face: Act IV, Scene V, line 75: Claudius: 'When sorrows come, they come not single spies, but in battalions.' I felt I had just won a treasure hunt. I phoned Alan, who was neither here nor there about it – 'I've never been any good with titles' – and then Richard Eyre, director of the National, who was very pleased indeed. I felt awfully smug, and still do. The cleverness of it! They were spies, they were single (as were the plays), and they came in battalions. Alan and I were an odd couple, Eeyore and Tigger, and no prizes for guessing which was which. I suspect that I was, as he says of someone in a book of his, 'too cocky for my taste', alarmingly ebullient for someone of his fastidiousness and self-discipline. It is to my credit, however, that, overruling his fastidiousness, I saved a wonderful line in the play, HMQ's observation that 'if Francis Bacon painted one, one would be a Screaming Queen', which Alan had thought rather obvious and camp and wanted to cut. I wrote about him in a review of his autobiographical collection, Untold Stories, in 2006.

There are times – rare, very rare – when as an actor or director you find yourself holding a piece of new writing which you know to be pure gold. It happened to me with a double bill of plays called *Single Spies*. The author was Alan Bennett, who would also appear in both plays and direct the other one, and it was clear that the central scene he had written between Blunt and the Queen – quite apart from any element of *lèse-majesté* – was going to create a sensation. It was a sublime piece of comedy which touched on a number of profound questions, the most penetrating that of authenticity, which, as it happens, is the central concern of *Untold Stories*, Bennett's magisterial and largely autobiographical compendium, sequel to the immensely successful *Writing Home*. The present volume is much the more revealing of the two, offering a comprehensive insight into a figure who, perhaps to his own surprise, has become a defining feature of the national landscape, part of what it is to be British – 'as British as Alan Bennett', as one might say.

He and I had a very successful working partnership, despite the anomaly of my directing the author in his own work while acting with him, a situation which Alan seemed to find perfectly normal.

Once the play had opened and transferred to the West End, we were gratifyingly successful, celebrities beating a nightly path to the stage door, but Alan couldn't bear any of it, and, safety helmet on head, he would escape, unrecognised, to his bike and thence home to supper by the television. He hated the socialising, which is not unknown in the acting profession, but he didn't much care for the acting either, which is rather less common. He would sit in the dressing room encircled with gloom. And yet as Blunt he was quite brilliant, and astonishingly consistent, provoking the same roars of laughter night after night. Sharing a stage with him was like sharing a stage with Paul Scofield: one feels a bit of a gooseberry. The public's lust for him knows no bounds. Perhaps that is what persuades him to appear so frequently before them, in one guise or another; he writes of himself as 'someone who has had to stand on stage [and read Larkin]'; had to, Alan? The ageless physiognomy is endlessly photographed, the subject an unwilling but stoical victim.

Untold Stories has little to say about him as a performer, but it is the last word about him as a writer, and as a man; he now speaks in unmediated form about his life. 'You do not put yourself into what you write,' he says, marvellously, 'you find yourself there.' But Bennett the writer offers the same paradox as Bennett the performer: a private man who is determined at all costs to go public. And we certainly want to know about him. The present volume both satisfies that appetite and explains it. Something in us wants to reach out to the boyish figure who he tells us is seventy but who to us is always that mop-topped egghead, spikily brilliant but somehow needy: he has described his late start, anatomically, not maturing physically till he was eighteen, a circumstance that has lent a quality of perpetual precocity to everything he does, seeming to warrant special admiration as if it were a wonder that he'd done it at all. His remarkable writing here about his parents – Mam and Dad, as he invariably refers to them – reveals the extent to which he is still their lad Alan. Their sense of the home as a fortress, their horror of attention-seeking, their rejoicing in their ordinariness, is shared by Bennett: he also shares his parents' disdain for the enterprise, the ebullience, the sheer extroversion of Mam's shop-assistant sister, Myra, and her 'desire to be different, to be marked out above the common ruck and to have a tale to tell'. One is inclined to warm to Aunty Myra but Bennett's – and Mam's and Dad's – disapproval is implacable. At the same time, without endorsing Myra, he seems tentatively to disapprove of the censorious person that he was; it seems to have taken him a lifetime to escape his parents' values – for most of us it takes a lifetime to appreciate them.

The book begins with an account of his mother's depressive illnesses which is unsparing both of her circumstances and gradual decline and of his attitude to the woman she had become: his coldness, impatience, indifference – and his sense of duty. He charts his frustrated rage with her delusions, determinedly trying to hike her back to reality, until eventually she dwindles into the sort of touchy-feely creature she would have been horrified by when she had her wits; he is dismally aware that the breezily generalised manner of the nurses probably suits her more than his attempts to communicate. He offers tart and pertinent comments on the diagnosis and treatment of mental illness, protesting against the general indifference to the plight of the routinely depressed, unless they present sensational symptoms: 'Mistake your wife for a hat and the doctor will never be away from your bedside.'

A thread of family insanity runs through the book, and the suicide of his grandfather looms large. But the precision, detail and pithiness of his writing – whose sententiousness owes as much to Yorkshire as it does to Oxford – plucks celebration from what might otherwise be merely depressing. There is a pervading wistfulness well expressed in his remark (not collected in the book) that he saw himself as an outsider, 'not in the Colin Wilson sense, more other people having fun and me not'; the prose too frequently has a dying fall: 'I have no nickname as there has never been any need for one.' This sometimes tips over, forgivably, into self-pity in the diaries, where, for example, he finds it impossible to believe that there will be any sort of gathering in his honour when he dies; in fact, though the diaries – five years' worth of them – fail to avoid a certain querulousness, they add up to a serious chronicle of our time, a valuable corrective to the babble of current affairs and opinion programmes. Sometimes he is unintentionally hilarious, as when citing reasons for being cheerful: 'Well, at least it's not Stalingrad. It's warm – I don't have lice.' And always he remains a great phrasemaker: the Queen, after Diana's death, is forced to go 'mournabout'.

The book is a house of many mansions, celebrating his enthusiasms and focusing sharply on what he deplores: he remains an Attlee boy, and can only see modern life as a *dégringolade* (especially under the present 'Labour' government, as he parenthesises it). His account of his own illness is strikingly restrained and all the more powerful for that, utterly eschewing sentimentality. In fact, what emerges from the book, and is perhaps the key to why he is so cherished, is a man who refuses to be anything other than who he is. He describes how, when he failed to become an officer during National Service, he identified himself: 'What I was not was a joiner. And so in due course not a CBE, not a knight.' Elsewhere he tells us that he is 'reluctant to be enrolled in the ranks of gay martyrdom, reluctant, if the truth be told, to be enrolled in any ranks whatsoever'. Except, of course, that he has joined the ranks of the non-joiners. Beyond all his varied brilliance, the wisdom and the profundity of so much of his work, it is his insistence on refusing to be other than who or what he is, that has made the British people take him under its wing. He is his own man. He sees the hilarity, however, when the National Gallery makes him a trustee on the grounds that he represents the man in the street. If only.

Alan was extraordinarily easy to work with, which, when you consider that he was being directed in his own play by the actor he was acting with, is remarkable. His only day of anxiety came at the technical rehearsals when the paintings that hung in the corridor of Buckingham Palace were first brought on. They were in an unfinished state, and Alan was told so, but he flew into a state of terrible agitation, all the more alarming because hitherto he had never once so much as raised his voice. No matter how often I explained to him that they would be hugely better very soon, he remained agitated to an almost medically troubling degree. Richard Eyre was sent for, and, talking him down very calmly, eventually restored his equilibrium. Later Richard told me that on Kafka's Dick, *which Richard had directed at the Royal Court, Alan had become obsessed by the suit which Jim Broadbent (Kafka's father) was wearing, until he had finally gone to Savile Row and bought him a new one with his own money. 'Displacement anxiety,' Richard said. A great artistic director; and a remarkable and somewhat unexpected man. I wrote this review of Eyre's diaries,* National Service, *in 2003.*

Richard Eyre is a strikingly handsome man, compact and perfectly groomed. He is physically and intellectually elegant at all times, unfailingly courteous and searchingly intelligent; whatever he says is perfectly phrased and shot through with self-irony; he is both fastidious and ascetic. His quiet authority is unmistakable, his kindness palpable; power and sensitivity are present in equal quantities. It would not surprise you, on meeting him, to discover that he was Head of the Foreign Office, a clinical psychologist, or an internationally acclaimed architect. In other ages, he might have been the personal confessor to a Bourbon monarch, or the master of a great medieval college. Sanity, balance, control are at his core.

So how did this man come to confide these words to his diary: 'I've started a course of an antidepressant, Prozac. I feel as if my brain has a number of compartments, like dog traps, out of which wild things emerge – insects, spiders, frogs, snakes and wolves, surrounded by a gnawing cold damp wind that permeates everything. The drug has closed these traps and I feel that sand, or snow, is piling up outside them. I'm not happy, just not in pain.' How did that man write those words? Why, because of the theatre, of course; more precisely because of The Royal National Theatre of Great Britain, that century-old dream turned into concrete nightmare. Eyre ran it for an extraordinary ten years, and for a large proportion of that time, he felt overwhelmed by the task. Coming across a list of the symptoms of depression, he ticks off four: insomnia; feelings of worthlessness; diminished ability to think; recurrent thoughts of suicide. Not that anyone would have known. 'I have to clam up at the theatre. Don't give the game away.' He kept a diary 'to remind myself that what is unbearable today will be bearable tomorrow'.

Running any theatre is a challenge, but the National is in a class of its own, both in itself and emblematically. When they were looking for a successor for him, David Hare briskly listed the three tasks of its director: 1 – plan a repertoire of seventeen shows a year; 2 – run the building; 3 – be a spokesman for the British theatre. The first of these demands, which seems perhaps the most straightforward, is, as Eyre puts it, like 'three-dimensional chess in the dark'. He describes the process to his board; they are, understandably, horrified and awed: 'Here's the equation: three theatres, three shows in repertoire in each theatre. If you want to play your successes and nurse your failures you need total freedom of manoeuvre, but if you cast an actor in two shows you restrict your freedom of programming, and if you cast one in another auditorium, you're scuppered. As you are if you want to tour a show. Or have an unusually complex set. Or stage a musical. You have to guess at the number of performances for each show, i.e. predict your successes, or worse, your failures. And if you want to transfer a show to the West End you have to anticipate getting an option on the actors. And the freedom to change the repertoire according to demand is restricted by the three-month print deadline of the brochure. If you shorten that you diminish the advance booking and therefore prejudice your cash flow. And so it goes...'

Why, he asks himself, did he ever take on the task? He lists the obvious motives: ambition, vanity, hubris, finally – conclusively – 'because it was there'. But when it comes to it and he is appointed to the job, at the press conference he feels as if he's 'performing a character called Richard Eyre about whom I don't have enough information to give a credible performance'. But this is temporary. He knows that at a deeper level 'I like danger. I like the feeling of having a gun pointed at my head: dance, perform, live a bit.' This is a very striking phrase, the theatre as an antidote to respectability, normality, complacency – safety, perhaps. Theatre as bungee jump. Well, if he wanted a gun at his temple he certainly got it: the daily dread of failing, both personally (in his own productions) and in his responsibilities to his company and his audience. Rarely has a director so nakedly described the panic that attends every production, the hopes, the fears, the minute-by-minute anxiety about the piece, the actors, his own work. He had a number of brilliant successes during his tenure at the National – *Richard III*, David Hare's trilogy, *King Lear* with

261

Ian Holm – but an equal number, by his own account, of abject flops. It's hard enough under any circumstances to live with failure but when you're running an organisation, and everything hinges on your judgement, to have to face your colleagues and find the necessary self-respect to continue to articulate policy with any authority is a very particular test of character.

Eyre's solution to the challenge is the only possible one, but rarer in practice than hen's teeth: 'The most important attribute for anyone who runs a theatre is generosity: you've got to be prepared to enfranchise people who are more talented, more successful, and just *different* from yourself.' This he did, consistently, during his tenure. It was harder to be generous with himself: 'I'm a Catholic in everything but religion – I believe in guilt, I believe in suffering as the cost of happiness, failure as the cost of success.' Public service is in Eyre's genes: his sense of duty exceeds every other impulse, and he was deeply loved by his colleagues for it. He worked unceasingly to balance the books, to maintain and exceed standards, to tame and liberate the beastly building itself (in the teeth of the uncomprehending resistance of its vainglorious architect Denys Lasdun and the Lasdunites who openly called him 'a barbarian'). He knew every one of his fellow workers by name (a feat not achieved by every director of the National Theatre); he forged a team.

This had been his first ambition for the theatre when he was appointed: 'to encourage a sense of community, a sense of family, a desire to share a common purpose: in short, to make the NT into something that was more than the sum of its parts'. Like many people in the theatre, he has sought to create in his working life what he never knew in his childhood. His magnificently awful father dies during the course of Eyre's time, but not before having finally manifested the tenderness he was incapable of showing when Eyre most needed it; his mother, too, is at last liberated from the twilight zone of Alzheimer's syndrome where she has dwelt for too long. He becomes an orphan, and sits with his wife and daughter reading *King Lear* by candlelight, finally grasping its meaning: 'I'm no longer prepared to judge, everyone's to blame, everyone can be forgiven.' The fine production of *Lear* for which this was preparation and by which it was so profoundly informed was his last at the National; released from his chains, he feels bereft, but at his farewell party, he quotes William Shawn: 'Whatever our roles we did something quite wonderful together. Love was the controlling emotion; we did our work with honesty and love.'

Everything Eyre did for the National and at the National, he did with honour and distinction. Intelligence and taste informed all his actions; his decisions were shrewd and often innovative. And of his love of the theatre, its processes and its denizens – actors, writers, designers, technicians, publicists, caterers – there can be no doubt. The man who emerges from these diaries, however, does not quite seem to belong to the theatre himself. He is like the very finest kind of colonial administrator who has fallen in love with the land he administrates and with its people, learnt the language to perfection, knows its history better than they do, and never wants to be anywhere else till the day he dies. But the people themselves have an emotional energy which is irrational, ancestral and dangerous, and this energy is not in his blood. He writes superbly about it: 'That's the true actor: the true professional – experiencing the state of possession, enduring passion and yet, like a firewalker, remaining untouched by the experience.' He quotes with approval a magnificent letter sent to him by that great beast of the jungle, Mike Gambon, raging against an attempt to make the National a no-smoking zone: 'A theatre isn't a place where you can impose rules on people, it's a dirty radical place where an actor can work with a fag in his hand, a place where someone like me or you if you felt the need can piss down the staircase... surely these people should go and work at IBM or Shell... screaming at night from the stage about the plight of mankind and the world would be ridiculed in a building where you can't smoke. The stage is like a war game and some wounded people have to smoke.' Exactly, says Eyre, but you won't catch him pissing down the stairwell.

Nor is this raging sense of appetite for life confined to actors. Eyre writes admiringly and a little wistfully of Peter Hall (who haunts the early part of the book) as possessing 'a prodigious energy, a kind of devouring greed and an edge of madness'. At the beginning of his tenure, Eyre and Hare rather soberly agree that it is necessary to 'to introduce a note of anarchy to the theatre', but then he adds, 'It's hard to make an anarchistic gesture now that isn't immediately assimilated,' not a thought, perhaps, that would occur to any self-respecting anarchist. The riot that is at the theatre's heart – the gaudy assertion of carnival values, upturning everything, embracing everything, roaring its pain and its bliss to the skies – cannot be reduced to a note, or a gesture. It springs from the primitive act of theatre – an actor and an audience – fuelled by an all-consuming, raging need on both parts of the equation, which is why a theatre that doesn't have a company at its centre will always, by one means or another, end up cerebral, and that spells death to the theatre.

Richard Eyre's book is a superlative record of a theatre, a man, and a time. There is unconscious comedy, as, desperately overburdened, he accepts more and more additional work, lecturing incessantly, becoming a Governor of the BBC. He wanted, at the beginning of his tenure, 'to live a bit'. Not too far along the line, he is crying 'I want my life back' and later, more poignantly, 'An unexamined life is not worth living (the unlived life isn't worth examining).' But responsibility will always come first. He is a natural member of the Great and the Good, being himself both good and great, and he has sat at life's High Table as of right. The book is filled with many wonderful conversations heard there; he has heard the inside riff and has transcribed it wonderfully. Not a page is without some fascinating and unexpected shaft; when he says something to somebody, as often as not, they reply with a quote from Cato the Elder. And some magnificent monsters stride across his pages – John Osborne, Maria St Just, Georg Solti, his father. Come to think of it, Eyre Senior ('Shakespeare is balls!') might have made a wonderful director of the National Theatre – carnival-style.

Single Spies was one of the great successes of Eyre's regime. The scene in Buckingham Palace, in Question of Attribution, *was, with impeccably credible canvases, the smash hit of the evening, all the more electric because it broke a centuries-long taboo prohibiting the representation of the monarch on stage. After the show, as Alan made his getaway by bike, all the famous people who came to see the show were ushered into* my *dressing room, where I filled their glasses with champagne and chatted urbanely about the play. I suspect that many of them thought I'd written it. I did nothing to disabuse my new best friends Shirley, Liza or Dustin, of their error.*

I left the play after three months in the West End because – why? – oh, yes – yawn – I had to direct Shirley Valentine *on Broadway – triumph (yawn) – and then I went to Hollywood to act in* Postcards *from the Edge with Meryl Streep, Gene Hackman and Shirley MacLaine (yawn, yawn) for Mike Nichols (no yawn, even as a joke). I wrote a sort of diary piece about the film for the* Independent.

Mike Nichols, whom I had never met, called me in my dressing room during the interval of *Single Spies*. Alan Bennett was in the room at the time, and groaned when I voicelessly told him who it was. 'Nothing like that ever happens to me,' Alan moaned. 'It's the first time it's ever happened to me,' I mouthed back. Nichols had just seen the play, and on the strength of it wanted me for a part in his new film. It might, he said, amuse me: an English director named Simon, directing his first film in America. It did amuse me; more than he could guess. Unknown to him, I, Simon, and English, was about to direct my first movie, in America. Beyond this astonishing and yet somehow completely meaningless coincidence, there was every reason to accept the part. The script, adapted by Carrie Fisher from her novel *Postcards from the Edge*, was as funny as the book, though in an entirely different way, being an extrapolation of only one of the characters' stories, that – presumably autobiographical – of Suzanne Vale, actress, drug addict, wit. This character was to be played by Meryl Streep, and it was she whom I would direct in the movie within the movie. I called Nichols back to tell him that yes, indeed, I'd do the part. 'Oh that's good,' he said, 'because when I saw you in *Single Spies*, I made a resolve never to make another movie without you in it.' 'That's quite a commitment, Mr Nichols,' I said. 'One I am happy,' he replied, 'to make.' Deals were struck, contracts signed. Three months later, I was summoned for a read-through in Hollywood, at the Burbank Studios.

Read-throughs are not all that common on movies, particularly not if, as on this one, the cast is spread around the globe. But there we all, or almost all, were, in one of the huge hangar-studios of Columbia Pictures, in the centre of which had been placed eight trestle tables piled high with scripts. Behind the trestle tables, there were other tables, sagging under the weight of a great deal of food: hot kippers and omelettes and steaks, served on silver platters. We all rapidly made our way to this feast, piling our plates high. There were Meryl Streep and Richard Dreyfus and Shirley MacLaine and Dennis Quaid and twenty others of us, passionately scoffing away at ten in the morning, as if eating were the reason we had come here from the four corners of the earth. Mike Nichols was not eating, preferring to smoke. He did this somehow tentatively, as if cigarettes were a novelty he was pioneering. He was the host of this teetotal party, and alone seemed impervious to the mania that seized the room, affably introducing his actors to each other. Meryl Streep, plucking at her hair as if there were wasps in it, teetered over, uttered some charming compliments, and then tottered off. 'Don't expect any sense out of Meryl,' Mike said, 'she has to sing.'

*

I remembered the last time I had been at Columbia Studios. It was 1980, I was in America for the first time, and my then agent thought it would be a good idea for me to show my face around the various studios. She arranged meetings with six casting directors. Los Angeles being Los Angeles, that took the whole day, and Los Angeles taxis being Los Angeles taxis, cost something over $300. My rounds were not encouraging. Nobody had the slightest idea who I was. I had acted in no movies, and though *Amadeus* was news in New York, it had as yet created no ripples on the West Coast, where the theatre is in any case regarded as a harmless hobby indulged in by actors who can't get serious work. '*Amadeus*,' said one of the casting ladies, 'what is that?' 'It's a play about the death of Mozart,' I said. 'The death of *Moss Hart*?' she replied, wide-eyed. No one was less than polite, but the lady at Columbia spoke for all her colleagues when, after a little polite chat about the art of acting ('Which do you prefer, Simon: comedy or drama?') she reached over to me, placed a hand on top of mine, and said, gently, 'What are you *doing* here, Simon? Go home. I beg you. Go home.' I did, and decided that the only way to come to Hollywood was in triumph.

*

By the time we sat down to read the script, sound recordists with their equipment were installed at the trestle tables. Our first stumbling efforts were thus immortalised. Actually, nobody stumbled much at all. Mike, still smoking in an experimental sort of way, made a charming speech of thanks to us all for coming to help them, him and Carrie, with the script, and we plunged in. Mary Wickes, playing Meryl's grandmother, eighty years old with *Now Voyager* and *White Christmas* among her credits, spoke her lines from memory, which is unusual in this situation, almost bad form, showing off. She apologised: two weeks before she had been struck temporarily blind; it would be a month before she could see again and so she'd been obliged to learn her lines from a tape recording. She was in an emotional state anyway, she confessed. The man at the gate had greeted her with 'Nice to have you back again, Miss Wickes'; it was thirty years since she had worked at Burbank.

The Misses Streep and MacLaine were magnificently certain, especially in their musical duel. Meryl, admittedly, started singing tentatively, but so did her character. Shirley brazenly eclipsed her; so did her character. Stephen Sondheim had revised his lyrics for 'I'm Still Here' specifically for her – 'In the Sixties / I burned my brassiere / And I'm still here' – and as she sang them, she worked her way round the table, ruffling hair, slipping her hand inside a jacket, finally flinging her legs over some happy man's shoulder. We cheered. The actor next to me said, 'This is magic. It's magic. It's like the great days. This one has that something, believe me. It's great.'

I myself was less conscious of the extraordinariness of the event than of the bruises on my right arm. They had been put there by Carrie Fisher, who, as her first line was read, sank her talons into my flesh, and left them there. Every laugh, every sob – and there were many of both – produced another steel spasm. After it was all over, she thanked me sweetly for the use of my body. The actors parted to their respective corners of the globe, to be pursued there by rewrites on pages of many colours. I went to various places in America before returning to England, and wherever I went, there would be a FedEx package waiting for me with the new stuff. Scenes were contracted, scenes were expanded; characters were sharpened, characters were softened. One page contained the pleasing information that my first entrance would now be made on a crane, murmuring the phrase, 'Hello darling. You look *wonderful*. Big Kiss.' The scene had been added in the light, I imagine, of my sly impersonation of A Certain English Director, which had produced laughter round the table as I drawled my Actions and my Cuts. This estimable gentleman likes to give the impression that directing is the least of his interests, a slightly vexing interruption of his elegant social life. Actually, he's a rather good director.

*

All the scenes I was involved in take place on a movie set, so naturally they were shot at Burbank. Any movie location is a little confusing – you can never be sure what's real and what was put there by the designer – but films about film-making are severely disorientating. Is that a grip or an actor playing a grip? Am I on the backlot of Burbank or the backlot of Burbank-within-the-movie? In the film I, Simon, was playing a director, Simon, directing Meryl Streep, who was playing an actress, based on the actress who wrote the script, who was standing behind the camera watching us. Meryl and I were being directed by Mike Nichols, himself a well-known performer. The confusion continued at all levels. As I stood at the refreshments table, a gaffer (a real gaffer) who was standing next to me said: 'It's okay, Simon, you're among friends, you can drop the accent.'

*

On American films, there is a never-ending supply of food at all times. This is not so on English films. We have tea breaks instead. Here we are sustained by a strange assortment of foodstuffs laid out on a trestle table: there are cupcakes, breakfast cereals all day long, jelly babies, M&Ms. What kind of food is this? I puzzled over it for a long time, and then I realised: it's food for a children's party. I suppose that must be somebody's – somebody UP THERE's – idea of what filming is.

*

Meryl *was* Suzanne Vale, or rather, she was Carrie. She had become Carrie. She was extrovert, outrageous, garrulous; things which I believe she, on the whole, is not. Carrie, meanwhile, was still Carrie, only rather more so. Dressed in a perfectly simple little black Azzedine Alaia number which should have been a crumpled mess as a result of her hyperactivity but wasn't, she presented a surprising combination of Dorothy Parker, Groucho Marx and the Princess Leia. An ebullient figure at the edge of things, she was rarely silent and never still. Once, I walked out of the studio where we were filming, to find Carrie – the real Carrie – the one not played by Meryl, that is to say – still in her Alaia outfit, lying on her back on the tarmac, with a puzzled expression on her face. She called me over and asked me a complicated question about Charles Laughton's sex life. I was unable to answer it to her satisfaction, so I left her, still puzzled, apparently oblivious to the danger of being run over by a passing lorry.

Meryl and Carrie were always together on the set. They were forever engaged in a curious duet, or maybe duel. Not that there was the slightest tension between them – on the contrary. They were like schoolgirl twins, whispering and shrieking together, spurring each other on. It was like seeing someone with a fantasised version of themselves: Carrie and super-Carrie – except that the fantasy version was the real person.

*

Mike Nichols had the air of a genial master of ceremonies. He had cast his actors and fixed his script, and he trusted both. Once, only once, I saw him slightly agitated. A prop man had set the wrong prop. 'Why is that chair there?' Mike demanded to know. 'Well,' said the guy, 'they said...' 'They?' said Mike. 'They? Who are they? *I* am they.' For the most part, he operated by wit and irresistible intelligence, and was unusually available to all comers. He spent, he said, a great deal of his time on a film just being pleasant to people. He needed to do this in order to remain human. 'Everything is geared to your becoming inhuman. You suddenly find you've turned into stone or Streisand.' Why do so many directors scream, he had asked himself? Because, like the President of the United States, they feel that they're at the very top of the pile, and yet still things don't happen they way they want them to. So, says Mike, he no longer screams. He prepares, to the last degree; but once he comes to shoot the scene, he arrives with a perfectly empty mind, and is generally delighted by what he sees. Even his trailer is called Komfort.

*

In Hollywood, they pay you better, the costumes are better, there are better facilities. Communications are better, and there are more people concerned for your welfare. But it is a factory, where the film you are making is one of many, past, present, to come. An independent film, or a film made on location, is, by contrast, a corporation convened uniquely for the object of making THIS film, a temporary empire whose end is contained in its beginning. That gives it a brave, adventurous feeling, however tough or hectic it may be. But Hollywood has seen it all before, is ready for everything. The machine works. Nichols & co. did their considerable most to make *Postcards* feel like a group of people who had a great idea for a movie and got together to make it. Nichols talks to you; he really talks. So does John Calley, the associate producer. They come to your caravan, and they talk. And when my scenes were over, the entire company, led by a lusty Streep and a finger-clicking Carrie, sang a song of farewell to me. Two hundred people looking into your eyes and singing a song of farewell is tough on the Anglo-Saxon temperament while it's actually happening, but it becomes heart-warming, a little tear-jerkingly so, only moments afterwards.

The real movie that I, the real Simon, was about to direct was The Ballad of the Sad Café, *some of the madness of which I described in a piece for the* Sunday Telegraph *magazine at the time of its release, 1991.*

Among the messages on the answer machine is one in the unmistakable voice, imperious and exotic, of Ismail Merchant. 'Simon. We think it's time you made your first film. Come to the apartment tomorrow morning to have breakfast with the screenwriter.' I phone Ismail at his office and discover a) that this is not a hoax and b) that the book in question is *The Ballad of the Sad Café*. It's taken him, he says, twenty-five years to acquire the rights, and now he wants me to direct it. I find a late-opening bookshop and buy this, the only Carson McCullers novel I haven't read. I find it moving in a primitive way, quite different from anything else she wrote. 'Southern Gothic' the back cover calls it, but the story seems to me more like Racine or Sophocles, a love trap devised by cruel gods to humiliate proud and pitiful mortals. The tone of the book, despite her singing cadences and steady rhythms, has the quality of a folk tale. It reads like a tribal myth, as if it were something brought back by an anthropologist from a forgotten people, a record of some ancient outrage.

At breakfast the next morning I meet the screenwriter, Michael Hirst, lean and intense, given to spasms of laughter which shake his whole frame and make him cough so much he has to light up another cigarette to calm it down. Urged on by enthusiastic cries from Ismail, we start talking about the story immediately, as if we were old collaborators. As we talk, the phone rings; it's Vanessa Redgrave. She's brought a group of Russian Jewish actors to London from Moscow to do a season at the Lyric Hammersmith, and she wants Ismail to take them all out to supper. He accedes immediately. The dinner, to be held at the Red Fort in Dean Street, is fixed for the following week . We must come too. He has suggested to Vanessa that she should play Miss Amelia in the film. She's wildly enthusiastic, but wants to meet me. Understandably. We know each other slightly from social gatherings and the odd benefit, but nothing in our previous acquaintance would give her any reason to believe that she should trust her talent to my uninitiated hands.

Why indeed should Ismail trust this project about which he cares so deeply to my uninitiated hands? I never asked him; he just did. I had never mentioned any desire to direct a film, though in fact I felt it quite strongly, ever since writing a book about Charles Laughton, in the course of which I saw over seventy films, and learned something of what he went through in making his only film as a director, *The Night of the Hunter*. I discovered that he had finally found his perfect *métier*. His strong visual instincts, his poetic temperament, above all his desire to collaborate with writer, cinematographer, designer and composer, had all reached their fulfilment. Being similarly inclined, I felt that maybe this was the *métier* I'd been looking for, too. Who on earth would ask me to direct a film, though? Mr Merchant, that's who. He'd intervened in my life once before when in 1985 he asked me to be appear in the film of *A Room with a View*, at a time when no other film-maker seemed to think that I could be contained on celluloid. He had seen and liked my work as a stage director, I knew. But this was a gamble even by his standards.

Michael Hirst and I started meeting regularly. He'd already done a draft of the script that he wouldn't show me; we began again from scratch. I wanted to be true to the novel's shape. I was convinced we should tell the story as much as possible the way McCullers had, creating her forgotten world and her strange people without reference to psychologising or explanation, as sparely as she had done. It is a ballad after all, a simple narrative of a town in which three powerful outcasts, a giantess, a dwarf and a criminal, work out their appalling destinies before the horrified gaze of the townspeople. Edward Albee, adapting the novel for the stage, had endowed these townspeople with the gift of tongues, enabling them to comment and moralise on events; in addition, as if that were not enough, he had created a narrator, to comment and moralise on the comment and moralisation. Mrs McCullers had not liked the play: 'There are barely fifteen lines of dialogue in my novel,' she said. 'In Mr Albee's play they never stop talking.' To be sure, in her persona as the writer, she says some enormously eloquent things, including some of the most famous and devastating words about love ever uttered; but it is impossible that the townspeople could know or say any of them. Michael and I struggled over many meals to find the true epic quality to the story. Halfway through our work, I discovered a letter of hers in which she described her novel as 'my strange fairy story', and that crystallised our thoughts. The script began to take shape.

Meanwhile there was dinner with Vanessa. I got to the Red Fort after a performance of *Single Spies*, and things were in full swing, with fifty Russian Jewish actors washing down their onion bhajees and tandoori quails with large gulps of Stolichnaya, as the Indian waiters looked on with anxious amazement. Ismail was in his element, and so, evidently, was Vanessa, making impromptu speeches which were immediately translated to great acclaim, the Stolichnaya flowing ever more merrily down the hatch. Ismail was introduced and so was I; we were cheered and toasted. Somehow, in the midst of all this, Ismail managed to pop the question. 'Vanessa!' he roared. 'Will you be our Miss Amelia?' he said. She turned her face, radiant and flushed with delight, to us. 'Why not?' she said, and threw back her head and laughed with roguish joy.

At this point, I felt a cold hand of fear on my heart because I knew it was all going to happen, and I would have to become a film director. Of course, nothing was signed. There was no money, apart from anything else. But the combination of Ismail's determination and Vanessa's joyful commitment, were curiously reassuring. In fact, whatever reservations one might ever have entertained about Ismail when it came, for instance, to negotiating one's fees ('We are not Hollywood! We make films for love!'), he has never, in my experience, said that something would happen which didn't. Michael and I continued to wrestle with the form and tone of the script; one day we had a breakthrough. Perhaps the Reverend Willin, a minor character in the novel, could attain an eloquence denied to his congregation. Perhaps, like a Graham Greene priest, he was a broken man whose head was wiser than his heart and he might be able to articulate McCullers's great truths about love. That, our only departure from the novel, gave us a great release, and we delivered a first draft which, with the addition of a few subtle *hommages* to *The Night of the Hunter*, seemed us to be a script that Mrs McCullers, had she been the screenwriter, and chosen to tell her story as a film, might have written. That was the criterion.

My next collaborator was Bruno Santini, with whom I had done many stage productions, but who had never designed a film before. We gathered our materials, starting with the astonishing photographs of Walker Evans, recording the bleak, blasted, but not unbeautiful lives of the people of the dust bowl in the 1930s. His images guided us in our search for locations. We had to find, somewhere in America, a town that time had forgotten. We knew we couldn't afford to build one, so we set off under our own steam, and at our own expense, to roam through the southern states of America. Received and patiently ferried around by the respective Film Commissions, we passed with increasing melancholy from Georgia (where Carson McCullers had been born and of which she often wrote) to Mississippi, from Louisiana to Texas. The dryness and the dustiness she describes were easy enough to find, but there wasn't a single site that hadn't somehow been invaded by the late twentieth century. As we took our leave wearily from the Film Commission in Austin, Texas, Bruno spotted a set of photographs of what appeared to be a Western Town. 'Oh, that wouldn't interest you,' they said, 'it's a movie set that Willie Nelson built on his ranch, for a movie he was in.' 'Well, we'd better see it,' we said, appalled at the idea of returning to England without having had even a glimpse of our nameless town. And so we drove out, and it was instantly evident that this was it – a little dusty street in the middle of – not nowhere, but an estate so vast that it might as well have been. Not a strip of tarmac, not a telephone pole, not a modern building in sight. Nothing daunted by the place's name (Willieville) we photographed it as lovingly and thoroughly as a lover, and returned, via steamy New Orleans, to London. Ismail immediately accepted that this was the location, with as little comment as he had offered on hearing that we were taking ourselves off on recce – with as little comment, indeed, as he had offered when I suggested that Bruno, who had never designed a film in his life, should design *Ballad*. If he trusts you, it appears, he trusts you. We reckoned that it would cost half a million dollars to convert Willieville into Carsonville. This was the first money talked on the project. It was becoming more and more real.

All of this took place in summer of 1989. There followed, for me, a period of American nomadism, going to Chicago to start work on a book about Orson Welles, to Kansas City to act in *Mr & Mrs Bridge* for Merchant Ivory, to Los Angeles to act in *Postcards from the Edge* and then to direct *Stevie Wants to Play the Blues* at the Los Angeles Theatre Center, finally holing up in the snow of Toronto to shoot a final scene for *Mr & Mrs Bridge* with Paul Newman, only really returning to England in February 1990. At every point (and especially in Kansas and Toronto, of course), Ismail was keeping me abreast of his struggle to raise money for *Ballad*. Nobody wanted to invest. His track record spoke, one would have thought, for itself, not to mention Vanessa's. Mine, I appreciated, left a little to be desired, but that, apparently, was not the problem. It was Carson McCullers. The novel, wrote distributors and producers from all over the globe, was not 'satisfactory' – was 'difficult'. A six-page letter from an Australian demolished the work, informing us that McCullers had set herself a task as a writer that she didn't have the genius to bring off; more candidly, a Japanese investor wrote to say that the story was 'too sad. At this time Japanese people want to be happy.' But still Ismail plugged on, setting dates for the start of filming and a schedule for editing and release.

I arrived in New York in March to start casting the rest of the film. Vanessa was in place, of course, and the crucial part of the hunchback dwarf, Cousin Lymon, was settled, too, on a happy inspiration. While we were in Los Angeles, my partner Christopher Woods had approached the casting department of the theatre and asked if they knew of any extraordinary 'little guys', as these actors are formally known in the States. They produced a photograph which showed a face of such mingled melancholy and mischief that we knew he must be our man; and lunch the next day, which added titanic appetite and pugnacious political argument to these qualities confirmed us that Cork Hubbert, stand-up comedian, was our man. Marvin Macy, the third of the trio, was another matter. Actors seemed to find it daunting – or was it the book? Or me and my inexperience? Or Vanessa and her genius? Then, with his usual dramatic fatefulness, Ismail stormed into the casting suite as we sat, surrounded by photographs and directories and clumps of our own hair pulled out at the roots in despair, and cried, 'Sam Shepard will do the part. Sam Shepard will be our Marvin Macy!' I knew Shepard a little and had greatly liked his work in various movies, but I had not thought of him for McCullers's bad angel. 'Well, I – ' 'We will have him,' raged Ismail, 'we will have him! We must!' and swept out.

'And who,' growled Shirley Rich, the veteran and brilliant casting director, in the ensuing silence, 'who do you want for the Reverend Willin?' 'Rod Steiger,' I said, moodily. 'You're joking,' she said, and, knowing in my heart that no one of his stature was going to consider doing a two-scene part in a tyro director's first outing, I said, 'I know, it's ridiculous, isn't it, but he's exactly the actor to turn what might be thought of as a speech into something someone actually said.' 'No,' she said, 'you don't understand. He's my friend. I'll get it to him tonight.' And the next day Rod Steiger called and we spoke and he said it was the most exciting thing he'd read in years – 'The shit you get sent! You wouldn't believe' – and that he'd do it. And that was encouraging. A few days later, Sam Shepard agreed to play Marvin Macy: Ismail's will-power at work again.

Money was still a problem. Ismail put me up in his apartment in New York during the casting period, and one morning as we walked down 52nd Street and across Fifth Avenue to the casting office, he told me that we were only halfway there financially, but that we would start shooting anyway. It wouldn't, he said, be the first time that had happened on a Merchant Ivory film. 'I want to just shoot the fucking thing. Shoot it! Get it on film! Then we can edit it later. When they see the footage, people will invest.' We hope, I thought, having somewhat less faith in my unshot masterpiece. He told me that he'd spoken to a group of potential backers the day before, and they had turned him down. He had rounded on them: 'You are fools! When all of you are dead and forgotten, *this film* will still be remembered.' How can he possibly have such confidence, I thought, beginning to twitch a little. But that's what he is: a confidence man, in the most literal sense, and possibly a few other senses too.

We cast the rest of the major speaking parts mostly from New York stage actors. One, an actress of great experience and distinction, had never acted in a film before. As for the townspeople, we would cast those from Austin, Texas. I was despatched to Philadelphia to meet the cinematographer, a senior English Director of Photography, now resident in America. He was very charming, and told me not to worry about technical matters, above all not to read any How To books, just look at movies and keep my wits about me. He professed himself excited by the novel, by the visual notions that I suggested, and by the world that I sought to evoke. Then he picked up the script – which he had not yet read, I'd just brought it with me – weighed it in his hand and said: 'It's too short.' 'How can you tell, Larry?' I said, thinking of *Gone with the Wind*: 'Scene 20: Atlanta burns.' 'I may be wrong, though I don't think you'll find I am. I reckon you need an extra half an hour.' Gulp. I went back to New York with this news and everyone thought he was probably right. Michael and I, desperate not to disrupt the bare language of the version we'd come to, introduced at the beginning of the film material that we'd decided to exclude; but everyone thought we'd cracked the problem very well, so no more was heard about it until much later.

Now finally we moved to Austin. Bruno had gone out the week before, and an army of carpenters had effected the transformation. I strode about feeling like Pharoah surveying the construction of the Pyramids, as one building was doubled in size and another was halved, one was demolished and another new one put in place. I was accompanied in my striding about by my first assistant director, Gary Marcus, thirty years old and a veteran of forty films. On a preliminary visit to Austin I had worked with Michael Peal, a brilliant storyboard artist (he had storyboarded the original *Texas Chain Saw Massacre*). I had suggested all kinds of shots, and, to my amazement, he thought they were feasible, even, well, rather exciting. He then drew them with wonderful dexterity and at lightning speed, so that by the time I returned to Austin, we were able to walk through a shot list in some detail. 'Can I put the camera here?' I'd nervously ask Gary. 'You can put it wherever you like,' he'd say, 'you're the director.' The original cinematographer, the speak-your-weight script-measurer, had fallen away, his current film running considerably over schedule, so Walter Lassally, an old associate of Merchant Ivory, an Oscar winner and a famously peppery character, had replaced him. He was, as many Directors of Photography are, distinctly unimpressed by the storyboard, and disinclined to create too detailed a shot list before seeing what the actors did with the scenes, but we walked through every scene, and found extraordinary locations, swamps and so on, and learned how to endure the unrelenting sun and to protect ourselves against the bloodthirsty chiggers, a demonic species of mite that bores its way into your flesh and itches you to the point of insanity.

Feeling the absence of an opportunity to address the whole cast the way I would have done in the theatre, I sat down and wrote a three-page document describing how I was going to approach the piece, and why. I detailed the style that we'd evolved, and the way in which we were going to shoot the film. Walter and I, in conversations in London, had decided on a manner, partly borrowed from John Ford but with reference to Eisenstein, of extreme close-ups and wide shots – tableaux shots, we called them – that we hoped would created the fairy-tale atmosphere. I also suggested the acting style that was called for. Too often in the theatre as well as on film, STYLE is something created by the production or by the design, but not actually embodied in the playing. I asked the actors to eschew psychological complexities and to accept a world in which things happen because they do. This document I distributed to everybody in the growing army which constituted the film: grips, gaffers, best boys, props people, set decorators, carpenters, accountants, secretaries, sound operators, caterers, security men, press officers, actors. I wanted everybody to know why we were here, and what we were trying to achieve. People were appreciative. I had no idea whether it would make the slightest difference.

My townspeople had been recruited by the appalling but necessary method called, surprisingly cheerfully by the participants, the cattle call. This was arranged by the local casting director – our second, after the first had been sacked by Ismail for dilatoriness ('Tell her to get out! This is not Hollywood! Tell her to sit in the Ganges!'). An ad was placed in the local newspaper showing a Walker Evans photograph over a caption say-ing: '*Can you look like this?*' They had turned up in their hundreds, all in some sort of costume acquired from the local Goodwill Store. We selected them by appearance alone, and then slowly discovered more about them, and whittled our group down to thirty, each of whom I spent a half an hour or more with, getting them to invent names, characters, relation-ships and life stories for themselves. This they did with astonishing speed and imagination and emotional power – astonishing considering that hardly more than two or three of them were professional actors. They were pastry chefs and cabinetmakers and farmers and psychiatrists and, in one case, a Professor of English literature. They came up to Willieville where they were ensconced in a large barn, converted into a series of cubicles, each one furnished – I insisted on this – with a large mirror. Across the road, there was another large barn, in which Christopher, who was in charge of costuming the townspeople, had set up shop. Here he established The Wheel of Fashion, in which each day the group would receive their costume from the sad, tattered garments of the people of Carsonville and pretend to be the delighted recipients of a game show prize; here too, they would have a cup of coffee, smoke a cigarette or two, and unburden their hearts.

Two days before we started shooting, Sam Shepard, with whom I had just had a long and enthusiastic phone call from Greece, where he was film-ing, fell ill, and withdrew from the part of Marvin Macy. We continued our preparations, but with heavy spirits. Ismail seemed, briefly and for the only time in all our acquaintance, to despair, and I sank down even further. It seemed that the entire film would collapse, and then: 'Simon! Wonderful news! Keith Carradine will play the part.' He had read the script and decided to rearrange his life to be with us.

We started shooting on a Thursday, without Vanessa. She was due on the Saturday, so we began with a key scene, that of the arrival of Cousin Lymon, one of our boldest visual statements, and a test of the actors' abilities to endure the slow and intense poetic playing that I was sure the film needed. Once the first shot was set up, I found myself unable to shout 'Action!' I left it to Walter, who was operating the camera as well as directing the cinematography. By the second shot, I found my voice, and Ismail appeared with a tray of sweetmeats, telling everyone to 'Eat! Eat!' It was, he said, a tradition, to celebrate the beginning of the film and draw down the gods' benevolence. Quite which Hindu god was the god of film-making this devout Muslim never quite explained, though I noticed that he had a highly ecumenical approach to religion in general. On arrival at Willieville, he discovered that some of Willie's staff seemed to have some traces of 1960's pantheism, 'but now,' he said, 'they have become converts to me.'

We finished shooting that first night at 4 a.m., and, quaffing the champagne he had given me (thus, presumably, getting Bacchus on our side, too), I shed a little tear. The next day was almost second night in feeling, but after we finished, early, Ismail had arranged another propitiatory event: a family of Pakistani musicians had been summoned to play for us and as they sat on the porch of Miss Amelia's house, chanting and playing their winding, ecstatic melodies under the epic and darkening Texan sky, it seemed that the ancient soul of an America that lived before the memories of men was called up, and that *The Ballad of the Sad Café* had found its proper home. Ismail turned to me and said, 'This raga is 1,200 years old. The words are exactly the same as Carson McCullers's: in love there is the lover and there is the beloved, and these two often seem to come from different countries.' At the height of the musical ecstasy, Vanessa, impossibly tall and wearing dark glasses, arrived out of the dark, her blonde hair flowing over her shoulders.

The next day, Sunday, Vanessa tried on her costumes, and her creative process began, standing in front of the mirror, tugging at the clothes, violently rejecting some, inhabiting others as if she'd worn them all her life, snatching up hats, bits of cloth, bags, staring at her own image with the fierce eyes of an actor deciding whether she can believe in the dual image of herself and her character. We went back to the set to discuss hair. Vanessa had brought with her two wigs, made at her own considerable expense, and she and the film's hairdresser started to shape one of them, hacking away at it, Vanessa urging him on. Again the sharp critical look in the mirror. She turned to Walter and to me and said: 'Could you leave the caravan for a moment?' When we went back she sat there, her shorn tresses on the floor, triumphantly gazing at her image, cropped, mannish, powerful, her blue eyes and blonde hair giving her the air of a Norse warrior. She stepped out of the caravan, into the sun, and stood there, laughing – roaring with the sheer joy of having refashioned herself into Carson McCullers's Miss Amelia. Not, to be sure, the physical description of her from the book, but the very soul of her. She became the soul of Willieville, too, building her own garden, befriending the mule, arranging her kitchen – and the soul of the film, permeating it with her poetic genius.

It took us eight weeks to film; it took another eight weeks to edit; sound editing and mixing took another five. The whole feeling and texture of the film depended on an actress's ability to create a mythic figure at the centre of it. It owes everything to the courage and imagination and love of mankind of the exceptional creature that is Vanessa.

The foregoing, though all true, is highly selective. In many ways, making the film was absolute hell. One day, when I was editing it (which was the worst hell of all), Jim Ivory said I must write a novel about it. I fully intend to.

The influence of Charles Laughton's only film on The Ballad of the Sad Café *is beyond* hommage*: it is, I'm afraid, sheer imitation. I console myself with Picasso's profound epigram: 'To imitate others is necessary, to imitate oneself, pathetic.' Before directing* Ballad, *I had started work on my next book, which was to be about Orson Welles's theatre, stories of which – especially the stirring early days at the Mercury – had inspired me as a drama student. That's the life for me, I had thought, working twenty hours a day, under the charismatic leadership of a young genius – stretching oneself and the theatre to the very limits, defying convention, electrifying the audience, changing lives.*

Citizen Kane was Orson Welles's greatest triumph, of course, but in some ways it was his greatest scourge, almost obliterating his other, innumerable and diverse, achievements. Next in order of his achievements in the public view were the *War of the Worlds* broadcast (whose notoriety was a happy accident), *The Third Man* (which, of course, he didn't direct and whose huge success at the expense of his own films profoundly irked him) and the Paul Masson advertisements, in which the great *bon viveur*, almost a parody of himself, endorsed a mediocre *vin ordinaire* in a thunderous purr which was widely and mockingly imitated. But before *Kane* and these other things came an extraordinary body of work almost unknown to the general public.

Above all, the hidden *oeuvre* is the theatre work. It was the theatre that was Welles's all-consuming passion from his earliest years, fed by a

Shakespeare-worshipping mother, and nurtured by the childhood gift of a toy theatre. He had the extraordinary good fortune to go to a school whose educational philosophy was that learning was best done by doing. The young Welles was accordingly let loose on their brilliantly equipped theatre and lighting board, with an army of schoolboy-slaves at his disposal to build and paint sets and then to act as supernumeraries in his productions, in which, needless to say, he played all the leading roles – including, when he was not quite fifteen, Richard III in his own adaptation of the Shakespeare History Cycle which he titled *Winter of Discontent*. He had intended to play Sir John Falstaff as well, but for once the Todd School put its foot down when faced with a probable seven-hour running time. Welles reluctantly confined himself to a ninety-minute canter through the career of the deformed Plantagenet.

He left school at fifteen, taking a year off before a putative application to university; he spent the year in Ireland under the guise of a painting holiday but in fact was simply determined to act, even offering to learn Gaelic on the off-chance that he might get a job in the Irish-language theatre in the West. Instead, he ended up in Dublin where he blarneyed his way into the Gate Theatre, run by the great team of Micheál mac Liammóir and Hilton Edwards, and here, at the age of sixteen, he learned not only how to hold his own in a company of experienced and temperamental actors many years his senior, but also something of the very latest developments in lighting and staging, for the Gate was a daringly avant-garde theatre with a radically different policy to that of the Abbey, still then under the control of Yeats and Lady Gregory. When, after his sensational debut as Duke Karl in *Jew Süss*, the parts began to get smaller, he returned to Chicago, where he wrote two plays, one a fevered, semi-autobiographical piece, *Bright Lucifer*, the other a worthy account of the anti-slaver, John Brown. Time hanging on his hands, he also produced, under the aegis of his ex-headmaster and warmest admirer, Roger Hill, an edition of three of Shakespeare's plays which they called *Everybody's Shakespeare*, furnished by the seventeen-year-old Welles with staging suggestions and a running commentary in dazzlingly cartoonic visual form; these highly original teaching tools were hugely successful and were still in use in the mid-Sixties.

Welles's career as an actor took off when at the age of seventeen he joined Katharine Cornell's immensely distinguished company, playing Mercutio to her Juliet. The performance was not judged a success (nor was the production) and when he came to New York in a revised version, it was in the role of Tybalt, for which he received moderate acclaim. But his performance was seen by the thirty-year-old director, writer, producer and ex-corn merchant John Houseman, who knew the moment he caught sight of Welles that he had encountered his destiny. They began to work together, and as soon as Houseman was put in charge of the Negro Theatre Project, an offshoot of the New Deal's Federal Theatre Project, in 1936, he invited Welles, now twenty, to stage *Macbeth* for him in Harlem. Welles changed the play's setting to Haiti in the reign of Jean-Christophe, creating a kind of barbaric cabaret which was an absolute sensation. Shortly after, he and Houseman together formed another branch of the Federal Theatre which they whimsically named Project 491; for it they staged *Doctor Faustus*, one of Welles's most technically dazzling shows, the zany *Horse Eats Hat* (from *An Italian Straw Hat*) and *The Cradle Will Rock*, Marc Blitzstein's radical pro-union agit-prop musical. This proved too controversial for a government-sponsored project, and Welles and Houseman founded their own Theatre, the Mercury, which they inaugurated with a Fascist interpretation of *Julius Caesar*, whose fame spread across the Western world. This was followed by *The Shoemakers' Holiday* (riotous) and *Heartbreak House* (respectful).

On a shoestring budget, the Mercury was staking a claim to be the American National Theatre. Young actors were desperate to be part of it, and Welles, both as actor, but more particularly as director, was universally acknowledged as the White Hope of the American stage. He was now twenty-three. The second and last season of the Mercury however was something of a disappointment: *Too Much Johnson* never transferred to New York after a hilariously chaotic out-of-town try-out; *Danton's Death* was beleaguered by technical catastrophe. Meanwhile the Mercury Theatre of the Air had begun its remarkable and innovatory seasons of classical adaptations; Welles quickly proved himself a master here, too. The broadcast of *The War of the Worlds* precipitated a panic which hit the world's headlines; Hitler made reference to it in a speech to the Reichstag. Welles's fame was now dangerously independent of his achievements, a self-generating phenomenon. While the brouhaha over the broadcast continued, the Mercury Theatre was quietly wound down, surviving only as a name for Welles's producing company, to the eternal regret and occasional bitterness of a generation of actors who had been inspired by Welles to believe in the possibility of a kind of theatre which was at once classic and radical, and a genuine alternative to the poetic social realism practised by the Group Theatre.

The Mercury had one last gasp: *Five Kings*, Welles's adaptation of the Shakespeare History Cycle, a second crack of the whip at the grand scheme that dwindled into *Winter of Discontent* at the Todd School. This was planned to be on two evenings, the first centring on Falstaff, the second on Richard III, both of whom, it is perhaps unnecessary to report, were to be played by Welles. In the event, only the first, Falstaff, half was produced, and then in nightmarish circumstances of primitive technology, manic rewriting and exhausted performers. But the play was very dear to Welles, and he not only had the set put into store for many years in the belief that he would revive the show, he also retained his Falstaff beard when he went to Hollywood, which he did in 1940; he was known, for his first few months there as 'the Beard'. Ironically, Hollywood had only seemed to really wake up to his potential when his fortunes were at their nadir. After the demise of *Five Kings*, he had quixotically embarked on a tour of the Orpheum Circuit's music halls with a cut-down version of William Archer's hoary melodrama *The Green Goddess*; the only noteworthy aspect of this bizarre venture was the use in it of film (something he had already attempted in *Too Much Johnson*) but the few people who paid to see him were profoundly baffled by what they saw, and unable to believe that they were witnessing the work of a man who had only eighteen months before been acclaimed as perhaps the most exciting talent ever to be produced by the American theatre.

Once he arrived in Hollywood on the contract of his – or anyone's – dreams, he discovered film and the potential of RKO Studios' craftsmen, and from then on the theatre was always essentially second fiddle to his cinematic aspirations. However, the theatre was deeply ingrained in his heart, and for at least another twenty years, he continued to return to his first love, with varying degrees of success, but always with imagination and originality. In 1942, for example, while desperately waiting for the release of *Citizen Kane*, he produced on Broadway a dramatisation of Richard Wright's uncompromising novel *Native Son*; his use of sound and light, the claustrophobic atmosphere he evoked and the overwhelming performance that he elicited from Canada Lee in the central role, allied to his deeply felt radicalism in matters of race, created an overpowering impression of urban angst. Four years later, at the polar opposite of the theatrical spectrum, *Around the World*, his *hommage* to the spirit of the nineteenth-century spectacular theatre, with a Cole Porter score, was a piece of sheer theatrical ebullience, panned by the critics ('Wellesafloppin'!') but today still admired by those who saw it for its dazzling effects and sheer élan. The next year, he staged *Macbeth* again, this time in a severely Scottish and pagan setting, in Salt Lake City, prior to filming it in a version which suggests that Welles's visual conception was curiously old-fashioned, with something of the feel of the Beerbohm Tree production at Her Majesty's Theatre some fifty years earlier.

Four years later again, in 1951, he came to London to act in and direct *Othello*, under Laurence Olivier's management; he had just finished shooting his magnificent flamboyant film of the same play. The stage version, by contrast, was sober in the extreme, with his own somewhat somnolent performance at the centre; *Citizen Coon*, Kenneth Tynan called it. By contrast with the reckless freedom of his early stage productions, and indeed with the radical recasting of the texts for his cinematic versions, Welles seemed increasingly to see the theatre as a rather serious place, at least where Shakespeare was concerned. His next theatrical outing, however, was a piece of sophisticated boulevard, a double bill titled *The Blessed and the Damned*, premiered at the Edouard VII in Paris, consisting of *Time Runs*, a version of the Faust story with Eartha Kitt as a particularly seductive Helen of Troy, and a rather dubious satire on Hollywood, *The Unthinking Lobster*. He then took *Time Runs* on tour in Germany with a second half consisting of a thirty-minute version of *The Importance of Being Earnest* (with himself as Algernon and Micheál mac Liammóir as Jack), and various Shakespearean scenes. The tour was bedevilled by Welles's frank dislike of his German hosts and his authorship of an number of hostile newspaper articles on the post-war persistence of Nazi sympathy.

Back in London, where he resided for some years in the Fifties and Sixties, he created his version of Melville's masterpiece, *Moby Dick*, at the intimate Duke of York's Theatre, in 1955. It was a triumph, critically, and his innovations of lighting, of musical integration, and of the Pirandellian framework (*Moby Dick* is being rehearsed by a group of actors), were greatly admired by his contemporaries. However, it ran for no more than three weeks at a substantial loss. Welles had lost some of his pull at the box office. The following year came his disastrous experience with *King Lear* at the City Center in New York. His spraining not one but two ankles certainly looked like carelessness and resulted in his playing the role in a wheelchair; but this was the only innovation in the production of the slightest interest. There was widespread dismay at what was perceived to be the decline of a once-great talent. *Lear* had been planned originally as part of a season to include *Volpone* with Jackie Gleason as Mosca; the chimera of an American National Theatre led by Welles once again – for ever this time – disappeared.

Late in 1959, Welles, all of whose waking and most of whose dreaming moments were spent engendering plans for films or plays, returned to his earlier obsession, *Five Kings*, and the role of Falstaff which meant so much to him. He also returned to his old partnership with Hilton Edwards from whom, in 1931, he had learned so much of his stagecraft. Together they put together the text which he now called *Chimes at Midnight*, a title reflecting his increasing melancholy about human affairs. Always precocious, he had settled, at the age of forty-five, into a sort of autumnal mood; his belief that the rejection of Falstaff signalled the death of Merrie England lent his interpretation a profoundly elegiac dimension. His physical bulk had now passed the point of simple fatness and had begun to become something of a phenomenon; this was, of course, no drawback in playing the part of Sir John Falstaff, which he did with some distinction, though the production itself, staged by Hilton Edwards on an impossibly overstrained schedule, was something of a flop *d'éstime* both in Belfast and Dublin where the reviews were respectful but failed to sell tickets. Welles's work on the part and the text, however, bore glorious fruit in the film of the same name which, three years later, he started to make, taking with him from the original production only Keith Baxter, his dazzling Hal.

There was to be one last theatrical venture, the same year as the stage version of *Chimes at Midnight*, 1960. Oscar Lewenstein invited Welles to direct Laurence Olivier in the English-language premiere of Ionesco's *Rhinoceros* at the Royal Court. As was his wont, he designed the play and created both the lighting and the sound plot, and as a physical achievement, the show was something of a triumph. His work with the actors was less happy, however, culminating in Olivier's exclusion of him from the final rehearsals. The first night was given an added surreal dimension – as if that were necessary – by the spectacle of Welles, on a primitive walkie-talkie, padding around the tiny theatre in Sloane Square, adjusting the sound levels in that uniquely audible voice. It is a curious end to a career in the theatre which had provided some of the most compelling productions of the century, and offered the promise of something quite exceptional which never quite materialised. It is a history, like much else about Welles, awe-inspiring, baffling and hilarious by turns.

After my near débâcle *with the Laughton biography, I went about my work with due diligence. I had been preparing for months, made all the contacts I needed, and secured appointments with all the relevant archives, including the great Lilly Library at Bloomington, Indiana. During the time of* Shirley Valentine *on Broadway, I went round all Welles's old theatrical associates – actors, designers, stage managers, secretaries, publicists – asking about their time with him in great detail. And a number of them said to me, 'Why just write about Orson's theatre? You're doing the work for a full biography. Write it – and we might recognise Orson from its pages. Because the Orson that people have written so far bears no resemblance to the man we knew.'*

The 'authorised' biography by Barbara Leaming had appeared, with wonderful timing for her, four years earlier, just before Welles's death. Although I had no intention of writing a book about him at the time, I happened to review the book for the Sunday Times, *in 1985. It is the first of many many hundreds of thousands of words I have written on the subject.*

When Orson Welles died, it was as if he had been relieved of some terrible burden, as if he could rest at last. Like a Flying Dutchman or a Wandering Jew, he had seemed condemned to roam the world expiating a nameless curse. From time to time he would appear on the world's stage, a living ruin, his preposterous girth somehow the embodiment of all the unrealised projects, genius turned into lard. Ancient Mariner-like, he seemed, with his wonderfully humorously haunted eyes, to be catching our gaze and saying, 'Look what happened to me,' as if the wind had suddenly changed and he'd stuck like that.

Never was ruined greatness so visible. The other great *auteurs maudits* of this century, Abel Gance and D. W. Griffith, disappeared into silence and oblivion. Eisenstein, not without his troubles, simply died young. Not Orson. Every time he trundled insincerely through some commercial for cheap liquor (he, the great *bon viveur*! He, to whom 'commercial' was a dirty word when applied to film) or one of the various mediocre manifestations of God with which he dignified other men's nonsense, he sent a pang through the world's heart. Poor Orson, we'd think.

Poor Orson. Pity, for the man who made *Citizen Kane*, at least three other masterpieces, and at least two lesser but exquisite short films? Pity, for the man who revolutionised radio, whose theatre productions have never been rivalled for audacity and innovation, whose acting performances in the few good films he made for other directors (*The Third Man, Compulsion*) will never be forgotten? Yes, pity for what might have been: the very thing that haunted Welles himself. 'Considering what I thought of myself at fourteen, I'm a mess,' he admitted. 'Where did it all go wrong?' is the unspoken question behind every utterance he ever made about himself, and it is inevitably the theme of Barbara Leaming's book. 'If only people knew the true story!' is Orson's constant lament, and this, up to a point, is it, the first biography to have been written with its subject's active cooperation, laced, indeed, with many conversations with Welles and his various intimates.

In fact there are few surprises. The stories have been often told, generally rather better than here, although there is a more extensive treatment of Welles's political activities than I have ever read before. (At one point he was quite seriously proposed for the Secretary-Generalship of the about-to-be-born United Nations.) The book originated in a *Playboy* profile, and it feels like it. Simple reportage, as of Welles's return to Hollywood to receive his Lifetime Achievement Award, is well done, but historical reconstruction is not Leaming's strong suit. Nor is she a stylist. She has a flat-footed way with an anecdote that threatens to turn even Orson into a bore. She is unable to give any impression of what the stage productions were actually like, how filming was conducted, even what his own performances were like. She never assesses him as an actor at all, Worse, she is unable to give the flavour of the man, let alone any account of the contents of his mind.

I suppose it is no accident that she is really viciously unkind to both John Houseman and Micheál mac Liammóir, who have left – Houseman in *Runthrough* and mac Liammóir in *All for Hecuba* and *Put Money in thy Purse* – glorious accounts of Welles beside which her Orson is a frequently trivial dullard. The truth, of course, is that really only Orson himself could have written the extraordinary book needed. He actually tells her the sort of book she should have written: an investigation à la *Kane*, probing him from every different angle, testing his account of himself against the others. And she should be in it, too, he says. Well, she is, but she doesn't really engage; under his spell, no doubt, which is forgivable, but not very satisfactory.

Her strongest suit, surprisingly, is in what she disparages in herself as 'pop psychologising'. Early on she correctly identities what she calls the key to Orson's personality: 'The past is more immediate to him than the present or any intervening period.' To person after person, he is a boy all his life. 'A monstrous boy' (Houseman). 'The boy wonder' (Virgil Thomson). 'The most talented fourteen-year-old I have ever known' (Robert Arden). This boyishness is the glory of so much of his work, and a large part of the delight of the man himself: the sheer joyful high spirits of it all, the fun and celebration of the medium.

In another, darker sense, he remained a boy all his life, the son of the brilliant Beatrice and the drunken Dick Welles. 'I always felt I was letting them down. That's the stuff that turned the wheels.' Children could be treated as adults 'as long as they were amusing'. But when Beatrice died, he felt 'shame'. And when Dick, drunk and desperate, died, alone because Orson had refused to see him until he sobered up, he felt terrible guilt: 'I don't want to forgive myself. That's why I hate psychoanalysis. I think if you're guilty of something you should live with it. Get rid of it – how can you get rid of a real guilt? I think people should live with it, face up to it.' And this guilt somehow permeates his life. Miss Leaming is unable to refute Charles Higham's thesis that Welles had a deep reluctance to complete anything. Time and again – on *The Magnificent Ambersons*, *Macbeth*, *The Lady from Shanghai*, *Touch of Evil* – he walked away from the film at a crucial moment, flung himself into something else, whether pleasure or work. Many of his personal relationships were similarly suspended – he just walked away from them.

The whole life as presented by Mrs Leaming is melancholy reading. To read of the studio's destruction of *The Magnificent Ambersons* is actually painful. In the end, Welles emerges as a somehow fated figure, not sure of what hit him. In this, and so many other ways, he seems to resemble another O. W., sipping himself to an absinthe death, telling the stories he was never going to write. *Bright Lucifer* is the title of an early play of Welles's. He certainly fell; but not before having soared higher and with more tangible results than any maker of our century. *Requiescat in pacem.*

I listened to the siren voices telling me that I should commit myself to a full biography, with the result that here I am, still writing it, twenty years on, two large volumes published and a third to come. One of the people who urged me on most passionately, God rest his soul, was the éminence grise of Condé Nast, Leo Lerman, the very embodiment of the old Manhattan, elegant, funny, informed, naughty. I wrote his obituary for the Guardian in 1994.

New Yorker Leo Lerman, who has died aged eighty, was an actor, a stage manager, a set designer, a biographer, a critic, and, through his work at Condé Nast, a legendary editor. He was also a man whose social network generated a salon that stretched across five decades.

Born in Harlem, educated at the Feagin School of Dramatic Arts, his Thirties career in theatre was followed in 1942 by his first *Vogue* article, on five women of the Renaissance. By the end of the decade he was working for *Saturday Review, Harper's Bazaar, House and Garden* and *Mademoiselle*, where he was a contributing editor for more than a quarter of a century. As a features editor at American *Vogue* in the Seventies he commissioned writers such as Iris Murdoch, Rebecca West and Milan Kundera. He reviewed dance, theatre, music and wrote biographies of Leonardo and Michelangelo and a prize-winning history of the Metropolitan Museum of Art.

Ismail Merchant introduced us seven years ago at the Connaught Hotel. The meeting was informed by a hectic gaiety characteristic of both men and not exactly alien to me. The fourth person present, Gray Foy, silver-haired, poker-backed, and sceptical at so much sudden energy, provided such stillness as was on offer. The feeling of an exploding nursery wasn't contradicted by the fact that the centre of all the uproar, Leo himself, was alarmingly frail and apparently ancient. Age was hardly to be gauged, since even then, on first glimpse, the physical circumstances of the chair-bound man – thick wisps of white hair around the chin, tufts of it on the back of the head, lightly mottled pink flesh, dainty hands, unreliable legs, heavy unyielding torso – had the air of wittily assumed disguise, an elaborate masquerade by a dazzling infant whose fearless young eyes stared at you exhilarated and challenging, through the hugely magnifying lenses of his spectacles. Regally seated in the middle of the room, he somehow had the air of a child in a high chair.

What was I doing? he wanted to know, impatiently, as if we had been reunited after too long an absence, though this was our first encounter. A book, I said, about Charles Laughton, and he beamed like the Pope hearing a perfect confession. Books were always to be encouraged. What kind of book? I've tried, I said, to make it like the book that Parker Tyler wrote about Tchelitchew. 'Tchelitchew!' he cried, clapping his hands. 'Tchelitchew! I never thought I'd live to hear his name again.' And then we were off on a conversation that never stopped till the day that he died, though an ocean and the rest of our lives made sure that we only ever really met half a dozen times.

He was my idea of heaven: a conduit of the brilliant dead who as he spoke entered the room more really than any hologram, Toscanini and Balanchine and Gertrude Stein and, yes, Tschelitchew, as vivid as if he'd just come off the phone with them. He'd lived at the hub (in his case the hubbub) of the world of art since he first arrived on the scene, as a personable young actor. He had been at every premiere, every *vernissage*, every *répétition générale*, was apprised of every scandal and had launched a few himself, knew everyone and had subjected them all to his X-ray analysis, wickedly unfair and then suddenly tender. He had gloried in it all, the carnival of personality, the drama of talent.

'Glorious!' was his favourite word. I have faxes from him which simply say 'Glorious, glorious, glorious. Love, Leo.' Ten days ago, I was sifting through some papers and found a photocopy he'd sent me of a page of *Vogue* magazine (where he'd reigned for so long as a sort of journalistic sybil, having soon abandoned the stage proper for the theatre of society). It was an account of New York, 1935. He'd scrawled across it 'See the lovely life I lived!' He was living it still, up to the last moment. The past was no nostalgic refuge for him: it was present – but so was the world in which he lived, in which his interest was absolute.

Frail though he was when I met him, he became eggshell delicate as the years went by. Not for one second did he let this interfere with the daily schedule he pursued around America – even, if necessary, to the unloved Los Angeles, always pronounced with a hard 'g' – and around the world until the brutal hassle of international travel became unendurable. At home, in New York, nothing would stop him. Across busy thoroughfares, up stairs and through rough throngs Leo and Gray would struggle towards the desired event, Leo dispensing a witty if barely audible commentary on the passing scene until finally, ensconced in his seat, aching, brittle limbs carefully arranged in front of him, he would turn his great child's head to the stage like a fledgling at feeding time, ever-expectant. Through those monstrously magnified eyes he took it all in, missing nothing, no image, no phrase, no gesture. All became part of the living record of his times that constituted his inner life. There were the parties, too, attended by him, blessed by him or given by him. Home – opposite the Carnegie Hall, where else? – was the last of the great salons, a vast apartment rammed to the ceilings with bibelots, a temple of bric-à-brac, 'all quite worthless,' Leo would say, 'but every one of them means something.'

Books, records, paintings, sculptures, fans, mantillas, boots, and there, in the centre of it all, Leo, wearing one of those embroidered caps favoured by Victorian bibliophiles, adding a perfectly appropriate touch of *Alice in Wonderland*. And at the centre of Leo was Gray, their adoring relationship on the knife-edge of passionate incompatibility, filled with an appalled fascination with each other. Each radiated immense strict caring for the other: the love was tangible. You could cut it with a knife. Love was the heart of it all for Leo. Years ago, I introduced him to a new amour of mine. After a brisk interrogation along Lady Bracknell lines, he beamed approval, then, as we left, grew suddenly grave. 'Be kind to each other,' he said with great precision, and we did our best to obey. Instructions of this kind were always forthcoming from Leo, and when they were, you listened. It seemed that he had berated, advised and admonished half of the Western world.

Leo was writing his memoirs at the end. He was a memoir himself, an antiquarian of our times, John Aubrey and Chips Channon, the Goncourt brothers and the Duc de Saint-Simon, rolled into one, made pink and snowy and put in an embroidered cap. He seized life greedily as it passed, hooting with delight when it pleased, utterly undaunted when it didn't, passing light and witty judgements on love and art and the times with exuberant delicacy, gay as a cricket, irrepressibly naughty, unerringly right. New York is scarcely going to be New York without him.

Faltering

With Ballad *in the can, I came back to England to direct my first musical,* Carmen Jones. *I wrote about it for the* Daily Telegraph *to coincide with the revival of 1994, which had an unusual tour: Plymouth and Tokyo.*

I was in the middle of rehearsing my production of *Die Fledermaus* in Glasgow when the producer Howard Panter called me and wondered whether I knew *Carmen Jones*. Well, of course I did – who hadn't seen Otto Preminger's movie, beaten out dat rhythm on a drum with Pearl Bailey and been to de café on de corner with Dorothy Dandridge, while Harry Belafonte told her about dis flower dat she threw his way? Panter wanted to know if I'd like to direct it: he was about to secure the rights from the Hammerstein estate. I gulped. The lyrics were undoubtedly brilliant, and the black setting a masterstroke, but there was something somehow ponderous about the film that made me wonder if it wasn't a period piece which was a great idea for its time but rather reach-me-down forty years later.

Then I read the script of the original 1943 Broadway production. I was struck all over again by the deftness and the rightness of Hammerstein's relocation of Bizet's opera to a black American Deep South setting; but I was also struck by a curious coincidence. He seemed to have done, triumphantly, what I was struggling to do with *Die Fledermaus*: in an attempt to cast off the middle-aged never-never-land air of most productions of that old chestnut, I had transposed it to a contemporary

Glasgow setting. I hadn't quite got it right, whereas Hammerstein had triumphantly hit the nail on the head, finding the perfect marriage of music
and setting. What had inspired him to make his version of *Carmen*?

Carmen Jones was, from the start, a labour of love. Writing a screenplay
based on the life of the grandfather (Oscar I) who had lost a fortune trying to promote accessible and dramatically coherent productions of opera
in an age of all-singing, non-acting stars, Oscar II became possessed of a
missionary desire to bring opera to the people, in English and with credible characters in recognisable situations. The choice of *Carmen* can't
have been difficult. The most popular of all operas, crammed with hit
numbers as well as having one of the clearest and best-told of stories, its
atmosphere is exotic and irresistible. Whether he was influenced in setting it among black people by other current black versions of famous
classics – Orson Welles's 1936 voodoo *Macbeth* or the *Swing Mikado* of
1938, or indeed by the Gershwins' *Porgy and Bess* – is hard to say, but
once hit upon, the idea of transferring the piece to the Deep South of
America must have seemed inevitable: the Gypsies, among whom so much
of the opera is set, have a perfect counterpart in black America. Foreign
and yet indigenous, a culture within a culture, passionate, physical,
colourful, musical, they were a perfect solution to the problem of making the people of the opera both American and exotic. The changed
setting was only a starting point. It needed to be worked out in detail;
Hammerstein's ingenuity in doing so led him to some radical results.

In transposing the four acts of the opera, Hammerstein presented a
greater range of black experience than had ever been shown on the
Broadway stage, let alone on film. Setting his first act in a parachute factory, with the workers and soldiers of an impoverished Southern black
town, he moved the second act to the very different world of a louche
and rather shady bar in the same town, a world of pimps and good-time
girls, where the world heavyweight champion drops by to pick up a one-
night stand, until his managers persuade him to think of his trainer's
instructions. For the third act (Bizet's Gypsy encampment) Hammerstein
takes us into rich middle-class black society, at the champ's elegant party
in his fabulous Chicago South Side mansion. The fourth act presents a
typical urban sports crowd, screaming encouragement at their hero
before he fights his latest engagement.

It was Hammerstein's theatrical instincts, rather than a commitment to
the black cause, that had made him choose a black milieu for the piece

(he announced, extravagantly, that he was thinking of devoting the rest of his working life to transposing operas, planning next to do *La Bohème* set in New York's Greenwich Village). But he was a committed liberal, and was concerned both to display what he called 'the huge wealth of black talent in this country', and to represent black life credibly. In the first act, for instance, he changes Bizet's dreamy chorus of factory girls extolling cigarette smoke into a celebration of one of the workers who has become a pilot – 'Flying Man'. The Broadway audience in 1943 would immediately have recognised the allusion to Roosevelt's recent enactment – under threat of a mass march on Washington by black activists – of legislation permitting blacks to train as pilots at a school specially established for them at Tuskegee Black University. Equally, his reinvention of the toreador Escamillo as Husky Miller, the coming heavyweight champion of the world, was clearly and squarely based on Joe Louis, whose visits to black neighbourhoods with his wife, the nightclub entertainer Marva Trotter, were described as being like royal visits – a scene exactly paralleled in Hammerstein's Act Two, set in Billy Pastor's bar.

The relocation of the opera seemed to stimulate his imagination at every turn. Part of the creative excitement of *Carmen Jones* derives from the need which drove Hammerstein when he wrote it. In 1942, when he set to work, he had endured ten years of flops, the great days of *Desert Song* and *Showboat* many years behind him. He withdrew to the countryside with the La Scala recording of the opera on twelve 78s, and, working to no commission and with no prospect of a production, rediscovered himself both as a musical-dramatist and as a lyric-writer. His work on *Carmen Jones* has a new directness and understanding of the idea towards which he had for years been striving: the idea of the organic show, where numbers don't stop the show for a song but grow directly out of the action and advance it. Only weeks after he'd completed his work on *Carmen*, and before he even had a producer for it, Hammerstein was approached by the Theater Guild to work with Richard Rodgers on an adaptation of the current Broadway hit *The Grass is Greener*. Out of this grew *Oklahoma!*, and out of *Oklahoma!* – it's not too sweeping a statement to make – came the whole of the modern American musical theatre, the direct fruit of the lessons he learned in writing *Carmen Jones*.

Getting the show on was no easy task. His contemporaries thought he was mad. How to find one hundred and fifteen black performers (his original cast) who were well-enough trained to sing Bizet's score? Because that, with a few minor alterations and cuts, was what he had used, transposing nothing and leaving all the musical excitement and challenge untampered with. Fortunately, he was introduced to the flamboyant and audacious impresario Billy Rose, who, on hearing of the idea, eagerly put his weight behind the project, which led his fellow producers to think that he had gone mad, too. A production of all the talents was immediately assembled: Howard Bay and Raoul Pène Du Bois to do sets and costumes, Eugene Loring to choreograph, Charles Friedman (of the left-wing Labor Project) to direct the book, Robert Shaw, then and now the greatest of American chorus masters, to work with the ensemble, and Joseph Littauer to conduct; the whole to be supervised by Hassard Short, English-born wizard of lighting and overall conception.

There was only one small snag: they couldn't find a cast. After three months of extensive auditions, the team had not found a single performer adequate to the show's musical demands. On the point of abandoning the project, they had the extraordinary good fortune to run into the legendary A&R man, John Hammond. Once he had ascertained that Hammerstein's version was a radical departure from the eyeball-rolling, happy-darkie nonsense that Broadway was pleased to purvey, Hammond put his huge knowledge of black talent at the team's disposal. Bit by bit, they found their cast: Luther Reed, a riveter and dockworker as Joe, Glenn Bryant, a New York cop who had to be relieved from his beat by central government intervention, as Husky Miller, and, finally, Muriel Smith, a twenty-year-old first-year music student at the Curtis Institute, the first ever black student to enrol there, as Carmen; she was working nights as a chemist to pay her way through college.

Billy Rose's blind faith was rewarded with staggering reviews, from both music and drama critics. Among the most perceptive was that of the *New York Herald Tribune*'s music critic, the composer Virgil Thomson, who hailed the show both as a reproach to prevailing standards at the Metropolitan Opera House and as a return to Bizet's original conception before it was transmogrified, on his deathbed, and without his consent, into a Grand Opera. Thomson's phrase to describe both *Carmen* and *Carmen Jones* – 'realistic proletarian melodrama' – is brilliantly precise. This is what gives both the opera and the 'musical play' (his own phrase) that Hammerstein adapted from it its feeling of coming from today's headlines.

We started work on *Carmen Jones* knowing that if we could capture a half of the excitement generated by the original show, we would set the town alight. In addition, there was the chance of working with an all-black cast – an ambition I'd long had, hoping to do a black version of *The Importance of Being Earnest*, but very happy with the hand that fate, Carmen-like, had dealt me. My starting point, like Hammerstein's, was the music. I knew and admired, from his recordings with the Royal Philharmonic Orchestra in the Seventies, the work of the black American conductor Henry Lewis. Never having met him, I had a powerful instinct that he was the man we needed; an instinct that proved right in various unexpected ways. I had forgotten that he had been married to Marilyn Horne, the voice of Dorothy Dandridge in Preminger's film, and thus knew the show and its special demands intimately; moreover he had conducted five different productions of *Carmen*, including most performances of the legendary one at the Met starring Horne, initially conducted by Leonard Bernstein.

At Sardi's one summer evening we decided the basic principles that have informed all our work on the show: it would be essentially realistic (psychologically and socially detailed, a story of real people in a real world), every word of Hammerstein's astonishing lyrics would be heard, and clearly heard, the orchestral sound would not mimic a symphony orchestra's, nor yet be a synthetic concoction, but would reproduce the sound of a Forties band. Dave Cullen, master-orchestrator of Andrew Lloyd Webber's shows, would arrange the score. In fact, Hammerstein's deliberate setting of the piece in the year of its composition, 1943, in wartime America, would be respected; Bruno Santini's designs would be completely in period. So far so good. But then we ran up against Billy Rose and Oscar Hammerstein's problem: where were we to find a cast?

The answer was simple: in America, for the most part. The original cast of the Old Vic production was mostly imported from the States; there simply were not enough British black performers with the vocal skills to fill the roles. The show opened with great success; as the show ran on we needed to recast. To our delighted amazement we discovered that more and more British black artists, fired by the example of the American artists in the show, had worked on their own on their voices, and were coming to us with their ranges and their stamina transformed out of recognition. Thus the present production – tighter, sharper, more direct than before – fields a cast which is one hundred per cent British. To be pleased about this is not chauvinistic: it is entirely in the spirit of Oscar Hammerstein's desire to celebrate 'the huge wealth of black talent' in his country. We had exactly the same ambition when we started out; that, and to tell the terrible story he had so brilliantly reclaimed from the stuffy confines of the opera house, of the maddeningly free spirit whose lover, unable to possess her, turns into her killer. *Fatal Attraction* indeed.

Two singers who played Joe were particularly remarkable: Gary Wilmot, hitherto known for light comedy and a long run in Me and My Girl, *and Anthony Garfield Henry, originally a dancer, who had started to do a little bit of singing in* Miss Saigon. *At his audition he sang 'Dis Flower', and he was frankly not up to it, so we said what we always said: 'Go away and work on it and come back and see us.' And he did, about a year later. He started singing, very quietly, and we started to wonder how soon we could stop him without bruising his dignity too much, when he slowly started to expand his dynamic range, till he was singing at triple forte, perfectly under control, perfectly in pitch, with absolute rhythmic control. He was a fully fledged singer, who when he came to do the show – and of course we cast him immediately – brought astounding power to the end of the third act and the final duet. A year or so later, when I was directing Puccini's* Il Trittico *at Broomhill Opera, I asked him to sing Luigi in* Il Tabarro, *a famous and very challenging Domingo role, and he was again magnificent; a year later he sang Don José for Opera North.*

The day after the reviews for Carmen Jones *came out, I was asked to direct* My Fair Lady, *which, of course, I did, with Edward Fox as Higgins, Helen Hobson as Eliza and Bryan Pringle as Doolittle. The choreographer was Quinny Sacks, the set designer David Fielding, the costume designer Jasper Conran, and the hats – those all-important hats – by Philip Treacy. It was a production of all the talents. Everyone did superb work – and it didn't work. This was due to a vast complex of reasons, but in the end I must carry the can, as the director always must. I wrote a perhaps overexuberant piece for the programme, some weeks before we had actually opened.*

In 1959, mother and I were living in the tiny town of Fort Jameson in the very large country of Northern Rhodesia in the middle of the vast expanses of Africa. We shared a sprawling house with another fatherless family, and among our proudest possessions was a gramophone player, in a fine-looking walnut cabinet; you had to wind it up when the battery ran down, and it was the very latest thing. We had just one LP: the Drury Lane recording of the original production of *My Fair Lady*, with a famously witty sleeve adorned with a cartoon in which a snowy-bearded George Bernard Shaw is shown manipulating Professor Higgins, who is himself manipulating Eliza Doolittle. We played it over and over, not just because it was all the rage, and because it was tuneful and witty, but because it was so perfectly and completely British. For a little boy from Streatham who felt himself to be alarmingly adrift in an incomprehensibly strange and different land, it was immeasurably comforting to listen to 'Wouldn't It Be Luverly' and 'Why Can't the English?'

I don't believe I realised for many years that it was in fact a Broadway show, directed by an American, that its lyrics were by another American, its score was by an Austrian, and that it would never have happened at all had it not been for a Hungarian. The very fact that it existed as a musical was a minor miracle, because Shaw loathed the musical theatre, and publicly denounced the only attempt to convert one of his plays into a show – *The Chocolate Soldier*, an operetta by Oscar Straus based, very loosely indeed, on *Arms and the Man*. A rather better composer than Straus, Franz Léhar, attempted to persuade the old man to let him adapt *Pygmalion*, but was sent off with a flea in his ear: 'I absolutely forbid such an outrage... *Pygmalion* is good enough with its own verbal music.' As if to prove his point, composers found it very difficult to adapt: Cole Porter and Rodgers and Hammerstein attempted to wrestle it into musical form, but gave up. In any case, as long as Shaw was alive (he died in 1950) there was no possibility of getting the rights; after he died, the Shaw estate faithfully maintained his position.

There was, however, a loophole, which is where the Hungarian comes in, in the fabulously picaresque person of the producer – director – entrepreneur, Gabriel Pascal. This was the man who had succeeded where all the moguls of Hollywood had failed: he had persuaded Shaw to allow his plays to be filmed. Hollywood had offered millions (in the 1920s) for the rights, but Shaw was convinced that his work would be at the very least diluted and at worst destroyed in the Dream Factory. It is all the more extraordinary, then, that Pascal, a caricature of the Eastern European con man, incomprehensibly mangling the English language, patently mendacious and profoundly untrustworthy in all matters pecuniary, should have magicked the rights out of the canny if by now elderly Irishman. Shaw adored him, above all, it seems, because he made him laugh. 'I have had to forbid Pascal to kiss me,' he said, 'as he did at first to the scandal of the village.' Pascal himself directed *Major Barbara, Caesar and Cleopatra* and *Androcles and the Lion,* confining himself to merely producing *Pygmalion.* For this, he commissioned Shaw to write a screenplay, but, taking advantage of the octogenarian dramatist's absence from the film set, Pascal and his collaborators, the director Anthony Asquith, and the star and co-director Leslie Howard, dropped several of the scenes he wrote, and (with the aid of three other writers) invented a couple of new ones. Some of these substantially diverged from the play and the author's passionately expressed view of the characters and their motives; most heretically, they had Eliza come back to Higgins at the end.

Why Pascal is relevant to the story of *My Fair Lady* is that the splendid old rogue had, by means of one of his familiar contractual conjuring tricks, managed to prestidigitate away from the aged Shaw not merely the film rights to these plays, but the rights to any further adaptation, on stage or screen. Quite out of the blue, in 1952, he approached Alan Jay Lerner, who had just had a modest success with *Paint Your Wagon,* to ask him and Frederick Loewe, his composing partner, to write a musical version of the screenplay. Nothing came of it at the time, but two years later, Pascal having in the interim died, they secured the rights from his estate and plunged in. Using the screenplay as their dramatic template, they were relieved of the impossible challenge of setting closely argued Shavian dialogue to music. It also gave them the chance of creating vivid and colourful numbers, not strictly integral to the play's action. With three exceptions – the Doolittle scenes (one in Tottenham Court Road, the other in Covent Garden), and the Ascot Gavotte, a re-siting of the tea-party scene in *Pygmalion* – all the 'new' scenes come from the film. These include some of the most famous scenes in the show: the 'Rain in Spain' scene (the phrases 'the rain in Spain' and 'in Hertford, Hereford and Hampshire, hurricanes hardly ever happen' are lifted directly from the screenplay); Freddy Eynsford-Hill's vigil outside 27a Wimpole Street; the Embassy Ball, in which the oleaginous Karpathy tries unsuccessfully to unmask Eliza; and, finally, most significantly, the last scene of all, in which Eliza returns to Higgins, who is discovered listening to the first recordings he made of her voice.

Lerner and Loewe were joined by a team of incomparable collaborators of innovative brilliance: Oliver Smith, designer of *On the Town,*

Brigadoon, Oklahoma!; Hanya Holm, choreographer of ballets, initially for her own avant-garde troupe, then for *Kiss Me Kate* and *The Golden Apple*; Cecil Beaton, famous for his costumes for *Lady Windermere's Fan*, *The School for Scandal* and *The Chalk Garden*, not to mention his standing as one of the world's great photographers; Abe Feder, the greatest lighting designer the American theatre has ever produced, who lit not merely Orson Welles's *Macbeth* and *Julius Caesar*, but also the Empire State Building. Before any of these, however, the producer Herman Levin had engaged as director the universally admired and loved Moss Hart, the writer and director who, in collaboration with George Kaufman and on his own, had been responsible for an unparalleled string of Broadway hits. This was the key appointment.

Hart's most pressing task was casting the – as yet unfinished – show. Henry Higgins was, of course, the big question. Noël Coward was asked; then Michael Redgrave. Both, for different reasons, turned the show down. Next on the list was Rex Harrison. After a great deal of persuasion, he accepted the part, even though, as he said with characteristic tact, only two out of the five songs were any good. The authors immediately began to frame the part according to his capacities and personality. Fritz Loewe reimagined his songs as *Sprechgesang* (speech-song), an idiom familiar to him from the musical avant-garde of his youth in Berlin, while Lerner imported Harrison's explosiveness and his incomprehension of the female sex (so many of whom he had married) into the lyrics. All other important roles were filled with veteran British performers: Stanley Holloway, a great variety star of the Thirties, was Doolittle, Robert Coote, a distinguished character man, Colonel Pickering, and Higgins's mother was played by Cathleen Nesbitt, who seemed to embody the vanished Edwardian age of which her first boyfriend, Rupert Brooke, had been the poet laureate. The cast was so overwhelmingly British that a tea break, hitherto unheard of in Broadway rehearsals, had to be introduced.

Only the all-important casting of Eliza remained. It was the toughest role yet written for a woman in the musical theatre, in which, hitherto, the greatest crisis a heroine had had to face was a dating problem, or the enumeration of the children of the King of Siam. Mary Martin turned them down – '*How* could it have happened,' she asked her husband after hearing the songs for the first time, 'how *could* it have happened? Those dear boys have *lost their talent*' – whereupon they offered it to Julie Andrews, from Walton-on-Thames in Surrey, twenty years old, and at that moment starring on Broadway in the latest import from London, Sandy Wilson's deliciously silly show *The Boy Friend*. They took a tremendous gamble on her lack of acting experience; and indeed, during rehearsals, the authors – and, without any attempt at concealment, her co-star – began increasingly to doubt their wisdom. Moss Hart, a wise and cunning old hand, kept his faith in her, suspending rehearsals for two days to teach her the role, gesture by gesture, inflection by inflection, line by line – a real-life Higgins to her real-life Eliza.

Inspiration ran very high. Beaton had sworn never to do another stage show, but was enchanted by the possibility of putting the elegant world of his childhood on stage. Oliver Smith, veteran of countless radical and innovative ballet designs, and later of highly successful musicals, used the inevitable succession of back and front cloths (the show has seventeen changes of scene) to evoke London interiors and exteriors in cleverly angled and stylised rooms and boldly painted vistas: the scene in the Covent Garden Market is an almost Expressionist vision of great arching roofs jostling each other at crazy tangents. Here was no tired realism, no chocolate-box charm. Hanya Holm likewise eschewed swooning waltzes and *Me and My Girl* knees-ups, finding instead a physical language of wit and droll allusion. The form of the piece, as devised by Alan Lerner (much aided by Moss Hart, who provided a similar service for him to the one he performed for Julie Andrews: a weekend-long seminar on structure and storytelling), was, with its quick succession of scenes, revue-like. Each scene required a brilliant visual image, a physical language which revealed the class and world of the characters, and acting which communicated vividly and amusingly.

We have one indispensable piece of evidence from that first production: the original cast recording, made on the Sunday after the Thursday opening. From the first note of the overture – dynamically propelled along by Franz Allers, another of the collaborators, the outstanding Broadway conductor of his day, a sophisticated musician who came from the world of classical music – the feeling is vital, brilliant, bold, theatrical. Harrison, still excited and challenged by the new medium, performs on a knife-edge, half speaking, half singing, his songs, almost seeming to improvise them. Andrews is suffused with rapture. Stanley Holloway brings a wholly authentic and grounded note of music hall to the proceedings, rough, real and earthy. Allers drives the score along at a delirious pace. The rhythms are pungent, the wit is always unexpected and the romance breathtaking, whether in Freddy Eynsford-Hill's effusions or Eliza's self-discoveries. Higgins's capitulation to feeling is tentative, unwilling and, ultimately, overwhelming.

In the 1958 recording from the London production at Drury Lane, the one I wore out all those years ago in our rondavel in Fort Jameson, everything has become a hundred times more accomplished; they had all been playing the piece for two years. Skill is supreme; and with it greater sophistication of feeling. Harrison's 'I've Grown Accustomed to Her Face' is a masterpiece of dramatic emotionalism. Something is missing, a certain edge; but in the face of so much brilliance, its loss is insignificant. In the film (1965), the tendency to smooth out, to varnish over, has become rampant. Oliver Smith, Hanya Holm, Moss Hart (who died in 1960, replaced for the film by George Cukor), Julie Andrews, have all disappeared. Cecil Beaton, now responsible for both sets and costumes of paralysing prettiness, Rex Harrison, a very different, mellower, softer Rex Harrison from the Rex Harrison of eight years before, Audrey Hepburn, ravishingly unconvincing either as flower-girl or as self-confident, independent and suddenly grown-up woman, and André Previn (seemingly determined to out-Mantovani Mantovani with his hundred-piece orchestra), rule the roost. The music has become slower and fatter; any attempt at stylisation in the settings has disappeared, without the introduction of any compensating realism; the choreography, by Hermes Pan, is entirely conventional. Paradoxically, the feeling of the film is theatrical: it seems to take place in Never-Never Land. The harsh elements of the story and the audacious wit of the stage show have become ironed out – the Cinderella dimension has become all, with the outcome never seriously in doubt.

My Fair Lady should have all the attack, all the brilliance, all the fun and wit, all the fresh beauty of that original production. But the theatre has changed, and so have we. We need new ingenuities to tickle our fancies, new jokes to make us laugh, a new kind of beauty to gasp at. My collaborators and I have tried to treat *My Fair Lady* as if it were a script that had just fallen through the letter box. And an astonishing script it is to read; we've tried to wipe off the patina time has put on it. The show is about all kinds of important things – class, language, independence, feminism, love – but it's always told by its multiple authors, Lerner, Loewe, and, of course, Shaw, with sharp, elegant wit. That's what we're after. Oh, and of course, we hope you'll have a little cry, too.

I was determined to break the mould established by the original production, but the new elements I had assembled – Fielding's witty sets, Conran's trenchant costumes, Sacks's offbeat and joyful steps – didn't quite add up by the time we opened. We needed more time: we weren't remotely ready. The production manager walked out, cursing the management from the stage before he did so: 'It's all your fucking fault!' The lighting designer had a nervous breakdown when it was discovered that he hadn't been noting down the lighting cues as he plotted them. Edward Fox, resentful of being amplified, ripped his microphone off and threw it into the pit. Because of the glamorous conjunction of Edward and Jasper, the national papers had insisted on reviewing (badly) the excruciating, faltering first preview in Manchester. One critic, Charles Spencer of the Daily Telegraph, *to his undying credit refused to go, whereupon his editor, Max Hastings, told him that if he didn't, he'd be out of a job. Charles went, and gave the show an entirely undeserved rave review. Before long, with constant work (always more difficult once a show has opened), things got better, and the individual elements started to cohere rather brilliantly, but a big show, once it's running, is like an ocean-going liner: turning it round is a massive undertaking. Finally, in Southampton, after four not-at-all unsuccessful months, financially speaking, and now attracting properly deserved rave reviews, the exhausted management decided to pull the plug, and the boat sank without trace – apart from the hats, which, from time to time, surface in costume houses across the land. For the first time in my career as a director, I had felt not entirely in command of the actors, who were an oddly disparate, wayward bunch who never gelled into a company. On the last day in Southampton, there was a farewell party, at which some of chorus had got up a satirical cabaret in which the stars and the creative team were none too affectionately sent up. I got a mention: 'Ah, the director – was there a director on the show?' How I laughed.*

A pattern was now establishing itself: I'd direct a show, then act in a film. Acting on stage was becoming the exception. On one rare, and mistaken, occasion, I directed myself in a play, Larry Kramer's autobiographical AIDS drama, The Destiny of Me. *The plan was to open in Leicester and then transfer to London. We had a superb cast: Ann Mitchell, Gary Waldhorn, Jason Durr, Patti Boulaye, James Kennedy, Peter Woodward. Rehearsals were rather exhilarating, although one day the author mysteriously absented himself and was never heard from again. After a moving and funny final run in the London rehearsal room, we moved to Leicester in high spirits. I was a little taken aback when, during the technical rehearsals (unusually taxing when you're in the play and directing it), the artistic director of the theatre asked if he could have a word with me. 'I hope,' he said, 'that you and the company won't be too upset if nobody comes to see the play.' 'I think we might,' I said. 'Why won't anybody come?' 'Because they never do,' he said. 'They never come to plays?' 'No'. 'So why do you do them?' I asked, not unreasonably, it seemed to me. 'Because the Arts Council likes it if we do.' 'What do they come to? Musicals?' The theatre had a deserved reputation for doing musicals. 'Oh no,' he said. 'Well, what do they come to then?' 'Compilations.' Kramer never had a chance. But the hardy few who came were deeply moved by what is a deeply felt, if poorly written, play by a man who, working flat out on the front line, must have saved, by his ceaseless and cussed proselytising, thousands and thousands of lives. To coincide with the play's opening, in the spring of 1993, I wrote this piece for the* Independent *(whose critic, incidentally, hated the show). The piece was called* The Theatre of Plague.

Recently, I was amazed and delighted to be asked to play the part of a middle-aged gay man who dies, not from AIDS, but from a heart attack induced by excessive Scottish dancing. It happens in a film called *Four Weddings and a Funeral* which will appear next year, and from a political point of view it is a very positive demise. Homosexuality has in the last ten years so become synonymous with illness and early death that it has begun to seem impossible not to allude to these things in the depiction of gay men. Just at the point when gay men and women were slowly beginning to be perceived as simply part of life's rich pattern, different but essentially made of the same common clay from which the rest of humankind is formed, we have suddenly become A Problem again.

For most gay men under thirty, the moment at which they discovered the existence of AIDS is for them the equivalent of Kennedy's assassination. I remember a supper, a little more than ten years ago, with my friends the playwright Martin Sherman and the actor Rupert Everett. Martin had just come back from New York and he said: 'There's a terrible disease sweeping through New York. It's a sort of cancer that only gay men get.' Rupert and I laughed. Nervously. It seemed absurd; a paranoid reflex of the puritan conscience, or else something medieval, some echo from a savage past. As Martin spoke, giving more and more disturbing details, a great weariness overcame us all. For the first time in living memory, gay women and men were beginning to be able to stop apologising, stop hiding, stop lying about themselves. And now, we thought, that day, it's all going to be spoiled. We're not going to be able to explore our new freedom, be allowed to make our mistakes, slowly mature from licentiousness into liberty. And so it proved. Gay people galvanised themselves and others into trying to deal with this disease. People gave up their entire lives to fight it. The immediate impact was luridly highlit by the prominence given to instances of the disease among the famous; it seemed that the arts were being singled out for the virus's scythe. The theatre's cruel losses were starkly embodied in the emaciated, pain-racked form of Ian Charleson, playing his unforgettable Hamlet at the National Theatre while the final ravages of the disease worked their way through his body. AIDS had finally made a personal appearance on the stage.

Theatre writers were initially winded by the new phenomenon. AIDS had the same impact on gay theatre-writing as Mrs Thatcher had on left-wing drama generally: impossible to write about, impossible not to write about. How do you write a play about illness, anyway? Terminal illness is terminal illness, gay or straight. It is not, so to speak, a fit subject for the drama. There are the dying and those who look after them; there is anger and resignation, courage and fear, hope and despair. Novelists, poets and short-story writers, Paul Monette, Thom Gunn, Adam Mars-Jones, have written brilliantly on the subject; but the emotional oscillations of the deathbed can scarcely be translated into theatre without descent into a static sort of sentimentality. There is the possibility of AIDS as a metaphor (in defiance of Susan Sontag's insistence that disease must never be viewed as anything but disease), though this has not yet really been attempted; and finally there is the political play. AIDS, unlike, say, cancer, or multiple sclerosis, has an intensely political dimension in that it predominantly afflicts – in the West, certainly – a section of the community unloved of the establishment. Why was so little done to find a cure? Why is so little still being done? A plot to let the gay population die off, or at the very least be exploited financially? More sinisterly, a form of chemical warfare deliberately engineered to wipe us out? All or none of these scenarios may be true; they are fuelled by the desperate, heartbreaking rage of individuals inexplicably struck down at incomprehensibly young ages for no cause other than ignorance of the workings of their own bodies and the seemingly Manichean workings of a universe inhabited by inexhaustibly mutating viruses bent on our obliteration. Were the God of Love not well and truly dead, buried at the Somme, Katyn, and Dachau, AIDS would surely have finished Him off.

This sense of apocalypse is behind the two major political theatre-writers on AIDS, Tony Kushner and Larry Kramer. Kramer was first on the scene with *The Normal Heart*, a unique piece of theatre in that it is a from-the-barricades account of the struggle by the leading – the founder – member of the American AIDS activist movement. Passionate, wordy, angry almost to point of incoherence, it is as if Daniel Cohn-Bendit had written a play about Paris 1968. Virginia Woolf maintained that 'one can never write in anger'. Larry, a sort of dramatist-pamphleteer, can never write in anything else. It may not be art, but it is certainly theatre. Kushner's *Angels in America*, a sort of apocalyptic soap opera, broadens the canvas, homing in on the bizarre figure of Roy Cohn, the gay-bashing gay lawyer at the very heart of the American political machine, while telling various interlocked stories of love in a time of AIDS. Kramer, continuing in his autobiographical vein, has now written *The Destiny of Me*, both prequel and sequel to the earlier play. The author is now HIV-positive himself, and his theatrical alter ego, Ned Weeks, checks into hospital at the start of the play to avail himself of a promising new technique for dealing with the disease. There he finds himself invaded by memories of himself when young. As the memories insist, he begins to piece together, in a sort of psychoanalytical detective thriller, the clues that may help him to understand who he is, what made him. Extraordinarily bold in theatrical technique, it is an instance of the mournful necessity in these terrible times for so many young and middle-aged men prematurely to take stock, to ask, as Ned does in the play, 'Does it make any sense, a life?' Encompassing fifty years and three generations, the play, the author insists, is not about AIDS; it is about the tenacity of human life during a plague, and thus becomes a celebration.

The protagonist himself seems doomed, however, lending the play an air of elegy, as he finally and spectacularly detaches himself from the continuing indignity of unavailing medical treatment. In the haunting words of 'the doleful ditty to the lute / That may complain my near-approaching death' from Thomas Nashe's *Summer's Last Will and Testament*, also written at a time of plague, bubonic, in this case:

Haste therefore each degree
To welcome destiny:
Heaven is our heritage,
Earth but a player's stage,
Mount we unto the sky.
I am sick, I must die:
Lord, have mercy on us.

As I note at the beginning of the foregoing piece, I had acted in Four Weddings and a Funeral *shortly before. It is worth remembering that that delicious and seemingly imperishable romantic comedy was written against a background of AIDS, and that the film's quest for a perfect mate in life was a symptom of the new monogamy that was being increasingly adopted – for a while, anyway – by people of all sexual persuasions. It hadn't occurred to me at the time quite what a remarkable thing it was of Richard Curtis to have placed a gay couple at the very centre of his film. John Hannah's exquisitely acted funeral oration for Gareth (on which I am often congratulated, though of course I wasn't there) was up to that date the most outspoken affirmation of the authenticity of gay love ever to appear in any mainstream film.*

Movies – and television, of course – no doubt have a much greater direct social influence than theatre, and since Four Weddings and a Funeral, *the situation has changed out of all recognition. I wrote this Foreword to* Out at the Movies *in 2008.*

As Steven Paul Davies notes in this fascinating volume, we live in interesting times as far as the gay presence in cinema is concerned. For him, *Brokeback Mountain* is the great breakthrough into the mainstream, and though some of us may quarrel with his interpretation of the movie itself, there can be no doubting the enormity of the leap it represented. For some of us, it stands in the long and by no means dishonourable homosexuality-as-problem tradition in the movies; indeed, it is arguably a film about the difficulties of bisexuality. But the fact that in a mainstream film two highly bankable and impeccably butch actors are shown making passionate love to each other, and that no moral judgement is made on this, and that the actors' careers were greatly advanced by appearing in it (one of them, of course, subsequently tragically curtailed but not remotely in connection with his work on the film) is a quite remarkable development, inconceivable to me thirty-five years ago when I started acting, much less when I started going to films fifteen years before that.

In those distant days, every homosexual was an expert decoder, as skilled as anyone at Bletchley Park. Messages were being sent to us, and we learned to read the signs, to infer the hidden communications, to sniff out the double meaning. This was not without its thrills, but it's no way for grown men and women to experience their lives. Little by little, things began to change. It had started already in the theatre, where illicit kisses had been exchanged, tortured psyches examined and what was now known as gay humour freely flaunted. The movies, as well documented by Mr Davies, began to deal with the troublesome matter of same-sex attraction with increasing subtlety and truthfulness to life: it is hard to describe how powerful was the impact on the gay community of films like Schlesinger's masterpieces *Sunday Bloody Sunday* and *Midnight Cowboy*. Nonetheless, the prevailing mood was summed up by a line from Mart Crowley's seminal – if I may so express myself – play, then film, *The Boys in the Band*: 'Show me a happy homosexual and I'll show you a gay corpse.' The notion of depicting the normal homosexual man or woman (as, by definition, most homosexual men and women are) was still thought of as dangerously radical. It must be said that perhaps homosexuals themselves contributed to this: the drama of being gay is central to many gay people's identities. And indeed it took major social changes before gay lives could in any way be described as normal.

Not that 'normal' was what all gay men wanted to be. It was one of the great debates of the 1970s and 1980s. Was homosexuality inherently radical? Was it of the essence of being gay that one was consciously distancing oneself from heterosexual norms? Were gay people born crusaders against conventional society, glorying in their otherness? Or was it our demand, indeed our right, to be accepted as part of society, just another strand of human existence, different in orientation but not in emotional experience, equal in the right freely to express our loves and desires, but not in any way superior? Militantly gay films are few, but many of the films described in this book fall naturally into one or other of two camps: those of a specifically gay sensibility, and those which attempt to depict gays as part of the general human situation. The specifically gay ones by no means necessarily advocate a separatist gay position, but they do insist on a viewpoint that sees the world differently, with homosexual eyes. The other kind of film seeks to integrate gays into the world at large. I appeared in what I suppose is one of the most important films of this kind, *Four Weddings and a Funeral*. Gareth, the character I played, was flamboyant but not camp; he belonged to no stereotypical category; and he died, not of AIDS, which was at that time ravaging the gay community, but of Scottish dancing.

When I read the script, it was immediately evident that this was a new kind of a gay character in films: not sensitive, not intuitive, kind and somehow Deeply Sad, nor hilarious, bitchy and outrageous, but masculine, exuberant, occasionally offensive, generous and passionate. He was also deeply involved with his partner, the handsome, shy, witty, understated Matthew. In the original screenplay, they were glimpsed at the beginning of the film asleep in bed. In the final cut, the film-makers removed this sequence, in order to allow their relationship to creep up on the audience. They were right to do so: before they knew it, viewers had come to know and love them individually, and were hit very hard, first by Gareth's death and then by Matthew's oration (with a little help from another splendid bugger, W. H. Auden). Perhaps the most important moment in the film from a gay perspective was Charles's remark after the eponymous funeral that while the group of friends whose amatory fortunes the film follows talked incessantly about marriage, they had never noticed that all along they had had in their midst an ideal marriage, that of Gareth and Matthew. It almost defies belief, but in the months after the release of the film, I received a number of letters from apparently intelligent, articulate members of the public saying that they had never realised, until seeing the film, that gay people had emotions like normal people. (I also had a letter from Ian McKellen saying how much more important *Four Weddings* was in gay terms than the simultaneously released *Philadelphia*, with its welter of chaste histrionics.)

Gay men and women have now entered the mainstream of cinema, losing their exoticness on the way. They are, increasingly, just a part of life, though still generally a somewhat marginal part. Sexual roles are less fixed, not in a 1960s androgynous way, but in the sense that it might be possible to have sex or even an affair with someone of the same gender and not compromise one's masculinity or femininity. Rose Troche's *Bedrooms and Hallways* (1998) played most entertainingly with this idea: a gay man joins a men's group, whose sexiest, most rampantly heterosexual member falls for him; the gay man himself later has a fling with the straight guy's girlfriend. A highlight of this film about sexual musical chairs is the speech by the hunk (James Purefoy) hymning the unexpected delights of being anally penetrated. I played the coordinator of the group – straight. In fact, not a single gay character in the film was played by a gay actor. One of the ironic side effects of the new dispensation in movies was that straight actors were queuing up to play gay, and it became increasingly hard for gay actors to get the parts for which they were uniquely qualified. This issue, though scarcely a subject of deep concern, raises interesting questions about authenticity. It is striking that not a single gay person had anything to do with *Brokeback Mountain*, from the author of the original novella, to the director, to the actors. (Perhaps someone in make-up or wardrobe slipped through? Who can tell?) Would it have been different had gay artists been involved? Better? Or perhaps, to return to my earlier point, it isn't really a film about being gay at all, simply about deep friendship which, under certain circumstances, turns sexual.

What, if anything, is missing from the gay cinematic scene? In fact, the single most significant piece of gay celluloid was a television series, *Queer as Folk*, which, in telling it like it is (at least for the young and pretty), broke so many taboos that almost everything else was left looking pretty silly. Russell T. Davies's stunningly witty and truthful script was an account of what it is to be part of the scene today. But of course, many – perhaps most – gay people aren't part of that scene. There is a gay world elsewhere. Early in the 1970s, as part of a theatre company called Gay Sweatshop, I appeared in a little play by Martin Sherman called *Passing By* which I still regard as one of the most radical gay plays ever written. It showed two men meeting, falling in love with each other, falling out of love and then parting. At no point did they ever mention the word gay or homosexual, there was no reference to mothers or even Judy Garland. They simply found each other highly attractive and one thing led to another. It was amusing, touching, sexy, and entirely normal. This little play has had few successors, on stage or screen. Jonathan Harvey's *Beautiful Thing*, the film version of which Steven Paul Davies describes very well in his book, was a sort of 1980s version of the same thing, though the youthfulness of the characters lent it a special poignancy; *My Beautiful Laundrette* showed another sort of a tender relationship which defied race and class in the most spontaneous, natural, innocent fashion. Ferzan Özpetek's exquisite *Hamam*, a film I think Davies is somewhat inclined to underrate, showed the gradual, delicate development of feelings between a heterosexual Italian and a young Turk, a story which conveyed the gentle seduction of one culture by another. These are all quietly persuasive, lifelike accounts of the birth of homosexual desire.

What I personally would like to see is a story of overwhelming passion, a gay *Antony and Cleopatra* or *Romeo and Juliet*, on a grand scale. For that I suppose we need a gay Shakespeare. The gay directors who might have told that story – Zeffirelli, Visconti, Schlesinger – didn't. Let's hope that their successors will take the plunge. And let's hope that two huge box-office stars who fully acknowledge their own gayness will be playing the leads. Meanwhile, Steven Paul Davies's book describes the astonishing, moving, witty (and sometimes blissfully silly) things that have been achieved so far.

If the honest representation of gay people on film is still not quite completely achieved, the pioneers had an infinitely tougher job. This is a review for the Guardian *in 2002 of Richard Barrios's* Screened Out.

'For Chrissakes, Charles,' moaned Leo McCarey in 1935 as he attempted the always difficult task of directing Charles Laughton (in *Ruggles of Red Gap* on this occasion), 'do you have to be so goddam *nancy?*' To which Laughton replied, pleasantly, 'My dear fellow, after five o'clock, a bit of it's bound to slip out.' Richard Barrios's new book is essentially a study of the bits of it that slipped out in American movie history. He covers the terrain from the beginning of movies to the mid-Sixties, stopping there because after *The Boys in the Band*, gays had finally occupied centre screen, rather than the peripheries. It is a fascinating and thoroughly documented study in subversion, as much social science as movie history, which reveals how ultimately irrepressible minorities are, regardless of the weight of opposition ranged against them. In the case of homosexuality and the movies, the opposition came both from within and from without. Few of the moguls who ran the studios were sympathetic to homosexuality as such (though many of their employees were more or less openly gay), while the Hays Office, established by the industry for self-protection, and its militant cousin, the Catholic Church's Legion of Decency, set their hearts implacably against any representation of what

MY LIFE IN PIECES

was officially deemed Sex Perversion, especially of what they invariably called the 'pansy' tendency. Under the influence of Henry J. Forman's best-selling moral tract *Our Movie-Made Children,* which warned against the corruption of the American mind, they attempted to impose their manically sanitised vision of American life on the country. This was a world view which thought the word 'pregnant' unacceptable for public consumption, waged furious war on cleavage, and denied even married couples the comforts of the double bed.

The Hollywood gay community, with exceptional ingenuity, determined to make its presence felt on film, not simply demanding acknowledgement for itself, but also propagating an alternative and antithetical view of human life where our impulses and aspirations refuse to conform to the arbitrary and unreal codes of the moralists – pan-sexuality rather than homosexuality. They played an extraordinary game of cat and mouse, and Barrios describes it with relish and some wit, in a prose style which sometimes slips into the chatty and even gossipy, but which is mercifully free of the structuralist, semiotic, and Saussurian modes which still dog so much writing about film. He is equally free of political correctness, and seeks to celebrate those gallantly effeminate actors ('sissified', in the language of their time) who from the earliest days of film embellished and enlivened the films in which they appeared. He sees them as the opposite of self-oppressive: they are rather, for him, gay guerrillas, fearlessly and cunningly bringing their sensibilities and subversions into the light. A tireless camp-hound, he hunts out these moments, just as gay audiences of the time must have done, looking for the hidden innuendo, marvelling at the outrageous excess. What, for instance, can audiences have made of George K. Arthur as Madam Lucy the (male) couturier in *Irene* crying, 'As I live and hemstitch, she's impossible!' Sound gave a voice to gays, and that voice simpered, hissed and lisped. In tracing the lavender thread that runs through film history, Barrios unearths some wonderful curiosities – the character Clarence (Clarence and Leonard were frequent giveaway names for gay men) in the 1927 silent film *Wanderer of the West* announced by a title card which says: 'One of Nature's mistakes in a country where Men were Men'; the passionate friendship between Richard Arlen and Buddy Rogers in *Wings* of the following year, in which Arlen cradles the dying Rogers in his arms and finally takes leave of him with a passionate kiss on the mouth; *Ladies They Talk About* (1933), the first lesbian prison drama; one pretty boy slipping a slave bracelet onto

311

the wrist of another in Noël Coward's *Cavalcade*; and *Dude Wrangler*, now sadly lost, billed as 'The Story of a Pansy Cowboy... *oh dear!*' Very often, lesbian elements were used for titillatory purposes, in, for example, the notoriously steamy *Naked Moon* sequence from *The Sign of the Cross*, directed by the magnificently hypocritical C. B. DeMille to be, he claimed, a dreadful warning, or in *Queen Christina*, where Irving Thalberg, inspired by *Mädchen in Uniform*, had specifically briefed the screenwriter to create as much intensity as possible in the relationship between the cross-dressing Queen (Garbo) and her lady-in-waiting.

The incidence of homosexuality on screen is thus a complicated two- or three-way traffic between the agenda of the gay performers, writers and directors (the famous 'Fairy Unit' at MGM musicals, for example), the commercial calculations of producers, and not rarely the professional instincts of performers who were often not gay. Gay roles are often fun to play; some straight comedians in the Twenties and Thirties specialised in 'nance' roles until they were no longer able to (one of the most famous ones – Bobby Watson – switched during the war to playing Hitler). Inevitably, film mirrored the prevailing social situation. There was, in the early Thirties, a brief period in which homosexuality emerged into the light, with thriving bars and clubs, especially in New York, where the glittering Pansy Club was the smart place to be seen, both for gays and straights. The supply of queer humour on the screen rose to meet the fashion. Paradoxically, this unexpected suspension of homophobia came to an end with the election of FDR and the ending of Prohibition. As Barrios remarks, it seemed as if America could take only so much vice, and from 1935, that was drink, and only drink. In a brilliant capsule, he notes that the framers of the newly enforced Production Code of 1934 declared war on Mae West, because she dared to treat sex as a joke: their demands 'denatured' her work, and caused it to flop. Before the enforcement of the new Code, West had been the greatest box-office draw; after it, it was Shirley Temple.

Barrios steers us through the Forties and Fifties, noting the development of the male bitch character as perfected by Clifton Webb, the tortured ambiguities of the relationship between James Dean and Sal Mineo in *Rebel Without a Cause*, the dramas over the filming of the pathetically mild *Tea with Sympathy*, Robert Walker's dazzlingly gay interpretation of Bruno in *Strangers on a Train* for Hitchcock, and the Legion of Decency's last great triumph, the excision of seven gay minutes from

Spartacus (now restored). The relative triumph of the commitment to film of Mart Crowley's *The Boys in the Band* is noted for what it was – a truthful account of some gay lives at a time of considerable oppression, though scarcely an affirmation of gay liberation. He ends by sombrely noting that six out of the nine actors in the cast have subsequently died of AIDS, a horror to eclipse any of the griefs endured by Crowley's Harold, the 'pockmarked Jew fairy' of the play, and his friends. AIDS of course has changed everything for homosexuals and our representation on screen, for better and for worse.

These developments are beyond the scope of Barrios's book. The story he tells is of hidden history and witty subversion and in that sense it is a positive one. For me, however, it is finally a little depressing. His subject is the American cinema, and it has to be stated that the inability of that industry to deal with the realities of life as it is lived – not simply gay life, but the whole spectrum of human desires and aspirations – is a dispiriting phenomenon. 'Movies are us,' he says, rather overexcitedly, 'we are the movies.' But all human life most distinctly is not there. Again and again it is foreign movies or foreign artists making American movies that have pushed forward the possibilities. In pre-war Hollywood, of course, the vast majority of directors were European, and they – von Sternberg, von Stroheim, Lubitsch, Billy Wilder, James Whale – pushed as hard as they could against the pressures of the small-town morality which held such curious sway over the lives and work of movie artists, but it was an unending and often unequal struggle. America has still yet to produce films on gay themes as grown-up as Almodóvar's *The Law of Desire*, or even the recently aired British film *Bedrooms and Hallways*. Britain, at least since the Sixties, has had a more impressive record altogether with films like *Victim, Sunday Bloody Sunday* and *Tchaikovsky*. And *Four Weddings and a Funeral*, apart from its other felicities, struck a really mighty blow by placing a gay couple acknowledged by all as 'the perfect match' at the heart of what has now become one of the most popular films of all time. As Charles, the Hugh Grant character says, 'If we can't be like Gareth and Matthew, maybe we should let it go.'

There still remains the dream of a film about a great and overwhelming gay love affair, not to proselytise, simply to affirm the eternal diversity and richness of human experience. Alas, it seems unlikely to emerge from a Hollywood in which apparently and miraculously not one single American gay actor is to be found, where historical characters' sexual preferences are still straightened out (as in *A Beautiful Mind*, one dreads to imagine what will be made of Alexander the Great's adored boyfriend Hephaestion in the forthcoming films of his life) and where the success and failure of movies is predicated on vast nationwide box-office returns, demanding the approbation of the lowest common denominator. In fact – and this is where Barrios's admirable book seems perhaps to be over-stating the importance of the movies – television, both here and in America, is again becoming a great engine for social change, more adept at reflecting realities than its older brother. *Queer as Folk*, both here and in its somewhat less bold transatlantic version, shot from the hip (if you forgive the slightly nancy innuendo) in a way one scarcely believed could ever be possible. Television is again the medium of the future.

A final note on Four Weddings and a Funeral: *the film had an almost impossibly ideal cast, some of the older members of which – Kenneth Griffith, Robert Lang, Rosalie Crutchley, Corin Redgrave – have since left us, as has one of the poster boys and girls, one of the core team, Char-lotte Coleman. Her death in 2001 was responsible for my only experience of being doorstepped: the tabloid press smelt a scandal. I refused to speak to any of them, but wrote this piece for the* Guardian.

I suppose Charlotte Coleman will be always remembered now as Scarlett, Hugh Grant's unexpectedly punk flatmate in *Four Weddings and a Funeral*, but for a generation of children presently growing into young adulthood she was Marmalade Atkins and for another whole section of the viewing public, she was Jess in the television adaptation of Jeanette Winterson's *Oranges Are Not the Only Fruit*. That was quite a range, although all these parts and almost everything else she ever played shared a wholly unforced quirkiness which was the essential her. I had known her for some years before we worked together in *Four Weddings and a Funeral*, when she was still a very young woman, and she always cut a striking figure – sartorially, to be sure, as a clothes horse for the teenage chic of the moment, her nostrils sometimes be-ringed, her hair radically transformed every time you met her – but it was the intensity of her per-sonality that caught you, wild with laughter one moment, plunged into deep melancholy the next, her huge sleepless eyes opening up deepest chasms of feeling. She was worryingly thin, but her energy was immense.

She spoke brilliantly and wittily of herself, begging one to shut her up – 'I know I'm emotionally incontinent' – but always conscious of absurdity, in herself or in others. She struck me as a Sally Bowles *de nos jours*, outrageous and vulnerable and impossible not to watch. I believed that she was going to be one of the great comic talents of our time, with the special gift of creating her own outlandish rhythms, which made everything she ever said as an actress seem new and original and hilarious. The loss is terrible, for her family and for all of us. Thank God there is so much that is wonderful to remember her by.

The only jobs I got out of Four Weddings and a Funeral *were to be the voice of the Ancient Green Grasshopper in* James and the Giant Peach, *and to play the villain in Jim Carrey's* Ace Ventura: When Nature Calls, *which shot in Charleston, Carolina, in 1996, and was not, to put it mildly, a joyous experience. But the long hours of waiting in a sweltering caravan were not wasted: I sat there in my jodhpurs (villains always wear jodhpurs in these sort of films), translating the screenplay of* Les Enfants du Paradis *and adapting it into a play for the Royal Shakespeare Company, for whom I was going to direct it. I wrote the following for the* Daily Telegraph *just before the opening night.*

Last spring, Adrian Noble asked me to direct *Widowers' Houses* for the RSC. It is a splendid play in its way, acerbic, trenchant, relevant, but Shaw has never excited me, neither as actor or director, so when I met Noble to talk about it, I brought a list of twenty-seven possible alternative options with me. After reciting them, I casually added, hardly expecting to be taken seriously, that what I really wanted to do was to put *Les Enfants du Paradis* on stage. The effect was electrifying. Noble jumped up, eyes blazing. 'My favourite film!' he cried, as so many people would over the coming months. He'd seen it at the Academy Cinema when he first came to London as a kid, going back again and again and again. We trotted down Memory Lane: the old movie house on Oxford Street, the Peter Strausfeld woodcut posters, the polyglot babble of the foyer, the all-pervading smell of coffee too long on the hob. Then favourite moments from the film and favourite actors – 'Arletty! Barrault! Brasseur!' – the names alone enough to evoke a vanished world of expression, one of the greatest films ever made which is at the same time one of the supreme celebrations of the theatre. 'Do you think it's possible?' Adrian asked and I said truthfully that I hadn't the slightest idea but that I'd find out.

What he didn't ask was why I would want to do it on stage, with the Royal Shakespeare Company. He didn't need to; it was obvious to both of us. It was an opportunity for actors and audience to encounter the French romantic tradition, with the human heart, eloquent, impassioned, at its centre. This form of writing calls for a very particular kind of acting, the head and the heart in perfect balance, in which the individual emotional experience is transformed, made mythic by force of personality, expressed in language both eloquent and concrete. Acting of this sort has not been seen on the English stage for many years, for the simple reason that the plays that call for it do not exist, or do not translate well. French nineteenth-century theatre has hitherto resisted attempts to find a satisfactory English form; the nearest experience of it English audiences have had was in Alan Badel's extraordinary performance of Jean-Paul Sartre's version of Dumas' play *Kean*, in which that astonishing and much-missed actor played the central role with a (rather un-English, in fact somewhat un-Kean-like) burnished articulateness, a smouldering eloquence, phrasing in huge paragraphs, exuding a sexuality of intellect, that was a perfect transmutation into English terms of a fundamentally French phenomenon. He did it again on television, in an adaptation of *The Count of Monte Cristo*, no doubt long since wiped, in which his Edmond Dantès, too, was full of the uniquely precise passion he so consummately distilled.

It was self-evident to me and, I guess, to Adrian Noble, that it would be a marvellous thing for a company like the RSC to explore this language of acting. It would be the sort of technical, imaginative and emotional challenge which is the lifeblood of ensembles. *Les Enfants du Paradis* is the work of a poet – the great popular poet Jacques Prévert, France's unofficial laureate for over thirty years. Though the film is not in verse (which immediately makes it more susceptible to translation) it is nonetheless of quite exceptional elegance and eloquence and fullness. The film's exploration of the devastating power of love, so particular to the characters and yet so unerring in its ability to embody the universal romantic experience, is one of the most comprehensive expressions in existence of that fascination with romantic love which is undergoing something of a shy revival at the present moment, in films like *Four Weddings and a Funeral*, and plays such as Jonathan Harvey's *Beautiful Thing* and David Hare's *Skylight*. The question was – would it work in the theatre?

I had no qualms whatever about transferring a text from one medium to another – the traffic from stage to screen dates from the earliest days of the cinema; why should it all be one way? Indeed, it had struck me forcibly while directing my film *The Ballad of the Sad Café* that there were several ways of conveying exactly the same script to the screen, mine being just one, even though I had actively collaborated with the screenwriter. Why shouldn't Prévert's wonderful material have a second innings? And why should the original interpreters have copyright on the material they first performed? After all, I wasn't pulping the film. It would always be there, and if people were terrified of a new performance or interpretation tampering with their memories, I suppose I'd just have to say, well don't come. If they did, though, they might have a whole new and complementary experience of the masterpiece, rather like – but only *rather* like – seeing Shakespeare's *Othello* and Verdi's *Otello* side by side. My only consideration was whether the material would work on stage.

I had a hunch that it would: certainly the plot, the spine of the action, is exceptionally well-wrought, with a symmetry and an ingenuity that rivals *Twelfth Night* (to name a somewhat comparable treatment of romantic experience). While love is unquestionably the theme – scarcely a scene or a character in the entire three-and-a-half-hour span is not concerned in some way with it – the context is that of the theatre. The action takes place largely in or around theatres of various kinds, offering extremely promising opportunities for staging – not to mention splendid value for money: three mime shows, a chunk of melodrama spoofed and a three-minute *Othello*. But all of this would be of no interest if the text itself were not dramatically conceived. I had not seen the film for fifteen years when I made my suggestion; to find out whether it was I went, not to the film, but straight to the screenplay.

Close scrutiny of the text revealed that, in a way unusual in film, every single speech both advanced the action and disclosed more about the characters. The director Marcel Carné – who was of course closely involved in creating the screenplay – was a strictly classical director; camera work per se was of no interest to him. He created the physical world of the piece in studios in the South of France and Paris, and then trained his cameras on it, in almost documentary style, always concentrating on the human figure; a vast amount of the film consists of single shots, two-shots and three-shots. Even tracking is used with great restraint. Putting *Citizen Kane* on stage would be absurd, or an exercise in visual theatre on the grandest scale. It lives entirely in its visual style. The essential test of a play, however, is whether or not it lives in its language, and this, *Les Enfants du Paradis* most decidedly and triumphantly does. Not only in its dazzling eloquence, but in its exhilarating commitment to the principle of action, which has nothing to do with action shots in a movie, and everything to do with the momentum of the characters and their needs.

The text we play is virtually intact. The action needed only a small amount of relocating to avoid restless cutting from scene to scene. There are nonetheless some fifty scenes in the play (not quite as many as *Antony and Cleopatra*, I reassured a gobsmacked RSC) and my brief to the designer, Robin Don, was simple: no scene-change must take longer than twenty seconds. He solved this monstrous demand with perfect sangfroid, and his solution was such as to make it quite impossible, even if one had been tempted, to reproduce on stage the physical life of the film; every scene had to be rethought in theatrical terms alone. In some ways, though, the approach to the play has been not unlike approaching a film: the costume requirement has been enormous – some three hundred and fifty costumes specially designed by Christopher Woods; musically too, it is an enormous undertaking. John White, avant-gardist of the class of '65, a musician of vast sympathies and irrepressible originality, has composed over two-and-a-quarter hours of new music, and is still at it. Steve Wasson, mime and teacher, last *assistant* of the great Étienne Decroux, has, to brilliant effect, taught the actors the essentials of a discipline that normally takes years to absorb, and created entirely new versions of the mime shows. At every level, the piece is an epic – a huge panorama on the subject of love created at a murky period of French history (1944) to affirm the essentially human values that had been compromised during an occupation out of which few French people had come unscathed.

My greatest anxiety once I'd translated the thing was how the young actors to whom I gave the script would respond. Casting actors more or less the age of the characters in the first half of the play – mid-twenties – rather than the forty-year-olds in the film (Arletty – *'une jeune fille'* – was actually forty-six), I had no idea what they would feel about this material, with its entirely direct acceptance of the premises of romantic love. The work is the antithesis of *cool*; the inverted commas which enclose a great deal of modern acting are of no use here. I shouldn't have worried. Every actor who received the script – many of them had never seen the film – walked into the casting office eyes glowing, scarcely being able to believe their luck at having material like this in their hands. Such work calls for acting of a particular commitment and freedom, which it immortally received from its first interpreters. Watching the RSC actors, all twenty-six of them, flower with it (and they were after all the starting point for the whole project) has been uniquely moving and exhilarating, the most remarkable experience of my working life in the theatre.

That article was one of the worst misjudgements of my professional life. My opening sentences about Adrian Noble jumping to his feet were quoted and requoted in review after review as an example of my pretentiousness and idiocy. Adrian and I became a kind of self-congratulatory mafia scheming to make fools of the public. The press were anyway quite determined to loathe the show: I knew this in advance because a perfectly harmless, scholarly fellow called Ronald Bergan, whom I knew slightly, and who had been deputed by the Guardian *to interview me, sat down, switched on his tape recorder and launched into some very spiky, confrontational questions. 'Hold on, hold on, Ronald,' I said, 'what's got into you?' He switched the tape recorder off, and smiled sheepishly. 'Sorry,' he said, 'only they told me: "Don't let him get away with it".' Well, I didn't. They made sure of that.*

Not only were the reviews bad, all attacking my temerity at tampering with a masterpiece, there were shock-horror state-of-the-RSC stories about how expensive it had been, how many actors had been specially hired for the production, and how I had disappeared after the (triumphant, as it happens, with curtain call after curtain call) first night. I had disappeared, but only because, thanks to the vagaries of repertory planning, there were no performances of the show for a week afterwards. I had the pleasure of reading the reviews the following morning at the airport as I departed for the cross-country American book-signing tour of the first volume of my biography of Orson Welles, The Road to Xanadu, *which was being serialised in the* New York Times, *had been joyfully received up and down the country, and propelled me on to every chat show in the land. There I was, being interviewed by the great Studs Terkel in Chicago, and Charlie Wilson in New York, and every hour, on the hour, it seemed, they were faxing me yet more bad reviews for* Les Enfants. *It was an oddly schizophrenic experience. I toyed with not going back to England. Ever. On my return to the Barbican, the stage management all greeted me warmly, none of the actors tried to punch me, and there were dozens of letters from the public to say how much they'd enjoyed it. As some sort of salve, the French critics who had seen the show wrote of it with high enthusiasm, only regretting that I'd been too respectful to the original. One shouldn't whine about failure, and as often as not it's deserved, in some measure (vide* My Fair Lady*). But this time, I think the show was better than it was said to be: too long, certainly, because we had had unending technical problems with the revolve, and been obliged to cancel a number of previews, which meant we could never work on the play on the set, and the cutting which I'd always known was needed had not been possible. After we opened, I slashed about twenty minutes, and of course it was better. In fact, the last night was like the first night: awash with tears and cheers, people saying that it was the best thing they'd ever seen and so on. Whatever else it was or wasn't, it was different: a different acting vocabulary, a different temperature, a different story.*

By now, it was clear that my honeymoon with the critics, such as it was, was over. I had been remarkably lucky, over the years; had, as Ronald Bergan's editor might have said, got away with it. But now there was a distinct feeling of 'Oh no, not him again' in the response to my work.

And in truth, I was fairly fed up with myself as an artist, insofar as I felt entitled to call myself that at all. I had sworn in public – in print, indeed, in the pages of Being an Actor *– that I would never become a jobbing actor; now I had become a sort of jobbing director, although, ironically enough, my latest, biggest flop had been a conviction project par excellence, born out of love of that film in particular, and of French acting in general, whose essence I had tried to bring to an English stage. I felt the need to stop, to think, to rediscover, to reconnect. Whenever I directed in America, I would tell the actors, before they went out in front of the public during previews, to remember why it was that they had wanted to be actors in the first place. Now I needed to give myself the same note. I found that I was just doing things in order to be doing them. Not even, really, to make money, just in order to be perpetually busy.*

Then I went to America to direct Cavalli's La Calisto *in Glimmerglass, in James Fenimore Cooper country, in the bear-inhabited forests of upstate*

New York, and something about being in that wild, pioneer landscape and working on one of the earliest of all operas, on a subject taken from the dawn of Western civilisation, changed my whole pulse as a director. To my slack-jawed astonishment, Jane Glover, conducting, orchestrated the music as she went along with her group of baroque instrumentalists, inventing it in the instant. I sat and listened, I encouraged the singers to listen – to each other, to the instrumentalists, to themselves – to allow the piece to breathe with its own inherent vibrations as naturally as the rhapsodic Orphic strummings of the theorbists in the pit. The production was simplicity itself, inspired, visually, by the paintings of Piero di Cosimo, which have a unique quality, seeming to be not generic evocations of the ancient world, as in so many Renaissance canvases, but an actual record of it, as if Piero had not imagined that world, but visited it. His fauns are not frolicsome or riotous as in Titian: they are rutty, iddy creatures, rough and hairy; you can almost smell them. Even the animals that emerge from the forest in The Forest Fire, Piero's great canvas in the Ashmolean, are weirdly miscegenated, still evolving, some with human faces, others with ancillary limbs. In La Calisto, Endymion's lovelorn addresses to his divine mistress seemed to speak of a purer, simpler world.

Immersion in this world was stirring something in me, a dissatisfaction with my life in art, to put it rather grandly. In fact, my feeling was that art was precisely what I was not making. While I was staying in Cooperstown, where Glimmerglass is located, I was writing an introduction to Snowdon's collection of photographs, Snowdon on Stage – it's easy, he had said, you just have to write everything that's happened since Suez – and this, too, forced me, in considering the evolution of the British theatre over the previous forty years, to question what sort of a contribution I thought I was making. I was painfully conscious of the erratic nature of my career as an actor: two Shakespeares, no Ibsen, no Chekhov, no Pinter, no Beckett. What kind of a path was I pursuing? Certainly not that of the classical actor I had set out to be. Hoping somehow to catch up, I leaped at Bill Alexander's invitation to go to the Birmingham Rep and play Face in The Alchemist, a play I had enjoyed seeing in the past. Once in rehearsals, however, I found that I loathed doing it. It was not a happy production, but the problem went beyond that. I found Jonson's world view so unrelentingly misanthropic, so contemptuous of the foibles of his fellow human beings, that I had a sort of physical reaction against playing the character. I had no real idea what I was doing, apart from hurling out a *lot of wilfully obscure language at a baffled audience and desperately trying to whip up some sort of comic energy. I felt as if I was idiotically prancing behind a huge glass pane, in front of an audience which was viewing me with resentful incomprehension. I feared that I was losing my pleasure in acting altogether, and resolved to step back from the theatre. In fact,* The Alchemist *had been my first play for five years; I hoped it would be at least another five before I did one again.*

Going Solo

At that point, in 1997, the producer Brian Brolly asked me to revive Micheál mac Liammóir's one-man play The Importance of Being Oscar *in the West End. I refused immediately, not just because of my vow to keep out of the theatre but because I felt that the play was inextricably bound up with his unique personality. I wrote this piece about him and it for the* Sunday Telegraph *in 1997.*

To a remarkable degree, my adolescence was dominated by Oscar Wilde: I only ever spoke of him as 'Oscar'. This was the man I wanted to be, generous, eloquent, intellectually brilliant, provocative, fun, and, of course, gay, though I kept rather quiet about that bit; this was, after all, 1963.

When I was about fifteen I borrowed a couple of LPs from the record library, their sleeves exotically printed in gold and black, the title printed in curling Beardsleyesque letters: *The Importance of Being Oscar*. The title was irresistible, of course, to a thorough-going Wildean, the presentation exotic and promisingly decadent; even the actor/author's name was fascinatingly foreign, not to say unpronounceable: Micheál mac Liammóir. What I heard did not disappoint on any of these counts. It was an astonishingly ripe and evocative odyssey through Wilde's life, spoken with a kind of immediacy, an intimacy, almost, that took one directly to the heart of the life and the work. The acting style was one I had never encountered before: its rhetorical sweep alternated, in a brilliant exercise in contrasted rhythms, with sudden throwaway quips that had the air of improvisation about them. The actor was playful and magisterial, conversational and ritualistic, high priest and cheeky altar server all at once. The Irish accent was like none other I had heard, too, neither upper-class cut glass, nor Dublin demotic, certainly not stage-Irish and yet not life-Irish either, but it was a supremely musical and utterly compelling, and I came to know its cadences as one learns a piece of music.

Time passed; I went to work at Olivier's Old Vic, in the box office, where I fell in love with actors and acting, and determined to make the theatre my life. I decided to go to university to find out whether I had any talent; there was not the slightest pretence that I would be doing any academic work. I had intended to go to Trinity College in Dublin – Wilde's Alma Mater, of course – but the British Government had just ceased to offer grants to go there so instead I went to Queen's University in Belfast, thinking, in my boyish innocence, that it would be much the same thing. It wasn't, but it was rather wonderful nonetheless, and the day I arrived I enrolled in the Drama Society, and proceeded to immerse myself in its work. Our year built towards the competition, in March, of the Irish University Drama Association, and presently it was announced that the adjudicator for that year would be Micheál mac Liammóir. I walked into the office of *Gown*, the student paper, and proposed that I interview the great man in Dublin, and found myself, furnished with a tape recorder the size of a large suitcase, on the train a week later.

What I found there, I described to the readers of the paper. I continued:

I went back to Belfast a changed man; I had been vouchsafed a glimpse of a whole other way of being, like something out of my reading, out of my dreams. Olivier's National Theatre, my *beau idéal* up to that point, seemed terribly dour after this; I knew then the real meaning of a phrase of Cocteau's that had stuck in my mind, 'red-and-gold sickness' – of a theatre of poetry and magic and a sort of opulence of spirit.

When Micheál came for the Festival I ferried him around Belfast, from play to play; I took down his verdicts on the performances, including my own as Trigorin in *The Seagull* ('not a born actor, I fear; a born writer perhaps'); above all, I dressed him for the two performances he gave of *The Importance of Being Oscar*, and saw for the first time something of the pity and terror of an actor's life, as well as its glory: minutes before the supremely self-assured performances, he was a shuddering wreck, invoking the Mother of God, Her Husband, Her Son, and all the Saints, to protect him through his ordeal. Once on, though, he was an absolute master.

When he left Belfast, he handed me a sweetly inscribed copy of *The Importance of Being Oscar*, and was gone – gone, in fact, out of my life for ever, in the flesh, at any rate. As a presence he has remained with me ever since, not as a model, for he was truly *sui generis*, but as a token of a sort of richness, a ripeness, even, that is quite absent from our new, improved stages. I wrote to him when I was about to graduate from drama school saying you won't remember me but... and he replied saying you're quite right, I don't, but what a very charming photograph. I auditioned for Hilton Edwards, but didn't get in, and that, you might have thought, would be that. But then I wrote a book a few years ago in which I described my encounter with Micheál in Belfast, and an ex-member of his company, Pat Maclarnon, wrote to me and said that I'd got him dead right, and as a reward he would be leaving me in his will Micheál's very first theatre design. Then, a few years later, I went to Dublin to make a radio documentary about mac Liammóir, and sought out Pat in his reclusive retirement, and after many clankings and bangings and sliding of bolts, the door opened and a man appeared, red of face and heavily bespectacled, struggling along on two sticks – this was the man, mind, who had played Dorian Gray to Micheál's Lord Henry Wotton – and said he wondered when I'd come, he had something for me, and he reached into a drawer and pulled out a gold ring, an exquisite thing, with a Celtic motif signifying love unto death, and he told me that it was Micheál's, that Micheál had designed it and Hilton had had it made up, and then he said, 'It's yours, it belongs to you.' And it fitted, and I have worn it ever since.

Nonetheless, and if that isn't An Omen I don't know what is, I resisted suggestions that I should revive *The Importance of Being Oscar*: how could I banish Micheál's lush cadences from my ear? Finally, grudgingly, I agreed to read the script, and found to my amazement that it was perfectly possible to play it very differently indeed from Micheál, and very rewarding. I understood for the first time the brilliance of Micheál as writer, which his brilliance as an actor had been masking, and I was able to make the piece my own. So although there is a certain charming symmetry to the notion that once I was his dresser, and now I'm wearing his mantle, in fact the show, like Wilde himself, seems a very different thing now. It remains one of the greatest stories ever told, and it has been an extraordinary experience telling it.

Even though I had made the show my own, Micheál was ever-present. Meeting him had had an understandably large impact on me at the time, but now, thirty years later, he was if anything more vivid in my mind. He carried so much with him, so much history: in terms of theatre alone, the fact that he had played Oliver Twist to Beerbohm Tree's Fagin, that he had been at the legendary pre-war London performances of the Ballets Russes, that he had seen and met Sarah Bernhardt, gave him a link to a mythic theatrical past. His vocal technique itself belonged to the Victorian theatre: even in his lifetime, Tree was thought to be a throwback, and he had been Micheál's first teacher. But he was connected to history in other ways, too: he had known Yeats and Lady Gregory intimately and been passionately involved in Irish Nationalism. He was the author, too, of the oldest Irish-language play still regularly performed. He had more or less invented Orson Welles; he certainly discovered him. The theatre he cre-ated with Hilton Edwards in Dublin was a blazing torch of avant-gardism, acclaimed across the whole of the theatrical world. To talk to him was to be plugged into a vanished world of art, wit and gossip at the very high-est level, as well as to be vouchsafed glimpses of a sort of a mysticism which he liked to say was Celtic, but which was rather more occult than that. His power over an audience was positively uncanny, magical and mysterious, spellbinding in an almost literal sense. The revelation in the late 1990s that he wasn't Irish at all, that his accent, his name and his supposed Cork childhood were all inventions, only compelled further admi-ration. What a supreme act of creative imagination to realise who you are in your essence and to reinvent yourself accordingly! Sitting in my dress-ing room one afternoon after the show, I discovered yet another dimension of this extraordinary man: a beautiful young woman with tumbling yellow tresses knocked on the door and announced herself as Valerie Rossmore, daughter of Brian Tobin, who had been, I knew, Micheál's manager and his lover. Her father having no gift for fatherhood, Micheál had adopted her, and she was brought up by him and Hilton at Harcourt Terrace – two flamboyantly gay men raising a thirteen-year-old girl in the middle of Sixties Dublin, one of the most puritanically Catholic cities in the world.

She and I immediately became fast friends, and so he continues to be a living presence in my life.

Doing The Importance of Being Oscar *proved to be my salvation as an actor. The play is a highly sophisticated and brilliantly effective piece of storytelling, and the contact with the audience was powerfully direct and eventually quite profound. They seemed mesmerised by the story I was telling, entranced by the spellbinding cadences of both Wilde and mac Liammóir. And, for the first time in what seemed like a very long while, like my singers in* La Calisto*, I was able to listen: to listen to what I was saying, listen to the audience, listen to the complex feelings that were passing through me. I could take the pulse of show. The form of the piece was deeply satisfying: this attempt to evoke a man and his work not by impersonating him but by summoning him out of the ether. In* The Importance of Being Oscar *the narrative formed a framework for sections of great virtuosity in which I would play several characters speaking to each other, or evoke the Victorian theatre (in the brilliant five-minute digest of* Dorian Gray*), or dazzle with a very flashy speech from* Salome *in the original French, always returning to the man, Oscar Wilde. With* Importance*, I had found myself again as an actor. It was nothing to do with a rejection of acting with other people, nothing to do with not wanting to do plays any more: it was a reassertion of the sheer pleasure of storytelling, a return of my delight in the power of language to evoke worlds, a renewal of the pact between me and the audience, a joyous rediscovery of the exhilaration of creating character.*

The end of the brief run of The Importance of Being Oscar *was perfectly timed to coincide with the anniversary of Wilde's release from Reading Gaol. The day after we closed, I went down to Reading and performed the whole of the* Ballad *outside of the gaol, which is now – how Wilde would have wept! – a remand centre for young offenders. A few friends came down and passers-by gathered round and we drank some champagne and ate smoked-salmon sandwiches and it was all very touching. Not the least touching thing was to discover that all the inmates of the remand centre were issued with copies of the poem on arrival.*

After The Importance of Being Oscar*, I started urgently thinking of another writer whose life and work would be suitable for the mac Liammóir treatment. The qualification was obviously that the life and the work had to be of equal fascination. I at once thought of Balzac, but rejected him – reluctantly: the particular sweep and fervour of French* *romanticism remains something I long to bring to life on a British stage, but it seemed perverse to do a writer in translation – and then turned, inevitably, as it now seems, to Dickens. Dickens had been my literary hero ever since at the age of twelve a copy of* The Pickwick Papers *had been put in my hands as I lay in bed trying not to itch the scabs that chicken pox had left all over my body. Once I started reading, I was never tempted to itch again. Later, I played Bob Cratchit and Scrooge, as I have recounted, in rep, and Micawber on television. More recently, again on television, I had recreated, for two consecutive Christmases, a number of Dickens's public readings. This was my first direct connection with the man himself. These public readings are central to an understanding of his personality and indeed his life. I reviewed Malcolm Andrews's* Dickens as a Reader *in the* Guardian *in 2006.*

Alongside the huge and ever-expanding tide of Shakespeare studies there is a more modest but equally interesting wave of Dickens studies lapping gently along. From a biographical point of view, the difference between these Titans is, of course, that we know so little about Shakespeare whereas – with certain crucial lacunae – we know almost everything about Dickens. Unlike the shadowy playwright from Stratford, Dickens lived his adult life in a lurid glare of publicity, much of it self-generated; he was a tireless speech-maker; his collected correspondence runs to twelve large volumes and his reading tours brought him into direct contact with his public both in America and Britain in a way that no author had ever achieved before (nor has any since).

His contemporaries were fascinated and sometimes appalled by him and many of them wrote of him with detailed discernment. In the matter of the readings – a key and central element in his output – there were no fewer than three books published while he was still alive describing what he did, how he did it, and why he did it. It remains an area of deep interest, not least because it underlines how perfectly unique he was in the annals of literature. There have been plenty of authors eager to read from their works – even in Dickens's own time Thackeray and others had had a go – but most of them were content, as Dickens wickedly put it, to 'drone away like a mild bagpipe'. What Dickens offered was a major histrionic event, brilliantly stage-managed, in which he electrified huge numbers of people in vast auditoria, creating stampedes for tickets, rousing his hearers to almost uncontrollable laughter or tears.

He had always had a taste for acting and the theatre, even contemplating a career on the boards. Famously, he cancelled an audition at Drury Lane because he had a cold, and before he could arrange another, his journalistic activities suddenly took off and he was lost to the stage. Instead, he indulged his passion for theatre in amateur dramatics, although there was nothing amateur about the all-consuming seriousness with which he took every aspect of the productions. At a charity benefit in which he participated, a stagehand told him, 'What an actor you would have been, Mr Dickens, if it hadn't been for them *books*.' The idea of reading from his novels came to him relatively late: his debut was in Birmingham in 1853, reading from *A Christmas Carol* for a benefit, and the success of that and subsequent readings led him to embark, five years later, on the arduous and very well-paid professional tours which continued until a few months before his death, to which they may well have contributed a great deal, at the age of fifty-eight.

In his subtle and probing study, Malcolm Andrews, acknowledging the great pioneering work of Philip Collins, examines every aspect of this phenomenon, and in doing so comes very close the heart of the mystery of Charles Dickens, at the same time offering some strikingly original insights into the nature of acting and performance. At the core of his analysis is his understanding of the nature of what might be called the Dickens enterprise. What was he up to? What sort of relationship did he seek to establish with his readers (and eventually his audiences)? Andrews acutely notes that Dickens was the most successful – indeed the only really successful – writer of novels in serial form: the directness of the rapport with his readers, the sense that he was coming into their houses on a regular basis, that every fresh instalment was, as the *Illustrated London News* observed, 'as if we'd received a letter or a visit at regular intervals from a kindly observant gossip', appealed to him greatly. In 1841, after *Barnaby Rudge*, he determined to write a novel without serialising it as he wrote, but when it came to it, he missed the regular rapport with his readers too much. He regarded the relationship between reader and writer as one of 'travelling companionship'. Andrews notes the sense of intimacy with his readers that approached collaboration: he was inundated by suggestions from the readers of *Pickwick* as to what should happen next. 'To commune with the public in any form is a labour of love.' He aspired to 'live in the household affections' and hoped that his characters would take their place 'among the household gods' – as they assuredly did.

It was a logical step from this to public performance. Logical to us, that is, but for a Victorian, there was the terrible stigma of the theatre to overcome. Dickens agonised over the propriety of appearing not only in public, but for money; his best friend John Forster argued strongly against it, but Dickens's compulsive need for direct communication with his readers overcame all objections. At first, the readings were relatively low-key: the characters lightly sketched in and a conversational narratorial tone maintained. Increasingly, however, his desire to escape into character prevailed. He learned the texts by heart and rehearsed them intensively. As a young man and aspiring actor he had been deeply influenced by the actor-writer Charles Mathews, whose wittily designated monopolylogues had the performer playing several different people, as well as the narrator. Like Mathews, Dickens came increasingly to delight in abandoning himself to the characters, and this aspect of his performances drew the astonished admiration of his audiences (many of whom were professional actors themselves). 'Assumption,' he said, 'has charms for me… being someone in voice &c. not at all like myself.'

Before the audience's very eyes, and without the aid of props or costume, he would become David Copperfield, Mrs Gamp, Fagin. 'The impersonator's very stature,' reported Charles Kent, 'each time Fagin opened his lips, seemed to be changed instantaneously. Whenever he spoke there started before us – high-shouldered with contracted chest, with birdlike claws, eagerly anticipating by their every movement the passionate words… his whole aspect, half vulpine, half vulture-like, in its hungry wickedness.' This description underlines the fact that acting is above all an act of imagination rather than of external representation: it is an overpowering mental connection which produces a physical result. Malcolm Andrews finely says: 'In order to get the right voice, in a concentrated way, Dickens had to move his full being into that of the character.' I can think of no better description of the art of acting, and Dickens's readings, bereft of any external aids, show this in particularly pure form. He explored in the flesh, as he had done in his novels, 'the fissility of self', the multiphrenia latent in us all.

It cost him dear. He spoke of tearing himself to pieces, seeing himself as some sort of Orphic figure: 'the modern embodiment of the old enchanters whose familiars tore them to pieces'. But his submission to this self-morcellation, as Andrews calls it, was in paradoxical service to the primary drive of his writing: reconstituting the sundered body of society. Every one of his readings was in that sense a paradigm of the great effort of his work: healing society, restoring it to oneness. There is something medieval in his sense of the interconnectedness of everything. The contemporary *Times* reviewer who described these performances as a 'return to the practice of Bardic times' correctly catches the oddly atavistic quality of Dickens. He was the enemy of Progress, in the Victorian sense, as much as he was of Poverty: alienation was what he set out to abolish, in himself as much as in society. When he read, the surge of affection from the public moved him to tears and helped, however, temporarily, to heal his own sense of internal estrangement; even I, a hundred and fifty years later, acting as a mere conduit for his work and personality, felt this massive affection for him rising up from the audience, the deep-rooted sense that he speaks to us and for us.

The readings gave him a spurious lease of life. His transformation from prematurely old, lame, frail man into energetic, vital, compelling storyteller was widely noted. It is something with which many of us in the theatre are familiar – Dr Theatre, we call it. But in this case, the treatment didn't cure him: it killed him. Andrews's last pages, describing the final reading – of *A Christmas Carol*, ending as he had begun – are inexpressibly moving. 'From these garish lights I vanish now for evermore with a heartfelt, grateful, respectful and affectionate farewell.' Andrews writes with deep imaginative sympathy of the phenomenon that was Dickens. 'In mid-Victorian towns and cities he arrived in person to conduct people nightly into a world where the great blaze of Christmas celebrations issuing from the red hearth of the reading platform threw giant shadows around the hall of listeners, and where, for Scrooge, Past and Present, reality and illusion became therapeutically confused.'

The more I read about Dickens, the more I sensed that he represented, both in his social attitudes and in his literary vision, a tradition which was almost pre-Shakespearean; Chaucerian, perhaps; carnivalesque, like Falstaff. (He had had rather a success as Falstaff, as it happens, in The Merry Wives of Windsor, *in his own fanatically well-rehearsed production.) This piece was written for the* Chicago Examiner *in 2003.*

When he was already well-established as the most prosperous and famous novelist of his day – not just in England – Charles Dickens was to be found stalking the streets of London at dead of night, witnessing for himself the atrocious conditions under which laboured the wretched of the earth. 'There lay, in an old egg box, which the mother had begged from a shop, a feeble, wasted, wan, sick child. With his little wasted face, and his little hot worn hands folded over his breast, and his little bright attentive eyes, I can see him now, as I have seen him for several years, looking steadily at us. There he lay in his little frail box, which was not at all a bad emblem of the little body from which he was slowly parting – there he lay quite quiet, quite patient, saying never a word. He seldom cried, the mother said, he seldom complained. He lay there, seeming to wonder what it was all about. God knows, I thought, as I stood looking at him, he had his reasons for wondering – and why, in the name of a gracious God, such things should be.'

His anger thus fuelled, Dickens turned it into incandescent words – hundreds and hundreds of pages of journalism, speeches up and down the country, and of course the great novels of his maturity, *Bleak House, Hard Times, Little Dorrit* – in which he puts Britain at its industrial zenith in the dock, prosecuting with savage ferocity those whom he held responsible for the iniquities he had witnessed. His compassion had never been in doubt from the very first – from the early sketches he wrote under the name of Boz, from *The Pickwick Papers* and *Oliver Twist* – but to this was added a kind of volcanic rage which made him more than ever publicly identified with the disadvantaged. With *A Christmas Carol* and its explicit attacks on the disparity between those who have and those who do not, he had given the conscience of the age a powerful jolt, but that was just a beginning. From his early forties until his death some fifteen years later, he never ceased to engage with the howling injustice he saw all around him. This is not in itself, of course, enough to make a great novelist. But when this sort of active, practical, radical determination to reform the system under which he lived is allied to a genius for storytelling and an incomparable imagination in the creation of character, you have a pretty potent combination.

There is nothing distant or cool about Dickens, nothing formal or academic. His structures are big and unwieldy; he seems to be making it up as he goes along, which of course is exactly what he did, writing in episodes, sometimes knocking off three or four at a time for weekly or monthly publication, as he pursued his active, not to say frantic, other life – corresponding, speechifying, editing (weekly journals and even, for a time, a crusading daily newspaper), partying, breeding (ten children by the time he was forty), performing conjuring tricks with nonchalant ease – the fruit of much serious rehearsal.

The thing that pulses through his work like an electric current is his almost carnal need to communicate with his readers. His relationship with them far exceeds in intensity any other relationship in his life: those with his children (devoted but formal), his wife (initially affectionate, ultimately disgusted), his friends (passionate but erratic), or even his hidden mistress Ellen Ternan, thirty years his junior; we can only conjecture at the nature of his feelings for her, though it is safe to say that an element of play-acting – he adopted the persona of 'Mr Tringham' to throw the curious off the trail – must have formed a large part of them.

His relationship with his public was something quite different, altogether more real. Simply put, he needed their love in order to exist. Like a lover, he responded instantly to their moods and to their wants; they for their part expected him to speak for them, to express their joys and their miseries, to create for them their monsters and their comic heroes. Almost shamanically, he was possessed by their spirit, the great popular carnival spirit. His playful, metamorphosing language – distorting, personifying, now engorging, now withering, transforming a city into a single breathing organism or an individual into a swarming mass of grotesque features – is the vernacular mode at its most extended and its most exuberant. He embodies appetite, glories in extremes. This is where he can most be compared to Shakespeare, his immediate superior in the pantheon of English literature – in this, and in his matchless creation of character. Only in the matter of sex is he oddly reticent, almost blank. In every other area, his inventiveness is almost surreal, which is why adaptations of his books, attempting to treat him as a social realist, or a psychological realist, are so rarely successful. The screen and even the stage have a confining effect on the psychedelic fantasias of Dickens's pen.

In true carnival spirit, Dickens's work is a performance, generous and unstinting, for his audience of readers. We never forget that it is him that is doing it, nor that he is doing it for us. And, on cue, we laugh, we cry, we moan, we applaud. Dickens is the writer as actor. In life, of course, he acted whenever he had the opportunity, finally, triumphantly, taking to the boards with great tours of England and America in which he 'read' his own work. His audiences (who also knew his books by heart and who were more or less chanting the words in unison with him) were in ecstasy: they thronged to him in their thousands and the performances became cathartic experiences, both comic and tragic, on a grand scale. They were unprecedented events, only to be compared today in their emotional fervour to rock concerts; but they were implicit in the novels themselves: the literal performance was the logical extension of the literary one.

Dickens wrote fiercely and pertinently about the abuses of his day, which are not, alas, so different from the abuses of ours. He attacked imbalances in income, indifference to mental suffering, the venality of lawyers, the heartlessness of capitalists, the death of the soul and the rape of the child. But it is not for this alone that we read him now; not even for the great generous heart, or for the unique literary voice. It is for his huge populist energy that we love him and need him, for his assertion of the glorious vitality of human life and the united diversity of society, for his denial of uniformity and his exploration of the unbounded manifestations of man and woman, both peccable and sublime. Dickens, the hero of his own age, reaches out to a tradition and a culture which long precedes it, which even antedates the Elizabethan period, and asserts, for our own age in which the twin horrors of globalisation and fundamentalism – both tending towards the standardisation of human experience – threaten to overwhelm us, the glorious, contradictory and unsuppressible bounteousness of the human experience.

Dickens's passion for the stage and indeed his own performances of his own work brought an inherently theatrical dimension to the enterprise. Although Peter Ackroyd is not a dramatist, his stupendous biography of Dickens, like much of his work, is theatrical through and through, full of mirrors and smoke, and with a superlative sense of the grotesque. He provided me with a wonderful play which at first he called Bring on the Bottled Lightning *(one of Dickens's descriptions of himself as a reader), a title we feared would not be immediately comprehensible. Instead, reluctantly, we settled on* The Mystery of Charles Dickens *(obviously on the model of* Edwin Drood*). In the event it turned out to be rather apt: the play grew into the title. I performed it all over the world, in Australia, in Ireland, in Chicago, on Broadway. This is the second part of the article I wrote for the* New York Times *in time for our opening there.*

As in *The Importance of Being Oscar*, the central event in *The Mystery of Charles Dickens* is, we hope, the raising of a ghost, in this case that of Charles Dickens. By the end of the show, we hope that you will feel that you have been swept up in and touched by the life and the unparalleled charisma of that unique author: that you will have spent time in the company of his characters, invoked not so much in rounded psychological depth as by the flickering footlights of the Victorian theatre in all its excess and power: and that you will have walked the dank London streets with him and experienced the vanished idyll of childhood which he so desperately sought to recover. G. K. Chesterton said of Dickens that wherever he went in the world, his journeys were always travels in Dickensland. Here is another, in the company of the author. The form of the piece is perhaps even better suited to Dickens than it is to Wilde. Wilde was a dramatist, which Dickens was not; his plays are peculiarly bad, lacking any individual touches. He was so utterly stage-struck that in his dramatic works, he simply and slavishly imitated the plays of the day.

But his novels, paradoxically, are supremely theatrical. 'Dickens enters the theatre of the world through the stage door,' as Santayana memorably remarked. He himself longed to go on stage, and participated, with some distinction, in innumerable theatrical productions as an amateur, playing a fine Falstaff and a better Bobadill; he even secured an audition with a famous actor-manager. The very form of his novels, the structure of his characters and the arc of his dialogue, are derived from popular theatrical forms of his time, in which he would play many characters in the course of an evening. Eventually, Dickens fused his talents in the public readings which dominated his last years, in the course of which he astounded huge crowds on both sides of the Atlantic with his histrionic genius, producing uncontrollable mirth and asphyxiating horror in his listeners, and inhabiting no less than eighty-nine characters in the course of eighteen different readings, seeming to become each in turn.

Dickens is the Writer as Actor, finally come to claim a Broadway stage. And in the course of the evening, this one-man play will introduce you to forty-nine characters, Charles Dickens and – ahem – me. Or me as invented by Peter Ackroyd: one more level of ontological jiggery-pokery. It's all done by mirrors, of course; it's a conjuring trick (one of which, perhaps, Dickens would have approved: he was a practised and dazzling magician himself, in the guise of the Unparalleled Necromancer Rhama Rhia Roos). Now perhaps it's a little clearer why we call it *The Mystery of Charles Dickens*.

I had been rather in love with Oscar Wilde, but Dickens took me over, body and soul. He is titanic: phenomenal, inspiring, appalling. He is generous and destructive, subtle and stupendous. To be in contact with him and his work is like standing in front of a blazing fire. He is a life force. In his journalism, Wilde affected an amused and fastidious disdain for Dickens's vulgarity and broadness. But when he was admitted to prison, the first books he asked for were Dickens's (though they did not include The Old Curiosity Shop, *of the death of whose heroine, Little Nell, Wilde had famously remarked that it was impossible to read without bursting into... laughter). From my point of view as an actor, I had the odd sensation that I had found my perfect author. He fitted me like a glove. This was a little regrettable in that he had neglected to write any performable plays, so I would always – or so I assumed – be at the mercy of adaptations. The distinction between drama and theatre is a profound one, and it is not a paradox to say that our greatest novelist is our most theatrical writer.*

Rethinking

The Mystery of Charles Dickens *was my first experience of the so-called* No. 1 Touring Circuit *in the British Isles, something to which I took with great enthusiasm. Apart from anything else, it was deeply satisfying to act in the remarkable theatres – most of them Victorian or Edwardian – which are still the underpinning of this country's remarkably healthy tradition. I reviewed John Earl's* British Theatres and Music Halls *in 2005.*

Theatres are architecture, to be sure, finished, achieved, but they house a living art and accordingly and inevitably are both influenced by the work that appears on their stages, and exercise an influence over it. The revelations offered by the reconstructed (or, more precisely, reinvented) Globe Theatre on the South Bank are the most vivid example of the interdependence of building and performance; whatever you might think of any individual production under Mark Rylance's richly idiosyncratic regime, no director or actor of plays by Shakespeare or his contemporaries can think of them in quite the same way again.

The relationship with the audience is the key. Any player will tell you that certain plays suddenly come to life in certain spaces, although it is by no means dependable that a small theatre will afford you intimacy or that a very large one will inhibit it. The whole business is something of a mystery, and it is hugely to the credit of John Earl's small but exceptionally nourishing volume on the subject that he acknowledges, as he traces the development of the theatre building from the sixteenth century to the present, that it has above all been a pragmatic process, and that certain individuals (the Edwardian theatre architect Frank Matcham perhaps the greatest of them) have mastered its secrets without being able to pass them on. He traces a steady chronological line, showing how the Elizabethan outdoor theatres evolved out of courtyards, how the move indoors immediately changed the habits of audiences and of practitioners, both actors and writers. He charts the regular decline and fall of enthusiasm for theatre, how regularly it seems to sicken, then on its very deathbed leaps up with new vigour.

He is particularly good on the growth of the music hall from mere incidental entertainment into a central and unique phenomenon, cutting across classes and giving rise to massive buildings of unparalleled splendour. The London Coliseum was the greatest of these, but, with characteristic vividness of phrase, Earl notes that in its very design 'it contained an infection that was to prove fatal' – a projection booth: film would kill the music hall and probably (with its housebound sister, television) for ever destroy theatre as a great popular art. He is no architectural nostalgic, cheerfully contemplating the complete reconstruction of Elisabeth Scott's unsatisfactory Shakespeare Memorial Theatre, though he professes a surprising enthusiasm for Lasdun's ugly, dysfunctional National Theatre.

It is astonishing how much information and stimulation Earl has packed into his sixty pages, and the illustrations are simply superb – plentiful, unhackneyed and magnificently reproduced. And very – improbably – cheap. The book should be put in the Tessa Jowell grab-bag of books that all schoolchildren are about to receive: it's an utterly alluring introduction to the passion that theatre buildings inspire both in audiences and actors. Now that the Sixties' conviction that red-and-gold auditoriums were elitist and alienating has quietly died, audiences have voted with their feet on the subject. The theatre building should be an entertainment in itself, an environment out of the usual run, an invitation into the world of the imagination. Earl admirably demonstrates the variety of forms that invitation can take.

Because the Dickens show, like the Wilde show that had inspired it, had such direct contact with audiences, the venue was of paramount importance. Facing the audience head-on of course creates an immediate and direct relationship with them which is matchlessly exciting.

Although the solo performances dominated so much of my professional life, and were so deeply satisfying, I was conscious that in a sense, they were divergences from the main path. I wondered whether I had abandoned the proper pursuit of an actor which is, after all, the interpretation of character. In my frustration with, and doubt about, acting, I had been reading and rereading various books on the subject, and had become fascinated by a good new translation of a book I had struggled with some twenty years earlier, To the Actor *by the great Russian actor and teacher, Mikhail (or Michael, as he called himself after he fled to the West) Chekhov, Anton's nephew.*

The more I read, the more I fell in love with Michael Chekhov, both as man and as teacher. Mostly through his writing, of course, but what little we have of his acting on film, and the electrifying descriptions of his stage work – even the photographs of his characterisations – are both inspiring and encouraging. If I cast my eye back over my own work as an actor, it was clear that I was at my best – Arturo Ui, Mozart, Molina in Kiss of the Spider Woman *– when I was able to be expressively free, not trying to offer photographic or realistic conceptions, but rather creating fantastical projections of character, each one a complete universe of expression in itself. This was the Michael Chekhov route. I attended Chekhov symposiums and weekends, meeting some of the leading practitioners in the world, Russian, American and Australian, discovering what the practical applications of the teaching might be. As a result of these encounters, perhaps, I was asked to write an introduction to a new edition of* To the Actor.

At the beginning of the twenty-first century, we are in the throes of a crisis in theatre acting. It is clearly not a crisis in talent: actors are as eager, as gifted, as attractive as they have ever been – perhaps more so. The stars are younger, their bodies are in better condition, they apply themselves energetically to all the physical aspects of the job. But something isn't happening. Audiences feel it; actors feel it. Disappointment is in the air. The theatre isn't delivering. Audiences over a certain age start to rumble about the Golden Age when actors were really *actors*, while actors for their part start to complain about the declining quality of audiences. All sorts of other theatre experiences become more interesting than those which focus on acting: the musical theatre, for example, with its combination of spectacle, noise, rhythm, and sheer energy, which can, properly manipulated, whip up an audience into a state of frenetic excitement; or what is called physical theatre – as if theatre, which is the word made flesh, could be anything other than physical! – which brings elements of dance, of acrobatics, of circus into play, taking the spotlight away from language and from character and into the realm of choreography. The search for new forms of theatre never ceases. What is curious is that no one ever discusses acting in this context.

*

The last time there was a full debate about acting in the British theatre was in the late Fifties and early Sixties of the last century, and it may be interesting to consider what came out of it. The debate was provoked by the revolution in playwriting at the Royal Court Theatre, which led to an urgent demand for new kinds of acting. The old guard of actors, whether suave exponents of drawing-room comedy, or high priests and priestesses of the classics (often they were the same people), had dominated the post-war theatre and they were now denounced as bourgeois, individualist, elitist, shallow, technical. Where were the new actors for the new plays? They were there, waiting in the wings, ready to swing into action, the generation famously trained by John Fernald at the RADA: working class, regional, feisty, real. For a while they and their mentors – the firebrand, mostly left-wing directors of the epoch – plunged into a heady exploration of the possibilities of acting. Sometimes from aesthetic, sometimes from political perspectives, they investigated mask work, improvisation, theatre games; they embraced the theories of Bertolt Brecht. Occasionally they threw a loving glance sideways to the pioneering work of Joan Littlewood at Theatre Workshop in the East End of London. With her unique mix of theory and sheer bloody-mindedness, she had offered an approach both to new plays and to the classics which was almost medieval in its vitality and impudence and demanded of her actors a kind of magnificent rough poetry.

In the early 1960s, some of the results of this exploratory work passed into the mainstream of the theatre; both Olivier, at the newly created National Theatre at the Old Vic, and Peter Hall at the Royal Shakespeare Company he had formed slightly earlier, absorbed the work of these directors and actors. Every so often these companies would present a piece of truly experimental acting – like, for instance, Robert Stephens's electrifying performance of the sun-god Atahuallpa in Peter Shaffer's *The*

Royal Hunt of the Sun, or Ian Richardson's Herald in the *Marat/Sade* –
but the dust soon settled, and a consensus began to emerge, a sort of new
realism: a kind of unvarnished, unsentimental manner in which real life
could be credibly presented, in plays both modern and classical. Above
all, this approach eschewed theatricality. Any sense that actors were
unusual or exceptional human beings was rejected. The job of actors was
now to be as like their audience, or their hoped-for audience, as possible: the man on the stage was now the man on the street.

What the revolution had really achieved was the absolute dominance of
the director. Experiment became centred on design and *concept*, both
under the control of the director. The actor's creative imagination – his
fantasy, his instinct for gesture – was of no interest; all the creative imagining had already been done by the director and the designer. The best
that an actor could do was to bring himself or herself to the stage and
simply be. Actors, accepting the new rules, resigned themselves to serv-
ing the needs of the playwright as expressed by his representative on
earth, the director. Of course they rebelled against this; they started to
sneak amusing and charming and original elements into their work. But
they had lost control of their own performances. And so they started to
desert the theatre. The financial rewards could never compare with those
of television or film; if there were to be no creative rewards, what was the
point? It seemed like very hard work for very little return. Most of the
celebrated actors of the recent revolutionary period disappeared into film.
They came back again, from time to time, on a visit, but the theatre had
ceased to be their natural habitat. It wasn't just a question of fame or
money: the stage had become unexciting to them. They were simply not
getting the response from their audiences. They were not satisfied by an
activity which now had neither the grandeur, the glamour nor the sense
of heightened emotional power of the old school, which had engendered
such intense energies in the auditorium, often taking the experience into
the realm of the primal. Audiences felt this too. Despite the frequently
challenging and inventive work of the dramatists, the designers and the
directors, the contribution of the actors – what might be called the acting enterprise – was circumscribed. It was all very rational and objective
and credible, but it was not markedly different from what was readily –
and more cheaply – available in the cinema or on the television.

The older actors – that fabled generation of Evans and Ashcroft, Olivier,
Gielgud, Richardson, Redgrave, Guinness – never gave up, of course. They

continued more or less unreformed, despite exposure – in the case of Olivier and Ashcroft – to the Royal Court during its fervent years; Gielgud and Richardson, in particular, became much loved as they ventured in extreme old age into plays by David Storey and Harold Pinter. But there was a clear shared sense that no one was going to replace these living national treasures: we were watching a gorgeous sunset without hope of a repeat. It was not the individuals that were dying, it was an entire view of acting and of actors. Above all what was disappearing was the idea that the actor was at the centre of the event; that his or her contribution was the core of the experience. Actors started to become embarrassed by their job; anyone who had the temerity to talk in public about the complex processes involved in acting, or to suggest that acting might be a great and important art, was remorselessly mocked. The phrase *luvvie* was invented by the British press to put actors in their place. Only those who claimed that there was no more to acting than learning the lines and avoiding the furniture were accorded any respect.

*

The roots of these developments are deep, and it is here that we need to mention the name of Konstantin Stanislavsky, a towering figure in the history of twentieth-century theatre, who – sometimes directly, sometimes more obliquely – has profoundly influenced attitudes towards acting. Deeply concerned to advance the art of acting itself, seeking to establish the conditions necessary for what he called creative acting, he studied the work of actors he admired and began to extrapolate theories from his observations. Little by little he formed a corpus of exercises and analysis which came to be known as the Stanislavsky System, the central tenets of which are brilliantly simple and convincing. In the Theory of Actions, he proposes that a play consists of a series of interlocking actions, or objectives, out of which the actor's path through the play is constructed; in the Theory of Emotional Memory, he maintains that the actor finds the truth of the role by using his own experiences, thus achieving a lifelike as opposed to a merely theatrical performance. These two ideas, most potently expressed in question form – What do I want? and Who am I? – formed a powerful tool for combating what Stanislavsky defined as the actor's worst pitfall: acting *in general*.

Stanislavsky had a naturally restless intellect and these simple formulations only satisfied him for a short time; striving to clarify, expand, diversify and enrich his system to accommodate his developing insights, he doggedly continued his quest for the key to acting until his dying day. Meanwhile, some of his earliest pupils, like Richard Boleslavsky and Maria Ouspenskaya, had left him at this formative stage, spreading the word in its most elementary form, particularly in America, where a technique rooted in emotional experience and deterministic action was eagerly received. The British theatre, too, though less susceptible, in its pragmatic way, to grand theories, quietly acknowledged that here was a way to reform the outmoded gestures and vocal mannerisms of the late Victorians and Edwardians, but also to counter the reliance on mere personality. The drama schools began to teach Stanislavskyan precepts in simplified form, and this began to filter through to the theatre in general. From the 1920s, the Moscow Art Theatre toured the West and astonished audiences with the detailed realism and emotional depth of its productions. The influence of Stanislavsky's ideas grew and grew. Like Freud's psychological theories, they swiftly established themselves as the common wisdom, passing into general currency among the population as much as among the profession, and they have since held sway in more or less diluted form in the theatre practice of the English-speaking world. All actors now aspire to give emotionally truthful, many-layered performances based on observation, utilising the raw material of their own lives; they aim above all for credibility. Whether they approach their roles from the inside out, or from the outside in, to use a familiar distinction, the desired end result is always the same: the recognisable truth. What else is there?

*

In Russia, the progress of Stanislavsky's ideas had taken a somewhat different path. Initially, his colleagues in the Moscow Art Theatre resisted the idea of the System, but bit by bit he wooed them – *bribed* them, in some cases, with the promise of this role or that – into accepting it. The System never became popular with the established actors, nor with the ever-sceptical Nemirovich-Danchenko, who finally sidelined his partner into running the Studio Theatre and School. Out of this institution emerged an extraordinary group of young actor-theorists who swallowed Stanislavsky's ideas whole and then spat them out again in radically different form. Meyerhold and Vakhtangov rapidly evolved into radical directors, as different from each other as they were from Stanislavsky, while Mikhail Chekhov, who had come to the Moscow Art Theatre when he was already a well-known actor at the Maly Theatre in St Petersburg, gave a series of performances for the Studio of startling originality. Stanislavsky unreservedly acknowledged him as the most gifted actor with whom he had ever worked, although at a certain point he dismissed him from his classes on account of his 'overheated imagination'. Together they achieved an enormous success with Stanislavsky's production of *The Government Inspector*, in which Chekhov endowed the central character with mystical and bizarre elements, underlined by a design of grotesque menace. But despite this happy collaboration, it was clear that they had radically different views about acting. In a sense, Chekhov – intuitive, audacious, infinitely flexible, apparently able to transform himself into any shape he desired – was the actor the careful, cautious Stanislavsky had always dreamed of being. He was also terrifyingly volatile in his private life, alcoholic, paranoiac, wholly unpredictable. But he too was on a quest of his own quite as urgent as Stanislavsky's, first of all to discover meaning for himself in his own life, then to understand the source of his art.

Groping towards this meaning and that understanding, Chekhov immersed himself first in the study of yoga, then in the anthroposophical works of Rudolf Steiner. He started to teach and to direct; in time he became the director of the Second Moscow Art Theatre School. His formulations were fundamentally different to Stanislavsky's. Their 'idealistic' and 'mystical' dimension caused violent opposition from some of his actors and from the state authorities; by now the first fine frenzy of the Russian Revolution, which had initially encouraged experiment and radicalism of every kind, had evolved into a controlling party bureaucracy which defined art in strictly political terms. Eventually, denounced as a 'sick artist', Chekhov was driven from Russia and commenced a lifelong odyssey during the course of which he sometimes seemed to be pursued, Orestes-like, by unrelenting Fates. From Riga to Berlin, from Paris to Dartington, from Connecticut to New York he moved. Time and again war, civil and global, forced him and his successive schools and companies into ever more distant hiding places, until he finally ended up in Hollywood, where he continued to teach, giving, before his early death, half a dozen charming cameo performances in various movies, among them *Spellbound*, for which he was nominated for an Academy Award.

*

Chekhov encapsulated his teaching in various publications over the years, culminating in the appearance of the present volume, *To the Actor*, which contains the essence of his working method. Another, more elaborate version of the same book has recently appeared under the title of *On the Technique of Acting*. The complex relationship of the two books to one another is described in Deirdre Hurst du Prey's introduction to the latter; both are indispensable handbooks, providing a detailed and practical guide to Chekhov's work. They were not, however, his first books. While he was still in Russia, he had described his early life and the development of his ideas in two remarkable volumes, *The Path of the Actor* and *Life and Encounters*. These earlier works of spiritual and artistic autobiography convey the pressure out of which his ideas grew, vividly portraying Chekhov's frustration with what he perceived to be the unnecessary limitations and inhibitions which cramp and ultimately destroy actors' creativity. Many of these limitations and inhibitions seemed to Chekhov to stem directly from Stanislavsky's System.

*

Chekhov revered Stanislavsky, as anyone who cares about acting must, both as a man, and for his deeply sincere lifelong quest to discover the laws of acting. But Chekhov's conception of acting was as different from the older man's as were their personalities. Stanislavsky's deep seriousness, his doggedness, his sense of personal guilt, his essentially patriarchal nature, his need for control, his suspicion of instinct, all found their expression in his System. At core, Stanislavsky did not trust actors or their impulses, believing that unless they were carefully monitored by themselves and by their teachers and directors, they would lapse into grotesque overacting or mere mechanical repetition. Chekhov believed, on the contrary, that the more actors trusted themselves and were trusted, the more extraordinary the work they would produce. For him, the child playing in front of his nanny, improvising wildly, generating emotions with easy spontaneity, changing shape according to the impulses of his fantasy, was the paradigm of the actor. Stanislavsky was unable look back on his own childish efforts without embarrassment. Stanislavsky believed that the only acceptable truth in acting was to be found within the actor's own experience, whereas Chekhov was profoundly convinced that the imagination was the key to all art. Acting, he said, should never be autobiographical; constant recourse to one's own experience would lead, he said, to 'degeneration of talent'. The imagination, once engaged, never lost its freshness and power, but the limited pool of individual experience quickly stagnated. The actor's work on himself should focus on encouraging and liberating his imagination, by consciously inventing and fantasising, rather than by dredging the subconscious. For Chekhov, fairy tales were the ideal material for his teaching: all plays, in his view, aspired to the condition of fairy tales.

As far as the text was concerned, Chekhov had an almost mystical relationship to language, crystallised by his exposure to Steiner's Eurhythmy. He insisted on the vital importance of sound, of the vibrations which were released within the actor and within the audience by the consonants and vowels themselves. Stanislavsky had a very different approach. Interestingly, he was what we would now describe as severely dyslexic, and always sought the subtext, the emotional life behind the words, rather than engaging with the words themselves, which he was notoriously given to paraphrasing. As for character, Stanislavsky believed it had to be constructed painstakingly, detail by detail. This was anathema to Chekhov. 'They call this work,' he wrote in *The Path of the Actor*. 'It is indeed work, it is tormenting and difficult – but unnecessary. The actor's work is to a significant extent a matter of waiting and being silent "without working".' To him the all-important prerequisite for acting was 'a sense of the whole'. In a parallel characteristically drawn from the natural world, he believed that character was like a seed which contained the whole future life of the plant within it; if you grasped one phrase, one gesture, of the character you had access to all the rest; everything would fall harmoniously into place. Here was the origin of his famous 'psychological gesture', the embodied essence of the character, a transforming and liberating principle of being which awakes the character into instant and complete life, and which then proliferates into a thousand details which spontaneously and harmoniously evolve. Stanislavsky believed that the actor must be wholly immersed in his character, who becomes a second 'I'. Chekhov, rather, believed that in a successful performance, the actor was always watching his character, moved by him, but never 'violating his personal emotions'. This *standing apart*, he said, 'enabled me to approach that state whereby the artist purifies and ennobles the character he is playing, keeping him free from irrelevant aspects of his own personality.'

Finally, and most significantly, Chekhov increasingly believed that the core of the theatrical event was to be found in the actor's relationship with his audience. For Stanislavsky, the audience was both intimidating and corrupting; he feared what he called 'the black hole of the auditorium,' but even worse he feared his own desire to pander to the audience. To solve this problem he erected the notorious imaginary Fourth Wall.

Chekhov saw it quite differently. It was vital, he said, to engage with what he called 'the will of the auditorium', to reach out to each member of the audience and share the creative act with him or her. 'I understood that members of the audience have the right to influence the actor during a performance and that the actor should not prevent this.' He spoke, mystically, of the actor *sacrificing* himself to the audience.

*

Stanislavsky's noble work has served its purpose; but it is Chekhov, it seems to me, who speaks to the crisis in our theatres. Audiences feel neglected. They are offered more or less naturalistic work which engages neither their imagination nor that of the actors. Prophetically, Chekhov wrote of naturalism: 'The legacy that naturalism will leave behind it will be a coarsened and nervously disordered audience that has lost its artistic taste; and much time will be needed to restore it to health.' He says that it breeds the necessity 'of giving its audiences a series of "powerful sensations" capable of arousing shock through a chain of pathological effects'. Since actors no longer think of themselves as creative artists they have lost their self-respect. To be mere interpreters of the written word is not enough for them, or for their public, though it may be enough for some writers and directors. This is why the public increasingly turns to what is called 'performance art', as if the theatre was not by absolute definition a performance art – as if the work of performance artists was expressive and imaginative, but that Marlowe, Ibsen, O'Casey, David Hare, required mere photographic realism. It is particularly absurd to attempt to perform the classics with a naturalistic technique, the very idea of which would have been inconceivable to a writer of the Elizabethan period: in the admirable epigram of the Shakespeare scholar Graham Holderness, 'An actor playing naturalistically in an inn yard is likely to be confused with a waiter.'

Michael Chekhov was a highly individual artist, and it would be wholly inappropriate to hope for a generation of Michael Chekhovs. On the contrary, the central purpose of his teaching is to encourage the actor's respect for his or her own imagination and the freedom to create from it. It opens up the possibility of a full and reciprocal relationship with the audience, who can once again be introduced to the idea that actors provide them not with photographic facsimiles of life, but with works of art in which the actors' voices, their bodies and their souls are the medium for the production of unforgettable, heightened creations. In the past, when ballet dancers originated roles, they would speak of them as 'creations'. 'Great acting is like painting,' Charles Laughton, an actor much after Michael Chekhov's own heart, said. 'In the great masters of fine art one can see and recognise the small gesture of a finger, the turn of a head, the vitriolic stare, the glazed eye, the pompous mouth, the back bending under a fearful load. In every swerve and stroke of a painter's brush, there is an abundance of life. Great artists reveal the god in man; and every character an actor plays must be this sort of creation. Not imitation – that is merely caricature – and any fool can be a mimic! But creation is a secret. The better – the truer – the creation, the more it will resemble a great painter's immortal work.' The possibilities are limitless, far beyond the demands of naturalism. Why should the art of the theatre be more restricted in genre than any other? In my first book, *Being an Actor*, I called for Cubist acting, Impressionistic acting, Secessionist acting (I said we perhaps had already had enough of Mannerist acting). Just as each of these painterly genres enriches truth's vocabulary, so might these different modes of acting.

All our lives in the theatre we have heard this maxim: LESS IS MORE. Most of the recent great explorations of acting – Brecht, Brook, Grotowski – have been directed towards this LESS: stripping back. But very often less is simply less, and more is actually MORE. We must overcome our fear of the theatre theatrical when it comes to acting. A theatre is where we are. The theatre is the place where extraordinary things happen, where you see people behaving, not as they do on the street, but as they might in your dreams – or your nightmares. When the shaman does his dance, nobody says: 'Could you do a little less, please?' When the great comedians, the great clowns walk on stage, we know we are in the presence of something else, something well known to us but outside of our experience. At the very least an actor should, as the great Irish actor Micheál mac Liammóir used to say, 'displace air'. But he should also transform the energy in the auditorium; he should invade the collective unconscious of the audience and bring them up short. He should not merely quite interest them, or quite amuse them. He should brand himself on their souls, breaking down the prison walls of logic. This used to be the job of actors, and of clowns. As Michael Chekhov would say, it requires a certain openness to the great forces of the universe to attempt it.

Film and television will perfectly satisfy the demand for realism. It is only when the need for something which goes further is felt that people have recourse to the theatre, an inherently poetic medium. Actor-poets are what the theatre as a unique art form needs. Why else bother to go to the theatre? The profound importance of Chekhov's work – he would have hesitated to call it a system – is that its aim is to breed just such a race of actor-poets. The beauty of his approach is that he offers a direct route to the actor's creativity by the simplest of means. Stanislavsky's anxiety about his own lack of creativity, his insistence that what Chekhov called 'inspired' acting was only available to the very few preternaturally gifted performers (of whom he did not consider himself one), and that only a cautious, logical method will pay dividends, is replaced by Chekhov's faith in the naturalness of the acting instinct, his conviction that if left untampered with, it will soar into the zones of human experience to which only the imagination has access. Using his work won't necessarily make you a great actor, but you will be approaching acting as an artist.

This exhortation was addressed more to myself than to anyone else. I tried to apply its ideas to the Falstaff I played at the Chichester Festival in Chimes at Midnight, *Orson Welles's conflation of the two parts of* Henry IV. *I saw the Fat Knight as Shakespeare's masterpiece in character, a figure at once mythic and real, but essentially pagan, a figure from carnival, part of what C. L. Barber calls 'Shakespeare's Festive World'. I wrote the following piece for the* Independent *to coincide with the opening of the production in 1998.*

Sir John Falstaff has been widely described as Shakespeare's greatest creation and his best-loved character, which in the circumstances is no mean claim. The adjective Falstaffian has long passed into the language. We all know what it means: fat and frolicsome, gloriously drunk, bawdy, boastful, mendacious; disgraceful but irresistible; above all, fun. Not only, as he says in *Henry IV, Part Two*, witty in himself 'but the cause that wit is in other men', Falstaff provokes cascades of comparisons both from critics and from his fellow characters in the play; to see him is to be irresistibly impelled to describe him.

Because of all this, we feel we are very familiar with the character, comfortable with him; we know who he is. It is easy to overlook quite how spectacularly original and unprecedented a creation Falstaff is. There is no other character in Shakespeare to match him; no other character in the whole of Western literature, as far as I am aware, quite like him. There are, of course, plenty of braggarts, innumerable sots, and repro-bates galore. In the theatre alone there is the *miles gloriosus*, the bragging soldier of the Roman comedy of Terence and Plautus; mischievous rogues are a staple of the city comedies of Jonson and his contemporaries; and comedy through the ages, from Aristophanes to Terry Johnson, could scarcely survive without the figure of the drunkard. There are even somewhat similar characters in Shakespeare: Parolles in *All's Well That Ends Well*, Sir Toby Belch in *Twelfth Night*, elements of the Thersites of *Troilus and Cressida*. But even to mention these other characters is to affirm the uniqueness of Falstaff. In his never-failing wit, the abundance of his appetite and the bigness of his spirit, he contains – embodies, indeed – a life force which is so overwhelming as to be beyond type, cer-tainly beyond morality and even beyond psychology.

Above all, he is extraordinary, in the two parts of *Henry IV*, because of the relationship he has with the young Prince of Wales, soon to be the great warrior-king, Henry V. Here is the seventeen-year-old heir appar-ent choosing to spend his days with a debauched, besotted, monstrously fat old reprobate in an East End brothel. It is as if the young Prince Charles had slipped away from Buckingham Palace to hang out with Francis Bacon – with the difference that Falstaff is not only debauched, he is positively criminal: he and his dubious cronies beat people up in dark alleys and take purses from innocent travellers; and the young Prince Henry is no constitutional monarch's son, he is the heir of the divinely anointed and all-powerful absolute monarch, who in his very person *is* England. What is going on, then? Is this mere truancy? Is the boy simply getting it out of his system, sowing his wild oats? Or is there something deeper going on? It seems there is.

It would be one thing if Hal were to have taken up the company of tarts and pimps, or to be slumming around with chums of his own age and class. But it is quite another for the prince to have adopted this old scoundrel not merely as a friend but as a mentor, and to have extended to him every appearance of love and tenderness. What do they want from each other, this odd couple? What Falstaff gets is, in a sense, obvious: the excitement of being so close to the heir to the throne, and the opportunity to practise his habitual *lèse-majesté* at the very closest quarters; and the delight of being connected to youth, the most gilded youth of all, clearly has a tonic effect on the old rascal. But what does Hal want from him? Alienated from his cold, anxious, controlling and guilt-ridden father, he has clearly chosen Falstaff as a surrogate father, an antidote to the sterilised atmosphere of the court, as commentators have understood from as early as Maurice Morgann, in the eighteenth century. He is liberated, relieved, made to think by this fallible, permissive, funny creature of animal warmth, who inverts all the pieties and the truisms he has had dinned into him. It is with Falstaff that he discovers his humanity, the common touch which enables him to do what his father has never been able to do, to unify the kingdom and to reach out to his subjects in a way which they can understand.

But clearly Falstaff is just a phase that he's going through, the supervisor of his rites of passage. To have this absurd, impudent figure at his side after he has ascended his throne would be out of the question, an embarrassment and a dreadful example. He has to go, as Hal understands from the beginning of the play; it is not a question of whether, but of when. The scene at the coronation in which Falstaff is rejected is both devastatingly upsetting and profoundly necessary; Old Hal makes way for New Hal. There is a sense of elation at the establishment of a new order, but also a tremendous sense of the price that has to be paid. 'Banish plump Jack,' Falstaff says in *Part One*, 'and banish all the world.' Not all the world, perhaps, but some rich, natural, flawed, human part of it without which we are all poorer. It is this theme that Welles stressed when he made his version of the two plays which, with consciously elegiac intent, he entitled *Chimes at Midnight*, focusing on the advancement towards kingship of Hal as he outgrows and outstrips both his fathers. For Welles, the rejection of Falstaff was the death of Merrie England, with its natural harmony, and the birth of the modern world, willed and coldly realistic.

This is a highly convincing and effective account of the plays. But as so often with Shakespeare, there is a sense of something else, deeper, stranger, behind the simple narrative, an impression of buried rituals, ancient lore, vanished conceptions, which account for the profundity of our response. With the Reformation, England had undergone a radical change just before Shakespeare's lifetime, and it becomes more and more clear that the old faith, and the even older, Pagan faith that it had absorbed, were still present in the dramatist's consciousness and that of his audience. The glorious, abundant, anarchic life in Falstaff, wholly credible within the world of the play, has an energy which is also somehow primitive, even primal. Shakespeare's sources for the character are, as always, diverse; first named Sir John Oldcastle, after the real-life rebel of that name, he was rechristened when Oldcastle's surviving family, the powerful Cobhams, vigorously objected to the scurrilous portrait Shakespeare presented. Sir John Fastolfe, whose name Shakespeare borrowed more or less at random, also really existed, but bore no resemblance, not even a faint one, to the character in the play. But behind these shadowy historical personages lay another figure, one often referred to in the course of the plays: the Vice of the medieval morality plays, with whom Falstaff is specifically identified again and again, corrupting the youthful hero until finally overcome himself. Dover Wilson's great monograph, *The Fortunes of Falstaff*, makes a very good and clear case for Shakespeare's reworking of this relationship.

Something in this interpretation does not quite ring true, however. It neither explains the loving warmth of Hal's feelings, nor does justice to the magnificence, the positively regal expansiveness, of Falstaff's spirit. It was a little-known American anthropologist, the late Roderick Marshall, who pointed to the existence of another tradition which is more likely to be the fundamental underlying matrix of the character and the relationship. He identified Falstaff with a figure common to many cultures, known variously as the Substitute King, or the Interrex. When the Divine King in these cultures becomes ill or incapable, a Substitute King is sought from among the banished descendants of the Divine King of the previously conquered peoples; once captured, 'this King for a day, a week or an indefinite period of atmospheric danger, has to perform rites of overeating, overdrinking and excessive coupling… to reinvigorate the reproductive powers of nature.' His job is to initiate the heir of the Divine King into the rituals necessary to make the conquered soil flourish – secrets unknown to the conqueror. The parallels with Falstaff, Hal and the ailing Henry IV are evident. Marshall identifies various figures in different cultures who correspond to the Interrex. Some are familiar and obviously Falstaffian. Silenos, grossly fat, drunken, debauched, followed, like Falstaff, by a dubious rout, was the tutor of Dionysos, and was one of the pre-Athenian gods, the children of Kronos, whose task was to shriek, dance, and copulate as noisily as possible after midnight to waken the sun which might otherwise slumber on indefinitely. Bes, the Egyptian god, tutor to Horus, is the god of life's pleasures, and presides over parties and children; he is described, in perfectly Falstaffian terms, as 'the old man who renews his youth, the aged one who maketh himself again a boy'. Janus, the Roman god, lord of the Saturnalia, is identified with the ancient god of sowing and husbandry, and presides over 'the golden age of eternal summer' – Merrie England by another name. At the Saturnalia the declining powers of the sun are encouraged by sympathetic magic: roles are reversed, the Mock King is appointed, and perhaps at some point killed. 'The whole state becomes childlike to encourage the sun to do the same.' And thus, at the court of King Falstaff, Hal is able to become the child that his father's chilly court refuses to allow him to be; and having been truly a child, he can then become truly a man.

These figures (and many more with striking similarities to Falstaff, always including great girth, bibulousness, hairiness, great age and seeming age-lessness, profanity, sedition and endless wit) suggest the profundity of the archetype: but how did they filter through to Shakespeare? Marshall suggests a link. Researching the seventeenth-century mummer plays, which almost certainly derive from earlier folk plays which Shakespeare may very well have known, Marshall was struck by the familiar pattern of the characters: the leading character simply called the Presenter but also known as the Recruiting Sergeant, Fool, Clown and Father Christmas; his wife Mother Christmas, also known as Dolly; the subsidiary characters Little Devil Don't and Old Tossip, the red-nosed drunk, his followers; and Saint George, also known as King George or any other English King, including Henry. Father Christmas is hugely fat, red-faced, wears bullock's horns and has a bladder. He is 'in many ways a bearded child who... though just turned into his ninety-nine years of age... can hop skip and jump like a blackbird in a cage'. Father Christmas helps the King to fight two battles, but, like Falstaff, he is dismissed and dies.

It is neither possible nor particularly valuable to quantify the elements which create a mythic figure like Falstaff, but it is unwise to ignore them in the interests of mere psychological verisimilitude. Falstaff is part of the great culture of fertility which underlies our entire civilisation. We may control fertility, chemically and socially, but the grand patterns of human nature will not be so easily manipulated. Hal's initiation and growth to responsible manhood can only be achieved as a result of a negotiation with nature, a negotiation which we have largely abandoned. It is salutary to think that as recently as four hundred years ago, the greatest genius of the language placed such a primitive figure right at the centre of his great saga of English life.

SIMON CALLOW

To try to create such a Falstaff was perhaps a little beyond my capacities at the time. Certainly it was not the way the critics wished to think of him, and they unanimously rejected my performance. They did so all over again when I tried to develop it a bit further in Merry Wives: the Musical *at Stratford-upon-Avon a few years later. They had all collectively fallen in love with Robert Stephens's famous performance from the late 1990s: expansive but frail, touching and affectionate, but lacking in grossness and the earth. All subsequent performances will be judged by this until someone comes along and breaks the mould, something I proved unable to do (though I'm damned if I'm not going to have another crack at it, in Shakespeare's plays, unadulterated). Critics are a fact of life that, like the existence of VAT inspectors, one can embrace intellectually, but the experience of being criticised – in my case, at any rate – remains acutely painful. I wrote this piece for the* Independent, *whose critics, as it happens, have rarely been able to find a good word to say about any of my work.*

Critics. Even as I write the word, a sort of hopelessness spreads over me, an inner voice whispers: '*You can't win this one.*' At the beginning of one's career (and in some cases, at the beginning, in the middle and at the end), one is so shocked to the core by the whole phenomenon of criticism as it is practised – the cavalier judgements, the slipshod reporting, the personal animus, the power of life and death over a show or an exhibition or a career – that one's instinct is to fight back, to have a showdown, to scotch the lie. Letters to the editor follow, and are sometimes published; interviews are given in which the artist's pain is expressed; in some cases, retaliatory action is attempted.

In every case, the effect is wholly counterproductive. When the critic of a Sunday paper devoted a whole paragraph of his vitriolic review of my production of *My Fair Lady* to denouncing my 'arrogance' and 'lack of psychological insight' for rearranging the order of the numbers in the score, I wrote a mild letter pointing out that the sequence was the standard sequence, exactly as written by Lerner and Loewe. The critic in question wrote one sentence by way of reply: 'I could have cried all night.' So I was now doubly in the wrong: making a fuss about nothing, and unable to take a joke. The critics' response to criticism is always measured: the critic was simply expressing his opinion. To the challenge

354

that some degree of expertise, some understanding of the matter in hand, might be appropriate, there is always the answer that the critic is the representative of the man or woman in the street, on whose behalf he or she is sending a report. This is particularly true of drama critics, for whom there appears to be no qualification whatever. It is generally assumed that music critics have some training in music, some capacity to perform it or analyse it technically, but this is not the case with drama critics, most of whom have neither acted, nor directed nor even so much as attended a rehearsal. Happy *métier*! – in which you may say anything you like with absolute impunity. Pontius Pilate is their patron saint; *quod scripsi scripsi* their motto: what I have written, I have written.

Does it matter? Is it not all part of the rough and tumble of what will always – we hope – be a controversial business? And was it not ever thus? Well, no, actually, it was once different, and the difference is the key to the changes that have overcome all the performing arts in this century. In a world in which audiences have lost all contact with the performance or creation of art themselves, they depend greatly on expert opinion – but the more this has become the case, the less expert the reviews and the more purely opinionated. Criticism has become the performing flea of journalism, an outlet for the prejudices of the critic, expressed in verbal cadenzas designed only to parade his or her coruscating brilliance; the work under review is the merest occasion for this exercise. This is not to say that the judgement is necessarily wrong: for the most part critics are intelligent, often highly committed people. But the substance of their reviews is rarely concerned with the specifics of the performance or production, and largely filled with general adjectival elaborations – superb, exquisite, heavy-handed, dull – of the simple proposition 'I liked it' or 'I loathed it.'

The result is that there is no longer any record of performance. Just as the art of theatrical portraiture – with the charming and very useful exception of William Hewison's cartoons in *The Times* – has died, the art of verbal reporting has disappeared. Theatre and dance remain ephemeral arts; the tradition can only be passed on by direct accounts, written or oral. I don't simply want to know whether Ian McKellen was good or bad as Dr Stockmann; I want to know what he did, how he attacked the part, what physical life he gave to it, how he stretched his own resources, what new dimension he brought to our understanding of the role. It is here, too, that the other crucial contribution of criticism is failing: the maintenance of standards. Hyperbolic reviewing, in which everything is either heaven or hell, has helped to create a great confusion both within the profession and in the public: things that are quite ordinary are acclaimed as great; things that are flawed but fascinating are denounced as heinously bad. The theatre will in the end only ever be as good as its audience, and the critical discourse is central to what the audience brings with it to the performance. The art of theatre-going needs to be rediscovered, and a new criticism must be an essential element of that rediscovery.

Bill Hewison is of course now long gone. The only person who still practises the art of theatrical portraiture, superbly, is Antony Sher. If anyone wants to know what Ian McKellen's Iago or Edgar or my Pozzo was really like, then they would learn as much from one of his paintings as from all the critics put together. I reviewed Tony's first book, Year of the King, *in the* Sunday Times *in 1985.*

Again and again in recent years Tony Sher has created astonishing and unforgettable images on stage and screen. Last year at Stratford, he created the most astonishing and the most unforgettable image of all: the paraplegic Plantagenet: Crookback on crutches. In so doing, he at last revoked the *droit du seigneur* over the role established forty years ago by the greatest actor–image-maker of the century, Laurence Olivier. *Year of the King* tells how he did it, providing at the same time a rich account of the temperament of the bravura actor – of which species he is the supreme example in his generation.

What is it, bravura acting? The unkind definition is: acting which looks like acting. A more generous, and more accurate, definition is: acting in which every aspect of the role is made physical, is externalised and crystallised and indicated by means of sensuous impact. The excitement of the performance – excitement is above all the aim of a bravura performer – is experienced through the audience's nervous system. Thus to speak of 'unforgettable images' is to touch on the essence of bravura. Anyone who thinks this is easily achieved, is a form of showing-off, or egomania, has only to read Tony Sher's book to be disabused. It is hard, hard labour, brain-, body-, and soul-busting work, requiring the mental application of

a policeman tracking a criminal, the physical fitness of an athlete competing in the decathlon and the competitive instincts of a presidential
candidate. It is an inherently ambitious undertaking – but ambition at its
best, for the art, for the performance. Sher reveals himself to be both
competitive and ambitious, haunted by other people's achievements and
the prospect of failure; but he is ambitious and competitive for his *performance*, in the way a mother might be (his mother was!) for her child.

This book, his journal, takes us from the moment when his Richard was
a mere misty glimmer in Trevor Nunn's eye to its triumphant birth and
acclaim by world. He details his growing obsession – how the thought of
playing the part invades his dreams and his waking moments alike; how
valiantly he tries not to contemplate it, not to discuss it, not to read it even
until it's absolutely certain – but his lust for the part overmasters him.
His mind, and even more remarkably, his sketch pad, swarm with monstrous shapes, he can't keep his hands off anything in print which might
relate to the object of his desire. It's hopeless; he's a goner; and before
long he's committed to the part on terms that he's sworn he'll never
accept. Wise friends advise him: wouldn't some nice quiet role, full of
inner confusion and unfathomable text be better for him? Or a film? All
meaningless to him: he must have that part. Not because he has some special affinity with psychopathic regicides, but because of what he could
do with the role. He goes back to his family in South Africa, a joyful and
sometimes baffling journey into his past and himself. He finds that in his
house 'I'm on display everywhere. Every inch of wall is covered in pho-
tos of me or my paintings or posters of plays. It makes me rather
uncomfortable; as if I've died and this is the shrine.' Later, his therapist
tells him, 'You still want to come home from school with prizes saying
"Look, Mommy, I'm best"... Bury all that.'

But there's one prize he must have. Even among his folk, on the other side
of the world, Richard is eating his mind out: he sees him everywhere: in
the landscape, even: in a mountain shaped like a hump. Back in England,
the serious work begins: research, investigation. He visits homes for the
disabled, he reads medical volumes, he sees documentaries. He becomes
obsessed by Dennis Nilsen and Peter Sutcliffe; he ponders the physical
lives of bulls, he examines the activities of insects. Anything to achieve
the shape of this man he's going to play. All the time he's haunted by Laurence Olivier. Well might he be, not only because of the dread memory of
the lank wig, the vulpine face, the steel whip of his voice: it's because

357

they're at the same game. Bravura calls to bravura across the decades. Tony is approaching the part just as Olivier might have done. Indeed, Olivier has often remarked that the motive for his 1944 performance was Wolfit's brilliantly silky success of the previous season. He was determined to be as different as possible; just as Tony rears away from Larry. But like Larry, he must ground his work in reality: he must find his frames of reference in the real world. No abstract nouns for him; no academic conceits.

And he must be fit. Despite a snapped Achilles tendon only a year before, he throws himself into bodybuilding; he gives up smoking; he submits himself to a hilarious health farm with a resident army psychiatrist who can be found in its swimming pool ('How are we to avail ourselves of his service...? Presumably plunging in and swimming alongside: "Ah, morning, Captain, I have this problem with foreplay."'). When rehearsals start he experiments with different kinds of crutches; he submits to having his spine cast in wax; he toys with different costumes. Finally the image has shape and reality and the production takes shape around it. Because, in a sense, the image has preceded the text, there is something of a struggle; but in the end there is integration, and integrity, and triumph.

This is a most wonderfully authentic account of the experience of creating a performance. It's full of delicate and sometimes moving observation; full of striking information (you'll know the difference between scoliosis and kyphosis by the time you've read it); full of the frustration and tedium and occasional tears of the unequal struggle of any of us flawed thespians with ourselves and a great role, and full of his own astonishing and unforgettable drawings. Images, images, images! What images!

Tony spectacularly hit the critical jackpot with his Richard. When he told Michael Caine that he hadn't read his reviews, Caine said: 'Read them? I thought you'd written them.' Like all of us, he has from time to time experienced the opposite.

A show of mine which provoked one of those feeding-frenzy attacks to which critics are collectively prone was Simon Gray's The Holy Terror. *Simon and I had been waiting to work together in the theatre for nearly twenty years. The night before the first night we had supper. The show had gone very well that evening but we both had a foreboding of doom, amply justified. Somehow this made the total crash of the play even more annihilating. The attack on Simon, whose* Smoking Diaries *had just been universally acclaimed by all the literary critics, was savage; the assault on me was only slightly less violent. I shall always particularly cherish the review by the legendarily witty Rhoda Koenig in the* Guardian: *the sight of me making love to Polly Fox at the end of the first act, she said, would give her nightmares for months to come. This is a piece I wrote for the* Guardian *about playing love scenes in 2009.*

It was reported the other day that an actress somewhere has walked out of a play because of some difficulty with a love scene. One has to sympathise. It's a tricky business. Despite the massive growth in recent years of touchy-feelyness and kisses on all cheeks upon the slightest acquaintance, and notwithstanding the supposed shamelessness of actors, extreme bodily intimacy remains a delicate issue. It is not a problem addressed by drama schools. As far as I am aware, there are no courses in Advanced Osculation or Girl on Boy Body Surfing, though it's a while since I was a student. At the Drama Centre in 1970, emotional nakedness was the order of the day, although it is true that in the world outside getting your kit off was more or less *de rigueur*, from *Hair* to *Oh! Calcutta!* to the Living Theatre's *Frankenstein*. But that was Epic Nudity, nudity as the exemplification of Innocence and Vulnerability, the bare forked animal. Love scenes are a different matter.

It may not strike you that love scenes have figured heavily in my curriculum vitae, but you would be wrong. I have tumbled with the best of them, and it has not always been easy. Partly, I suppose, in my case, the problem has been to imitate heterosexuality convincingly. Is one getting it quite right? Just what *do* heterosexuals get up to in bed? But in truth, it's always tricky, whatever the orientation.

With neither drink nor drug nor meal nor relaxing social ambience to blur things, there you are, face to face, in all your unadorned physicality. The feeling is more morning-after than night-before. There was a scene in *Shakespeare in Love* which was particularly unlovely in that way. The character I played, Sir Edmund Tilney, is having a quick poke when he is interrupted. It's a brief scene, but it needed to be urgent, animal, groiny. The schedule was behind, it kept getting pushed further and further back, it looked as if we wouldn't get to it, then suddenly it had to happen and it had to happen NOW. The actress and I were hurtled through make-up. The shot list was very simple, the action obvious – so much so that they were already discussing the next shot while we rehearsed. I was introduced to the actress, there was a brief, practical discussion about how much would be exposed (my bum, her tits) and how long it should last (thirty seconds), the furniture was quickly adjusted, the director called 'Action!', whereupon, like a couple of mating dogs, we leaped on each other, our climax topped by the director's 'Cut!' Great satisfaction all round, lens checked, hands shaken, and off we went, as the crew raced to the next set-up. I never saw the actress again, and indeed, to my embarrassment, I can't quite remember her face, let alone any other part of her anatomy. A typical one-night stand, in fact. At least it all happened so quickly that there was no self-consciousness.

Passionate scenes at least have their own momentum. Romantic encounters are a different matter. It needs a special kind of trust to express physical tenderness with a stranger. Some people, of course, have a gift for instant intimacy, and it's never quite who you might expect. Thirty years ago, I was in a BBC production of *La Ronde*, Schnitzler's famous play in which each character has sex with someone and then moves on to another person who, in turn, moves on to someone else. So all the actors have two sex scenes. Mine were with the very young Amanda Redman and that remarkable and distinguished actress Dorothy Tutin, then nearly sixty. I was naturally very relaxed about Amanda and very anxious about Dottie: the idea of embracing her seemed like *lèse-majesté*. In the event, it was Dottie who hurled herself at me with thrilling rapacity, while Amanda was rather shy. These differences are clearly visible in the finished product. Not that Amanda looks at all reserved: but with her it was technique, whereas with Dottie it was feeling. As in life, so on screen.

Sex on radio is something else again. In the 1970s, Anna Calder-Marshall and I played lovers in a play by Fay Weldon: as soon as her husband left home, I slipped between his sheets. These were the days of Method Radio, so there was a bed, and blankets, and pillows. Anna and I duly clambered into the bed and set about us with gusto, puffing and grunting and lip-smacking, all the while trying to turn the pages of our scripts noiselessly. The result was a cross between sumo wrestling and origami. The trick was not to catch each other's eyes, or we would have collapsed. So far so good. Unfortunately, the scene was not just between the two of us: there was a dog in it, trained by the jealous husband to stop us from making love. The production couldn't run to a real dog, but we had a barking Jack Russell on a separate speaker, held by a rather tubby stage manager, who attempted little jumping-up-and-down movements, scampering around the studio, running at us, speaker in hand, every time we essayed a little passion. Tears of laughter spurted out of our eyes as we squealed our lines, the hysteria quickly reaching orgasmic heights. The director leaped out of his booth to berate us savagely, like schoolchildren. When we finally did the scene, the lovemaking was – how shall I say? – tight-lipped.

And then there was the play I did, very early in my career, for Gay Sweat-shop. It was a two-hander, a simple romantic (but for the time radical) tale of two young men who fall in love with each other and then drift apart. Inevitably, perhaps, a rather torrid offstage romance developed between us. In the central scene, we were in bed together, naked. Then we had to get out of bed. The ingenuity expended on concealing the very obvious pleasure we took in each other's proximity led to rather baffling improvised choreography involving cushions and hats.

Well, we were young. Nowadays, the problem is much more one of engendering arousal than of suppressing it. You're doing this in front of other people, remember – the director, the camera crew, props, make-up, continuity – for other people, sometimes millions of other people, and it'll be up there for all time, to be watched dozens, even hundreds of times on DVD. For some, that might, in itself, be a turn-on. But, like everything else in film – and, one is tempted to add, in life – it boils down to tech-nique. And it's astonishing what can be done with mirrors and smoke and a little smart editing.

During the tour of The Holy Terror, *I appeared, as the stage directions required, naked, but I think we all decided that I was getting a little old for it. Y-fronts were firmly in place by the time we hit the West End. But one never learns. I wrote the following for the* Sunday Times *in 2003.*

In *Through the Leaves* at the Southwark Playhouse I play Otto, an alco-holic steelworker who is engaged in a sometimes clumsy, sometimes brutal attempt to thrash out some sort of relationship with Martha, a woman offal-butcher. Things, for the most part, do not go well, but after the most savage scene of the play, there is a curiously haunting scene in which Otto takes a bath. Martha comes into the bathroom while he is flannelling himself. It is evidently the first time she has seen him fully naked. The following exchange occurs: Otto: 'What you staring at?' Martha: 'Nothing.' Otto: 'Like what you see? Shoulda seen me when I was younger. What a physique. I was quite the athlete.' Martha: 'Pity you don't do more outdoor sports instead of you know what.' Otto: 'No blubber anywhere you look.' Martha: 'What's that there – on your tummy?' Otto: 'Don't talk crap. That's sheer muscle.'

The scene proceeds with her gently scrubbing his back. For perhaps the only time in the play their defences are down and a kind of ease prevails between them. So: a delicate, intimate scene, which the designer and director have staged behind a gauze, warmly and rather dimly lit. There was no question in anyone's mind but that I should have to be naked for the scene: indeed, Otto's nakedness is the point of the scene. No reviewer so much as bothered to mention it; it is a seamless, integral part of the whole production. The day after the first performance, the *Evening Standard* Diary carried a piece whose headline blared 'NAKED CALLOW LEAVES TOO LITTLE TO THE IMAGINATION'. With lewd innuendo the writer claims that theatregoers 'are getting a tiny bit more of Simon Callow than perhaps they bargained for', describing a nude scene 'so protracted it proved too much for at least one member of the audience' who allegedly left the theatre during the scene. (In fact, the individual in question left during the previous scene to go to the loo, thus missing the offending scene, returning in time for the next one.) 'The expansively built actor suddenly stripped naked under the spotlight, leaped into a bath and enthusiastically kneaded his flesh,' the piece continues. A seasoned theatregoer was questioned about 'the ordeal'. 'It didn't really add to the drama, it was highly disgusting and at least three minutes long,' said the unhappy customer.

Now, regular readers of the *Standard* Diary would not for a minute have supposed that this item bore any resemblance to the truth. We all know that the Diary of any newspaper is its crèche, where infant journalists – not old enough to be exposed to real news yet – totter about with their building bricks, desperately trying to engineer Stories where none exist. The genre has its laws, as inflexible as those of the syllogism or the Zen koan: first invent a scandal, then invent someone outraged by the scandal, then invent their complaint. It is quite whimsical, rather *Alice in Wonderland*, like life seen upside down. I don't complain; it's just a bit of bunting that comes along with being in the public eye in whatever capacity. The follow-up to the story in the *Daily Mail* was in the same vein, but somewhat more unpleasant, of course. Having rehashed the supposed outrage, the *Mail* diarist invented a 'Lady Bracknellish' companion who remarked: 'How strange that a man with such a big voice should have such a small endowment.' The *Standard* returned to the fray the next day, quoting from a satirical book by Nigel Planer called *I, An Actor*, whose glossary contains the line 'Callow, verb, to expose one's genitals in the name of art.'

Boys, boys, boys! *Get over it*. The eleven-year-olds seem to have taken over. We are now out of the crèche and into the playground, where body humour is the staple of all discourse. 'Fatgut, fatgut, fatgut,' is the cry of the eleven-year-old wit. As a desperate protection against the self-consciousness of adolescence, every body part is remorselessly denigrated, regardless of its actual dimension or shape. The *Mail* item started – my personal trainer is suing – 'Flabby fifty-three-year-old actor Simon Callow…'

It is true that it has chanced that in the thirty years of my career I have appeared four times on stage without clothes (the late Jack Tinker, with delicious hyperbole, if also with underlying tragedy, once remarked that he was more familiar with my genitals than with his own), and once, rather memorably, on film, with the equally naked but rather lither Julian Sands and Rupert Graves – two gazelles pursued by a hippopotamus. The last time I did so on stage was in Goethe's *Faust*, emerging from the cauldron divested of age and scholarly gown as a newborn babe. It seemed absolutely the right image – and besides, this being a David Freeman production, everybody else was naked too, at one time or another. Fifteen years on, I thought I had put all that, so to speak, behind me, until I read *Through the Leaves*, and realised that there was nothing else for it. It never occurred to me that a press now exposed to, among others, a nude Kathleen Turner, Jude Law, David Haig (whose penis was repeatedly fondled and prodded in *Dead Funny*), Stephen Dillane (as Hamlet), Ian Holm (as King Lear) and the entire football team in *Take Me Out* at the Donmar Warehouse, would even notice the gentle four-minute scene at the Southwark Playhouse.

The playground banter is getting seriously out of hand. In *The Times* last year, that fine and serious actor Willem Dafoe, founder and co-director of the radical Wooster Group, ventured to express himself on the subject of acting. The interviewer utterly dismissed his views and indeed his right to have any. So what *did* the journalist want to talk about? Why, Dafoe's genitals, of course. Was it true that because of the hugeness of his penis, some takes of *The Last Temptation of Christ* had been spoiled when the unruly member slipped out of his loincloth as he hung on the cross? Willem pleasantly declined to answer, but the interviewer persisted. Nothing, it seemed, could have been of more interest to the readers of *The Times*. It sometimes does seem as if our culture, in Harold Wilson's memorable phrase, immatures with age. Or is it just journalism?

Our attitudes to bodies have of course changed radically in the last ten years or so. I wrote Actors and Their Bodies *for the* Sunday Times *in 2003: Kate Winslet had shocked the world by putting on a few pounds.*

There is a curious paradox best expressed, in one of her finest *aperçus*, by the late Bette Davis: 'You don't have to be neurotic to be an actor,' she said, 'but nobody who *liked* themselves ever became one.' She's right, and it's a safe rule that the lovelier or more handsome the actor, the less likely they are to like themselves. And yet here we all are, hauling ourselves – our tired old bodies, our hated faces – in front of the cameras and the footlights for close inspection at every available opportunity. This inevitably gives rise to a certain gloomy narcissism in the profession; when your face is your fortune, or at the very least, your living, you are compelled to take note of its evolution, the processes of decay, the evidence of excess. Bags and jowls appear, eyes get smaller, brows furrow permanently, lips lose their firmness, and with each development, another whole line of parts disappears. 'Mirror, mirror on the wall, am I holding it together at all?' There is nothing that can be done at a deep level to arrest this melancholy progress; only superficial transformations can be wrought, and even to the miracles of *maquillage* there are limits. Occasional resort is taken to the knife, but – quite apart from the ultimate unreliability of almost all facial surgery – the results are doubly unhappy, firstly because even the smallest tuck or nip limits flexibility of expression of the single most communicative part of the body, and secondly, because it's not you any more.

And that's the nub. Another of the paradoxes of acting is that in order to play another person, you have to be very fully in touch with yourself. *You* have to be the starting point. If the starting point is an artefact, all you can do is to superimpose another artefact on top of it, and so become doubly unreal. The body of the actor, every bit of it, has to carry information and expression. It does not necessarily have to be beautiful. Charles Laughton was a famously ugly man – 'I resemble,' he said of himself, 'a departing pachyderm' – but his amorphous, blubbery bulk was alive with meaning: an astonishing range of intention is conveyed throughout his physique. This capacity for revelation is the heart of the actor's skill. Fatness or thinness has nothing to do with it, until either becomes a block to expression. Orson Welles, trying to fill an awful void in himself with food, became too fat to act with anything except his voice and his face – which still left quite a lot, but not enough. He was trapped inside himself. Somehow, Welles's outer self had lost touch with his inner self, a thing which never happened to Laughton.

Many heavyweight actors have succeeded in losing substantial amounts of avoirdupois, only to find that their careers have whittled away, too. Sometimes the thing you want to change most is the essential ingredient of yourself, the fuel of your talent. Old timers will tell you that nothing Peter O'Toole did after having his nose altered to play Lawrence of Arabia comes within a mile of what he achieved in the glory days at the Bristol Old Vic and the Royal Shakespeare Company when, as Peter Hall says, he led with his nose. Noses, being so unavoidable, are something of a focus for obsession. Barbra Streisand's refusal to tamper with her stupendous natural endowment was a heroic gesture, the greatest blow for nose lib since Cyrano de Bergerac. Men are often embarrassed, for crudely Freudian reasons, it would appear, by smallness in that department. Orson Welles almost never appeared on stage or film without prosthetic enhancement of one sort or another. Anxiety about overendowment remains more common. Welles told the tragic story of Everett Sloane, Mr Bernstein in *Citizen Kane*, who thought he looked older than he was. Longing to be a *jeune premier*, or at least a leading man, he decided that his nose was the obstacle. He began, as Welles said, 'bobbing it'; twenty operations later, with no discernible improvement in his career, he killed himself.

Any devotion to an external image must surely tamper with the actor's freedom. The present cult of the body beautiful, especially among men, is terribly dangerous. The *summum bonum* of a worked-out body is a tight stomach; ab fab, indeed. But a free, relaxed stomach is vital for the free expression of emotion. The stomach, rather than the heart, was held by the Elizabethans to be the centre of the emotions; almost any emotional reaction – fear, anger, lust – is experienced first through the stomach, so anything which turns the stomach to steel must limit the actor.

Every era has its *beau idéal*, a physical matrix which we all – consciously or unconsciously – measure ourselves against. This body fascism has started to create cloned actors. They all look the same. Attending a recent performance at that excellent drama school, the Drama Centre, I was struck by how much more physically athletic the actors were than in my day, a quarter of a century ago. 'But where are the fat ones?' I wanted to know. 'Where are the long spindly ones?' I wonder whether we'll ever see the likes of Margaret Rutherford or Ernest Thesiger again. They'd be down at the gym, valiantly eliminating what made them such fascinating representatives of the human race. Actors take huge delight in transforming, popping up as someone different. A romantic leading actor like Brad Pitt metamorphoses as frequently and as radically as a self-confessed character actor like Dustin Hoffman, changing his appearance every time, altering the colour of his hair, the colour of his *eyes.*

Yet, somehow, it's still old Brad up there, not because his exquisite physique remains the perfect creation that it is, but because his imagination has merely exercised itself on his appearance, not engaging with his centre. Some years ago, Robert De Niro was hugely admired for his performance as Jake la Motta in *Raging Bull,* above all for having gained a couple of stone to play the character. To the extent that all anybody thought about while watching the performance was: 'Gosh, what a lot of weight he's put on!' Similarly, in Kenneth Branagh's film of *Mary Shelley's Frankenstein,* we marvelled at Ken's new body – almost more impressive than Dr Frankenstein's creation of the monster – but were thus barred from entering the obsessed brain of the young scientist; while Rupert Everett's work in progress on that sculptural masterwork, his torso, leaves us awed by the hours spent on the Nautilus machines, but some way away from the haunted husband in *The Comfort of Strangers* (as well as having given him a rather strange swaying gait – so much muscle must be hard to move around).

Far from credibility being enhanced, attention is drawn away from the character onto the actor. This is surely not what is meant by character acting. That self-confessedly plain woman, the late Edith Evans, with minimum recourse to the make-up box, made thousands of spectators believe that she was beautiful. Laurence Olivier, a man of medium height and slight build, appeared on stage to be a giant. While they were acting, they were, respectively, beautiful and gigantic. This is the true mystery of acting; it is the magic of transformation. The part of the brain that is the essence of the actor's gift has not yet been identified by medical science, but it is that part with which, by thought alone, the mind transforms the body. So that body has to be ready and waiting. Nothing more is required of it.

Stamina and the ability to perform whatever you demand of your body is of course indispensable to actors, especially in musicals, in which actors are far more liable to appear than they once were. I made my all-singing, all-dancing debut on stage very late in the day, in The Woman in White. *I thought at the time that for me this was the theatrical* ne plus ultra: *I had never dreamed of appearing in a musical. I never dreamed of appearing in a pantomime again, either, but coming back to* Aladdin *was outrageously exhilarating, as Ian McKellen had discovered the year before. I wrote this for the* Guardian *in 2006.*

Last year, after a gap of thirty-two years, I returned to one of the commanding peaks of dramatic literature: Abanazar in *Aladdin*. This was by no means a case of seeking to relive a joyous experience: *Aladdin* in Lincoln was one of the more alarming chapters in my professional life, dodging flying Coca-Cola bottles and other weapons of mass destruction expertly lobbed by the infant audience, accompanied by cries of 'Fook off, poof'. These juvenile critics were not entirely unjustified in their lack of enthusiasm for what they were witnessing: we had no idea what we were doing. I based my performance on the late great Bill Fraser, Widow Twankey gave a very creditable impersonation of Frankie Howerd, and everybody else did whoever or whatever they could do. A feeling for the form was largely absent. I'm not sure any of us had actually seen a panto. Over the years, I've caught up, seeing the great pantos at the Glasgow Citizens' in the Seventies, fresh as paint, the Martin Duncan ones at Stratford East, so wittily designed by Ultz, Danny La Rue's extravaganzas, Ian McKellen's saucy postmodern romp at the Old Vic. I was not especially tempted to appear in any of them, delightful though they all were: my secret yearning was to be part of a panto which was head-on traditional, with a dame built like a brick shithouse, a very leggy girl as principal boy, and me as a madly braying villain with a heart of pure malice.

When I was offered Abanazar in the *Aladdin* at the Richmond Theatre, I didn't need to ask whether it was traditional or not: Christopher Biggins was directing it and in it, so of course it was (although even he was unable to swing the principal boy thing. It may be a political correctness issue. Instead we got Rosa Luxemburg's grandson Henry. Go figure). The script was entirely satisfactory: the storytelling was brisk, the jokes appalling, the characters familiar. There were a number of references to television and to supermarkets, which is quite proper: Victorian pantos were similarly strewn with points of reference from everyday life, but there was no attempt to drag in characters from other media. It was the authentically bizarre but consistent world of comic-book China, a never-never land filled with everything oriental the Western imagination had ever encountered: the Willow pattern, Chinese laundries, pigtails, rick-shaws, an Emperor (who speaks with a Japanese accent), take-away dim sum. The design, despite having been round the block a few times, was really rather exquisite, with delicately painted backcloths and flats, which are so uncommon in the theatre these days as to be positively radical. The musical score was the usual hotchpotch of songs from other shows – *Annie, Mamma Mia!* – plus, as the big number, 'Show Me the Way to Amarillo', a song to which I was then a stranger but which is now for ever engraved on my brain.

I was appearing in another show almost up to the first night, but the rehearsal schedule was easily accommodated, since, basically, there is none. We showed up every day for a couple of hours and bashed out the routines, but as almost everything is inextricably bound up with the spec-tacle, the main achievement was to have learned it. Everyone had done panto before, and they marked their parts, under the amiable leadership of Biggins, who would from time to time bawl out instructions like a fair-ground barker, when he wasn't actually in a scene, and even then he used to bawl out instructions, often to himself. In adjacent rehearsal rooms, Susan Hampshire and Richard Wilson were engaged in a similar process for *Cinderella* at Wimbledon: the rather austere Jerwood Space in South-wark where all this was taking place became, for a couple of weeks, a panto factory. The Donmar was rehearsing *The Wild Duck* there at the same time; I never did find out who was playing the Dame in that. Or was that *Mother Goose?*

We threw it all together in a scarily short time in Richmond. The scenery was put through its paces at reckless speed; seamstresses were applying rhinestones to costumes as their wearers ran on stage; cash-flow crises were resolved by raiding the box office; dancers snatched warm-ups wherever they could find a vacant square yard (in the corridor, mostly), singers yodelled in their dressing rooms and all in all it resembled every backstage movie you've ever seen but the like of which I had never, till then, experienced in real life. Biggins was in field-marshal mode throughout, and being barked at by a large man in a frock is a strangely galvanising experience. Eventually, at the dress rehearsal, he reverted to merely playing the Dame. The producer watched the show and afterwards said some very hurtful things about it and then we were on.

To be precise, *I* was on. Accompanied by a loud bang, a flash of gunpowder and a lung-threatening quantity of dry ice, the curtain whisked up to reveal the vision of nastiness that with the application of a lot of mascara and greasepaint I had become. 'HahahaHA!!!!' I roared, but was quite inaudible over the noise coming from the audience, who booed and hissed like maniacs for nearly five minutes before I could speak. Very gratifying. This was not a hostile audience, like Lincoln's: this was an audience playing the role of an audience at a panto. It's a wonderful sight, to stare out over the stalls and watch an audience overacting. Finally I am able to persuade them to shut up for a bit while I tell them about this magic ring I have which will summon the genie. But how? I invite suggestions as to what I should do with my ring. 'Rub it, rub it, RUB it,' they all scream – all of them, all ages, genders, classes, races – roaring and shrieking. 'You want me to *rub my ring*?' I ask, eyebrows arched in disbelief. 'An unusual suggestion, but I might as well give it a try.' They're howling away, and over the roar one wit shouts out, 'It's behind you!' That's the great thing about panto: you don't even have to make your own jokes.

After a spot of vigorous rubbing, much applauded, there's more gunpowder and yet more smoke, and – da-dum! – Patsy Kensit is standing there in all her loveliness and there's a sort of tidal wave of pleasure from the auditorium because there she really is, off the telly and out of the papers, there before their very eyes, in person, not a facsimile, only feet away from them. This celebrity factor is an indispensable ingredient of the event, a touch of glamour, a piece of real magic. We whisk off to find Aladdin; Widow Twankey is on next, and Biggins unleashes his personality on the audience who are suitably overwhelmed by it. He has (as in life) a genius for creating immediate intimacy. It's as if he's in their front room, a bit bossy, incurably curious, asking them all sorts of personal questions, getting some hapless chap up on stage to hand over his coat, which is then thrown in the washing machine, to be returned to him in shreds. '*What* a good sport you are!' cries Biggins, as he all but throws him down the stairs back into his seat.

Wishee Washee, played by the brilliant young comedian Frankie Doodle, seems to come from another age, a more innocent one than Biggins or Kensit or me. He teaches the audience some odd chant with which they're to greet him every time he walks on stage, which they obediently do. They're up for it all. I can see the front ten rows very clearly: it's very touching to see families together, sometimes four generations from the smallest kid to his great-granddad. Fathers generally take the most warm-ing-up, they're there as a chore, and stare at us moodily but after a quarter of an hour, they've given in completely. The children mostly have toys with flashing lights that they buy in the auditorium and they switch these on and off quite arbitrarily. Normally, the slightest fidget in the auditorium vexes me, but here, it's Liberty Hall. Anything, pretty well, goes. They talk, they shout out, they stand up and walk about. As long as they're awake and looking in the general direction of the stage, it's fine by me. They are invariably ecstatic when the flying carpet hovers over them, and the toilet-roll sequence is pure paradise. What's astonishing is how passionately the kids care about the outcome of events on stage. When Aladdin momentarily considers giving Abanazar the lamp, they scream themselves hoarse, as if his life were at stake. How they hate me. How pleasing this is.

Biggins is particularly good at teasing the audience, stepping in and out of character, or rather in and out of the characters of Biggins and Widow Twankey. His interviews with the children, though always kindly, carry a slight air of disapproval. His questions concern their homes and what Santa will bring. One child confidently declares that this year Santa will bring him a toilet. The embarrassment of the child's parents and the crowing of other parents in the audience are full of the anxiety which lies behind all comedy. When John, the chap who lost his overcoat in the first half, comes back up to get it (dry-cleaned, Biggins assures him, though it is no such thing), Biggins announces 'And now the moment we've all been waiting for: John will sing "Show Me the Way to Amar-illo",' and he does, but only with the rest of us as part of the curtain call.

The audience is made to get on its feet, and there was never a show when I wasn't moved almost to tears by the sight of them all on their feet, belting out this corny old rouser, all the generations, all the ages, all the races – more than once I saw a large Indian family in the front rows who were obviously utterly captivated by the whole thing, beaming at everything with great dazzling smiles, and it occurred to me that it must be like the Kathakali drama with its gods and demons, desperate lovers and pesky old parents. Or perhaps just Bollywood. Whatever else it is, it's like nothing else in the theatre. It is the last remnant of the *Commedia dell'Arte*, the final refuge of the music hall, the ultimate flourish of burlesque. It depends on strong, clear plots, larger-than-life characters, surreal verbal comedy. It can allude to television, but it cannot be of it. It is the theatre theatrical in all its living glory.

A couple of years later, I did Peter Pan – *or rather* Peter Panto. *But despite the vaudevillian elements, and the fact that Peter was played by a girl (that living legend, Bonnie Langford), the show kept a great deal of Barrie's text, even managing to retain something of the play's dark mystery. The play itself, not just the part of Hook, is full of terror and anxiety. It is a unique example of what might be described as profound whimsy, full of a dark playfulness which sometimes seems to foreshadow the magnificently offhand brutality of Roald Dahl's world. Peter's famous cry – 'To die would be an awfully big adventure!' – is a startling sentiment to find at the heart of a children's play. The play is, of course, a dream, and as dark and as liberating as only dreams can be. 'It has something to do with the riddle of his being,' says Barrie's profound final stage direction. 'If he could only get the hang of this, his cry might become "To live might be an awfully big adventure!" but he can never quite get the hang of it, so no one is as gay as he is. With rapturous face he plays on his pipes... he plays on until we wake up.' I loved doing Pan, despite sixteen shows a week and an entrance singing Michael Jackson's 'Bad' which threatened to destroy my larynx for ever.*

Pantomime is famously the only thing that can never fail in the theatre. For a moment one glimpses a sort of theatrical Garden of Eden, a prelapsarian world where the contract between audiences and actors still obtains. Something like it still obtains on tour. I went on the road with Equus *for eighteen weeks, to every major theatre in the country. The tour*

– like the play – was specially targeted at young people, and the effect on them was thrilling. They'd shuffle resentfully into the auditorium, and then, thanks to Shaffer's unerring sense of theatre, the moment the lights went down and the four horsemen strode forward to put on their silver horse heads, they'd be gripped in an iron grasp. As one trudges around the country, getting tireder and tireder, the greeting that almost without exception awaits one on checking in to theatre, and the kindness and generosity of local audiences, makes one feel involved in a very ancient relationship. 'My lord, the actors are come.' 'Buzz buzz.'

I played Garry Essendine in a production of Present Laughter *directed by Michael Rudman, which similarly toured for quite a long time and which set every theatre where it played on a roar. Except Birmingham, that is, where the mournful press officer asked me how the first preview had gone. 'Not many in,' I said. 'No,' she said, 'Birmingham doesn't like Coward.' 'Why, then,' I asked her, 'are we doing three weeks here?' 'That's what we're all asking ourselves,' she replied, in that uniquely melodious accent of the Midlands.*

Rudman dug into Coward's play and found unsuspected seams of truth in it. I had been nervous about working with him: we were friends, and that is not necessarily the best basis for a working relationship. We all know from bitter experience that some of the warmest social relationships can come to grief on the floor, so to speak. He asked me to be present at all the auditions, which was a good way of getting the hang of each other's approach, and I always found myself agreeing with him, but still...

The moment we started rehearsals, I knew that everything was not just going to be all right: it was going to be wonderful. Without even noticing it at first, I found that something rather good was happening to my acting. Michael, always laconic, never didactic, was, by means of languid jokes and wicked anecdotes, adumbrating an approach to acting which was the perfect antidote to all my latent tendencies of bombast and energetic overkill. His blocking made it virtually impossible not to look at the person one was addressing, which was immediately a liberation. Everything suddenly had a very specific focus. He would say, drily, 'I'm not against shouting. Shouting can be very effective. But choose your shouts.' Or, 'Let's see how quietly we can play this scene. Just out of interest.' No theory; no big stick. Everything done with a sprinkling of excellent and often self-deprecating anecdote. We both became deeply interested in the speed of thought at the heart of the play. One fine day he proposed that we play a scene we were struggling with as quickly as humanly possible and the play immediately yielded up all its laughs and all its truth. The delight and approval of a man naturally given to ironic understatement were peculiarly gratifying. As we padded around the country with the show, the reviews everywhere said the same thing: 'This play is much better than anyone gives it credit for.' I can't think of more satisfying praise. It was entirely due to Michael. He trusted the play; he trusted us. Whenever he came to see the show on the tour – which was almost everywhere; I think he only drew the line at Milton Keynes for his own mysterious reasons – he would work it a little further and our game would improve. I began to realise that his aim was a very simple one: to get the production – and the acting, which, in an important sense, for him WAS the production – as good as possible. This is a surprisingly rare objective in the theatre. People have all sorts of agendas, but not often that one.

I by now knew that I had found that rare thing: a director with whom I had an almost perfect rapport. After his pastoral visits he and I would dine together and chew over the show, and I realised more and more that under that raffish and languid exterior beat the heart of a true theatre romantic. This also is rare – too rare. Among directors there are visionaries, ten-a-penny; there are careerists, ditto (often the same people, oddly enough). But there are few who deeply and tenderly love the theatre and love actors. Our conversations often summoned up shades of actors and of productions gone, and Michael's love and knowledge of them was comprehensive and profound. This was a strong enough bond, to be sure, but it turned out that our sympathy was based on something even greater than that. I shyly disclosed one day that I am an Honorary Citizen of Texas, a sublime honour bestowed on me in an absent-minded moment by the Mayor of Austin, on the last day of shooting of The Ballad of the Sad Café; *Michael is a native of Dallas. It is as Texans that we approached the work of Noël Coward, and as Texans that we will approach all our future work, which I trust will be voluminous.*

As we toured, by odd coincidence, I was writing a television screenplay for HBO about Noël Coward and Gertrude Lawrence. In time-honoured fashion it was shelved just before we started shooting: guess what? Too expensive. Who could have imagined that a film about two of the biggest theatre stars of the 1930s and '40s would cost money? But my fascination for Coward grew and grew. I wrote a review of his letters for the Guardian.

Noël Coward, who had a very vivid sense of his own significance, might nonetheless be slightly surprised at the hold that not only his work (which is never off the boards) but also the minutiae of his life continues to hold on the English-speaking public. The monumental *Theatrical Companion to Coward*, four interesting biographies (one of which, by Philip Hoare, probes very deep indeed), the autobiographies, the *Diaries* and now the *Letters* mean that we know as much about him as he did about himself – maybe more so, since he preferred not to dig too deep into his inner self, or anyone else's, for fear, as his childhood friend and playwriting collaborator Esmé Wynne-Tyson remarks in one of many striking letters in Barry Day's riveting edition of the correspondence, that it might 'interfere with your way of living, or alter your attitude towards life... I used to think,' she adds, 'your habit of evading a logical issue to an argument through abuse or humour was weakness. I'm now convinced it's a protective armour.'

Day's inspired decision to include other people's letters to Coward as well as his to them has resulted in a richly complex portrait of the man across the whole of his astonishing career. (A slightly less inspired decision, perhaps, was the creation of epistolary cul-de-sacs within the chronological progression. Thus the whole of Coward's formative relationship with Wynne-Tyson – it is their passionately stormy friendship, not the one with Gertrude Lawrence which is the inspiration for *Private Lives* – is examined over its whole forty-year course immediately after her first mention; we then resume where we were when she entered his life.) He was, as John Osborne famously noted, his own greatest invention, and as often with such people, the invention was so successful that it masks the sheer oddity of the man. Certainly his achievements have no parallel in their diversity: revue artist, actor, director (both film and stage), playwright, screenwriter, novelist, composer, lyricist, even – for a couple of hair-raising performances – conductor. In all of these spheres he achieved the utmost distinction. Nor was he confined to any one genre: he wrote sketches, songs, operettas, musical comedies, epics (*Cavalcade* attempts no less than a history of the British Empire from 1899 to 1930, which also happens to be the exact span of his own life up to the point that he wrote it), sentimental comedies, wartime adventure stories; he wrote the songs that rallied Britain during the war; and a half-dozen of his plays rank among the best of the twentieth century. He was a peerless performer, who eventually mellowed into a superb actor; above all, perhaps, he was a unique and uniquely charismatic personality.

All of this is to be found in the handsomely produced pages of this book. The vividness and urgency of the epistolary form, his triumphs and set-backs, are revealed in all the immediacy of the circumstances that gave rise to them. Day offers a detailed running commentary on the events and individuals concerned and provides a potted history of Coward's life and times. This last is sometimes a little genuflectory; though Day is not uncritical of the work, he backs off describing some of the uglier episodes – the catastrophic Broadway revival of *Tonight at 8.30*, starring his then boyfriend Graham Payn, for example, or Coward's unrelenting pursuit of a young heterosexual actor at a late stage of his career. Sex, though it was a major pastime of Coward's, doesn't get much of a look-in (as far as can be discerned, the only reference to it in the letters is 'I managed to get one satisfactory bit of nuki'): Day approvingly notes that 'To the end of his life… he remained private in his private life, a deci-sion,' he adds, 'that one wishes today's gay community would honour,' a particularly idiotic remark as a response to *A Song at Twilight*, Coward's last play, whose entire point is the terrible price to be paid for living in the closet. In fact, though he spared us the anatomical details, Coward was, for the time, remarkably brave in not pretending to be anything other than what he so clearly was, one of the many anomalies of his career.

His appeal to middle England was immediate and visceral; even at his most frivolous he seemed to speak for England: what he found absurd, they found absurd, and satire from his pen – 'Mad Dogs and Englishmen', for example, or 'Don't Make Fun of the Festival' – seemed to appeal to the most dyed-in-the-wool Disgusted of Surbiton, while his overt patriotism galvanised the nation. One wonders whether these admirers would have laughed so heartily if they thought that they were being entertained and stirred by a homosexual atheist of the most militant kind: a letter to his mother on the early death of his brother out-Dawkins Dawkins: 'I'm say-ing several acid prayers to a fat contented God the Father in a dirty night gown, who hates you and me and every living creature in the world.' More benignly but equally dismissively, he tended to refer to the Almighty as 'Doddie'. Coward's letters to his mother occupy a good slice of the book. They are not always the most interesting – for the most part he writes to her like a schoolboy – but they are a striking testimony to his absolute devotion to her and their sense of solidarity against the world, nowhere more vividly expressed than in the wartime letter she sends him wishing that she could line the whole of the Allied Government up against a wall and shoot them because of their slighting treatment of his attempts to make a serious contribution to the war effort.

The question of 'how best to employ my brittle talents in the cause' exercised him greatly; he took it very seriously, becoming enamoured of the phrase 'something rather hush-hush'. The whole of this extraordinary interlude during which Coward, Cary Grant and various other luminaries were trained up as spies is an hilarious, almost surreal episode; it got as far as Coward having serious personal briefings with Roosevelt. Coward's outraged feelings, his bitterness at the position he had been put in and his contempt for the 'stupidity' of the government agencies are vividly expressed in letter after angry letter; in the end, of course, he got on with doing what he did best, as Churchill had rather roughly suggested to him he should from the beginning. He did heroically, acting in three new plays one after another, making the quintessential rallying film of the war, *In Which We Serve*, delivering heroic speeches and comic songs across the war zones of the Middle and Far East. He had a private supper with Churchill a day or two before VE Day at which he and his fellow guests stood up to toast the great man; but it was Churchill who, on the grounds of a minor and involuntary currency offence, blocked his knighthood.

The section of the book that follows the war charts his increasing disaffection with England and with his own public ('Idiotic public for letting me down. They ought to have known better'), his return to popular acclaim as a cabaret artist, the rediscovery of his early plays and, finally, the knighthood; he was dead three years later, safe in the knowledge of his own immortality. The letters give report of his daily life, his many voyages, his frustrations and his disappointments, his falsely raised hopes and his cruelly dashed spirits. Above all, they are a record of his friendships. Notoriously, he knew *everyone*, from Virginia Woolf to T. E. Lawrence to Anthony Eden to Lionel Bart, and wrote to them all. Perhaps the most amusing letters are those to his secretary Lorn Lorraine, often in verse ('Pretty pretty Lorn / Timid as a haunted faun / This engaging little rhyme / Merely serves to pass the time'), and to Alexander Woollcott, full of nonsensical playfulness ('The bluebells are out and I sometimes throw myself among them laughing'). In his self-elected role as 'psychiatrist and nurse governess' to his friends, he wags his finger, more often than not telling them, as he does an anguished Marlene Dietrich, 'Snap out of it, girl!' Dietrich paints an unforgettable portrait of abject infatuation (with

Yul Brynner, whom they nickname Curly): 'Thank God I am German or I would have jumped out of the plane.' Bemoaning her linguistic incompetence, she offers a superb definition of *amitié amoureuse*: 'Friends who use lovers' tactics.' Garbo writes perfectly Garboesquely: 'That fluttering, tired and sad heart of mine has been in such a peculiar state...' Among the richest exchanges in the book are with the young radical writers of the Fifties and Sixties whom at first Coward denounced but then came to respect: Wesker, Pinter, Albee, Osborne. His enthusiasm for Pinter – 'I love your choice of words, your resolute refusal to *explain* anything, and the arrogant, but triumphant demands you make on the audience's imagination' – gives a clue as to Coward's continuing vitality today. He may have marginally outlived his own talent, but he slipped away with all his instincts intact, including that of a well-timed exit: 'I've never wanted to be the last to leave any party,' he said.

The truth is, I suppose, that nothing theatrical is alien to me, though my taste for showbiz – or perhaps my gift for it – is severely limited, as I realised when I directed The Pajama Game. *I tried, as I had tried before with* My Fair Lady, *to reproduce the circumstances of the original production, in the case of* The Pajama Game *the fascinating combination of modern dance, vaudevillian skills, and political radicalism; I felt, too, that musical revivals of 1950s shows needed to get away from irony and archness. The Fifties, it seemed to me and my producer, Howard Panter, were, from a visual point of view, all about joyful abstraction; musically they were about liberation from old forms. So, without any difficulty and in a very short space of time, we recruited that supreme saxophonist and musical explorer John Harle to arrange the piece, David Bintley, of the Birmingham Royal Ballet and a passionate aficionado of musicals, to choreograph it, and Frank Stella to design it. Frank Stella! After Howard and I left his studio in New York we literally hugged each other, and went and found the largest bottle of champagne money could buy. Exhilarated by the work, and quite forgetting what had happened after my effusion on the subject of* Les Enfants du Paradis, *I wrote a note for the programme book.*

The musical can be many things: it can be stylish or sombre; epic or harrowing. There is no bar to it addressing Great Themes, or taking Specific Political Positions; it can break your heart or change your mind. But the thing at which it is absolutely unrivalled is cheering you up. And of all the many joyful, throw-your-hat-in-the-air, set-your-foot-tapping-and-send-you-out-into-the-cold-night-air-with-a-grin-a-mile-wide-on-your-face musicals ever written, *The Pajama Game* is pretty near the top of the pile. The story is satirical, in theory: it sends up labour relations in a pyjama factory in the Midwest in the 1950s. The protagonists are Sid, the Works Supervisor, and Babe, the Head of the Union's Grievance Committee, so it's also a kind of Romeo and Juliet story, love across the picket line. But what it really is, is a paean to life, a celebration of its young creators' fertile inventiveness, and a non-stop triumph of theatrical panache. For all its craftsmanship, it has a kind of anarchic dynamism lending it an innocence which – despite all the grim historical evidence to the contrary – the 1950s still seem to us to possess: an exuberance, an optimism, a sense of liberation.

The show has a sensational sequence of hit tunes – 'Hey there, you with the stars in your eyes', 'Steam Heat', 'Hernando's Hideaway' – unrivalled in the annals of musical comedy, except, perhaps by *Guys and Dolls*, whose composer, Frank Loesser, was the great mentor of the young hopefuls, Richard Adler and Jerry Ross, who wrote *The Pajama Game*. It is very much in the tradition of Loesser's show – witty, snappy, vernacular lyrics, poignant ballads, streetwise and hip to the moment, bursting at the seams with sex. The action proceeds with a kind of zany anarchic freedom which owes something to vaudeville and everything to its original director and co-book-writer, George Abbott, who more or less single-handedly maintained the spirit of burlesque (in which he had grown up so many, many years before: he was already sixty-seven at the time of *The Pajama Game* and had another forty years' active life ahead of him) into the postwar musical theatre. It is no accident that his work is full of clowns, male and female, and their extended comic routines, and that love at first sight is at the heart of the plots. The long and glorious tradition of popular comedy – celebrating the comeuppance of curmudgeons and the triumph of youthful sexual desire over the world's strictures – the tradition of the *Commedia dell'Arte* and the ancient Roman comedies, of Benny Hill and Frankie Howerd, of the Marx Brothers and *Up Pompeii!* – lives in *The Pajama Game*; not for nothing was Hines (the insanely jealous, drunk, ex-vaudevillian time-and-motion study man who is the show's master of ceremonies) played in the first London production by Max Wall.

Combining these strands – the political story, the love story, and the comic subplots – with the mastery born of long, long practice, Abbott created a late flowering of a genre whose thrust is above all optimistic: the wilful lovers come together while the zanies weave their mad patterns through everyone else's life. What about the workers? They win. It is all very satisfying. It is a form of theatre that calls for freewheeling invention and rigorous craftsmanship, hard, hard work and a deep love of life. The extraordinary creative team of the present production has worked itself to the bone in the name of fun and they're still smiling, which must mean something.

My no doubt overebullient words were again seized on and savagely mocked by the critics, as was the whole venture. It was the biggest single disaster of my career. 'Diiiiiiiiiiiiiiiiire,' said the critic of the Mail on Sunday, *though the first-night audience had cheered to the echo, and the co-author, Richard Adler, not a man reckless with praise, had told me that it was one of the best evenings of his life. We ran for a month, and lost £3 million.*

I suspect that my love of popular theatre lies more with individual performers than with the musical theatre as such. No doubt it is something atavistic, some echo of my great-grandfather, which draws me to the idea of clowns, but the lure is irresistible. In childhood I idolised the great Coco; but in my youth, I was bitterly disappointed by what happened to the traditional clown. In middle-life I rediscovered my enthusiasm thanks to Slava Polunin, the reinventor of Russian clowning. His Snowshow *distills the essence of circus clown, in a setting of the utmost poetry, turning the entire audience into children. A photograph of him and me together is among my most cherished possessions, staring at each other in mutual incomprehension, as all clowns do. I wrote this piece for my regular weekly* Sunday Express *column (rather oddly named* The Outside Edge*) in February 1997.*

I never expected to feel again in a theatre what I felt last Tuesday in the Peacock Theatre off Kingsway in London, and I am still reeling. The show is called *Slava's Snowshow* and it counts among the two or three greatest things I have ever seen in a theatre.

Slava Polunin is a Russian clown and his show is a loosely connected series of sketches to which I was drawn out of mere curiosity. I'm not a big fan of clowns, or of circuses. I like plays, and acting, and beautiful design. I had heard good things about the show, certainly. But nothing that I had heard remotely prepared me for the poetry, the anarchy, the hilarity and the human tragedy that this man and his colleagues unleashed on us all that night.

His skill is supreme, but that's not it. He performed the old routine of hanging a coat up on a rack and sliding one of his arms through the sleeve and caressing himself voluptuously with his own hand. He did it superbly, supremely well. The disembodied arm seemed to have a life of its own, to belong to someone quite different from his other arm. And we roared with laughter, we shouted and brayed until we were hoarse.

But why were we crying, too? It was because we somehow knew this man, and knew his need for love, and knew, above all, about his terrible loneliness. The moment he walks on stage, we know him: he is us. Man, alone in the universe. And again and again through the evening, he made himself known to us – without a word, of course, with only a flick of the eye, a tiny gesture of the hands.

Every emotion, every impulse was crystallised in a gesture. Gesture is *the* art of the actor, or it always was. We have been misled into thinking that emotion and external imitation are its essence: looking and feeling the part. It's not. It's the thought made flesh, and at this Slava is a genius. We see his shock at encountering another clown, we sense him being appalled and intrigued, we understand his amazement that such a grotesque could exist (even though the other clown is almost identical to him), we get Slava's initial delight in the clown's company, then his growing frustration, his resentment, even hatred, of the other clown, the other clown's banishment, his delight at being alone again, then his sudden engulfing loneliness: this is the whole history of the human heart played out before us.

His leaps of imagination are bold, but they are always rooted in reality. When he takes a train, he does so by running round in circles, with smoke pouring out of his stovepipe hat. I never saw a more train-like train. Towards the end of the show, snow starts to fall on stage, then, magically, it starts to fall in the auditorium too, onto the audience.

The effect of this is extraordinary, moving in some ineffable way: one instantly becomes a child again. Then, as the opening of *Carmina Burana* pounds out, Slava whirls all the stage flats round till it becomes a great snowscape, while a battery of lights blazes into the auditorium, the stage cloths flap furiously before the wind machine, and Slava in the centre of it all turns round again and again and again, delirious with joy.

How can I make you understand that this is the single most beautiful thing I have ever seen in a theatre in my life, that as I watched it I felt my eyes opening so wide they seemed about to fall out of my head, as my mouth opened wider and wider with amazement, while hot tears coursed down my face?

That finale was of course, the end – but for one thing. From behind the stage now emerged three huge helium-filled beach balls looking like giant Christmas-tree baubles. Out into the audience they came and as if on cue, the audience stood up to bounce them, and they stayed bouncing them for ten, fifteen minutes; for all I know they are bouncing them still, players in the game now, no longer spectators. Solemnly, the clowns lined up on stage to watch them.

This is theatre. Naïve and profound, childish, in one sense, but deeply human. Theatre is not really the place for ideas. It is a playground for the imagination, a gymnasium of the soul, the heart's stadium. Every child in that theatre on Tuesday, and every adult too, now knows what theatre can be. Pray God they aren't disappointed in it too often in the years to come, and forget.

Since my early encounter with Max Wall I have been addicted to comedians, although there is some overlap between them and clowns, as in the case of Tommy Cooper, for example, about whom I directed a play called Jus' Like That, *the brainchild of my old friend from* The Beastly Beatitudes of Balthazar B, *Patrick Ryecart, and written by John Fisher. Jerome Flynn uncannily reincarnated Tommy, unleashing waves of laughter in the theatre quite as engulfing as those provoked by Tommy himself. I wrote about him for the* Observer *in 2003.*

Technically speaking, Tommy Cooper flourished after the music hall had died, but he embodies its spirit as almost no one else within living memory. Perhaps Max Wall with his simian presence was an even more characteristic expression of its world of extremes, but Cooper, the zany giant, fumbling magician and surreal raconteur, continues in a richer, more universal degree the great tradition of that comic Eden. It was the last flourish in the West of the immemorial carnival spirit, uniting all classes and degrees of men and women in a celebration of daily experience which was both life-affirming and highly subversive, obsessed with the bizarre and the odd, but endlessly asserting the common lot of all mankind. The comedy of the music hall was filled with a wild poetry, sometimes almost surreal, which had nothing elite about it, its laughter a transformation into prancing hilarity of the (on the whole) depressed and frustrated existences of both its artists and its audiences. The terms of reference are almost all mundane: everyday encounters with authority figures – doctors, policemen, lawyers; the difficulties encountered with fractious landladies and waiters in restaurants; the tyranny of objects; the treacherous mysteries of language; the never-ending caprices of the libido. It is a response to the exigencies of real life, but it is rarely topical. It creates another world, an upside-down image of life where everything is resolved in laughter. To be able to laugh at something is to be undefeated by it.

All this Tommy Cooper embodies, baffled as he is by life in general, by the intransigence of his own body and by the magic tricks which he has so carefully rehearsed but which constantly rebel against him, even when he follows the instructions. The magic is a sort of metaphor of the unprivileged life: the doomed attempt to gain power, to be impressive, to dominate the world. No matter what you do, how much you spend on your tricks, how diligently you practise them, you will fail: they have a life of their own. And we in the audience can see that Tommy Cooper is the last man on earth who should ever have been allowed to pick up a wand; the very idea is gloriously preposterous. He knows it too. He is everyone in the audience who has ever entertained the notion of being a magician, of surprising and astonishing the family and the neighbours (as the instruction booklets so glibly promise). When one of his tricks succeeds, we rejoice for him as we would for ourselves. The magic has another function, though, within the canny mixture which constitutes Tommy Cooper's act. It is a kind of a narrative, engaging our conscious minds, lowering our defences as we try to work out what has just happened and why, and allowing the comedy to attack us at the subconscious level, leaving us helpless to resist. In other words – T. S. Eliot's, to be precise – the magic is the objective correlative of Tommy's act. It functions like the bone the burglar throws to the dog of reason, keeping it happily engaged while the artist works his darker, deeper purposes, emptying the safe of the unconscious. Verbally, Tommy may not exactly be Shakespeare, but the flights of his imagination are no less wild. The result is that his comedy unhinges us, generating a kind of delirium which is extraordinarily restorative.

There are of course other comedians who do this. Ken Dodd asks nothing more of an audience, he says, than to let him 'muck around with their minds for an hour'. He represents another aspect of the halls when he breaks into mellifluous sentimental song; you will find no such thing with Tommy Cooper. If Tommy sings, it is to draw attention to his own lack of abilities in that department, but also, by extension, to the absurdity of singing. Mad as a snake though Dodd certainly is – Dodd the performer – and as compulsive a motor-mouthing, free-associating, stream-of-consciousness merchant as any Shakespearean clown, his personality lacks the grandeur of Tommy's. Tommy is, as Carson McCullers might say, 'afflicted'. He is doomed to failure at first sight. Our heart goes out to him. He is us. Dodd is a fool, a brilliant and obsessed madman, whereas Tommy plays the fool, because what else could he do? He is that person in every social group who takes it on himself to create laughter by stressing his own ineptitude. Just as his magic lets him down, so does his comedy. He offers a running commentary on the success or failure of his jokes. If necessary, he repeats them ('I've got a cigarette lighter that won't go out.' Pause. 'I'VE GOT A CIGARETTE LIGHTER THAT WON'T GO OUT.'). He doesn't just give away the mechanism of his tricks; he exposes the tricks of his comedy, too. 'More, more!' he shouts behind his hand, fanning applause; he identifies the beginnings of a promising laugh: 'Ripple, ripple, ripple.' He eggs us on to greater heights with encouraging gestures. And then he roars with laughter at his own idiocy; he is his own best audience.

All of this is deeply touching, which is not a necessary component of a great comedian, but is an essential one of a clown, which is what Tommy Cooper is, at heart. The invention of a clown is a great creative act, identical in sort to the great creations of literature, to a Falstaff or a Don

Quixote, a Leopold Bloom or a Captain Grimes. Chaplin's creation of The Tramp is a supreme example among comedians. Buster Keaton and Grock are others. And as such are they not susceptible of revival, just as you might have another go at playing Quixote or Bloom? It was the actor Patrick Ryecart, the co-producer of *Jus' Like That*, who had the seminal thought that turned into the show: wouldn't it be wonderful, he said, if we could sit in a theatre and be part of Tommy's audience now. It was not a question of impersonation – one of the indices of the man's enduring popularity is that virtually everyone in Britain who can speak can do their version of the man, if only to say 'Jus' like that', with appropriate hand gestures – or even of reconstruction, but of tapping into the unique energy that Cooper generated. I suppose you could say we wanted to bring him to life again.

That may be why they approached me to direct the piece. I have spent quite a large part of my working life being what Dickens in *A Tale of Two Cities* calls a 'resurrection man'. As a biographer, but also as an actor, I have often been involved in trying to revive the dead (usually the great dead). In my time I have played Mozart, Handel, Schumann, Oscar Wilde, Verlaine, Rousseau, Juvenal, Dr Johnson, Napoleon, Galileo, Dickens. It has generally proved to be a rather emotional business. I am not of a mystical turn, but whenever I start to play one of these geniuses, I am aware of a curious sense of responsibility towards them, as if they expected me to give the best account of them I could, to plead their cause. They take hold of you, put a pistol to your head, and force you to tell their story the way they want it told.

Working on *Jus' Like That* has touched on some of these same emotions. Tommy was one of those few performers, a tiny handful, who go beyond being simply entertainers, helping to pass the time, but become part of our mental landscape, as known to us as family. Their very presence – their very existence, you might say – warms us and their gorgeously familiar routines never fail to unlock the accumulated tensions of our lives. They are as cheering and as crucial to our well-being as wine and food; they put us firmly back into the present moment, that split second at which the laughter breaks, and we surrender our rational defences, giving in to the riot of mental mayhem where nothing makes sense any more, nor does it have to. Everything one has been holding together collapses. This intellectual liberation – this temporary insanity – produces physical joy, and a sudden breakdown of barriers between individuals.

Nothing melds people more swiftly. In the grip of this sort of laughter, it is nearly impossible to avoid catching one's neighbour's eye; sometimes it is essential to grasp him or her by the arm.

Working on the show has been a curiously moving experience. Given a performer as deeply connected to Tommy Cooper as Jerome Flynn is, as skilled and as funny, it has been no surprise that the comedy and the magic work triumphantly. What has been extraordinary, and surprising to all of us, as we've toured around the country, is – beyond all the glorious gags and the tricks – the sheer affection in which Tommy was held, the delight in his grandeur of spirit and his great cosmic laugh. There is a feeling that someone has returned who should never have gone away; that his spirit is abroad again, that something very personal, something that belongs to them, has been restored to people. He is a genuine Folk Hero, and his return is as welcome as that of Robin Hood or John Bull. (But they never got a laugh in their lives, as Tommy would say.)

Tony Hancock, too, was somewhere between comic and clown – with more than a little of the actor about him in the bargain. I wrote about John Fisher's biography of him in 2009, in the Guardian.

John Fisher is the roving commissar of comedy, the peripatetic Professor of Pandemonium, the Ancient Mariner of the Music Hall. He knows where all the bodies are buried and where the connective tissue is; nothing escapes his eagle eye, nothing slips away from his all-retentive memory. For years, he has been writing comprehensive studies of comedians he has seen, as well as affectionate evocations of those of whom he has merely heard. Though most of his professional life has been spent producing television programmes, including such milestones as *The Tommy Cooper Show*, and although he has a keen sense of the practical aspects of comedy, it is essentially as a fan, a gurgling, joyously chortling fan, that he comes to his task. In *Tony Hancock: The Definitive Biography*, he gives a touching picture of himself as a seven-year-old boy in the Gaumont Southampton, glimpsing Tony Hancock – then an up-and-coming radio star – hurling himself about the stage with hilarious precision; thereafter, he followed him through his brief but momentous career, and was numbed by his lonely, early death. But when the first book about Hancock appeared – a lurid account by his second wife, the publicist Freddie Ross – Fisher was utterly shocked by the unlovely details of his hero's decline, and tried to protect his very respectable and loving mother and father from learning them.

Something of this innocence betrayed haunts the present book. Fisher charts the comedian's rapid rise with jaunty brio, vividly recounting plots, analysing gestures, turns of phrase. But you sense that he is dreading the inevitable hints of trouble, tragedy's unrelenting finger beckoning, beckoning. When it all starts to go wrong for Hancock, he gallantly finds a redeeming moment here, a nicely timed gag there, but he gazes on helpless as the man he refers to again and again as 'the lad himself' slips deeper into the morass of alcohol and self-laceration. The final days as described by Fisher are almost unbearable to read because the author is so upset himself, as if Hancock were a close personal friend bent on a course of doom.

He gives us a lively account of the early life in Bournemouth, where Hancock's parents, who were intermittently in show business, bought an hotel where, like one of his heroes, Charles Laughton, he helped out. His father died; he was sent to public school and walked out at the age of fourteen. He tried to follow in his father's footsteps as a comedian and failed at the first hurdle; there was a succession of hopeless jobs; then his first faltering successful steps on stage. The breaks and the disasters are duly recorded against the background of a vivid and deeply affectionate account of the variety theatre of the day.

Eventually, after a dreary war as a clerk in the RAF, Hancock was discovered, like so many others, by Ralph Reader of the Gang Show, and equally inevitably, found his way to the Windmill Theatre, six shows a day, six days a week, where he learned 'to die gracefully, like a swan'. His confidence was growing; people began to sense that he had something special. He got into radio as a running character in Peter Brough's *Educating Archie*. His catchphrase 'Isn't it sickening?' was on everyone's lips, soon followed by 'Flippin' kids!'; an innocent age indeed. The crucial event in his life as a star was when he met the writers Ray Galton and Alan Simpson, who uncannily channelled the essence of the man Hancock into the character Hancock, boastful, aspirational, intolerant, out of place almost everywhere he finds himself, but nonetheless possessed of a certain grandeur. This character is surely one of the great inventions of twentieth-century comedy, the love child of these two writers and the actor they served. Just as surely as Archie Rice or Jimmy Porter, Hancock (as created by Galton and Simpson) expressed the age – the post-war accidie, the sense of vanished dreams, of alienation and angst, the rage against conformist greyness – but through the rumpled and familiar form of the man the writers in an inspired moment christened Anthony Aloysius St John Hancock. (In one of a million astonishing details in the book, Fisher reveals that Hancock was seriously courted to play Jimmy Porter in the film of *Look Back in Anger*.)

As a boy I was besotted with Hancock, especially after his transition to television, for which medium his infinitely expressive, melted-down features were made. Indeed, I identified with him, recognising in him a middle-aged child not so very unlike the middle-aged child I felt myself to be. There is so often a child at the heart of any great comic creation, and Hancock was gorgeously, outrageously infantile. The part was bespoke: the scripts follow the contours of Hancock's natural melody so perfectly that to read them on the page is to hear them. Fisher is exceptionally good on the odd interpenetration of character and man, and shrewdly observes that it was this that began to gnaw at him. As Fisher puts it, there were times 'when he felt cheated of his real identity'. He began to feel that the character was merely him, and that therefore he wasn't proving himself; he started to become increasingly introspective about his work. Like someone picking a scab, he felt compelled to worry at it till he bled, pulling a thread in a cardigan till the whole thing came apart. Like the lad himself, he had *des idées au-dessus de sa gare*: he started to think of himself as an Artist, which, of course, he was, but a deeply instinctive one – to the extent that he never used to read the radio scripts until the morning of the transmission, and then gave flawlessly timed and inhabited performances. The blitheness of radio – where scripts don't have to be learned, props don't have to be mastered and the actors have an easy camaraderie across the microphones – left him blissfully unselfconscious. Television, where everything had to happen for real, started the process of endless self-analysis which, his brother noted, killed him.

He was invited to appear on the notorious *Face to Face* series in which a quietly unrelenting John Freeman, shrouded in shadow, interrogated him as the camera dwelt on his face. It was a form of public confession – without absolution – which did him irreparable damage, tipping him over into a sort of anguished contemplation of his own limitations and an insatiable determination to innovate. He was determined to become a

Chaplin or a Keaton, a universal and international figure. This meant the immediate dismantlement of Hancock as we knew him, the departure from East Cheam, the abandonment of his co-stars (Sid James the first to go), and, catastrophically, the dismissal of his writers. From then on – despite occasional successes like his film *The Rebel* – it was a slow and increasingly excruciating professional suicide. His consumption of alcohol while on the job, which had begun when he was playing in variety theatres, began to destroy his talent: he could no longer remember lines, and, most poignantly, as his physical condition got worse, that uniquely expressive mug became as rigid as Mount Rushmore. In life, he and his wives and mistresses plunged headlong into a sea of booze; at one point he chained himself to the railings of Primrose Hill. Often things turned violent. One wife happened to be a judo expert, so he rarely inflicted any damage on her; the other protected herself by frequently (and with diminishing impact) attempting to kill herself.

In Australia to shoot a television series, he gave a dazzling read-through of the first episode, then retired to his dressing room to tank himself up on vodka and pills, and after that 'he didn't know who or what he was'. Finally, he did sober up, but one day he went down to get something from his neighbour, who was also his producer, only to find him out. That sudden reminder of his aloneness was enough, it seems, to have tipped him over the edge. 'Things seem to have gone wrong just too many times,' he wrote, and then administered a lethal dose of the vodka and pills that had been his constant companions for so many years. He had often talked of suicide; as early as 1957 he had suggested a mutual suicide pact to Charlie Drake, who declined, observing that 'Hancock wanted out of the game, even then. He was totally lonely, even with people.'

The roots of this epic loneliness are hard to deduce from Fisher's pages. In them you will find a brilliant and much-needed account of Hancock's extensive theatre work and its originality, just as he celebrates the audacity of the television work, with its formal inventiveness and its constantly Pirandellian playing with the frame, and a kind of voyage round the comedian's mind and the nature of his comic enterprise. But he fails to probe his crucial relationships, especially with his mother, Lily, to whom he was immensely close. She supported him financially in his early years in the business; she was the go-between when his marriages broke down; she was the last person in his mind when he killed himself. Fisher lets slip the astonishing fact that two weeks after he finally did for himself, Lily took a pleasure cruise to Turkey. There's something very very complex in that relationship which remains for future Hancock biographers to probe. Meanwhile, Fisher has written an indispensable book about what he rightly calls 'the most expansively idiosyncratic of recent British comic heroes'.

I never met Hancock or Tommy Cooper, but I did encounter one of my comic heroes, which proved to be a little alarming, as I reported in the Guardian *in 2004, in a review of* Frankie Howerd: Stand-Up Comic *by Graham McCann.*

Conversation with Frankie Howerd was peculiarly disorientating. There he stood, in his usual stage uniform of brown suit and crumpled shirt, his toupee (as Barry Cryer memorably remarked) going up and down like a pedal bin, his eyebrows soaring up to join it, the face getting longer, the eyes looking wildly askance in horror or disbelief, the vowels extending and distending – being, in fact, in every particular, the Frankie Howerd we all knew and loved. Except that he was not at all, not even remotely, for a single second, funny. What he was saying was almost identical to what he had said on stage the night before and the night before that to such side-splitting effect – a list of complaints, paranoias and resentments – but for some reason, while on stage it was the acme of hilarity, off it the laughter froze on your lips.

We had a little bit of an *histoire*, Frankie and I. One night, after the Olivier Awards, where he had made his traditional superb speech – 'This afternoon I spoke to my agent, who thinks I'm dead,' it had begun – I was chatting to someone in the foyer and suddenly there he was, gloomily alone, half-listening to us. He said: 'Are you going to this party?' and of course I laughed, because to hear him was to laugh. He didn't laugh back, so I quickly said that I was, with my partner Aziz. He said, 'D'you want a lift?' I said that would be lovely, and off we went. He sensed we were a couple. 'Do you love each other?' he asked, without preamble. 'Yes, sir,' said Aziz. 'Very much,' said I. 'That must be nice,' he said sourly. 'Give me your hands.' In the dark of the back of his car he peered at our respective palms and rattled off some somewhat sobering – and not entirely inaccurate – observations about our personalities and what we had to offer each other. By now we were at the party, which consisted predominantly of playwrights. Having downed most of a bottle of vodka in about ten minutes, he announced: 'Why don't any of you lot write something for me?' Out of the babel of writers' voices offering their services, one dominated, that of Peter Nichols. 'But I have, Frankie. You turned it down.' 'What play was that, then?' '*The National Health.*' 'Oh, that. That was an awful play, a terrible play. It was all about death. You don't make fun of death. Write me a proper play, a funny play.'

Soon afterwards he said: 'Let's get out of here. I'll give you a lift. Where do you live?' When we arrived, he said: 'Aren't you going to ask me in?' I was thrilled, of course, at the idea of having Frankie Howerd on my sofa. The same thought had obviously occurred to him, but in a slightly more literal sense, because after a few minutes of rather strained chat, he said: 'Why don't we have an orgy? Just the three of us.' I laughed, but it was terribly, terribly clear that he wasn't joking. 'Well?' he said, implacably. 'I don't think so, Frankie,' I said, 'I mean, it'd be so embarrassing afterwards.' 'What d'you mean?' 'We're so tired. It'd be hopeless.' 'I'm not fussy.' 'No, Frankie, no, really, I have an early call tomorrow.' 'All right, all right, I get the message.' He headed crossly for the door, then paused for a moment. 'Not a word about this to anyone,' he said. 'There's a Person Back Home who would be very upset.'

The Person Back Home was Dennis Heymer, who now, in Graham McCann's fine new study, emerges from the shadows – but only just. Heymer is described as the love of his life, whom Howerd met when he was beginning to despair about his career and his physical attractiveness. Heymer had unshakable faith in Howerd's talent, and spent his life extending his support in every way imaginable, most importantly by providing a domestic framework that reproduced the cosy and nurturing environment of his childhood home. Beyond these bare facts, however, we learn nothing of him. In fact, we learn little about Howerd, the man, either.

There are occasional tantalising glimpses of his friendships (with, for example, Rebecca West), but for all McCann's memorably ghastly anecdotes about him descending on chums such as Cilla Black and Barry Took with his sister and a bag of supermarket food, demanding that his reluctant hosts cook it for them while the visitors watched television, the sense of what he was actually like remains elusive. In a chapter entitled 'The Closeted Life', McCann gamely attempts to sketch the broad outlines of

Howerd's sex life, but beyond giving examples of the unattractive impatience of the sexual late-starter – Frankie bellowing 'You don't know what you're missing!' at the rapidly escaping object of his unwanted advances – he refuses to add to what he considers to be the prurient and unfounded speculations of the tabloid press; sensibly, he regards Howerd's homosexuality as extrinsic to his comic persona, which, camp though it was, was no more gay than that of his deeply heterosexual and equally effete hero, Jack Benny.

Filth was, of course, at the heart of his comedy, part of the same great British tradition as the Carry On series, which enabled him occasionally to join the team. But unlike Sid and Ken and Babs and co., he was a great comic innovator, and it is in describing the evolution of young Frank Howard from Eltham into 'Frankie Howerd' that McCann comes into his own, guided by his subject, whose brilliantly titled autobiography, *On the Way I Lost It*, reveals an exceptionally acute and articulate self-awareness. This is partially the result of his many encounters with psychiatrists and analysts – including one who used LSD extensively – in his continuing struggle to find meaning in his life. McCann describes his agonisingly slow start (he was twenty-nine before he got his first professional job), followed by his commensurately quick rise, which made him a national star within ten weeks of that first job. 'A completely new art form,' his first producer told him after his successful audition for radio's *Variety Bandbox*. Thanks largely to his performances, the show had a radio audience of nearly half of the total adult population. This was achieved not without enormous effort, accompanied by tension, rows and dread.

His initially successful style of 'anti-patter' had soon begun to stagnate; thinking hard, he realised that he was giving a stage and not a radio performance. He taught himself mastery of the microphone, painstakingly acquiring his characteristically wide vocal range, squeezing hilarious nuance out of a vast array of intonations. He discovered in Eric Sykes the first of many fine writers, commissioning from him the scripts which, building on his persona, invented the 'one-man situational comedy' ('I've had a shocking day') that stood him in such good stead for the rest of his career. He thought about every detail of his act, even changing the spelling of his name to make people look twice, thinking it must be a misprint.

Ordinariness was the key. He eschewed the flashiness of Max Miller or Tommy Cooper's exotic troglodytism, creating the impression that 'I wasn't one of the cast, but had just wandered in from the street... ' He had turned his perceived disadvantages as a performer – the unconventional appearance, the stammering, the forgetfulness – into comedic triumph, the stand-up comic as a paradigm of the oppressed little man. 'I played against the show,' Howerd wrote, 'as though its faults were all part of a deliberate conspiracy against me: I was being sabotaged by *them* – the cast, scriptwriters, management – and was striving to rise above it all.' Michael Billington, writing in this paper, was moved to describe him as 'arguably the most Brechtian actor in Britain', though Pirandello would surely have been equally delighted by the act.

His restless intellect (Aristotle and Aquinas were bedtime reading), and a profound conviction that the public could never be satisfied for long with what he was giving them, drew him to explore new forms and even new *métiers*, resulting in extreme vicissitudes in his popularity. Audiences were no longer sure who or what he was; for a while he was convinced that his real destiny was as an actor, a view shared by neither critics nor public.

Peter Cook rescued him when he persuaded him to appear at the Establishment club, which resulted in appearances on *That Was the Week That Was*, and a wholly unexpected new reputation as a satirist. The last few years were a sort of golden summer, in which he was finally reassured of the public's love. 'Can you believe I've been doing the same old rubbish for years?' he cheerfully asked Barbara Windsor during his last tour.

He was not easy to work with, and he seems only rarely to have experienced what most of us would call happiness, except when performing. McCann records Howerd's own (otherwise unsubstantiated) conviction that he was physically and sexually abused by his father, which would certainly be consistent with his eternal sense of self-rejection. The book's extensive transcripts from the act, with every um, yes, ah, liss-en, you see and no missus! in place, instantly evoke his unique comic creation, making one laugh out loud. However unloved Frank Howard may have felt, Frankie Howerd, this book clearly demonstrates, remains for ever ensconced in British hearts, a quintessential part of us, in the presence of whom it remains impossible to be titterless.

*Even more than Frankie Howerd, Mrs Shufflewick played dangerously on
the edge of what was acceptable to a heterosexual audience. I reviewed
Patrick Newley's monograph* The Amazing Mrs Shufflewick *for the*
Guardian *in 2007.*

By the time I started going to the theatre, the music hall had long gone,
except in the wretchedly bastardised form of television's *The Good Old
Days*, absurdly recreating the externals of the halls with an audience in
fancy dress acting and performers ghoulishly attempting to exhume the
great acts of the past. But every now and then someone would attempt to
put together a bill of acts, which, if not technically of the music hall, were
in the spirit of the thing. By amazing luck one evening in the early Seventies I caught one such programme at the Greenwich Theatre, seeing
among others Max Wall, and the then to me totally unknown Mrs Shufflewick. Wall was a great grotesque, a cross between an ape and a concert
pianist, and his comedy was surreally sublime, but Shufflewick was funnier, this tiny little man dragged up into the semblance of a faux-genteel
cockney charlady, sitting at a slight angle to the table with her drink in
front of her, generating and swelling and perfectly controlling laughter
such as I have never heard before or since. The man next to me eventually tipped out of his seat and into the aisle, still roaring.

It was absolute filth, but delivered with the utmost delicacy and a mastery
of *entendres, doubles, triples et quadruples*, that created mayhem in one's
mind. 'Do you like this fur, girls? It cost two hundred pounds. I didn't pay
for it meself; I met two hundred fellas with a pound each,' starts one of
the riffs usefully quoted in Patrick Newley's deeply enjoyable little mem-
oir/profile. 'This is very rare, this fur,' Shuff continues. 'This is known in
the trade as "untouched pussy" – which as you know is unobtainable in
the West End of London at the moment. And I don't think there's much
knocking around here tonight.' That little sequence would last up to five
minutes, the laughter teased out more and more by his comic genius, until
you felt almost literally sick, throat aching from the delirium he provoked.
It wasn't just the timing. Shufflewick was one of those comic creations that
are so complete that they seem always to have existed, to have sprung from
that timeless place from which all deep comedy springs.

In what he would certainly not have thought of as real life, the man who
was Shufflewick was a foundling dumped on the steps of Trinity College

Hospital in Greenwich, and adopted by a well-off couple from Southend called Coster, whose name he took. He had no particular ambition or talent, until, drafted into the RAF at the age of eighteen, young Rex Coster joined the famous Gang Show (at the same time as Tony Hancock) and proved an immediate hit. Where he learned his skills, as comic and singer, we are left to guess. Rex felt he had arrived in heaven, but not especially because of the job. 'This is marvellous, this life,' he said to himself, according to an interview, 'getting pissed all the time and not having to turn up for work in the morning.' Alcohol was already mother's milk to him, so much so that when he had to change his name because of the success of the singer Sam Costa, he chose to rechristen himself after a famous brand of whiskey. After the war, he was discovered by the Bryan Michie *Happy Hour Show* which toured Granada Cinemas (part of the vanished world of post-war show business lovingly described by Newley) and swiftly prospered. He invented Shufflewick on the spur of the moment for BBC radio, whose moral guardians had rejected his vicar sketch the moment they heard its first line ('Ah good evening to you my flock, and now you can flock off.') Mrs Shufflewick's much greater lewdness was less explicit, and she became a star, the interesting distinction of being radio's first drag artist, or at any rate the first to drag up for the microphones.

On the back of his radiophonic fame, he was hired by the Windmill for three years, at their top whack of £50 a week, doing six shows a day, on the hour every hour, alongside Hancock, Sellers, and Secombe. The marvellous sexual ambiguity of drag allowed for extraordinarily risqué material and the supposedly undeviatingly heterosexual audience of that establishment were hugely amused. 'I was standing at the bar, minding my own business, and all of a sudden the door opened and this sailor walked in. I think he must have been in the Navy because he kissed me on both cheeks. And I was doing me shoelaces up at the time.' Perhaps some of the audience literally failed to realise that the dainty little raconteuse with a mind like a sewer who was so royally entertaining them was actually a man: Shufflewick was always billed without reference to Rex. In the routines, sex is never far away but some of them verge on the surreal. 'Last night – I must tell you this – I was sitting up in bed at about half past seven, mending a puncture. I had a blow-out. I was sticking this patch on when all of a sudden I had it coming on again. You know, one of me hot flushes. Do you get them? Ooh I do. I have to blow down my blouse on the buses.'

Surprisingly, in the mid-1950s Shufflewick met with equal success on television, without significantly varying his repertoire. He triumphed both in the clubs and in big variety theatres; but by the mid-Sixties changing tastes and increasingly erratic professional habits brought him to the point where he was often performing for a bottle of whiskey, which he would anyway consume during the course of the show. It was then that the author, only twenty-five and with scarcely any experience in management, took him on and masterminded a revival which started with Shuff's appearance on one of Dorothy Squires's self-financed comeback nights at the Palladium. It was Rex's night as much as hers, and from then on he earned a decent living, as a cult figure in gay clubs and from the sort of music-hall nights I saw in Greenwich, with names like *Pure Corn*.

Newley, who had the heroic task of pouring him out of dressing rooms and on to the stage, writes affectionately of what must have been a nerve-racking relationship. He gives a vivid if depressing picture of Rex's personal life – cottaging and bar pick-ups as well as a curious intense long-term partnership (apparently non-sexual, but highly volatile) with a labourer – and offers glimpses of his domestic life in a miserable tip of a flat in Kentish Town. As Newley says, he was as far from the popular idea of a drag queen as could be imagined. He read the *Mirror* and the *Sporting Life*, ate meals in greasy spoons, liked betting on horses and watching *Carry On* films, smoked Woodbines, wore a flat cap and bought his clothes in jumble sales. Part of his genius was precisely because of his rootedness in ordinary life, the world of pubs and buses and low-grade lust and unreliable bodily functions, to which he brought a fantasy which crept up on you slowly but ended up in the wildest realms of zaniness. He was like Ken Dodd in that, but more real: Dodd is a fool, a jester. Gladys Shufflewick (to give her her full name) was just an old biddy in the snug, 'broad-minded to the point of obscenity', to be sure, but entirely recognisable.

Shuff finally shuffed off in 1983 on the way to the Theatre Royal Stratford East where she was due to top the bill, felled by the same booze which had been the real enduring love of her life. 'I can't find out what's wrong with you,' the doctor said. 'I think it must be the drink.' 'Never mind, doctor, I'll come back when you're sober.' Shuff never actually played the halls, but that gag alone is quintessential music hall. Patrick Newley has done us all a great favour by producing this admirably succinct memoir, with its rare photographs, outrageous anecdotes, transcribed routines and perceptive affection. One of the greatest comic geniuses of the last century comes alive all over again.

Clowns, comedy and music hall coincide in Waiting for Godot, *in which I played Pozzo for Sean Mathias, with Ronald Pickup as Lucky, and Ian McKellen and Patrick Stewart as Gogo and Didi, through the first half of 2009. Three years before, I had written in the* Guardian *about the play, which I had known since schooldays.*

Now that its influence has begun to wane, and it ceases to remind us of its imitations, we can again see the most influential play of the second half of the twentieth century for what it is. *Waiting for Godot* has lost none of its power to astonish and to move, but it no longer seems self-consciously experimental or obscure. With unerring economy and surgical precision, the play puts the human animal on stage in all his naked loneliness. Like the absolute masterpiece it is, it seems to speak directly to us, to our lives, to our situation, while at the same time appearing to belong to a distant, perhaps a non-existent, past. In his subsequent plays, Beckett created a number of ineradicable images of the human condition, but it is his first performed play, which had its British premiere fifty years ago this year, which has joined the select stock of myths by which we understand ourselves.

That Samuel Beckett should have chosen to write a play at all is something of a mystery. 'You ask me for my ideas on *Waiting for Godot* and my ideas on the theatre,' he wrote to Michel Polac on *Godot*'s publication a year before it was produced. 'I have no ideas on the theatre. I know nothing about it. I never go. That's reasonable. What is rather less so,' he added, 'is… to write a play, and then to have no ideas on that either.' Despite a youthful fondness for the art theatre in his native Dublin, and for the variety theatre anywhere, he was no buff, and his writing up to this point, inspired by the example of his literary masters, James Joyce and Marcel Proust, had consisted of fiercely difficult novels, poems and short stories. True, in 1930, he had written *Whoroscope*, a verse monologue in the voice of René Descartes, but it was never intended for performance. After 1940, his work had undergone a radical change. If he was to write about

MY LIFE IN PIECES

impotence and ignorance, which he now conceived to be the essential experience of human life, he must, he said, abandon rhetoric and virtuosity. The English language having a natural propensity for both of these, he abandoned it, henceforward writing in clean and analytical French, swiftly writing three great novels, *Molloy*, *Malone Dies* and *The Unnameable* in his adopted language, each of them in the form of a soliloquy; none of them knew any immediate success, and indeed, it was almost impossible to find publishers for them. His decision to write for the theatre was, the Beckett scholar Lawrence Graver acutely noted, a part of this stripping away: in doing so, he eliminates the voice of the narrator.

It seems that it was also partially the lure of immediate returns, however modest, from the box office that suggested to the impoverished Beckett that he might write plays. His first was *Eleuthéria*, a clumsy and overambitious experiment full of prefigurings of later Beckett – the hero is called Krap – which he immediately followed with *Godot*, in which his touch is infallible. The two plays were touted around unsuccessfully until Beckett's friend Suzanne Deschevaux-Dumesnil took them to a progressive actor-director, Artaud's old associate Roger Blin, who plumped for *Godot* because it had only five actors and one tree. Characteristically, Beckett was delighted to find that Blin's current production was playing to half-empty houses, which he took to be a guarantee of integrity. It took two years for Blin to raise the money and get a theatre; finally, when the play opened in January 1953, four years after it was written, at the nearly defunct Théâtre de Babylone in Montparnasse, it was greeted with a mixture of critical bewilderment, some active audience hostility, partisan enthusiasm from highly influential quarters (Jean Anouilh, the most successful French dramatist of the day, called it the most important theatrical premiere in forty years), and straightforward delight from the paying audience, who attended the show in ever-growing numbers. It was word of mouth that swung it.

This curious paradox – the play's ability to frustrate intellectual criticism with its apparent elusiveness while gripping with a vice-like hold those who neither know nor particularly want to know what the play *means* – was repeated in London and on Broadway. It is a remarkable fact that both in America and in England, commercial managers were keen to do the play; the problem here was that none of the great actors approached would commit to it. Sir Ralph Richardson was among them; he reproached himself for the rest of his life for turning down 'the greatest play of my generation'. Instead, the young Peter Hall cannily picked the play up, doing it at his Arts Theatre with a young and unstarry cast. The overnight reviews were dismissive, whereupon the legendary play agent Peggy Ramsay, using the guerrilla tactics for which she was famous, persuaded Hall to send a copy of Beckett's novel *Watt* to Harold Hobson, the powerful critic of the *Sunday Times*, before he wrote his review: the result was a panegyric, business built and eventually a successful West End transfer ensued.

Of course, the play did not appeal to everyone: Peter Bull, the first English Pozzo, recollected a matinee at which, during one of his longer speeches, an elderly lady penetratingly observed to her companion in the fairly wide-open spaces of the stalls, 'I wish the fat one would go.' But by instinctive genius, the tyro playwright had produced a work of absolute originality which was so sure-footed in its theatrical sense that despite defying all contemporary expectations, it communicated effortlessly with audiences, distilling its truth with the simplicity and profundity of a great poet who was also a sublime humorist. Beckett's informed love of the great vaudevillians – especially Laurel and Hardy and Chaplin – enabled him to produce a work which stirs the heart of anyone who has been moved to laughter or tears by clowns, who, like Vladimir and Estragon, oscillate between the dread of being alone and the horror of dependency. Eric Bentley remarked of the first New York production that 'highbrow writers have been enthusiastic about clowns and vaudeville for decades, but this impresses me as the first time that anything has successfully been done about the matter.' Of course, it helps if the actors playing Vladimir and Estragon are great clowns or vaudevillians themselves. Bentley saw Bert Lahr – the Cowardly Lion from *The Wizard of Oz* – in the role of Estragon, 'the perfect execution,' he said, 'by a lowbrow actor of a highbrow writer's intentions'; twenty years later, in Manchester and London, Max Wall performed the same service in the role of Vladimir. Such casting is a bonus but by no means essential: the play's opening image, of a tramp/clown in his bowler hat, tugging at his boots, with a solitary tree behind him, shortly joined by his identically attired comrade, provokes the sort of deeply stirring emotion that the first sight of a great clown produces. These men – like all the great theatre images: Mother Courage with her cart, blind Gloucester, Falstaff wrapped around Doll Tearsheet – come from our dreams, from deep in our unconscious memories. We are them; they are us.

There is indeed a good case for thinking of the play as a dream play in its repetitions, its circularity, its sudden absurdities, its arbitrariness, its nagging pursuit of unanswerable questions. Estragon can barely keep awake: and sleep is a blessed state because the sleeper is oblivious of life's terrible reality: 'He is sleeping. He knows nothing. Let him sleep on.' The characters themselves seem to shift shape oneirically: out of the blue, Vladimir becomes an eloquent philosopher, quoting Latin tags; Estragon announces that 'We are not caryatids'; for no known reason Pozzo is suddenly blind, Lucky suddenly dumb. An uneasy sense of unreality pervades everything: 'You're sure you saw me?' Vladimir asks the boy. 'You won't come back tomorrow and say you never saw me?' Just as in Strindberg's *Dream Play*, where Agnes's repeated cries of 'Poor, suffering mankind!' pierce the action, Didi and Gogo constantly cry out, apropos of nothing in particular, 'What'll we do! What'll we do!'

But perhaps the dream is the dream of theatre. Beckett's play is as conscious of its own theatricality as any by Brecht, by Pirandello, or – the comparison is inevitable and apt – Shakespeare. Theatrical imagery pervades the play. Vladimir, shocked at Pozzo's treatment of Lucky, accuses him of chucking him away 'like a – like a banana skin', to be stepped on, no doubt; when Pozzo delivers one of his lectures, he sprays his throat like an opera singer or a boulevard star; Vladimir and Estragon play-act to fill the void, doing old routines with hats; Vladimir takes on the role of Lucky, putting on his hat and walking up and down like a mannequin; when Estragon is terrified of being beaten up, Vladimir pushes him towards the auditorium: 'There! Not a soul in sight! Off you go.' Estragon recoils in horror, dreading the idea of becoming part of the audience, a fate worse than death. Even the twilight itself is, according to Vladimir, 'nearing the end of its repertory'. Instantly, Beckett, in his first performed play, understood every possibility of the theatre as metaphor. Slyly self-referential, he gives his tramps an exchange in which they say 'Charming evening we're having.' 'Unforgettable.' 'And it's not over.' 'Apparently not.' 'It's only beginning.' 'It's awful.'

His characters are as much of a mystery to Beckett as they are to us; that gives them a great part of their fascination. They are archetypes, who have emerged, ancient and novel, from tradition. No doubt, as James Knowlson perceptively observes in *Damned to Fame*, Beckett coloured their situation with his own wartime experience of living in the sticks, in Roussillon, waiting, waiting for the war to end before life could begin again. No doubt Pozzo has qualities of the concentration-camp *capo*. But the characters' existence is beyond history, beyond logic. 'I know no more about this play than anyone who just reads it attentively,' Beckett wrote. 'I don't know what spirit I wrote it in. I know no more about the characters than what they say, what they do and what happens to them… everything I have been able to learn, I have shown. It's not a great deal. But it's enough for me, quite enough. I'd go so far as to say that I would have been content with less… Estragon, Vladimir, Pozzo, Lucky, I have only been able to know them a little, from far off, out of a need to understand them. They owe you some explanations, perhaps. Let them unravel. Without me. Them and me, we're quits.'

Although I stand by everything I wrote about the play then, the experience of actually doing it proved, as always, completely unpredictable – an unimaginably difficult journey into the heart of this richest and most disturbing of plays. Playing Pozzo ranks as one of the most perfectly satisfying experiences of my career and one of the most intense rehearsal periods – to say nothing of the piquancy, for me, of the fact that I had sold tickets for each of my fellow actors; first, Ronnie Pickup at the National, then Ian McKellen at the Mermaid Theatre and finally Patrick Stewart at the Aldwych; I had known Sean Mathias since he was mere lad. I turned sixty, Ian seventy, during the production; Ronnie and Patrick were both about sixty-nine. We must have had the highest average age, per capita, of any West End cast, and for once were the approximate ages of the characters, which made a profound difference to the event. Rehearsals were incredibly hard for all of us, but I have never known a rehearsal room in which the actors' egos were less prominent. We got on with it, like war-scarred veterans. The reward was extraordinary, first on the tour, then in the West End, where people queued for the front-row seats, which were held back, from three in the morning. Sometimes they were so tired when they got to their seats that they fell asleep. But they were the only ones sleeping. I wrote this programme note for the 2010 revival of the production in which Pozzo was played by Matthew Kelly and Vladimir by Roger Rees. I called it On the Road with Vladimir and Estragon.

I have known *Waiting for Godot* quite well since I was sixteen; I have seen productions of it all over the world, in several languages. A few years ago, when Peter Hall's production of *Waiting for Godot* came to London, I was asked by the *Guardian* newspaper to write a piece about it, and in preparation for the piece, I reread the play and browsed through a biography or two and some critical studies. So you might have thought that I was pretty well prepared when Ian McKellen, Patrick Stewart, Ronnie Pickup, Sean Mathias and I assembled to rehearse the play.

In fact, as we read it, I realised that I had never understood the play at all. Not in the sense of failing to grasp it intellectually: contrary to its reputation, it is fairly transparent from that point of view. Nor was the form of the play so very difficult. Partly under its influence, plays have become far more exploratory both in terms of language and of technique. No, what I had absolutely failed to realise until I sat down and read it with my fellow actors was the scope of the action: the scale of the journeys made by each of the characters and the epic, even heroic energy that was involved in doing it. I'd written in the *Guardian* that 'like the absolute masterpiece it is, it seems to speak directly to us, to our lives, to our situation, while at the same time appearing to belong to a distant, perhaps a non-existent, past.' Yes, indeed, perfectly true, Professor, but actually doing it, staking out that path, working through all the stages along it, following every twist and turn, ending up in the extraordinary place to which Beckett takes the characters, was quite another matter. After the first read-through, I turned to one of the producers, Arnold Crook, and said 'I haven't the faintest idea how to do this.' Again, it wasn't that the character was hard to recognise or that his emotions were obscure: it was a question of how one would rise to them, how one would make them real and overwhelming – of whether I could, as the old actors used to say, 'come near it'.

I have never been more terrified of any play. I am aware that this sounds like luvvie-speak, but it is terrifying to contemplate one's own inability to do justice to a part. And Beckett, like the Greek tragic dramatists, offers no carefully graded development, no psychological entrée into the emotions depicted: you simply have to open yourself up to them and let them course through you; you have to become their conduit. And the way to do this, we quickly discovered, is by absolutely mastering the text and then letting it do its work. This is how it is with musicians; and Beckett is as much a composer as he is a dramatist. In the first weeks, we talked through every line, every phrase of the play. But it was when we stood up and began to find the play's music that it started to seize our souls. And this meant listening with extraordinary intensity, to ourselves and to each other. Increasingly, we were reminded of Beckett's famous reply to an actor who had asked him, 'What does this line mean?' 'What does it say?' he had answered. Not 'What is it about?' – 'What does it say?' And the more we attended to what the characters actually said, the more astonishing the play became. Again and again Sean would say: 'I think there's more to that speech. Keep digging in.'

Once we hit the road, we were hugely relieved to discover that the audiences that came to the play in their coachloads were quite undaunted by *Godot*'s fearsome reputation. They were immediately intrigued by these two dropouts: they knew exactly what they were saying, their anxieties and their meagre hopes; they enjoyed their jokes and their domestic frustrations; and then they were horribly disturbed by the sudden eruption on to the stage of a blustering man brandishing a whip, with another, silent man at the end of a rope. The audience, as audiences always do, taught us the story. The play has been haunted by a remark by one of the play's first admirers: 'In *Waiting for Godot*, nothing happens, twice.' But the audience's response told us that, on the contrary, in *Waiting for Godot*, Pozzo and Lucky happen, twice, and each of their appearances has a shattering effect on the other two characters. On the road, the response to the play was astonishing. I believe it is true to say that we never consciously tried to make the play funny, but the more we played what the lines said, the louder and louder the laughter rang round all those great regional theatres, and the deeper and deeper the awe with which the terrible truths Beckett exposes was received. He once said: 'I know no more about the characters than what they say, what they do and what happens to them.' Nor did we. But the audience got it, loud and clear.

It was not until the third week of the tour of Godot *that I began to feel wholly on top of the physical demands of Pozzo: the props, the rope, the coat, the eating. These had to be absolutely precise. Until they were, there could be no movement forward. Once they were, and the text was deeply rooted in my brain, it became possible to try to discover what was really there. Following Beckett's advice, I simply looked at what the characters said. Pozzo's account of himself is astonishing – he speaks of having* slaves, of taking Lucky to the market to sell him; especially surprisingly, he speaks of Lucky having taught him all he knows, of having been his tutor ('knook'). He hints at some terrible catastrophe that reduced Lucky to the subhuman creature that he is. Ronnie Pickup and I began to build a deep, complex, murky relationship. It was as if Pozzo and Lucky were a married couple: the second married couple in the play, because Didi and Gogo are similarly spliced. But the more we played the play, the more clearly it seemed to me that what happens in the play is that Everyman and his twin brother pool their anxieties, and then human history erupts on stage: a man enslaved by another man. This is the essence of Empire. I reread Heart of Darkness: Pozzo seems to share, as well as Kurtz's crazed colonial savagery, his sense of primal horror. Idi Amin came into my mind, a tyrant who, like Pozzo, desperately needed an audience, wanted to bask in approval; a man who had waded through blood. Pozzo's manic-depressive descents into abject melancholy had to be real, almost life-threatening. And yet, from somewhere he always finds the impulse to continue. 'On, on!' is his great cry. I listened to music of epic breadth: as I walked around the streets I sang – to the alarm of passers-by – the great brass chorale of the last movement of Sibelius's Fifth Symphony at the top of my voice, to expand my instrument; and then I remembered the terrible third movement of Shostakovich's Eighth Symphony, which seemed to me precisely to describe Lucky and Pozzo's journey across the blasted landscape, the strings' savagely ticking ostinato pierced by shrieks of pain from the woodwind. Every time I ever did the show, I listened to this music, had it running in my head as I stepped on stage. When Pozzo comes back in the second act, blind and broken, both physically and vocally, I wanted to show his frailty, certainly, but behind that his indomitability. I replaced his stentorian basso profundo with the querulous but penetrating and determined voice of my old friend Frith Banbury, who had just died at the age of ninety-six. 'What do you do when you fall over far from help?' asks Vladimir. 'We wait until we can get up,' says Pozzo, impatiently, 'and then we go on. On!' Beckett demands a huge impersonality, truly epic acting. Despite my dread and uncertainty, I felt licensed to go down this path by Beckett's own choice of actor for the part: when asked by Roger Blin who in an ideal world he would like for the roles, he said, 'For Vladimir, Buster Keaton, for Gogo, Chaplin, and for Pozzo – Charles Laughton.'

I felt that I had really done something with Pozzo, that it was, as Laughton would say, 'a creation'. I like to think that Michael Chekhov might have *approved of it; it sits with half a dozen other performances – Arturo Ui, Mozart, Molina, Falstaff, Verlaine, Lord Foppington – by which I would ask to be judged at the theatrical pearly gates.*

While the revival of Godot *was playing at the Theatre Royal Haymarket, I was acting at the Riverside Studios in Hammersmith in* Dr Marigold *and* Mr Chops, *two monologues by Dickens. He performed them as public readings, in his habitual tails at the lectern, but spoken in the first person, in character and in costume, they amount to monodramas. At last I had found the Dickens plays he had neglected to write, so much more satisfactory, as Michael Billington pointed out in the* Guardian, *than 'cut-and-paste jobs adapted from the novels'. Written in the last decade of his life, at the very height of his powers, they have the full span of Dickens at his most extended.* Dr Marigold, *in particular, in its tumultuous narrative flow, swooping in and out of sentiment and comedy with breathtaking speed, exemplifying the technique he called 'streaky bacon', affected audiences in Hammersmith as much as it had affected the Victorians, who loved it second only to* A Christmas Carol. *I wrote a piece for the programme about one of Dickens's great inspirations: I called it* He do the police in different voices *(the original title of* The Waste Land, *as it happens).*

As a young man, Dickens's appetite for theatre-going was insatiable. He claimed that for a three-year period during his young manhood, he went to the theatre every single night. His taste was catholic, embracing variety, melodrama, Shakespeare and sentimental comedy. But his favourite by far was Charles Mathews, an extraordinarily original performer who pioneered a form of theatre he called *monodramatics* – one-man pieces in which he played a dozen or more characters. The first of these pieces he called *At Home*; all his subsequent plays were known generically as At Homes. They were in two halves, in the first of which Mathews appeared as himself, narrating a journey, in which he described and increasingly became the characters he encountered. The second half – a straightforward farce made unusual by the fact that he played all the characters – was dubbed by Mathews (ever the enthusiastic neologist), a *monopolylogue*. They were no mere show-off pieces. Leigh Hunt observed that 'for the richness and variety of his humour,' they were 'as good as half a dozen plays distilled'.

As the characters in the monopolylogue came and went they changed costume, taking the performance to a high pitch of virtuosity, for which he must have combined the transvestite skills of Arturo Brachetti with the ear of Mike Yarwood. In *Youthful Days*, a big hit of the 1830s, he played, in rapid succession, a servant, a dandy, a French organist, a knight (Sir Shiveraine Scrivener), Monsieur Zephyr, a stout Welshman (ap Llewellyn-ap Lloyd), a skinny snooker player (Mark Moomin), and, finally, Moomin's wife Amelrose. It could so easily have been a generalised blur of stereotypes, but the quality his contemporaries above all admired in Mathews was his verisimilitude. He departed entirely from the set types of comedy, thereby, according to E. B. Watson, introducing 'what later would have been called "character acting"'. He toured America, where he is credited with introducing demotic language into local playwriting: a piece he wrote specially for the tour, *The African-American*, in which he performed, in blackface and in dialect, a version of 'Possum Up a Gum Tree', had a surprisingly liberating effect on contemporary American drama. He died at fifty-nine, in 1835.

This is the extraordinary performer Dickens so admired; indeed, he had memorised a chunk of one of the monopolylogues to perform at the audition for the Covent Garden Theatre he had so fatefully to cancel because of the flu. But Mathews's influence stayed with him, and was recognised as such; indeed, when *The Pickwick Papers* appeared, he was roundly accused of plagiarising the character of Jingle from Mathews (by then dead), which is as may be. But his art is felt throughout Dickens's novels in the constant sense of vocal virtuosity, of projected performance. Like Sloppy in *Our Mutual Friend*, and like Mathews before him, Dickens – the author as actor – did the police in different voices.

Even in his models, Dickens is unexpected. In some unfathomable way, I feel deeply connected to him; in 2012, the year of his bicentenary, I'll be playing the character in all of Dickens that I love most: Mr Pickwick. To embody that bonhomie, that profound optimism, that eternally springing hope that Dickens placed at the centre of his first novel, trying to convince himself against all the evidence of his early experience that the world is essentially benevolent, fills me with joy. As the Inimitable puts it, inimitably: 'And in the midst of all this, stood Mr Pickwick. Let us leave our old friend in one of those moments of unmixed happiness, of which, if we seek them, there are ever some, to cheer our transitory existence here. There are dark shadows on the earth, but its lights are stronger in the contrast. Some men, like bats or owls, have better eyes for the darkness than for the light; we, who have no such optical powers, are better pleased to take our last parting look at our visionary companions, when the brief sunshine of the world is blazing full upon them.'

*

One of the most pleasing things that has ever happened to me is the superb translation into French of my first book by Gisèle Joly, a French actress who learned English in order to perform the task, and who furnished the new edition with a comprehensive glossary of all the people mentioned in the book, which thus stands as a sort of monument to all my colleagues and partners in crime over the thirty-five years of my life in the theatre.

Two years ago, some actors from the Comédie Française read out passages from the translation at the Maison de Molière itself, to a large audience of actors, who responded with recognition and hilarity. That the book I wrote twenty-five years ago could reach this entirely new audience, and that that audience felt that what I had written was both true and funny, was deeply satisfying. I end the present book with these words I wrote for the French edition.

When I wrote *Being an Actor*, my first book, hoping to paint a truthful portrait of life in the theatre I used autobiographical form, because I believed that only by giving a precise account of my own journey through the theatre, blow by blow, could I convey anything worth telling about my life as an actor and the lives of my fellow actors. This was a gamble. Not all actors' lives have been like mine, and when I remarked at the beginning of the book that I hoped actors would say, '*That's* what being an actor is like,' I knew that there was a very good chance that they might say, 'Oh no it isn't.' As it happens, to my infinite gratification, it seems that despite my really rather brief experience then of the theatre and acting – I wrote the book when I had been professionally employed for only nine years – I had told a truth that many of my fellow thespians in the British theatre were able to recognise. I never expected that it could speak to actors from other countries and other traditions. Again, I was most happily surprised. A successful American edition followed quite soon after the book's appearance in Britain, and then, astoundingly, the first half of the book was translated into Russian; a few years ago an intrepid translator even rendered it into Slovenian (*Biti Igralec*). Again, the results were warmly received. Actors in these different countries seemed to feel that I had hit the nail on the head in two main areas: the experience of actually performing, and the things that lead one to become an actor. And I have begun to feel that, despite the wildly dissimilar structures and even aspirations of different theatrical cultures, there are some universal elements that we can all recognise.

I am especially delighted that this book is finally being translated into French. My grandmother was French – her father, an English teacher in Lyon, was said, according to family myth, to have taught Sarah Bernhardt the part of Hamlet – and I have always been profoundly engaged by French culture. French is the only foreign language I speak and I love the music of it, its shapes, its constraints, its passionate precision, its analytical aptitude, its innate intelligence. I have translated four plays from the French (Cocteau's *La Machine Infernale*, my stage version of Prévert's *Les Enfants du Paradis*, Milan Kundera's *Jacques et Son Maître* – a play originally written in French, not Czech – and *La Crampe des Écrivains*, a little squib by the composer Camille Saint-Saëns), and my hope has been to try to convey something of their essential Frenchness – even in the Kundera, which is after all inspired by Diderot. There are certain attributes of French acting, too, that I have longed to see on the British stage, above all what might be called the sexiness of the intellect, that capacity possessed by some actors – Pierre Brasseur, for example – to surrender no part of their brains when playing lovers (or actors). In my youth, I was lucky enough to see many great French actors of different kinds on stage – Marie Bell, Madeleine Renaud, Edwige Feuillère, Jean-Louis Barrault, Jacques Charon, Robert Hirsch – and, different as they were, all of them were characterised by this keenness of wit, this penetrating power of thought. The great companies I was able to see, like the Compagnie Barrault-Renaud, Planchon's TNP, Mnouchkine's Théâtre du Soleil and the Comédie Française at various times over the last forty years, were also wonderfully nimble and dashing in their use of language. Nowadays I am more likely to see French actors on film, and they are among my favourite. (I have even acted in a French film, in French: *Le Passager Clandestin*, one of Simenon's *outre-mer* stories.) My training was deeply influenced by Michel Saint-Denis (one of the founder members of the Royal Shakespeare Company, as it happens, and Patron of my drama school) and through him by his master, Copeau. Many of the best and most provocative books about acting, too, have been French, characteristically emphasising the philosophical and the exploratory: from Diderot's *Paradoxe* to Coquelin's *L'Art et le Comédien* (the introduction to the English edition by Sir Henry Irving, no less), the autobiography of the divine Sarah, books of reflection by the great trinity of Antoine, Copeau and Jouvet, Barrault's several volumes and Vilar's single masterpiece, to say nothing of the visionary manifestos of the fiery angel, Artaud, and Saint-Denis' seminal work, *Theatre: the Rediscovery of Style*, echoes from which will be found in the preceding pages. In fact, it is impossible to think of the theatre without thinking about the contribution of the French.

I offer my book to the French public, and perhaps especially to the French profession, with all due modesty. It offers no system, whether analytical or prescriptive: it is a book of observation, mostly, I confess, self-observation. It came from an almost anthropological fascination with the world I found myself in, and with the particular and unique experiences I underwent while in it. It is predicated on a conviction that acting and the theatre are central to the human situation and illuminate a great deal more than themselves. Finally, it is, despite occasional outbursts of melancholy and even rage, an optimistic book, and an idealistic one. The theatre has the power of transforming lives, sometimes on a simple level, sometimes profoundly. It has the capacity to restore us to ourselves, to waken the part of ourselves that has gone to sleep, to throw off life's oppressions. This is a noble calling. One of the most touching expressions of this is to be found in Guitry's charming play *Deburau*. The great mime is pining for love of Marguérite Gautier, to the extent that a doctor is summoned: he seems to be dying. A medical examination reveals nothing untoward, so the doctor, who has not been told the name of his patient, says 'I prescribe a visit to the theatre. Why don't you go and see Deburau? He can banish the deepest depression.' (Deburau of course leaps out of bed and rushes down to the theatre to resume his career, but it is too late: he is booed, and hands his name over to his son, who triumphs. The scene in which the old man instructs his son in what might be called the etiquette of acting will bring a tear to the eye of anyone who loves this profession.)

A crucial element in what led me to write *Being an Actor* in the first place was to remind actors that they were not the slaves of either directors or authors or of The System, but autonomous creative artists who had control over their destinies, and who had grave responsibilities towards their audiences. I believe that they should occupy a central part in determining the functioning of the organisations to which they belong. For various historical reasons, in England, the phrase actor-manager has become a term of derision. But in the land of Jouvet, of Antoine, of Planchon, the idea expressed in the manifesto at the end of *Being an Actor*, which caused such a scandal on its first publication, that actors might resume control of their art, will scarcely provoke anything other than an unsurprised nod.

Envoi

I am almost embarrassed to have written so much about acting, the theatre and film: this book contains only a fraction of the hundreds of thousands of words that have poured out of me over the past thirty years. If I sometimes seem combative, it is largely because there is, as I say elsewhere more than once, no broad debate about these matters, no sense of differing passionate views. The consensus prevails. As I did when I wrote Being an Actor, *I feel that more, so much more, can be asked of actors and of acting. Occasionally an actor emerges who is in himself so original, whose choices are so unexpected that, like Charles Laughton eighty years ago, he shakes up the whole concept of what an actor can do. In the present time, Mark Rylance is such an actor. But what would be thrilling to me would be if whole companies were inspired by their own particular vision of acting. In* Being an Actor *I made a comparison with orchestras: why could acting companies not be self-governing, as orchestras were, hiring their own directors just as the musicians hired their conductors? But there is a more melancholy orchestral comparison to be made now: with every passing year, orchestral standards get higher and higher, but it becomes harder and harder to distinguish these orchestras from each other, except in terms of corporate excellence. This multinationalism has affected singers too: it is so very much harder now to recognise a singer by individual timbre. Similarly actors, especially in the theatre, seem all to be singing from the same hymn sheet. Once, the National Theatre and the Royal Shakespeare Company stood for very different things: now their work – of undisputed excellence – is essentially indistinguishable. Once, the Royal Court pioneered a style of acting that served a new generation of authors, but also served us to make us see the classical theatre afresh, as, in radically difficult form, did Joan Littlewood. Now it, too, has adopted the lingua franca of acting.*

My plea is only the old Maoist prescription: let a hundred flowers blossom. After the preceding four hundred pages, it is pointless to deny that I am a romantic about the theatre, which has been the centre of my creative life for forty years. My view is a rather Chestertonian one, dreaming of guilds of actors, each fiercely loyal to each other and passionately convinced of the rightness of their own approach, engaging the public with their different wares. Most people, probably most actors and directors and audiences, are just grateful for good work, and good work is undoubtedly being done. But one could say about performances exactly what Orson Welles used to say about movies: 'what's the point of making a film unless you make a great one?'

*

While we were playing Waiting for Godot, *it fell to me to arrange the memorial service for Paul Scofield, who had died a year before. As I have said, his death hit me hard, not because of our personal relationship, but because of what he represented. What I had said in the* Guardian *about the end of an epoch was cause for great reflection. By the time of the memorial service, I was sixty, and in some ways felt myself to be part of a vanishing world.*

The service took place in St Margaret's Chapel in Westminster Abbey before a congregation packed with his colleagues stretching back over sixty years. I believe we did him honour. The choir sang Vaughan Williams; Eileen Atkins, who acted with him in his last public performance, spoke the end of the last of Eliot's Four Quartets:

> *Quick now, here, now, always –*
> *A condition of complete simplicity*
> *(Costing not less than everything)*
> *And all shall be well and*
> *All manner of thing shall be well*
> *When the tongues of flame are in-folded*
> *Into the crowned knot of fire*
> *And the fire and the rose are one.*

Ian McKellen spoke the Lesson (from St John: 'In the beginning was the Word, and the Word was with God, and the Word was God.'). Scofield's widow Joy Parker read Hardy's 'Afterwards': 'He was one who had an eye for such mysteries'; his son Martin read his father's favourite speech from Shakespeare, Henry VI's lament:

> O God! methinks it were a happy life,
> To be no better than a homely swain;
> To sit upon a hill, as I do now,
> To carve out dials quaintly, point by point,
> Thereby to see the minutes how they run...
> Ah, what a life were this! how sweet! how lovely!

Seamus Heaney read Beowulf's funeral – 'They extolled his heroic nature and exploits and gave thanks for his greatness' – from his own translation of the great poem, and at the very end, before we filed out, Paul's matchless voice, Prospero renouncing his art, echoed round the chapel:

> Ye elves of hills, brooks, standing lakes, and groves,
> And ye that on the sands with printless foot
> Do chase the ebbing Neptune, and do fly him
> When he comes back; you demi-puppets that
> By moonshine do the green sour ringlets make,
> Whereof the ewe not bites; and you whose pastime
> Is to make midnight mushrooms, that rejoice
> To hear the solemn curfew; by whose aid –
> Weak masters though ye be – I have bedimmed
> The noontide sun, call'd forth the mutinous winds
> And 'twixt the green sea and the azur'd vault
> Set roaring war; to the dread rattling thunder
> Have I given fire, and rifted Jove's stout oak
> With his own bolt; the strong-bas'd promontory
> Have I made shake, and by the spurs pluck'd up
> The pine and cedar; graves at my command
> Have wak'd their sleepers, op'd, and let 'em forth
> By my so potent art. But this rough magic
> I here abjure, and when I have requir'd
> Some heavenly music, which even now I do,
> To work mine end upon their senses that
> This airy charm is for, I'll break my staff,
> Bury it certain fathoms in the earth
> And deeper than did ever plummet sound
> I'll drown my book.

I gave the Address. I suppose it sums up a great deal of what I've been saying in this book.

Greatness – and from almost the very beginning, there was no question that Paul Scofield, for whose life and work we are giving thanks today, was touched with greatness – takes many forms. In the middle years of the twentieth century, there was in the British theatre an unprecedented outcrop of great actors: the roll call is astounding: Thorndike, Evans, Richardson, Gielgud, Olivier, Ashcroft, Wolfit, Redgrave, Guinness, all born within a few years of each other, each radically different from the other. The theatre revolved around these great figures: this was the golden age, not of directing or writing, but of acting. The actors were themselves managers and directors; the theatre was in their hands. Their fame made them public figures, 'The glass of fashion, and the mould of form / The observ'd of all observers.'

After the war, everything changed, not immediately, of course, but inexorably. And in the theatre, this meant that in the attempt to build the theatre anew, producers, directors and writers now increasingly became the central figures in the theatre. The great actors were still in their prime, and had great work still to do, but they were less and less leaders, more and more part of the team. Into this brave new world, the young Paul Scofield emerged. He was, in many ways, an actor for the new times. He was without managerial ambition, he had no desire to direct, he was utterly uninterested in the social position that fame conferred. What interested him was acting, and only acting. Discovering at an early age, as so many actors before him have done, that his scholastic gifts were meagre – a discovery that may have been an uncomfortable one, given that his father was the headmaster of the school he attended – he fell with inexpressible relief on acting, for which his gift was instantly apparent. Scofield was not in the least a boastful man, and not given to hyperbole, so we may believe him when he says that his thirteen-year-old Juliet was 'a sensation'. Other sensations of a similar kind followed, and as soon as he possibly could, he left school to train at various modest establishments purporting to inculcate the dramatic arts, where he learned, he said, not so much technique as an understanding of his instrument.

From a physical point of view, the young actor had quite exceptional advantages: he was tall and commanding, his face – uncommonly handsome, but in a highly individual way, mingling sensuality with severity, the eyes capable of great warmth and great coldness – was powerfully expressive. As for his voice, it was simply phenomenal, with more stops than any organ, from piping treble to full-throated diapason. Over the next sixty years, the critical thesaurus would be ransacked to describe its astonishing variety of registers: the sometimes grating, sometimes caressing, often sumptuous, sounds he seemed effortlessly to produce. But they were not just sounds: he had an intense relationship with language: he spoke of letting words loose in the echo chamber of his mind, where they would resonate with untold possibilities of meaning.

There is a danger in such a prodigious endowment for a young actor, the temptation of mere virtuosity, or indeed of laziness, a reliance on mere physical impact. But the defining thing about the young Scofield was that he was never tempted by easy effectiveness. He seems always to have had an innate maturity, knowing that if he was to do his work as an actor he must painstakingly learn to understand and master his physical instrument, however superb; above all he must nurture the source of his work: his imagination, his inner life. Though charming, courteous and full of naughty fun by nature, he instinctively knew that the social life on which most actors thrive would be the enemy of his work. His delight in that work was so complete, his fulfilment by it so absolute, that to abandon the social round for its sake was nothing to him, especially after he found his life's companion in the actress Joy Parker. They married and had two children, and Scofield wrapped his family round him like a strong fortress, enabling him to engage ever more deeply with his inner world.

At an impressionable age, he had received a number of jolts to his system which had opened his eyes to the possibilities of the art to which he was devoting himself. He saw Sybil Thorndike playing Medea on a tour of mining villages, an experience which he described as shattering and life-changing. Later he joined her company. Turned down for military service, as a very young man he worked constantly in touring companies, learning, learning, learning, often from distinguished older actors and directors who, like him, had not been called up, acquiring as Christopher Fry said of him at that age, 'a quiet mastery of his skills'. Luckily for him, though properly appreciated, he was allowed to serve his apprenticeship unmolested by the overheated attentions of the press. After the war, he went to work for that great manager, Sir Barry Jackson, at the Birmingham Rep, where he met the twenty-two-year-old Peter Brook, and a great artistic partnership started. Brook, Scofield said, taught him above all that he must learn to think, to connect with the thoughts of the character and ultimately with those of the author: how to lay what he called the groundwork of the character, the parameters of a role. His plan was to push these parameters as far as he possibly could, to create the richest, most complex and lifelike character feasible. He had success after success in an extraordinary range of parts, each one etched with a precise brilliance which seemed to release the very souls of the characters: the fantastical *hidalgo* Don Armado, followed by an earthy, dangerous Mercutio, and a tender and scholarly Horatio.

At the age of twenty-six he played a Hamlet at Stratford-upon-Avon that for many people was the most perfect of post-war performances of the role. With Brook he proceeded to exquisite romantic comedy in *Ring Round the Moon*, a second *Hamlet*, which was the first British production to play in Moscow since the Revolution, and the role of the whisky priest in *The Power and the Glory*, a performance which Laurence Olivier, not reckless with praise of other actors, described as the most perfect he had ever seen. He played a sleazy agent in the musical *Espresso Bongo*, Lord Harry Monchesney in *The Family Reunion*, and a number of well-wrought West End plays which he transformed with his power to astonish. His reputation grew and grew, steadily but greatly; after his remarkable performance in *A Man for All Seasons* transferred to Broadway he was increasingly spoken of as the greatest actor in the English-speaking world.

The more the acclaim, the further he withdrew from the social world, immersing himself ever deeper in his private life. He was a countryman by temperament; his horse, his resolutely untameable dog Diggory, his garden, his reading, his wife, his children: these absorbed him deeply and renewed him. His connection with nature was profound; he listened to its pulses, and through them, to his own, enriching in every way he knew the fertility of his inner soil. On horseback, or striding across the Downs for hours on end alone or with his hounds: it is an unexpected image for an actor. But Scofield was nothing if not his own man.

At the unusually early age of thirty-nine, with Peter Brook as his director, he played *King Lear*, perhaps Shakespeare's greatest role for a man, and his hardest. Rejecting any attempt to reproduce the external details of old age, he transformed himself into the ancient king by sheer power of imagination, a terrifying and pitiable bull of a man. His voice seemed to be made of granite, granite which cracked and splintered under the pressure of his inner dissolution. This performance, in Brook's shockingly radical production, toured the world; it was one of the early productions of Peter Hall's Royal Shakespeare Company which established it as among the greatest theatre companies of the world, and it set the seal on Scofield's own greatness. In rapid sequence, from the early 1960s he took on the widest variety of roles, tragic, comic, classical, modern, each transformed by his profound and fantastical imagination: embittered Athenian plutocrats, drunken Russian nobodies, gay barbers in Brixton, German petty criminals revenging themselves on authority, kidnapped diplomats, heartbroken provincials, foxy Venetian con men, mediocre and ultimately homicidal composers, pesky old New Yorkers, deranged ancient mariners, each with their characteristic and extraordinary voices.

All these, of course, for live audiences. He had his successes on film – for his Thomas More he won an Oscar – but his satisfaction was above all to be found working with an audience. The extraordinary surges of power he created in the theatre electrified not only his public but his fellow players too, particularly so because his force was so tightly harnessed. He banked down his flames, for the most part, allowing them to smoulder. But if he unleashed a thunderbolt at you, you knew all about it. He might easily have dominated his audience, but that was not what he wanted. He sought to draw them into the human life he was incarnating, to bring the character's entire inner world on stage with him, and allow the audience to experience the man for themselves. Wherever you looked in his performances, you found layer upon layer of complexity and depth, amounting to a complete transformation. Laurence Olivier once declared that his life's work had been to interest the public in the art of acting. Scofield's might be said to have been the exact opposite: to make the audience forget the art of acting. Above all, he wanted them to forget about him. He said that he was very secretive about his personality: it was not for public consumption. In giving thanks for his life and work, we should be grateful that he flourished in a time when it was still possible for excellence to be admired without its sources being dismantled, dissected, raked over, torn apart.

He guarded his God-given talent like a tiger; his loyalty to it was fierce and without concession, and he was willing to give up a great deal for it. His talent was, indeed, a secret, in all senses of that word: it was the source of his success, it was private, and it was a great and abiding mystery. He takes it with him to his grave, but he has left behind an enduringly inspiring example of what an actor who is also an artist might achieve: a body of work of such depth, breadth, imaginative and indeed visionary power that it rivals that of any great artist in any sphere. At the age of seventy-five, he took his leave of the stage he had commanded so incomparably for so many years with one of his very greatest incarnations, John Gabriel Borkman, 'a man,' as Scofield said, 'frozen and trapped by the past, embracing his own obsessive drive towards an anarchical climax, proclaiming his mad preoccupation with the forces and spirits of the earth, until his brain and body simply crack under the force of his avid desire to dominate his own small kingdom.' That was the scale on which Paul Scofield worked, that was the breadth of his canvas, addressing nothing less than the human condition, head-on.

That is what the theatre, what acting, can and should be.

Acknowledgements

Learning

p2.	*Peter Pan*	*Country Life*, 1997
p4.	Shakespeare and Me	Programme for a Sonnet show, Stratford, Ontario, 2008
p6.	Learning to faint backwards	*Zambia Spotlight*, 2005
p11.	Shakespeare and Me II	Programme note for *There Reigns Love*, Stratford, Ontario, 2008
p14.	The Old Vic	Unknown source
p15.	Kenneth Tynan	Review of Dominic Shellard's biography in the *Sunday Times*, 2003
p20.	Opera and Me	The *Independent*, 1995
p24.	Charlie Chaplin	Programme for London Philharmonic Orchestra concert, 2003
p27.	Peter Ustinov	Review of John Miller's biography in the *Sunday Times*, 2002
p31.	David Garrick	Review of Ian McIntyre's biography in the *Sunday Times*, 1999
p34.	Henry Irving	Review of Jeffrey Richards' biography in the *Guardian*, 2005
p40.	Diana Boddington	Entry in the *Dictionary of National Biography* (OUP), 2005
p44.	Laurence Olivier	Entry in *Cassell's Encyclopaedia of Theatre in the Twentieth Century*, 2002
p47	Companies	*The Times*, 1997
p49.	John Gielgud	Review of Sheridan Morley's biography in the *Guardian*, 2001
p56.	*Next Season*	Introduction to paperback edition of Michael Blakemore's novel (Applause Theatre Books), 1996

*

My greatest debt, of course, is to the editors who commissioned most of the pieces collected here. For the last eight years, I have been under exclusive contract as a book reviewer to the *Guardian* newspaper, and my editor there, Claire Armitstead, has been a model of patience and tact. I'd also like to thank Claire Tomalin who, as Books Editor of the *Sunday Times*, gave me my first book to review, and spare a grateful thought for the late Charles Wintour, father of Anna, who, as editor of the *London Evening Standard*, commissioned my first printed pieces. Matt Applewhite and Jodi Gray of Nick Hern Books have put a sprawling and much-modified manuscript into wonderfully elegant form; my secretary Fiona Wilkins has devoted many hours to deciphering ancient and yellowing cuttings and typing them up. That fine actress Gwendoline Christie gave up a good deal of her spare time to do the initial research, which greatly helped to shape the book. Finally, I must thank Nick Hern – AGAIN. This book was his idea, as was my very first book; Simon Callow, author, was, in fact, more or less his invention. His forbearance over what has been, even by my standards, an uncommonly protracted gestation period, has been admirable, as he read and reread literally hundreds of pieces of sharply varying merit. His advice and encouragement have been indispensible, to say nothing of his unerring identification of error or clumsiness. Nearly thirty years of warm friendship and close professional collaboration lie behind this book, which is, among other things, a monument to our unfailingly happy working partnership.

Index

424

McKellen, Ian 74, 181, 188, 193, 228, 308, 355, 356, 367, 396, 400–1, 411
Mackintosh, Cameron 216
Mackintosh, Kenneth 171–2
MacLaine, Shirley 264–5, 267
Maclarnon, Pat 325
mac Liammóir, Micheál 66–70, 97, 168–9, 280, 283, 286, 323–8, 348
MacMillan, Kenneth 62
Mad World My Masters, A 132
Mädchen in Uniform 312
Mademoiselle 288
Maeterlinck, Maurice 99
Magic Flute, The 156, 230–1
Magnificent Ambersons, The 287
Magnani, Anna 87
Mahler, Gustav 254
Mail on Sunday 237, 379
Major Barbara 298
Malmgren, Yat (Gert) 89–91
Malone Dies 397
Maly Theatre (St Petersburg) 250–4, 343–4
Mamet, David 92
Mamma Mia! 368
Man for All Seasons, A 111, 162–3, 415–16
Marais, Jean 243
Marat/Sade 85, 341
March, Elspeth 186
Marcus, Frank 78
Marcus, Gary 275–6
Marguerite and Armand 64
Marlowe, Christopher 54, 84, 281, 347
Marowitz, Charles 127
Marriage of Figaro, The (play) 103
Marriage of Figaro, The (opera) 142, 156, 158
Marriner, Neville 230
Mars-Jones, Adam 304
Marshall, Roderick 352–3
Marston, John 134
Martin, Mary 299
Martin Chuzzlewit 330
Marx Brothers 230, 268, 378
Mary Barnes 138
Mary Poppins 189
Mary Shelley's Frankenstein 366
Mask of the Gorgon, The 157
Masks and Faces 92
Massine, Léonide 90
Mastersingers of Nuremberg, The 22
Matcham, Frank 338
Matchmaker, The 180
Mathias, Sean 243, 396, 400–2
Mathews, Charles 330, 404–5

Maugham, W. Somerset 15
Maurois, André 245
Mayor of Zalamea, The 111
Me and My Girl 296, 300
Measure for Measure 121
Medea 414
Meehan, Thomas 368
Melancholy Jacques 215, 220
Melville, Herman 283
Mendelssohn, Felix 82
Merchant, Ismail 234–7, 239–42, 270–8, 288
Merchant of Venice, The 23, 36, 38, 45, 79, 109, 145, 149, 202
Mercury Theatre (company) 279, 281–2
Mermaid Theatre (London) 74–5, 80, 128, 167, 400
Merrison, Clive 219
Merry Wives: The Musical 354
Merry Wives of Windsor, The 331, 335
'Method, The' 64, 92, 102, 104–7, 137, 360
Metropolitan Museum of Art (New York) 288
Metropolitan Opera House (New York) 84, 139, 147, 294–5
Meyerhold, Vsevolod 82, 89, 104, 343
Michelangelo 288
Michie, Bryan 394
Middleton, Thomas 81
Midnight Cowboy 307
Midsummer Night's Dream, A 10, 58, 81–7, 162, 163, 183, 188
Miles, Bernard 74, 80
Miller, Arthur 170
Miller, John 27–30
Miller, Max 73, 391
Milligan, Spike 169
Milton, Ernest 84
Milton, John 77
Milva Canta Brecht 132
Mineo, Sal 312
Minnelli, Liza 228, 264
Misanthrope, Le 146
Miss Saigon 296
Mr & Mrs Bridge 273
'Mr W. H.' 175–7
Mitchell, Ann 126–7, 302
Mitchell, Julian 188, 190
Mitchum, Robert 225, 226
Mnouchkine, Ariane 407
Moby Dick 283
Modern Times 25
Molière (Jean-Baptiste Poquelin) 15, 48–9, 146, 185
Molière 98
Molloy 397
Monette, Paul 304

Monroe, Marilyn 106
Monsieur Verdoux 25
Moore, Dudley 54, 228
Moore, Stephen 171
Morahan, Christopher 154
Morgann, Maurice 351
Morley, Sheridan 49–55
Morris, Beth 128
Moscow Art Theatre 88, 94–105, 342–4
Moshinsky, Elijah 179
Moskvin, Ivan 99
Mostel, Zero 145
Mother Courage 161, 398–9
Mother Goose 368
Mountebank's Tale, The 79–80
Movietone Cinema (London) 23
Mozart, Wolfgang Amadeus 34, 54–5, 139–43, 155–7, 195, 210, 266, 339, 384
Mozart and Salieri 139
Much Ado About Nothing 14
Murdoch, Iris 177, 288
Murmuring Judges (see Hare Trilogy)
Musgrave, Thea 22
Mussorgsky, Modest 62, 84
My Beautiful Laundrette 309
My Fair Lady 216, 296–302, 320, 354, 379
My Life in Art 91–104
My Life in the Russian Theatre 97–8
Mystery of Charles Dickens, The 334–9
Mystery of Edwin Drood, The 334

Narrow Road to the Deep North 123
Nashe, Thomas 305–6
National Film Theatre (NFT) 24, 26, 132–3, 223
National Health, The 390
National Portrait Gallery (NPG) 41
National Service 260–4
National Theatre (London) 11, 13–15, 19, 39–46, 48, 52, 55–6, 59–60, 66, 72–4, 80, 81, 85, 108, 110, 124, 130, 142–50, 154–5, 166–73, 179–80, 192, 227, 240, 256, 260–4, 304, 324, 338, 340, 400, 410
Native Son 282
Neagle, Anna 87
Negro Theatre Project 281
Nelson, Willie 273, 278
Nemirovich-Danchenko, Vladimir 94, 96–104, 343
Nesbitt, Cathleen 299